A CRITICAL HISTORY OF CONTE

A Critical History of
Contemporary Architecture

1960–2010

Edited by
Elie G. Haddad and David Rifkind

ASHGATE

Published by
Ashgate Publishing Limited
Wey Court East
Union Road
Farnham
Surrey, GU9 7PT
England

Ashgate Publishing Company
110 Cherry Street
Suite 3-1
Burlington, VT 05401-3818
USA

www.ashgate.com

British Library Cataloguing in Publication Data
A catalogue record for this book is available from the British Library

Library of Congress Cataloging-in-Publication Data
A critical history of contemporary architecture : 1960-2010 / [edited] by Elie G. Haddad and David Rifkind.
    pages cm
  Includes bibliographical references and index.
  ISBN 978-1-4724-2937-7 (hardback) -- ISBN 978-1-4094-3981-3 (pbk.) -- ISBN 978-1-4724-2938-4 (ebook) -- ISBN (invalid) 978-1-4724-2939-1 (epub) 1. Architecture, Modern--20th century. 2. Architecture, Modern--21st century. I. Haddad, Elie, editor of compilation. II. Rifkind, David, 1968- editor of compilation. III. Laurence, Peter L., 1936- Modern (or Contemporary) Architecture circa 1959.
  NA680.C745 2014
  724'.6--dc23

                                                                    2013033625

ISBN: 978-1-4724-2937-7 (hbk)
          978-1-4094-3981-3 (pbk)
          978-1-4724-2938-4 (ebk – PDF)
          978-1-4724-2939-1 (ebk – ePUB)

MIX
Paper from
responsible sources
FSC
www.fsc.org   FSC® C013985

Printed in the United Kingdom by Henry Ling Limited,
at the Dorset Press, Dorchester, DT1 1HD

Contents

List of Illustrations

1   Modern (or Contemporary) Architecture circa 1959

1.1   "The Death of CIAM" at the last CIAM meeting, Otterlo, Holland, 1959. Peter Smithson, Alison Smithson, John Voelcker, Jacob Bakema, Sandy van Ginkel; Aldo van Eyck and Blanche Lemco, below. Image courtesy of Adam Voelcker

1.2   The demolition of the Pruitt-Igoe housing project in St. Louis was not "the death of modern architecture," as some claimed, but a testament to the accuracy of urban design critiques made decades earlier. Image courtesy of Getty Images

1.3   According to some of the Generation of '56, Le Corbusier's Chapelle Nôtre-Dame-du-Haut at Ronchamp (1950–55) represented a "crisis of rationalism" for modern architecture. Image courtesy of Peik Li Pang

1.4   In contrast with Le Corbusier's Ronchamp, Mies van der Rohe's post-war work, such as Carr Chapel at Illinois Institute of Technology (1949–52), represented a static, and obsolete, definition of functionalism. Image courtesy of Mike Schwartz

1.5 and 1.6   The popularization of modern architecture in the 1950s in works such as Gordon Bunshaft/Skidmore, Owings and Merrill's Lever House (1950–52), above, and Morris Lapidus's Fontainebleau Hotel (1952–54), below, exacerbated the post-war crisis of modernism architecture by conflating it with the International Style. Images courtesy of Getty Images and Library of Congress, respectively

1.7   The last CIAM meeting in Otterlo, Holland, 1959. José Antonio Coderch, standing behind Aldo van Eyck and Giancarlo De Carlo (seated at the center), speaks into the microphone. Among the group are Ernesto Rogers, seated far left; Peter Smithson, standing third from left; Jacob Bakema (obscured) and Alison Smithson, both seated. On the far right, John Voelcker stands behind Kenzo Tange. The meeting's organizing committee included Bakema (as chair), John Voelcker, Rogers, Alfred Roth, and André Wogenscky. Image courtesy of NAi

1.8   Selected projects from CIAM '59 in Otterlo represented the diversity of approaches that emerged at CIAM's end. Aldo van Eyck's Children's Home (1955–60); detail of Kenzo Tange's Kagawa Prefectural Office (1955–58); Kiyonori Kikutake's Tokyo Bay project (1959); passive cooling strategies for Jerzy Soltan's Polish Exhibition Pavilion (Damascus, 1956). Images courtesy of Oscar Newman, CIAM '59 in Otterlo (Stuttgart: Karl Krämer Verlag, 1961)

1.9   Sharply criticized at CIAM '59 at Otterlo, Ernesto Rogers and BBPR's Torre Velasca (1950–57) was nevertheless an important experiment in expanding the language of modern architecture along regionalist lines. Image courtesy of Marco Varisco

1.10   Representing another failure of modernist urban design, Paul Rudolph's Lower Manhattan Expressway Project (1968) was the conceptual climax of the line of megastructural thinking that emerged around the time of CIAM '59. Image courtesy Library of Congress

1.11   Ten years after Rudolph's LoMEx project, Charles Moore's Piazza d'Italia (1978) represented another extreme direction, and manifested the fears of some of the Generation of '56. Image courtesy of Lisa Heindel

1.12   Celebrated as a work of regionalism in the age of globalization, Enric Miralles and Benedetta Tagliabue, Santa Caterina Market adaptation (1997–2001) models a combination of urban and architectural design, historic and contemporary architecture, site specificity and connection to the larger world. Image courtesy of Getty Images

2   Post-Modernism: Critique and Reaction

2.1   Robert Venturi, Vanna Venturi House, Philadelphia, 1964 (photograph Rollin LaFrance). Image courtesy of Venturi, Scott Brown and Associates, Inc

2.2   Robert Venturi, Vanna Venturi House, Philadelphia, 1964 (photograph George Pohl). Image courtesy of Venturi, Scott Brown and Associates, Inc

2.3   Venturi, Scott Brown and Associates, Sainsbury Wing of the National Gallery, London, 1991 (photograph Matt Wargo). Image courtesy of Venturi, Scott Brown and Associates, Inc

2.4   Aldo Rossi, Teatro del Mondo, Venice, 1979. Image courtesy of La Biennale di Venezia

2.5   Paolo Portoghesi (curator) and collaborators, Strada Novissima, Venice, 1980. Image courtesy of La Biennale di Venezia

2.6   Michael Graves, Portland Municipal Services Building, Portland (Oregon), 1980–82. Images courtesy of Michael Graves & Associates

2.7   James Stirling Michael Wilford and Associates, Neue Staatsgalerie, Stuttgart, 1984 (photograph Alastair Hunter, RIBA Library Photographs Collection). Image courtesy of RIBA Library Drawings & Archives Collections

2.8   James Stirling Michael Wilford and Associates, Neue Staatsgalerie, Stuttgart, 1984 (photograph Alastair Hunter, RIBA Library Photographs Collection). Image courtesy of RIBA Library Drawings & Archives Collections

2.9   Taller Ricardo Bofill, Les Espaces d'Abraxas, "L'Arc" and "Le Palacio," Marne la Vallée (France), 1982. Image courtesy of Ricardo Bofill Taller de Arquitectura

2.10   Charles Moore, Piazza d'Italia, New Orleans, 1978. Image courtesy of Charles Moore Foundation

6   Postcolonial Theories in Architecture

11   Metaphorical Peripheries: Architecture in Spain and Portugal

15   Architecture in Africa: Situated Modern and the Production of Locality

16   Global Conflict and Global Glitter: Architecture of West Asia (1960–2010)

16.12   *c*.2000 skyscrapers of Gulf Cities (from left to right): Adrian Smith from SOM, Burj Khalifa, Dubai, UAE, 2004–10; MZ Architects, Aldar Headquarters, Abu Dhabi, UAE, 2010; SOM, Infinity Tower, Dubai, UAE, 2006–13; Jean Nouvel, Doha Tower, Doha, Qatar, 2005–12; Aybars Aşçı from SOM, Al Hamra Tower, Kuwait City, Kuwait, 2003–10. Image courtesy of Esra Akcan (own photo)

16.13   Rem Koolhaas and OMA, Waterfront City, Dubai, UAE, 2006-ongoing. Image courtesy of OMA/AMO

17   Old Sites, New Frontiers: Modern and Contemporary Architecture in Iran

17.1   The National Bank of Iran under construction, 1929. Image courtesy of the Center for the Study of Modern Iranian History; visual archives No. 019/31

17.2   Sandbag Shelters in Ahvaz by Nader Khalili, 1995. Composed of arches, domes and vaults, these single- and double-curvature shell structures in Ahvaz invoke the ancient mud brick architecture of the region. While barbed wire strengthens the structures against earthquake, their aerodynamic form resists hurricanes; sandbags themselves are resistant to flood, and their earth content is fireproof. The structures are particularly suitable for temporary shelters because they are cheap and can be quickly erected by unskilled labor. Above all, this system is sustainable. image courtesy of Cal-Earth Institute and the Aga Agha Khan Award for Architecture

17.3   Dezful Cultural Center, 1995 (photograph Farhad Ahmadi). View across the courtyard fountain. Image courtesy of the Agha Khan Award for Architecture

17.4   Dowlat II Residential Complex, 2007. View of the façade with opened wooden panels. Image courtesy of the Aga Khan Award for Architecture

17.5   Rafsanjan Sports Complex in Rafsanjan (an eastern desert city and the capital of Rafsanjan County in the Kerman Province), 2001. From top to bottom: elevations and façade; below: northwest view. Drawing by Naghsh-e Jahan Pars; photograph M. Rezaie. Image courtesy of Aga Khan Award for Architecture

17.6   Shahyad Arya-Mehr (now Azadi) Monument, 1971

17.7   Milad Tower, 2008. Image courtesy of Mohammad Tahsildoost

17.8   An article from daily newspaper *Abrar-e Eqtisadi* highlights the tent-like structure of the conference hall. The caption to the image of the computer-generated model of the building reads: "The Summit Conference hall shines, like a symbol of peace, in the middle of Tehran." *Abrar-e Eghtesadi*, January 31, 2001

17.9   Iranian Embassy in Berlin, 2005 (Photographs by Darab Diba). Above: detail of the roof; below: view from south-west. Image courtesy of the Agha Khan Award for Architecture

17.10   Mural by artist Mehdi Ghadiyanloo, demonstrating a pedestrian bridge that leads nowhere, Tehran, district 10, 2007. Image courtesy of the Organization for the Beautification of the City of Tehran

18.14   Modest yet intelligent "existence minimum" housing on the periphery of Jakarta. Andra Matin Architect, Rental Housing, Bintaro, 2002–03. Image courtesy of Andra Matin Architect

19   Internationalism and Architecture in India after Nehru

19.1   The School of Architecture at Ahmedabad was a direct outcome of the conjunction of entrepreneurial institution-builders and foreign technical and cultural aid that made Ahmedabad a nexus of international exchange in the 1960s. Built incrementally beginning in 1966 to designs by founding director, B.V. Doshi, the campus and its buildings embodied a dialogue between Doshi, Le Corbusier, and Kahn, with both of whom the architect had enjoyed a close working relationship. Image courtesy of Amit Srivastava

19.2   The interior of architect Hasmukhbhai Patel's own residence (1969) in Ahmedabad is a typical modernist living space from the period, with traditional Indian textiles and craft objects juxtaposed with iconic Modern furniture including chairs by Eames and Mies. Image courtesy of HCP Design & Project Management, Ahmedabad

19.3   The curved bangle roof form of the Azad Bhawan building, designed for the Indian Council for Cultural Relations by Achyut Kanvinde (1958–61), is an early example of experimentation with regionally associated forms by an established modernist architect. Image courtesy of Lakshmi Krishnaswamy

19.4   View of water court with brick jali work in the Centre for Development Studies, Trivandrum (1972–75), designed and built by Laurie Baker. Baker's inventive path-breaking work with low-cost building materials in the south Indian state of Kerala marked a return to Gandhian ideals in the 1970s, and concurrent engagement internationally with the Appropriate Technology movement. Image courtesy of Vikram Bhatt

19.5   The housing for the Electronics Corporation of India Ltd. (ECIL) in Hyderabad designed by architect B.V. Doshi (1971) was an influential prototype on which many later company 'townships' and public housing projects were based. Image courtesy of Vastu-Shilpa Foundation, Ahmedabad

19.6   The Permanent Exhibition Structures designed by architect Raj Rewal for the 1972 International Trade Fair in New Delhi embodied a tenuous marriage between hi-tech aspirations and humble means. Image courtesy of Raj Rewal Associates, New Delhi

19.7   The SCOPE government office complex, New Delhi (1980–89) by architect Raj Rewal employed sandstone polychromy and undisguised references to the *chatris* and ramparts of historic Rajput fortresses to ennoble the labour of the army of humble civil servants employed within. Image courtesy of Raj Rewal Associates, New Delhi

19.8   In his design for the Jawahar Kala Kendra (1986), a multifaceted centre for visual and performing arts in the historic Rajput city of Jaipur, architect Charles Correa employed ancient Hindu cosmological diagrams as planning grids and pattern-generators, enabling the superposition of traditional and modernist design reasoning to be felicitously exploited for both pragmatic and aesthetic purposes

20   Architecture in China in the Reform Era: 1978–2010

Introduction
Modernism and Beyond: The Plurality of Contemporary Architectures

Elie G. Haddad and David Rifkind

> *History – exactly like Freudian analysis at its core – is not merely a*
> *therapy. By questioning its own materials, it reconstructs them and*
> *continuously reconstructs itself. The genealogies it traces are therefore also*
> *temporary barriers, just as analytic work is anything but shielded from the*
> *conditionings of signifying practices or modes of production. The historian*
> *is a worker "in the plural", as are the subjects on which he performs his*
> *work … Operating on its own constructions, history makes an incision with*
> *a scalpel in a body whose scars do not disappear; but at the same time,*
> *unhealed scars already mar the compactness of historical constructions,*
> *rendering them problematic and presenting themselves as the "truth."*[1]

The second half of the twentieth century witnessed an unprecedented pluralism in architecture, following the spread of modern architecture around the world, in various interpretations, and the subsequent wave of movements that came in its wake. No previous period had seen an equivalent diversity of architectural production, nor a comparable volume of building construction on such a wide scale.

In the last few decades, the proliferation of studies on what constitutes modern architecture confirmed Manfredo Tafuri's characterization of the "historical project" in architecture as a work in progress, subject to multiple and successive layers which cannot obliterate the traces of previous operations. And true to the predictions of Tafuri, it seems as if the "body" on which these operations were being inscribed and re-inscribed remains the historical project of modernity, a project that has been subjected to various dissections, interpretations and misinterpretations.

In one of the reference works on this topic, Fredric Jameson related the project of modernity to its technological pole, which still appears sometimes as its hidden double, sometimes as its mask, and at other times as a pure semiotic index. In this respect, Jameson also reminded us of the intimate relation between this version of Modernism as ideology, and the appearance of the "new," through the aesthetic of shock. The attraction of the new characterizes much of what has been produced under the label of "contemporary" architecture, which in Jamesonian terms may be nothing more than the revival of the "modern" under new guises. This re-emergence of a new "Post-Modern" Modernism, consciously markets itself through the techniques of "shock", making it possible for emerging economic centers to instantly place themselves as equal partners on the global map of the new capitalist order. Yet in our view, this remains a modified or hybrid version of Modernism, stripped of any social or political objectives.

Another issue of interest that Jameson raises is this continuing dialectic between "two moments" of Modernism, which alternate historically in all fields from architecture to music and painting, as in the early movement from Jugendstil to Bauhaus. This can be also traced in our own times in the fluctuating movement back and forth, between two opposite strands: neo-expressionism on one side (from Scharoun to Gehry and Hadid) and neo-rationalisms on the other (from certain Swiss and German versions to Parametric design), with a wide spectrum of hybrid tendencies in between. Yet all of these in a sense partake of the same impulse, even while denying it, of a strong drive towards the "original" or the "new" that ultimately refers them back to the historical project of modernity as articulated by Jameson:

> Here, the force of the imperative to innovate or "to make new", the powerful and central presiding value of the New as such, has always seemed to constitute the fundamental logic of modernism, which replicates Schelling's dynamic of modernity in its powerful expulsion of the past in the name of a search for innovation as such and for its own sake, which can be an empty and formalist fetish.[2]

This condition of modernity, which Jameson connects to the "crisis of representation" in language, seems to parallel the same crisis in architecture, where a similar disconnection between architectural elements, bodies, and places appeared as a result of the increasing pressures exerted by the "forces of differentiation." The utopian time of an ideal unity, despite the futile attempts of some earlier "Post-Modernists," finds itself irrevocably shattered, giving way to a multiplicity of architectural codes (or styles) that gravitate between the two poles of technological rationality and subjective autonomy.

Due to this inherent complexity, we have consciously approached the task of attempting to write a "history" of contemporary developments in architecture, by opening up a few breaches in the wall of established "histories" of modern architecture, and by extension of their current manifestations. Through this process it becomes possible to sort through the multiple offspring that had extended beyond the confines of the "original" locus of operation, i.e. the Western world, to all corners of the world.

The extraordinary expansion started to happen at a time when the modernist consensus of the immediate postwar period began to fray in the late 1950s and early 1960s. Modern architecture faced multiple critiques both from within and from without (the Post-Modern reaction), which ushered the way for new experiments, dealing with both spatial syntaxes and semantic layers, as well as with an attempt to probe deeper into the very foundations of the discipline. At the same time, an "other" discourse appeared on the horizon, leading to the emergence of regionalist tendencies that would be translated in various forms, as a "critical" approach from within the main modernist course, or as forms of revivalism that cater to a popular search for identity.

The newly independent states that emerged after de-colonialization participated in this active search for new directions, producing a diverse range of architectural works, designed to meet the needs of emerging societies, sometimes resorting to a hybrid architectural language that synthesized international Modernism with regional or national patterns. In parallel, political movements in the West contested elite culture and centralized state power, finding expression in various forms of non-traditional practices, from community participation to self-built architecture. The period that followed the initial turmoil of the '60s and '70s was marked in the West by a movement towards reclaiming history as a form of contestation of "grand narratives," while the accompanying prosperity expanded the privilege of architectural patronage to new actors with diverse tastes and aspirations, resulting in the dissemination of the notions of plurality, difference, and heterogeneity. Towards the end of the century, the sudden collapse of Communism dramatically transformed the political and economic context in a vast geographical zone, extending from Eastern Europe to all the previous Soviet republics. This was further compounded by the adoption of the capitalist market economy model by the last major communist country, China, turning it into a global economic power and one of the major experimental fields for contemporary architecture and urbanism.

Architects responded to the various challenges of this era of global capital expansion by simultaneously engaging different architectural paradigms, some of which were revivals of previous traditions including a rehabilitated Modernism, while others came out as syntheses of opposite tendencies. What once appeared as contradictory positions under the banners of "Modernism" or "Post-Modernism" could now be found juxtaposed in the synthetic works of such architects as Frank Gehry, James Stirling, Rem Koolhaas, Rafael Moneo or Peter Eisenman. The various historical surveys of this period often brought together conceptually opposite architects under the same umbrella, and in some cases readjusted their position within a certain movement to suit different theoretical agendas, and particular exhibitions. Major institutions and museums continued to play an important role in the dissemination of new trends and movements, which led some theoreticians to the extreme position of calling once again for a unifying and overarching "style."[3]

In the midst of this cultural "mosaic," this work attempts to sketch a multiple history, composed of two parts: in the first part, a presentation of major movements in architecture after 1960, during a period when "grand narratives" including Post-Modernism still held sway; and in the second part a geographic survey that covers a wide range of territories around the world, in what seems to be a spreading hybridization of universal norms and tendencies simultaneous with a search for the specific and the particular. Although such partitioning may fly against the contemporary blurring of geographical zones under the effect of a widespread globalization which has led to the expansion of certain "major" practices and architectural firms across the world, we nevertheless believe that this survey would constitute a first step towards a critical evaluation of the current condition of architecture, at a time when the de-ideologization of architectural discourse has resulted in a stylistic celebration of different works without any critical examination. And since we also believe that a comprehensive history is more and more impossible to write by a single author, we turned this project into a collective project, with all the discrepancies, or "fault lines", that such an endeavor would inevitably produce, from overlaps to historical and geographical "voids."

The starting point of our project was set around 1960. This choice is not absolute, and does not imply that architectural developments around the world take a radical new turn specifically at this time, but it was simply used as a benchmark from which to re-assess later trends in architecture. The period is important in that it followed the last CIAM meeting, which signaled a turning point for the Modern Movement, and witnessed the emergence of contesting theories penned by Aldo Rossi, Robert Venturi and others, as a prelude to the first revisionary movement following Modernism. Some recent works did attempt to cover these developments, but in a rather fragmentary way, covering a specific region or movement, without attempting to weave a critical history out of these multifarious developments. Other studies attempted to address architectural developments by splitting them into arbitrary time frames, neglecting to address other parts of the world which are still considered to be of relatively "weak" importance, remaining essentially centered on the Western world.

This work will therefore present a more diverse reading of contemporary developments, opening up questions that originate from the different perspectives of their respective authors. And while we aimed to cover as much territory as possible, we recognize the limitations that such projects entail, and the unavoidable discrepancy in the coverage of different areas. An example of this is the wider importance given to Europe, warranted by the variety of approaches and problematics that architects in Europe have explored in our times, which manifests itself particularly in the growth of three important "traditions" within the European context: the Dutch, the Spanish–Portuguese and the Swiss; which have exerted a significant influence on architecture around the world. The impact of these three traditions has led to a variety of approaches in contemporary architecture, ranging from a concern with local traditions, to a continuing faith in a technological utopia, which has become more feasible through the dissemination of digital tools of production.

This book therefore reflects the different perspectives of its various authors, but it also attempts to chart a middle course between the "aesthetic" histories that examine architecture solely in terms of its formal aspects, and the "ideological" histories that subject it to a critique that often skirts the discussion of its material aspects. For some historians, the contemporary condition merely represents a "late" phase of the Modernist project, which remains unfulfilled. For others, it confirms our presence in a genuinely Post-Modern condition, which had been previously misrepresented as a return to historicism and neo-classicism. The final judgment will remain suspended on this issue, as the writing of a history-in-progress remains a "temporary" construction, an incomplete and precarious project, subject to the ever-evolving conditions of the present.

NOTES

1   Manfredo Tafuri, "The Historical Project", Introduction to *The Sphere and the Labyrinth*, MIT Press, 1990.

2   Fredric Jameson, "Modernism as Ideology", in *A Singular Modernity: Essay on the Ontology of the Present*, Verso, 2002 (151).

3   A case in point is Patrick Schumacher's recent *The Autopoiesis of Architecture: A New Framework for Architecture*, Wiley, 2011.

PART I
Major Developments after Modernism

1

Modern (or Contemporary) Architecture circa 1959

Peter L. Laurence

When did "modern" architecture become "contemporary" architecture? Although 1968 is often singled out as a turning point in the history of the twentieth century, as Jean-Louis Cohen did in *The Future of Architecture, Since 1889*, other historians push the transformation of twentieth-century modernity to an earlier moment.[1] 1959, for example, has been called "the year everything changed," a claim historian Fred Kaplan has supported with a long list of that year's many extraordinary events, which included the launching of the Soviet spacecraft, the approval of the birth control pill, the start of racial desegregation in the United States, and the sale of the first business computer by IBM. It was the year, Kaplan argued, when "the shockwaves of the new ripped the seams of daily life, when humanity stepped into the cosmos and commandeered the conception of human life, when the world shrank but the knowledge needed to thrive in it expanded exponentially, when outsiders became insiders, when categories were crossed and taboos were trampled, when everything was changing and everyone knew it—when the world as we now know it began to take form."[2] Although one must take exception with Kaplan's hook, that 1959 was *the* year that everything changed, his description of the historical moment is an example of recent histories that recognize the 1950s, and not just the 1960s, as a time of momentous change.

Architecture culture of the 1950s has also become better appreciated with greater distance from the 1960s and the "postmodern" period that followed it. While Charles Jencks famously dated "the death of modern architecture" to the demolition of the Pruitt-Igoe housing project on July 15, 1972, historians have since then explored the complexities and contradictions within architecture culture of the decades preceding Jencks's declaration. These accounts emphasize the "critiques and counter-critiques," "extension and critique," and "continuity and change" in the 40 years between the founding of the Congrès Internationaux d'Architecture Moderne (CIAM) in 1928 and 1968.[3] The very title of William Curtis's *Modern Architecture Since 1900* emphasized the continuity of modern architecture into the present. As Curtis noted in the preface to the third edition of his book:

1.1 "The Death
of CIAM" at the
last CIAM meeting,
Otterlo, Holland,
1959. Peter
Smithson, Alison
Smithson, John
Voelcker, Jacob
Bakema, Sandy van
Ginkel; Aldo van
Eyck and Blanche
Lemco, below

> When the first edition of Modern Architecture Since 1900 was published, it was
> common to hear that "modern architecture is dead" … Despite the rhetoric about
> the "end of an era", postmodernism proved to be ephemeral. In reality there was
> yet another reorientation in which certain core ideas of modern architecture were
> re-examined but in a new way.[4]

Recent research has continued this reexamination of modern architecture before
and after World War II, uncovering the heterodoxies of the modern movement and
challenging the exaggerations of its early proponents, contemporaneous critics,
and subsequent interpreters. For example, Jencks may have been right that *a phase*
of modern architecture expired finally and completely in 1972, after having been
"flogged to death remorselessly for ten years by critics such as Jane Jacobs," but,
like most others, Jacobs was unaware of the consequences of modernist urbanism
and supportive of urban renewal in the early 1950s.[5] Moreover, by the time Jacobs's
Death and Life of Great American Cities (1961) was published, her critiques of modern
architecture and its figurehead Le Corbusier were somewhat anachronistic. By
1956, CIAM had all but collapsed—in part because Le Corbusier and others of the
"Generation of 1928" felt that the organization had had its day, in part because
of dissention about CIAM's principles of modern urbanism, and in no small part
because modern architecture by this time was better characterized by heterodoxy
than orthodoxy—despite the totalizing claims of 1960s critics to the contrary.[6]

In retrospect, we can see that the cultural lag between modern architecture's
avant-garde experimentation in the 1930s and the popular acceptance of
modern architecture in the following decades was followed by a subsequent lag
between internal critiques of modern architecture in the late 1940s and 1950s and
a corresponding popular rejection of it in the 1960s, '70s, and '80s. As observed

1.2   The demolition of the Pruitt-Igoe housing project in St. Louis was not "the death of modern architecture," as some claimed, but a testament to the accuracy of urban design critiques made decades earlier

in the following pages, modern architecture was already in crisis in 1950, and by 1959 a new generation of modern architects had already come to reject "modern" architecture in favor of "contemporary" architecture, a term used to distinguish their work from CIAM modernism and favored in the later decades of the century.

So to better understand the forces and ideas that transformed the "modern" architecture of the first half of the twentieth century into the "contemporary" architecture of the second half, we must consider the 1950s and reasons for the decade's architectural crisis. Moreover, with increasing distance from postmodernism's historical and populist tendencies—which were lines of inquiry that thoughtful architects of the 1950s rightly believed would come to a dead end— there are new points of connection to earlier decades. An examination of changes in the thinking of both the "Generation of 1928" and the "Generation of 1956" in the post-war period suggests that modern architecture had the capacity to transcend the dogmatism of its early years through a diversity of perspectives and approaches. Moreover, some of these so-called "contemporary" post-war tendencies, such as regionalism and the high-tech, remain current today, representing a continuity of design thinking that suggests a larger history, and future, for modern architecture.

CONTEMPORARY ARCHITECTURE AND THE GENERATION OF '56

The transition from "modern" to "contemporary" architecture was a generational shift. In planning for CIAM 10, the organization's tenth international meeting, which was held in Dubrovnik in August 1956, CIAM's leadership decided that it was time to turn over the organization's fate to what they called the "Generation of 1956." At a moment of "crisis or evolution," as Le Corbusier described it, only this younger generation was "capable of feeling actual problems, personally, profoundly, the goals to follow, the means to reach them, and the pathetic urgency of the present situation."[7] With his keen historical consciousness, Le Corbusier understood that there were significant differences in the experiences of the Generation of '28, most of whom were born in the 1880s and came of age in the 1920s and '30s, and the new Generation of '56, most of whom were born in the 1910s and '20s.

As children of the Machine Age, the younger generation—among them Jacob Bakema, Aldo van Eyck, Alison and Peter Smithson, and John Voelcker—were too young to have witnessed some of the urban squalor characteristic of the exploding cities at the turn of the century, or to have experienced modernity as "one of the great metamorphoses of history," as Le Corbusier's generation had.[8] Indeed, as early as CIAM 6 in 1947, a meeting intended to be a post-war "reaffirmation of the aims of CIAM," Bakema and van Eyck had criticized many of modern architecture's fundamental principles, particularly those related to city planning. Rather than support the reaffirmation document, van Eyck rejected much of CIAM's La Sarraz Declaration (1928) and Athens Charter (1933), seeing them as symptomatic of a "mechanistic conception of progress" that was incompatible with his belief that a new civilization would emerge in the post-war period.[9]

In 1950, the editors of *The Architectural Review* summarized this post-war disillusion with the idea of progress as follows:

> *Perhaps the most extraordinary thing about 1950 is that it is no longer possible to treat as silly (as it was in the nineteenth and even the early twentieth century) the people who take a poor view of the future of man. The most sinister thing about the atom bomb is not so much that it may go off as that whether it goes off or not, its effects tend to be the same. Western civilization rests on its oars, awaits the issue. Result, a very appreciable slowing down of what used to be called Progress or the March of Events.*[10]

While Le Corbusier's generation was by no means blind to these concerns about the future, the younger generation was less invested in CIAM's work of the preceding decades. Thus, in the early 1950s, van Eyck and Bakema were joined by John Voelcker and the Smithsons in attacking CIAM's long-standing functionalist city planning principles with the kind of iconoclastic statements usually attributed to the critics of the 1960s. At CIAM 9 in 1953, Voelcker and the Smithsons presented a project on "Urban Reidentification" which observed that the short, narrow street of the slum often succeeded where spacious redevelopment failed, a sociologically oriented observation typically associated with 1960s urban theory.[11] Soon thereafter, the group presented the "Doorn Manifesto" (1954), which intended to replace the narrow functionalism of the Athens Charter with an emergent understanding of the "ecological" complexity of the city.[12] Undermining two decades of work by the Generation of '28 to promote modern architecture and city planning ideals, these architects of the new generation rejected CIAM's Functionalist City concept, with its "Four Functions" of dwelling, working, recreation, and circulation. In 1955, the Smithsons summarized the change in thinking by sharply stating: "we wonder how anyone could possibly believe that in this lay the secret of town building."[13]

In the context of such an attack, it is hardly surprising that the Generation of '56 was determined to bring CIAM to an end, and following a final meeting in Otterlo in 1959, the organization was declared dead.

Terminating the organization, however, was only part of a larger critique of modern architecture. By 1959, even the term "modern architecture" had become suspect among this generation of architects for having become negatively associated with post-war urban renewal projects. As Jacob Bakema explained:

> In our Dutch circumstances we no longer like the word l'Architecture Moderne. But why? Why don't we like it? Because we think that after the war, towns have been built, streets have been built, in a way that makes them look like what people associate with l'Architecture Moderne: we have mass repetition of blocks, [and] houses are placed in these blocks in military fashion ... [14]

However, rejecting the term "modern architecture" necessitated the invention of a new terminology, and a new conception of architecture.

Expanding on his critique of the "mechanistic conception of progress," van Eyck made a case for moving beyond the positivism of the 1920s and '30s, arguing that architects and city planners must get out of their deterministic or "Euclidian groove." He observed that compared with science, positivistic modern architecture and urbanism had been failures. Architects, he believed, had been out of touch with reality and had, in his words, "sidetracked the issue of contemporary creativity."[15] He thus recommended that architects follow the example of such "non-Euclidian" artists and scientists as Picasso, Mondrian, Joyce, Le Corbusier, Schoenberg, Bergson, and Einstein, whose work he described not as modern, but "contemporary."

Making a case for "contemporary" as opposed to "modern" architecture, van Eyck believed that when architects again discovered the world anew, they would discover a "new architecture—real contemporary architecture."[16]

FROM THE "FUNCTIONAL NEUROSIS" TO THE NEW EMPIRICISM

After CIAM '59, it became increasingly common to distinguish the "contemporary" architecture of the late twentieth century from the "modern" architecture of the first half. However, being nearly synonymous terms, the preference for one over the other indicated continuity as much as change. Indeed, while van Eyck went to some rhetorical lengths to make a case for a new contemporary architecture, his inspiration came from modern era figures including Picasso, Mondrian, and Le Corbusier, whose work he described as "contemporary."[17]

To use the term coined by Thomas Kuhn around 1959, the semantic shift from "modern" to "contemporary" represented a paradigm shift, a transformation in thinking which, according to Kuhn, does not require the complete rejection of the previous paradigm. Rather, lingering inadequacies and the increasingly evident failures of a paradigm eventually spark a "crisis"—a word which became increasingly common in architecture culture starting around 1950 and grew exponentially in common usage from around 1956.[18] Intellectual crises, according to Kuhn, are fueled by the contest of those seeking to preserve orthodox beliefs and others desirous of highlighting the inadequacies in prevailing theory and engaging in "extraordinary research"—a nice term to describe the varied and often fleeting architectural trajectories, and cultural phenomena, of the 1950s and the following decades.[19] Ultimately, however, the changes to the challenged paradigm may be more evolutionary than revolutionary, as Kuhn pointed out in *The Structure of Scientific Revolutions* (1962).[20]

The fundamental paradigm that changed in the 1950s was functionalism, but to follow Kuhn's hypothesis, it was not necessarily one that had been unanimously accepted as a concept, insofar as some had recognized its shortcomings earlier. Nor was it simply rejected. Indeed, debates over functionalism, a concept closely associated with modern architecture, spanned much of the twentieth century, continuing well into the 1970s, transcending the stereotypical historical boundaries between architectural modernism and postmodernism.

In the early twentieth century, critiques of functionalism dogged modern architecture. In 1923, for example, Adolf Behne criticized architectural functionalism by distinguishing the utilitarianism of builders from the functionalism of architects, observing that a true functionalist would make a building into a "pure tool" and arrive at a negation of form.[21] In 1932, Philip Johnson and Henry-Russell Hitchcock similarly defended their aesthetic interpretation of the new "International Style" by similarly arguing that Functionalists denied that the aesthetic element in architecture was important.[22] And in the same year, Douglas Haskell used Peter Behren's apartment at the Weissenhof-Siedlung, which had weathered and deteriorated greatly in just five years, to argue that functionalist architecture was inevitably metaphoric, an "architect's fairy tale."[23] By 1936, Leicester B. Holland could describe functionalism as a "cult," presciently adding that, like other architectural cults, it was soon to become "the trivial plaything of magazine advertisements."[24] Anticipating problems related to the popularization of modern architecture in the coming decades, Holland observed that if the function of functionalism was to combat the popular desire for period decoration, it was fighting a losing battle against straw men, and would only substitute one fashion for another.[25]

The end of World War II was a turning point, as functionalism seemed associated with mechanization and thus the destruction wreaked in Europe and Asia. In 1946, the same year van Eyck and Bakema criticized the aims of CIAM, Ernesto Rogers posed his famous question: "do we want to define ourselves as functionalists?"[26] These early post-war critiques were followed, in the early 1950s, by an outpouring of writings on the subject of functionalism and alternative architectural expressions by Lewis Mumford, Robert Woods Kennedy, Paul Zucker, Edward De Zurko, and others.[27] The debate would continue into the mid 1960s with Robert Venturi's and Aldo Rossi's critiques of "naïve functionalism" and essays by Mario Gandelsonas and Peter Eisenman in the 1970s.[28]

As indicated by the continuity of the debate, functionalism was not abandoned in the 1950s or '60s. "Contemporary" architecture would emerge from its reformulation. As Joan Ockman observed in her introduction to *Architecture Culture*

1943–68, architectural thinking of the time was characterized by "a reconciliation and integration of functionalism with more humanistic concerns: symbolic representation, organicism, aesthetic expressiveness, contextual relationships, and social, anthropological, and psychological subject matter."[29] The process, which was a crisis because it required revisiting the prevailing definitions of modern architecture and coming to terms with the failures of urban theory, involved the reconsideration of such important but neglected topics as history, popular culture, regional traditions, and the city.

In fact, although new interpretations of functionalism were not readily accepted because of the implications and scope of the task, alternatives to pre-war functionalism came quickly after the war. Among the first of these was J.M. Richards's "New Empiricism," a concept that sought to address the "aesthetic expression of functionalism." Although Richards initially applied the term to the regional modernism of Sweden, he observed the New Empiricism to be an international inclination in an eponymously titled essay:

> That this tendency is not purely a Swedish one is obvious from the concern
> being expressed in other countries, where other empiricists apparently fear
> that the enormous post-war opportunities of rebuilding may too easily result in
> the stereotyping of the functionalism of the thirties under the old argument of
> establishing it as the international vernacular.[30]

Richards's idea was quickly taken up by Lewis Mumford, who quoted from "The New Empiricism" in his famous essay "Status Quo" (aka "the Bay Region style"), which in turn prompted the Museum of Modern Art to organize a symposium titled: "What Is Happening to Modern Architecture?"[31] There Alfred Barr and Henry-Russell Hitchcock derided Mumford's "native and human form of modernism," describing Mumford's model Bay Region Style as the "New Cottage Style" and seeking to maintain the supremacy of their own International Style, which they affirmed as generally "synonymous with the phrase 'Modern Architecture.'"[32]

After that things quickly changed, however. In 1950, Richards articulated the feeling that was soon on everyone's mind by observing that, "The present is a moment of crisis, not any longer because we need modern architecture, but because we have got it."[33]

Indeed, in the early 1950s, many of the modern masters also answered "no" to the question "do we want to define ourselves as functionalists?" Sigfried Giedion wrote that the special task of architecture was to leap from a rational-functional mode to an irrational-organic one, and discover a way to save society from being overwhelmed by the onslaught of technical processes.[34] José Luis Sert stated similarly that modern architecture needed to move beyond simply expressing function and develop a more complete architectural vocabulary.[35] He argued that, "the need for the superfluous is as old as mankind," and concluded that architecture needed to move beyond the "stern architectural standards of the twenties."[36] And, in 1954, Walter Gropius made a similar argument as part of an *Architectural Forum* series of articles on "the crisis in architecture."[37] He argued that the portrayal of the early pioneers as rigid men addicted to the glorification of the machine and indifferent to human values was obsolete and outdated. Rather than accept reductive histories and static labels, he urged an understanding of modern architecture as one of continuous growth, responsive to the changes in life and to regional expressions derived from specific environments, climates, landscapes, and customs.[38]

Though resonant today, such changes in the thinking of the old masters were not uniformly welcomed by the younger generation. In the mid 1950s, for example, James Stirling opined that Le Corbusier had derided and betrayed modern architecture. Writing about Ronchamp Chapel (1951–55), Stirling attacked the old master for abandoning the correct use and expression of materials, using decorative motifs that did not advance formal, structural, or aesthetic aims, and otherwise overturning architectural principles that he had so convincingly promulgated in his early work. According to Stirling, with Ronchamp, Le Corbusier had "called into question what is modern" and triggered a new "Crisis of Rationalism."[39]

Indeed, the combination of the corporate and popular embrace of modern architecture in the early 1950s—represented by SOM's Lever House (1950–52) and "Googie" architecture, on one hand, and the apparent rejection of modern architecture by Le Corbusier, on the other—presented unhappy prospects for the "Angry Young Men" of the Generation of '56. As indicated by Reyner Banham's 1953 critique of a modest apartment building by Luigi Moretti, Casa del Girasole (1949–50), for the use of abstract historical and regional references, the new generation of modern architects was faced with an almost impossibly narrow operative space between functionalist dogmatism and expressive eclecticism.[40]

Although there was general agreement about the shortcomings of modern architecture of the early twentieth century, architecture culture in the 1950s remained deeply conflicted by what Robin Boyd described as a "Functional Neurosis." Modern architecture, Boyd observed, was torn by remorse and doubt because it was ready to renounce functionalism, but had no other conviction to replace this "god of its youth."[41] Modern architecture had produced an overabundance of "glass cubes" in the model of Mies van der Rohe's Farnsworth House (1951) and Seagram Building (1954–58), buildings Boyd believed had done little to extend design thinking beyond that of the 1920s. However, at the point when modern architects were ready to renounce functionalism and were tempted to build from the heart, and not from the head, he observed that they had the uneasy feeling that they were "somehow letting the old side down."[42] It would take at least a few decades, and another generation, for this feeling to pass.

THE NEXT STEP: TOWARD A FUNCTIONALISM OF THE PARTICULAR

In the 1950 essay in which J. M. Richards described the crisis of modern architecture, he also took a prescient look forward into the architecture culture of the next half-century. Seeking to find some common thread among an assortment of new catchwords, tendencies, and orientations, Richards summarized these as addressing a "functionalism of the particular." It was an idea that functionalist architecture

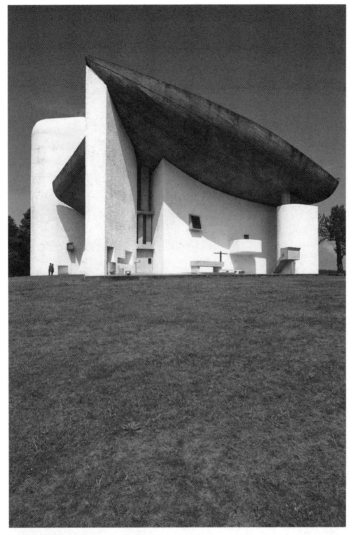

1.3 According to some of the Generation of '56, Le Corbusier's Chapelle Nôtre-Dame-du-Haut at Ronchamp (1950–55) represented a "crisis of rationalism" for modern architecture

1.4 In contrast with Le Corbusier's Ronchamp, Mies van der Rohe's post-war work, such as Carr Chapel at Illinois Institute of Technology (1949–52), represented a static, and obsolete, definition of functionalism

1.5 and 1.6   The popularization of modern architecture in the 1950s in works such as Gordon Bunshaft/ Skidmore, Owings and Merrill's Lever House (1950–52), above, and Morris Lapidus's Fontainebleau Hotel (1952– 54), below, exacerbated the post-war crisis of modernism architecture by conflating it with the International Style

needs not to be abandoned, but better related to the essential particulars of time and place and purpose. In his words:

> There is therefore no call to abandon functionalism in the search for an
> architectural idiom capable of the full range of expression its human purposes
> require; only to understand functionalism itself, by its very nature, implies
> the reverse of what it is often allowed to imply: not reducing everything to
> broad generalizations—quality in architecture belongs to the exact, not the
> approximate—but relating it ever more closely to the essential particulars of time
> and place and purpose. That is the level on which humanity and science meet.[43]

Though this seems an acceptable description of the multivalent nature of modern architecture since then, it was a frustratingly vague architectural manifesto to replace modern architecture's dogmatic founding principles. Indeed, while the Generation of '56 recognized that early modernism had many absurd aspects, they feared that the baby had been thrown away with the bathwater.[44] They also understood the consequences of heterogeneity on modern architecture's collective project. After what James Stirling regarded as three decades of the assimilation and personalization of modern architecture, he thus hoped that a period of diffusion was coming to an end, and that it would be possible to find a new synthesis.[45]

It quickly became clear that a single new narrative for modern architecture would not emerge, however. As Reyner Banham observed in his 1955 essay on "The New Brutalism," new ideas were coming too fast for this to happen. Speaking of the "new" in the New Empiricism and the combatant New Brutalism, he observed:

> This usage, like any involving the word new, opens up a historical perspective. It
> postulates that an old empiricism can be identified by the historian, and that the
> new one can be distinguished from it by methods of historical comparison … The
> ability to deal with such fine shades of historical meaning is in itself a measure
> of our handiness with the historical method today, and the use of phrases
> of the form "The New X-ism"—where X equals any adjectival root—became
> commonplace in the early nineteen-fifties in fourth-year studios and other places
> where architecture is discussed, rather than practiced.[46]

Despite the proliferation of new isms, for Banham, the Smithsons, and others, the "New Brutalism" was an important challenge to the "New Traditionalism" described by Stirling in the 1957 essay "Regionalism and Modern Architecture." Whereas the New Regionalism, the New Empiricism, and the New Palladianism (a tendency inspired by Rudolph Wittkower's *Architectural Principles of the Age of Humanism*, 1949) raised questions of formalism and historicism, New Brutalism—a term Banham described as "something between a slogan and a brick-bat flung in the public's face"—was determinedly contemporary.[47] And with the "postmodern" experiment on the horizon, those architects resistant to popular and historical allusions were perhaps right to worry: it would take more than two decades to cycle through the postmodern experiment bookended by the regionalism of the 1950s and the critical regionalism of the 1980s.[48]

By CIAM's final meeting in Otterlo, however, the stage was set for a wide range of "extraordinary research" into contemporary architecture. Along with CIAM, the idea of a unified master narrative was reluctantly accepted as a historical artifact. Although some modern architects continued to believe in the ambitious goal of "total architecture," the paradigm was clearly shifting toward the increasingly situated topography indicated by Richards almost a decade earlier.[49] By 1959, the force of different ways of thinking was undeniable; CIAM's demise was well summarized by Bakema's observation that in order to "intensify the attempts for finding a new architectural language, individuals and groups must work in their own way."[50]

Indeed, the diverse projects presented at CIAM '59 were remarkably prescient. Herman Haan put forward an anthropological inquiry into architectural essentials through his studies of the settlements of Saharan Africa. Aldo van Eyck, who had also traveled to Africa to study the architecture of the Dogon, presented his multivalent, fractal-like Children's Home (1955–60), later analyzed for its structural, anthropological, experiential, and utopian dimensions.[51] Kenzo Tange presented Kikutake Kiyonori's plan for the expansion of Tokyo, an early Metabolist project in which the metaphor of a tree was used to describe a "structural" system characterized by permanent and ephemeral elements, with the city (or house) being compared to the tree, and apartments (or the house's technical plug-ins) compared to its impermanent, but renewable leaves. Oskar Hansen presented a high-tech art gallery, notable for expressing structural and mechanical systems and for being an addition to a historic building, as well as a moving memorial for Auschwitz. Jerzy Soltan presented a flexible pavilion system for hot climates notable for passive cooling strategies familiar again in today's "sustainable" design.

Among other urban schemes for the extension and renewal of cities, Eduard Sekler's modest housing project for Vienna was groundbreaking in its

1.7 The last CIAM meeting in Otterlo, Holland, 1959. José Antonio Coderch, standing behind Aldo van Eyck and Giancarlo De Carlo (seated at the center), speaks into the microphone. Among the group are Ernesto Rogers, seated far left; Peter Smithson, standing third from left; Jacob Bakema (obscured) and Alison Smithson, both seated. On the far right, John Voelcker stands behind Kenzo Tange. The meeting's organizing committee included Bakema (as chair), John Voelcker, Rogers, Alfred Roth, and André Wogenscky

understanding of the difference between architecture and urbanism. More of an urban design scheme than a robustly developed architectural proposal—but representative in this way of the development of the new discipline of urban design in the 1950s—Sekler argued that, "*urbanity* is a characteristic which is not necessarily architectural."[52] Though his project was attacked by Peter Smithson for a lack of regional and site specificity, Sekler's notion of urbanity was very different from the CIAM approach to housing and urbanism, and the prevailing trend toward suburbanization and decentralization, which characterized the Smithsons' housing projects and much of urban theory at the time.[53]

Finally, John Voelcker, Giancarlo de Carlo, Ralph Erskine, Kenzo Tange, and, most notably, Ernesto Rogers all presented various regionalist concepts and projects, among which BBPR's Torre Velasca (1950–57) caused the greatest consternation for incorporating historical references into a building type that had come to epitomize modern architecture, the skyscraper.[54]

Rogers was, unsurprisingly, attacked at Otterlo for the Velasca Tower: with flying buttresses, a pitched roof, and chimneys, the building could be read as not just challenging, but mocking functionalist aesthetics and modern architecture. Peter Smithson agreed with Rogers that it was no longer possible to take up an anti-historical position, but he believed the design went too far. He recognized it as a dangerous precedent:

> You, in a way, created a model here which has included certain consequences which, if you had been aware of your position in society and your position in the development of things, you would have seen as dangerous. Such a development contains the possibility of other people's doing similar things in a worse way.[55]

Rogers, however, explained the design as being intimately related to the site's physical and historical context, and as exemplary of a sweeping challenge to the prevailing attitudes toward architectural and urban form, program, regional and local site specificity, and history. Challenging both modernist architecture and urbanism, he argued that to build in a preconceived modern style was as absurd as the modernist abandonment of architectural history, and that modernist urban proposals too often resulted in schemes antagonistic to existing cities and ways of life. In contrast, he called for architectural and urban plans that would respond to local climate and terrain, existing architectural and urban conditions, and the immense patrimony of inherited experience embodied in the city.[56]

1.8   Selected projects from CIAM '59 in Otterlo represented the diversity of approaches that emerged at CIAM's end. Aldo van Eyck's Children's Home (1955–60); detail of Kenzo Tange's Kagawa Prefectural Office (1955–58); Kiyonori Kikutake's Tokyo Bay project (1959); passive cooling strategies for Jerzy Soltan's Polish Exhibition Pavilion (Damascus, 1956)

1.9   Sharply criticized at CIAM '59 at Otterlo, Ernesto Rogers and BBPR's Torre Velasca (1950–57)
was nevertheless an important experiment in expanding the language of modern architecture
along regionalist lines

Rogers's argument for the history of architecture and place was a moral one that extended beyond empiricism and beyond the design project. He believed that a historical consciousness was necessary to be both modern and human:

> To be modern means simply to sense contemporary history within the order of all of history and thus to feel the responsibility of one's own acts not from within the closed barricade of an egoistic manifestation, but as a collaboration that, through one's contribution, augments and enriches the perennial contemporaneity of the possible formal combinations of universal relationship.[57]

NEO-RATIONALISM, NEO-REALISM, NEO-REGIONALISM, AND NEO-FUNCTIONALISM

Many modernist architects of the 1950s recognized the need to transcend the limits and legacy of functionalism, as revealed by their nascent research into vernacular architecture, urban form, anthropology, sociology, technology, structuralism, metabolism, and regionalism, and the other "New X-isms" identified by Reyner Banham. Nevertheless, the popular acceptance of modern architecture in the 1950s made it difficult for some to imagine the backlash that was to come in just a few years. As Jerzy Soltan put it in one of the concluding conversations of CIAM '59: "Everybody, everywhere seems to express the desire to be 'modern.' There is no longer a war between the old and the new—the old, it seems, has ceased to exist."[58]

Many modernist architects thus believed that the primary task of the post-CIAM era was to hold the line against historicism and populism. Whereas the task of early modernists had been to fight an external opposition, post-war architects saw the need to fight an internal threat, and to separate the "new modernists," who sought to satisfy popular tastes through superficial stylizations and regressions into history, from "true modernists," as Soltan labeled them.[59]

By contrast, others among the Generation of '56, like Aldo van Eyck, believed that the real threat to modern architecture was an internal enemy of a different kind: modernist urbanism and the system of thought behind it. As van Eyck put it:

> what is really wrong stems from the other enemy—the enemy of a system of analysis of "city"—of a creation of four keys, keys which don't fit the lock … You can go to Amsterdam and drive for hours through kilometers funktionnelle stadt made up of the four keys of CIAM—but you cannot live there. That is our enemy. The enemy is this terrible, rational, one track mind.[60]

In retrospect, both schools of thought were justified in their respective concerns about architectures that catered to popular tastes, whether historical or honky-tonk, and those that were so unconcerned about their contexts as to destroy the cities that they inhabited. The 1960s and '70s would be characterized by both extremes, with Charles Moore's Piazza d'Italia (1974–78) representing the former, and Paul Rudolph's Lower Manhattan megastructure project (1967–72) the latter. Between these two idioms—characterized in 1973 as a debate between "grays" and "whites"—the "postmodern" was, of course, the more publicly palatable.

1.10   Representing another failure of modernist urban design, Paul Rudolph's Lower Manhattan Expressway Project (1968) was the conceptual climax of the line of megastructural thinking that emerged around the time of CIAM '59

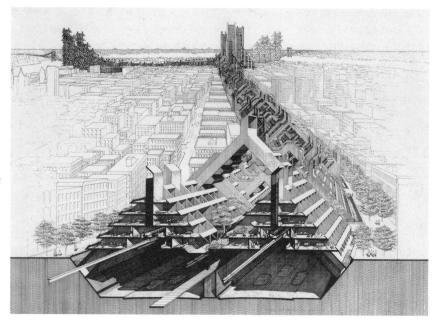

1.11   Ten years after Rudolph's LoMEx project, Charles Moore's Piazza d'Italia (1978) represented another extreme direction, and manifested the fears of some of the Generation of '56

Pushed by a populist movement that imagined architecture without architects, in the 1960s and '70s, architecture culture took up questions of architectural autonomy, historical reference, and popular taste, with a neo-realist position represented by Robert Venturi's work and a neo-rationalist position represented by Peter Eisenman's self-referential architecture characterizing two ends of the semiotic spectrum. Recognizing the situation as dysfunctional, Mario Gandelsonas

1.12 Celebrated as a work of regionalism in the age of globalization, Enric Miralles and Benedetta Tagliabue, Santa Caterina Market adaptation (1997–2001) models a combination of urban and architectural design, historic and contemporary architecture, site specificity and connection to the larger world

proposed a synthesis of neo-realism and neo-rationalism in the form of "neo-functionalism" in 1976, but the proposition added little to the ideas about functionalism put forward by Behne in the 1920s or Richards in the 1950s. It represented the restatement of a fundamental problem of modern architecture by a new generation.

Lagging more than a decade behind critiques that emerged from the late 1950s, such as Jacobs's *Death and Life of Great American Cities* (1961), it was not until the late 1970s, when many cities were at their nadir, that the Generation of '68 began to synthesize a new approach toward architecture and the city.[61] However, the CIAM '59 debate as to whether populist architecture or modern urbanism was the bigger problem would remain unresolved: the twentieth century would close without reconciliation between Leon Krier's utopian "Atlantis" (1986) and Koolhaas's anti-utopian "Generic City" (1994).[62]

Nevertheless, the twentieth century did not witness the complete triumph of either historicism or the "generic city": the unevenness of globalization, historic preservation and heritage movements, and the inherent inertia of people and places all provided some opposition to such forces. Moreover, more traditionally functionalist approaches continued to coexist, and to compete with, architectures that embrace time, place, and purpose. This seems to be an enduring state of affairs. The International Style coexisted with the Bay Region style and other regional styles in the late 1940s, in ways not unlike the coexistence of Classical and Gothic architecture; as Liane Lefaivre and Alexander Tzonis have observed, regionalism has a very long history.[63] Richards's 1950 vision for architecture in the second half of twentieth century has been vindicated: such approaches, regionalism among them, transcended the post-war transformations from "modern" to "contemporary" to "postmodern" architectural ideas. Through a common thread of "new empiricism"—

evident in the projects from around the world in the following chapters—modern architecture outlived reports of its untimely death and developed in response to the never-ending challenges of specificity and contemporaneity.

ACKNOWLEDGEMENTS

Special thanks to Adam Voelcker, Herman Gelton, Max Risselada, Dirk van den Heuvel, Tange Associates, Liane Lefaivre, Alexander Tzonis, and the photographers for their courtesy.

NOTES

1   Jean-Louis Cohen, *The Future of Architecture, Since 1889* (New York: Phaidon Press, 2012), 404.

2   Fred Kaplan, *1959: The Year Everything Changed* (New Jersey: John Wiley & Sons, 2009), 1.

3   See, for example, Kenneth Frampton, "The Vicissitudes of Ideology: CIAM and Team X, Critique and Counter-Critique 1928–68," *Modern Architecture: A Critical History* (New York: Thames & Hudson, 1980/92), 269, and William J.R. Curtis, *Modern Architecture since 1900*, 3rd edn (New York: Phaidon, 1996), 471. Similar to the third edition of Kenneth Frampton's canonical history, the 3rd edition of Curtis's book added chapters that expanded the history of twentieth-century architecture to cover regional and global aspects of modern architecture.

4   Curtis, *Modern Architecture since 1900*, 9, 16.

5   Peter Laurence, "The Unknown Jane Jacobs," *Reconsidering Jane Jacobs*, T. Mennel and M. Page (eds) (Chicago: Planners Press, 2011), 15.

6   Max Risselada and Dirk van den Heuvel's *Team 10: In Search of a Utopia of the Present* (Rotterdam: NAi Publishers, 2005) is an essential work for understanding architecture culture of the 1950s, '60s, and '70s.

7   Oscar Newman, *CIAM '59 in Otterlo* (Stuttgart: Karl Kramer Verlag, 1961), 16. See also Joan Ockman, *Architecture Culture 1943–1968: A Documentary Anthology* (New York: Columbia Books of Architecture/Rizzoli, 1993), 13–24; and Eric Mumford, *The CIAM Discourse on Urbanism, 1928–1960* (Cambridge, MA: The MIT Press, 2000), 248.

8   Le Corbusier, *Cathedrals*, 34.

9   Aldo van Eyck and Oscar Newman, "A Short Review of CIAM Activity: Bridgwater 1947: CIAM 6," *CIAM '59 in Otterlo*, 12.

10   J.M. Richards et al., "The Functional Tradition," *The Architectural Review* 107 (Jan. 1950), 3.

11   [John Voelcker, Peter Smithson, Alison Smithson], "Aix-en-Provence 1954: CIAM 9," *CIAM '59 in Otterlo*, 14.

12   Jacob Bakema, Aldo van Eyck et al., "Doorn Manifesto," *Architecture Culture 1943–1968*, J. Ockman (ed.) (New York: Columbia Books of Architecture, Rizzoli, 1993), 181–3. These concepts about the ecology and biology of the city had precedents. Volker Welter outlined some of the influences of Patrick Geddes's thinking in *Biopolis, Patrick Geddes and the City of Life* (Cambridge, MA: MIT Press, 2002), 253–4, and in *Team 10: In Search of a Utopia of the Present*.

13   Alison and Peter Smithson, "The Built World: Urban Re-Identification," *Architectural Design* (June 1955).

14   Jacob Bakema, "Introductory Talks," *CIAM '59 in Otterlo*, 21.

15   Aldo van Eyck, "Talk at the Conclusion of the Otterlo Congress," *CIAM '59 in Otterlo*, 216.

16   Aldo van Eyck, "Is Architecture Going to Reconcile Basic Values?" *CIAM '59 in Otterlo*, 26.

17   Ibid.

18   The common use of the word 'crisis' in English and some other languages can be analyzed with the help of Google's ngrams database (http://ngrams.googlelabs. com), which shows a precipitous rise in the use of the word around 1956, which peaked, curiously, around 2000. See http://ngrams.googlelabs.com/ngrams/ graph?content=crisis&year_start=1800&year_end=2011&corpus=0&smoothing=1. Thomas Kuhn's use of the term in his theory of intellectual change thus seems part of this context, but also gives some sense, if his theory has merit, of how the turmoil of the 1950s led to the revolutions of the 1960s.

19   Thomas Kuhn (1962), *The Structure of Scientific Revolutions*, 2nd edn (Chicago: University of Chicago Press, 1970), 82.

20   Ibid., 170–73.

21   Adolf Behne (1923), *The Modern Functional Building (Der moderne Zweckbau)* (Santa Monica, CA: Getty Research Institute, 1996), 123.

22   Henry-Russell Hitchcock and Philip Johnson (1932), *The International Style: Architecture Since 1922* (New York: W.W. Norton & Company, 1966), 39.

23   Ibid., 373.

24   Leicester B. Holland, "The Function of Functionalism," *Architect and Engineer* 126 (Aug. 1936), 25, 32. Presented at the 68th Convention of the American Institute of Architects, May 1936, and also reprinted in *Octagon* 8 (Jul. 1936), 3–10.

25   Ibid., 32.

26   Ernesto Rogers, "Program: Domus, The House of Man," *Domus* (Jan. 1946), reprinted in *Architecture Culture*, 77.

27   Robert Woods Kennedy, "Form, Function and Expression," *Journal of the American Institute of Architects* 14 (Nov. 1950), 198–204. Paul Zucker, "The Paradox of Architectural Theories at the Beginning of the Modern Movement," *Journal of the Society of Architectural Historians* 10 (Oct. 1951), 8. Lewis Mumford, "Function and Expression in Architecture," *Architectural Record* 110 (Nov. 1951), 108. Edward R. De Zurko, *Origins of Functionalist Theory* (New York: Columbia University Press, 1957).

28   Robert Venturi (1965), *Complexity and Contradiction in Architecture* (New York: Museum of Modern Art, 1977), 34. Aldo Rossi (1966), *The Architecture of the City*, D. Ghirardo and J. Ockman (trans.) (Cambridge, MA: MIT Press, 1982), 46. Mario Gandelsonas (1976), "Neo-Functionalism," *Oppositions Reader*, K. Michael Hays (ed.) (New York: Princeton Architectural Press, 1998), 7; Peter Eisenman (1976), "Post-Functionalism," *Oppositions Reader*, 9.

29   Ockman, *Architecture Culture*, 13.

30   J.M. Richards, "The New Empiricism: Sweden's Latest Style," *The Architectural Review* (Jun. 1947), 199.

31   Lewis Mumford, "Status Quo [The Bay Region Style]," *New Yorker* 23 (Oct. 11, 1947), 106. As Liane Lefaivre and Joan Ockman have observed in works cited here, Mumford's interests in regionalism may been traced to *Sticks and Stones* (1924), but J.M. Richards and *The Architectural Review* were influential: Mumford quoted J.M. Richards's essay "The New Empiricism" in "Status Quo" and seems to have been inspired by his ideas.

32   Museum of Modern Art, "What is Happening to Modern Architecture? A Symposium at the Museum of Modern Art," *Museum of Modern Art Bulletin* 15 (Spring 1948), 9.

33   J.M. Richards, "The Next Step?," *Architectural Review* 107 (Mar. 1950), 166.

34   Quoted in J.M. Richards, "The Next Step?," 181.

35   José Luis Sert, "Centers of Community Life," *The Heart of the City: Toward the Humanization of Urban Life* (London: Lund Humphries, 1952), 13.

36   Ibid., 14.

37   Walter Gropius, "Eight Steps Toward a Solid Architecture," *Architectural Forum* 100 (Feb. 1954), 156-57ff. See also Eero Saarinen, "The Six Broad Currents of Modern Architecture," *Architectural Forum* 99 (Jul. 1953), 110–15; Robert Woods Kennedy, "After the International Style – Then What?" *Architectural Forum* 99 (Sept. 1953), 130–33ff..

38   Gropius, "Eight Steps toward a Solid Architecture," 156.

39   James Stirling, "Ronchamp: Le Corbusier's Chapel and the Crisis of Rationalism," *The Architectural Review* 119 (March 1956), 160–61. See also James Stirling, "Garches to Jaoul: Le Corbusier as Domestic Architect in 1927 and 1953," *The Architectural Review* 118 (Aug. 1955), 145–51. Despite critiquing Jaoul Houses (1954–56) for irrationality and other flaws similar to Ronchamp, Jaoul served as a model for Stirling and Gowan's Ham Common (1955–58).

40   Reyner Banham, "Casa del Girasole: Rationalism and Eclecticism in Italian Architecture," *The Architectural Review* 113 (Feb. 1953), 77.

41   Robin Boyd, "The Functional Neurosis," *The Architectural Review* 119 (Feb. 1956), 85.

42   Boyd, ibid.

43   Richards, "The Next Step?," 181. See also Harwell Hamilton Harris's 1954 essay *"Regionalism and Nationalism,"* which can be found in Harry Francis Mallgrave's *Architectural Theory*, vol. 2 (Malden, MA: Blackwell Publishing), 288–9.

44   James Stirling, "Regionalism and Modern Architecture," *Architects' Year Book* 7 (1957), reproduced in Ockman, *Architecture Culture*, 248. Stirling was quoting British writer John Wain.

45   James Stirling, "Regionalism and Modern Architecture," *Architects' Year Book* 7 (1957), reproduced in Ockman, *Architecture Culture*, 248.

46   Reyner Banham, "The New Brutalism," *The Architectural Review* (Dec. 1955), 356.

47   Ibid.

48   Kenneth Frampton expanded Alex Tzonis and Liane Lefaivre's notion of "critical regionalism" in "Towards a Critical Regionalism," *The Anti-Aesthetic: Essays on Postmodern Culture*, H. Foster (ed.) (Seattle: Bay Press, 1983), 20.

49   Jacob Bakema, "Introduction," *CIAM '59 at Otterlo*, 10.

50   Ibid.

51   See Chapters 10 and 11, Nathaniel Coleman, *Utopias and Architecture* (New York: Routledge, 2005).

52   *CIAM '59 in Otterlo*, 186. For an outline of developments in urban design in the 1950s, see Peter Laurence, "The Death and Life of Urban Design," *Journal of Urban Design* 11 (Jun. 2006).

53   Ibid.

54   See *CIAM '59 in Otterlo*.

55   Ibid., 95–6.

56   Ernesto Rogers, "Preexisting Conditions and Issues of Contemporary Building Practice," *Architecture Culture 1943–1968*, J. Ockman (ed.) (New York: Columbia Books of Architecture, Rizzoli, 1993), 200–201.

57   Ibid.

58   *CIAM '59 in Otterlo*, 197.

59   Ibid.

60   Ibid.

61   Represented by such works as Colin Rowe's *Collage City* (1972–78), Venturi, Scott Brown, and Izenour's *Learning from Las Vegas* (1972), Rossi's "Analogical City" (1976), Bernhard Tschumi's "Manhattan Transcripts" (1976–81), Anthony Vidler's "Third Typology" (1977), Leon Krier's "Reconstruction of the City" (1978), and Rem Koolhaas's *Delirious New York* (1978).

62   Leon Krier, *Atlantis* (Brussels: A.A.M. Editions, 1988). Rem Koolhaas, "Generic City," *SMLXL* (New York: Monacelli Press, 1995), 1239.

63   Liane Lefaivre and Alexander Tzonis, *Architecture of Regionalism in the Age of Globalization, Peaks and Valleys in the Flat World* (New York: Routledge, 2012), 3.

2

Post-Modernism: Critique and Reaction

David Rifkind

As the modernist consensus of the immediate post-war period gave way to skepticism in the late 1950s and early 1960s, modern architecture faced critiques both from within (e.g. Team X) and without (Post-Modernism). The political crises and social transformations (civil rights and colonial independence movements, cold and hot wars, and economic upheavals) of these decades, alongside the not-quite-utopic results of a once radical modernism which was increasingly absorbed into capitalism and the state, precipitated profound reconsiderations of the ethical basis of architectural practice. By the early 1960s, many architects and intellectuals responded to a perceived homogeneity in Western architecture by seeking new vocabularies for architectural production. Some sought to bring new energy to modern architecture by adopting non-Western formal languages, others argued that vernacular architectures, which had already been celebrated by Le Corbusier and others, represented a "native genius" that had been suppressed by modernism's pervasive technological determinism, while others still called for a return of ornament and figuration in order to enable architecture to fulfill its historical role as a conveyer of meaning and marker of social order.[1]

Numerous architects challenged the professional codes of the discipline by pioneering new practices that stressed direct involvement of community groups in the design process, or by overturning the elitist structure of the discipline through popular participation in the fabrication and transformation of buildings.[2] These efforts coalesced in the 1970s with the emergence of a new trend in architecture, often Neoclassical in its overall tendency, characterized by the use of ornament, a concern with public space and historical context, and an effort to enliven streetscapes and bring drama to roofscapes. What became known as "Post-Modernism" in architecture was as diverse and pluralistic as the theoretical and aesthetic concerns that animated its principle advocates, from Robert Venturi and Denise Scott Brown to Charles Moore, Aldo Rossi, Philip Johnson, Michael Graves, James Stirling, Ricardo Legorreta, Robert Stern, Cesar Pelli and Ricardo Bofill.

Post-Modern architecture was not a single cohesive movement but rather a range of overlapping interests. In addition to describing a broad spectrum of design practices, Post-Modernism covers a wide variety of critical stances toward modernism that have been fueled by such extra-architectural sources as literature, philosophy, popular culture and the performing arts. A concern with questions of language and meaning and a desire to restore architecture's communicative function provoked explorations into semiotics and spurred research into history, sociology and anthropology. Post-modernism responded to the revolutionary rhetoric of modernism with the same suspicion that Jean-François Lyotard criticized as the meta-narratives underpinned by faith in science and reason.[3] Skeptical of modernism's utopian faith in architecture's ability to transform societies and individuals, Post-Modern architecture frequently extolled pluralism, playfulness, excess and ambiguity.

ROBERT VENTURI AND ALDO ROSSI: THE WAY OUT OF DOGMATIC MODERNISM

Of the numerous critical studies of modernism that appeared in the mid-1960s, the most noteworthy were Robert Venturi's *Complexity and Contradiction in Architecture* (1966), and Aldo Rossi's *Architecture of the City* (1966). These two seminal texts left a profound impact on architectural education and practice.[4] Within a decade, Venturi, Rossi and other architects were at work on large public projects that attempted to deal concretely with symbolism, history, precedent, typology, public space and urban planning.

Robert Venturi's *Complexity and Contradiction in Architecture* has frequently been misread as an apologia for eclecticism. Venturi's "gentle manifesto for a non-straightforward architecture" criticized the reductive logic and universal claims of orthodox modernism, and argued in favor of "an architecture that promotes richness and ambiguity over unity and clarity, contradiction and redundancy over harmony and simplicity." The book's trans-historical criticism, focusing on architectural qualities that are common to different historical epochs rather than tied to specific cultural contexts, became a common theme of Post-Modern thought. *Complexity and Contradiction* had the rare virtue of being both accessible to a general audience and significant as well to those versed in architectural history. The book offered scores of historical examples, organized thematically according to spatial and formal qualities, to elaborate the concepts of complexity and contradiction.[5]

Some of the ideas elaborated in *Complexity and Contradiction* were earlier applied in the house Venturi designed for his mother in the neighborhood of Chestnut Hill in Philadelphia (Figures 2.1 and 2.2). Completed in 1964, the Vanna Venturi House is densely layered with references to the work of a diverse range of architects who would feature in Venturi's polemical masterpiece, including Michelangelo, Le Corbusier, Frank Furness, Louis Kahn and Luigi Moretti. The juxtaposition of these formal gestures exemplifies Venturi's search for a "difficult unity of inclusion" rather than an "easy unity of exclusion." The broad gable and the recessed front porch of the Vanna Venturi House's principle façade present an iconographic representation of the American home. Yet numerous gestures, such as the displaced chimney and irregular windows, undermine its symmetry and the stability it signifies. The play of near symmetries imbues the house with tension through the ironic suggestion, but then elision, of a central focus—a technique Venturi identified in the work of both Michelangelo and Moretti. The house alludes to the bifurcated entry of Furness's Pennsylvania Academy of Fine Arts, a disquieting gesture Venturi had admired in *Complexity and Contradiction*, which also played an important role in the contemporary Guild House (completed in 1964). The front façade's Corbusian-inspired ribbon window opens onto the kitchen—the space

2.1   Robert Venturi, Vanna Venturi House, Philadelphia, 1964

2.2   Robert Venturi, Vanna Venturi House, Philadelphia, 1964

not coincidentally associated with Taylorist efficiency, Weimar-era gender concerns and the modernist cult of hygiene—announcing another theme of Post-Modern architecture, that of its capability to absorb in its discourse some of the elements of modernism.

Denise Scott Brown, Venturi's collaborator and spouse, injected a concern with social engagement and popular culture into the firm's design work and writing, which manifested itself in *Learning from Las Vegas*, published in 1972.[6] This study presented the streetscape of Las Vegas as an American vernacular that demonstrated a clarity of signification that modernist architects neglected, leading to the impoverishment of the built environment. Scott Brown and Venturi, along with their long-time collaborator Steven Izenour, argued in favor of an "ugly and ordinary" as opposed to a heroic architecture. They criticized the overwrought formal lyricism of high modern buildings that represented their programmatic function through idiosyncratic gestures, as in the work of Paul Rudolph. They eschewed these buildings, which they labeled "ducks," in favor of simpler structures—which they called "decorated sheds"—whose applied ornamentation communicated clearly, in the manner of billboard advertisements.

In *Complexity and Contradiction*, Venturi's interest in popular culture was filtered through the medium of Pop Art, whereas in collaboration with Scott Brown and Izenour, the firm's work engaged more directly with the material culture of everyday life. Taken from a more populist position than the literate criticism of Venturi's earlier book, *Learning from Las Vegas* involved a systematic study of Las Vegas strip architecture and signage. The book recorded work by Venturi, Scott Brown and their Yale graduate students, who combined the documentary-format photography of Edward Ruscha with empirical research and analytical methodologies drawn from the social sciences. *Learning from Las Vegas* made the honky-tonk streetscape a serious subject of study in American architecture schools and introduced a new popular vocabulary to architects steeped in the heroic traditions of orthodox modernism.[7]

After the populist Guild House, Venturi and Scott Brown realized a number of prestigious projects, including Gordon Wu Hall (1983) and Thomas Laboratories (1986), both at Princeton University, the Seattle Art Museum (1991), and the Sainsbury Wing, a controversial addition to the National Gallery in London (1991) (Figure 2.3). This significant work followed Prince Charles's criticism of the proposed addition by Ahrends Burton Koralek, which he likened to "a monstrous carbuncle on the face of a much loved and elegant friend." Venturi and Scott Brown responded with a design that matched the scale and materials of William Wilkins's 1838 building by inventively re-assembling the original structure's Neoclassical ornamentation in a manner that seems to draw equally from Baroque facade compositions and video editing techniques. The Sainsbury Wing mirrors and transforms the older building's Corinthian order columns; its ornamentation becomes more three-dimensional the farther it sits from the original building, echoing its full column-engaged column-pilaster sequence, yet compressing the elements into a series of layered pilasters at the point where the two buildings come closest. This gesture paradoxically emphasizes both the joint between the buildings and the parts of the façade farthest from it, introducing a compositional tension that rewards careful contemplation from Trafalgar Square. The Sainsbury Wing inverts the National Gallery's relationship to the ground by drawing the monumental stair indoors and opening the expansive main doors at sidewalk level in a gesture of accessibility.

In Europe, Aldo Rossi developed a broadly influential strain of Post-Modernism, rooted in a compelling historical critique of modern architecture and urbanism. Focusing on the notion of typology as a source of architectural form, rooted in both classical and industrial vernacular traditions, Rossi proposed an architecture of primary geometries whose simplified forms evoked an almost archaic timelessness. Rossi was a central figure in the Italian *Tendenza* movement, also-called Neorationalism, whose source material ranged from interwar Rationalism to rural farm buildings. In his seminal *The Architecture of the City* (1966), Rossi reaffirmed the importance of the traditional European city as a model of an integral collection of artifacts whose textures, scales and formal traditions must be respected by any new work of architecture. Paradoxically, his architecture was formalist and projected itself as "autonomous", even though it was inspired by works deeply immersed in the social life of their urban contexts. *The Architecture of the City* explicitly rejected the reductive principle of "Functionalism", a central tenet of modernist thought since Louis Sullivan, the roots of which extend all the way back to A.W.N. Pugin. Instead, Rossi argued that all major artifacts go through many transformations in time, alternating functions and adapting to different usages, which does not reduce their architectural significance. Instead of "function,"

2.3   Venturi, Scott Brown and Associates, Sainsbury Wing of the National Gallery, London, 1991

Rossi argued, it is the concept of type which could be more useful as a tool for the production of a legible and coherent built environment, which becomes a living record of a society's collective memory.

One of the earliest projects by Rossi to express this new "tendency" was the San Cataldo Cemetery in Modena, a competition he won in 1971 that required an addition to the city's nineteenth-century cemetery. Rossi and Gianni Braghieri designed the cemetery as a solemn ensemble of buildings—almost diagrammatic in their formal simplicity—housing different programs, including a large ossuary, columbaria and a common grave. Though only partially realized, San Cataldo expressed the metaphysical quality that often emerged from Rossi's typological investigations. The ossuary cube that dominates the complex has neither a roof nor glazing in its windows, as if the sheltering function of architecture were suspended for the dead.

The significance of Rossi's typological method was translated in a number of other projects, from town halls and museums to public libraries and social housing, among which figure prominently his projects for housing in Berlin on Wilhelmstrasse (1981) and Paris at la Villette (1986), the Town Hall in Borgoricco (1983), the Bonnefanten Museum in Maastrich (1990), and the residential complex at Schutzenstrasse in Berlin (1998), which restored a complete block of the city's urban fabric, using a variety of urban types in a single complex.

Rossi's ephemeral project for the Teatro del Mondo, built for the 1979 Venice Bennale, offered the architect an opportunity to reinvest architecture with the ability to produce and sustain collective memory (Figure 2.4). Rossi resurrected an eighteenth-century building type—the temporary floating theater—as a space of public appearance.[8] The building's massing is deceptively simple: a nearly cubic volume houses the theater-in-the-round, flanked by rectangular stair towers and topped by an octagonal lantern and cap. The wood exterior, painted in bright, theatrical colors, clads a metal scaffolding structure left exposed on the interior to celebrate the building's temporality. The paradigm of the urban theater as a space of public interaction recurred frequently in Rossi's work, especially through the device of the broad flight of stairs-cum-grandstand in such projects as the Monument to Sandro Pertini (Milan, 1990) and the Hotel Il Palazzo (Fukuoka, 1987).

As media for developing architectural ideas, drawing and painting were as important to Rossi as writing. The architect's graphic works frequently depicted building types afloat in idealized cities, imbued with the disquieting silence of a landscape populated with effigies. Often described as evocative of De Chirico's paintings, Rossi's metaphysical streetscapes can also be compared to the work of John Hejduk, whose built projects similarly draw from a cast of recurring figures that first appeared in his drawings and watercolors.

Rossi's significance in the development of this brand of Post-Modernism, with its clear Neorationalist accent, was not limited to these projects that he built, but also extended to his influence on a whole generation of architects, from Giorgio Grassi to Oswald Matthias Ungers and even Jacques Herzog and Pierre de Meuron, who elaborated and developed the principles that he advocated.

NARRATING POST-MODERNISM/ EXHIBITING POST-MODERNISM

2.4   Aldo Rossi,
Teatro del Mondo,
Venice, 1979

Architectural historians, critics and pedagogues played significant roles in developing a theoretical basis for Post-Modern architectural practice. Colin Rowe occupies a particularly important position among the intellectuals who provoked a radical rethinking of modernist orthodoxies. Rowe's trans-historical analyses of architectural form-making, beginning with his seminal essay "The Mathematics of the Ideal Villa", comparing the compositional strategies of villas by Palladio and Le Corbusier dissociated architectural languages from their cultural contexts and refocused design on primarily aesthetic, rather than ethical, concerns.[9] Rowe's skepticism toward the utopian aspirations of modern architecture and his analytical stance toward existing city fabric impacted the work of architects as diverse as James Stirling and Peter Eisenman.

In 1973, Rowe collaborated with Fred Koetter on *Collage City*, an important analysis of traditional city form and critique of modern urban planning doctrine.[10] *Collage City* challenged the central modernist notions of tabula rasa and utopia. Instead, Rowe argued, architecture had an obligation to engage the existing fabric of the city and to respond to its textures and heterogeneity. The traditional city developed over long periods of time through the overlapping and collision of independent fragments, he maintained. In his rejection of social engagement,

Rowe developed a formalist theory based on architecture's disciplinary autonomy. Rome figured prominently in *Collage City*, where it served as an example of a richly textured urban context whose synthetic form stands in opposition to the ideal of the tabula rasa, favored by the modernists. For Rowe, Hadrian's Villa in Tivoli exemplified the concept of bricolage, especially when contrasted against the proto-modernist utopian planning of Louis XIV's Versailles.[11]

Contemporary with the publication of *Collage City*, Rowe participated in the exquisite corpse of *Roma Interrotta* (1978) in which a dozen architects and critics reimagined the plates of Nolli's 1748 map of Rome. Giulio Carlo Argan and Christian Norberg-Schulz curated the project, which was exhibited in 1978.[12] The formal manipulations of *Roma Interrotta* and its focus on Rome fueled a growing interest the historical structure of public, urban space and the possibility of engaging the metropolis in ways that respected their historical context.

As the self-proclaimed apostle of the new movement, Charles Jencks played a central role in promoting Post-Modern architecture.[13] Jencks's 1977 book, *The Language of Post-Modern Architecture*, outlined the diverse formal and conceptual practices that comprised the nascent movement.[14] He saw Post-Modern architecture as self-consciously "double-coded," and catalogued the use of poetic tropes— such as irony, metaphor and simile—to convey meaning on multiple levels.[15] *The Language of Post-Modern Architecture* went through many reprints and over time was revised to accommodate new material and new projects. Jencks argued that Post-Modernism more accurately reflected the pluralism of contemporary culture, and thus embraced heterogeneity, discontinuity, and conflict. In a nod to populist rhetoric, Jencks opened *The Language of Post-Modern Architecture* with a spectacular, if misleading, account of the demolition of Minoru Yamasaki's Pruitt-Igoe Housing in St. Louis (built 1952–56) in 1972—an event he singled out as the moment of death of modern architecture.

Urbanism remained an important part of the Post-Modern reaction, and exhibitions were a key medium in which to test and diffuse ideas. When the Venice Biennale added a sector for architecture in 1980, Italian architect Paolo Portoghesi invited 20 architects to create facades along an imaginary street—the "strada novissima"—as the centerpiece of an exhibition whose theme, "The Presence of the Past," spoke to the growing concern with traditional forms and spatial relationships throughout the Western world(Figure 2.5).[16] Along with Portoghesi, who stepped in to replace Christian de Portzamparc, the other architects were Venturi Rauch and Scott Brown, Frank Gehry, Rem Koolhsas, Hans Hollein, Arata Isozaki, Michael Graves, Robert Stern, Leon Krier and Maurice Culot, Ricardo Bofill, Oswalt Mathias Ungers, Costantino Dardi, Franco Purini and Laura Thermes, Alessandro Anselmi, Thomas Gordon-Smith, Studio GRAU, Charles Moore, Stanley Tigerman, Allan Greenberg, Massimo Scolari, and Joseph Paul Kleihues. The facades, which became full-scale portals opening onto monographic displays of each architect's work, lined both sides of an urban thoroughfare running through the Corderie dell'Arsenale and demonstrated simultaneously the Post-Modern concern with signification and public space. Portzamparc later added an entry when the facades traveled to Paris and San Francisco.

2.5   Paolo Portoghesi (curator) and collaborators, Strada Novissima, Venice, 1980

The work exhibited at the 1980 Biennale prompted German philosopher Jürgen Habermas to write a pointed critique of Post-Modern architecture's retreat from the Enlightenment goal of rationally reorganizing social life. Reason, logic, objective science and universal morality were part of modernity's "incomplete project," which architecture could not abandon, argued Habermas.[17] Other philosophers and social critics have followed Habermas's spirited defense of modernism, including Frederic Jameson, who largely dismissed Post-Modern architecture as a pastiche which serves as the superstructural production of late capitalism.[18]

In parallel, some philosophical concepts also lent intellectual support for Post-Modern architecture. Christian Norberg-Schulz attempted a phenomenological interpretation of architecture based on the later writings of Martin Heidegger. Norberg-Schulz's influential books, beginning with *Existence, Space and Architecture* (1971), posited the need for architecture to relate to, and make manifest, the specific nature of a place.[19] In his later works, Norberg-Schulz would develop the concept of *genius loci* as a means to revive the essential qualities of "place," as opposed to the universal notion of "space," arguing that it ought to inform every work of architecture, from the micro scale of tectonics to the macro scale of site and landscape.[20] Later, in his *The Concept of Dwelling* (1985), Norberg-Schulz would more explicitly call for a revival of the "figural" quality of architecture, endorsing the Post-Modern revival of figurative architecture.[21]

Christopher Alexander played a significant, though marginal, role in the Post-Modernist discourse of the 1970s with a detailed critique of the practice of architecture which extended beyond questions of style or meaning. Alexander's *A Pattern Language* (1968) combined insights from systems theory with social sciences methodologies to form a generative grammar for architectural design, and to propose a new way of building, akin to traditional vernacular practices around the world, which he argued would create more humane and socially meaningful environments. One of the essential tools for such a radical revision of design would be the act of involving the collective in the design process, and reducing the role of the architect to that of a coordinator of the design process.[22] Alexander applied his design theories in a series of projects in California, Latin America, and Europe, among which figures the Linz Cafe in Austria (1980).[23] His strongest influence on the profession was through his widely read and often cited writings.

CIVIC AND CORPORATE IDENTITY

Many of the key Post-Modern architects began their careers as modernists. Of these Philip Johnson, may be the best example. As co-curator of the 1932 International Style exhibition at the Museum of Modern Art, Johnson played a key role in the introduction of international modernism into North America. As designer of the Glass House in New Canaan, CT (1949), and collaborator with Ludwig Mies van der Rohe on the Seagram Building (1958), Johnson helped define and promote the image of orthodox modernism in America. Yet Johnson was already moving toward a revival of classical forms by 1964, the year he completed the New York State Theater at Lincoln Plaza, a project whose Michelangelo-esque plan by Wallace Harrison, chief architect of the United Nations complex, reveals a larger move toward more conservative ideas of organizing civic space among American architects. Johnson (along with partner John Burgee) made one of the most important contributions to the emergence of Post-Modernism with the construction of a new headquarters tower for the American Telephone and Telegraph Company (AT&T) in New York City. The skyscraper was the iconic building type of modernity, if not necessarily of the Modern Movement. To a later generation of Post-Modernists, the ornament and whimsy of New York's Art Deco towers—above all the Chrysler Tower and the Empire State Building—struck a chord composed of artful massing, decorative arts and corporate identity. Yet by 1958, the year Johnson and Mies completed the Seagram Building, the skyscraper had come to represent the complete assimilation of modernism by corporate capitalism. Johnson's AT&T building (designed in 1978 and completed in 1984) announced Post-Modernism's acceptance by the nation's commercial elites, who would soon embrace ornamented architecture as another medium of publicity and a means toward establishing brand identity.

Michael Graves, another pioneer of the second generation of American Modernists, was a member of the short-lived New York Five, a movement that set out to revive the formal principles of 1920s European Modernism in projects that elided the social, technological and functional concerns of their antecedents. Graves established his modernist credentials with a series of Corbusian-inspired villas, beginning with the 1967 Hanselmann House in Fort Wayne, Indiana. This elegant Purist exercise includes an entry sequence which draws the visitor through a series of spatial layers defined by facades and lines of structure, drawing as much on Colin Rowe's analyses of Corbusian space as on the 1920s buildings to which Rowe referred. Graves explored architectural themes as a painter—a large mural is integral to the design of the Hanselmann House—and by the mid-1970s, Graves had begun a gradual shift towards a playful, neoclassical Post-Modernism, employing abstracted classical motifs and a rich, polychromatic palette of pastels and earth tones.

Graves revived the debate over the appropriate form of public buildings with his landmark project for the Portland Municipal Services Building (1980–82), popularly called the Portland Building, a project he won through a competition, in which Philip Johnson was a jury member (Figure 2.6). Graves challenged the bureaucratic indifference exuded by the monotonous government office buildings built after the second world war with a project that wrapped a heavy, polychromatic masonry veneer around an otherwise conventional structure. While the building did not relate specifically to the architectural heritage of Portland, it attempted to invest this public structure with a decorum appropriate to its civic function. Jencks cited the Portland Building, which figured prominently on the cover of one of his editions of *Post-Modern Architecture*, for its

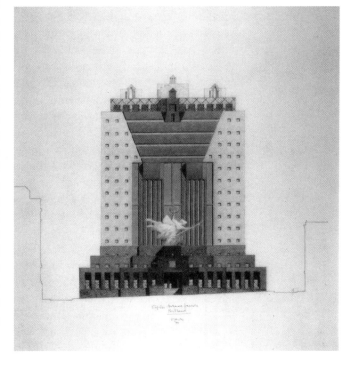

2.6   Michael Graves, Portland Municipal Services Building, Portland (Oregon), 1980–82

sense of scale, use of symbolism, and commitment to fostering civic identity, which he contrasted against the AT&T building's concern with corporate identity.[24] Formally, its four facades read as independent graphic exercises that make little effort to engage the neighboring city hall, nor the large square which it faces to the east. Yet the Portland Building's importance lies in the influence it had on governments worldwide, which commissioned major Post-Modern projects like the Missisauga City Hall (Jones and Kirkland, 1982–87), the Beverly Hills Civic Center (Charles Moore, 1988–90) and the new Parliament House in Canberra (Mitchell/Giurgola, 1988).

POST-MODERNISM AND GLOBALIZATION

In Europe, and in parallel with the Italian movement led by Rossi, an equally momentous shift was made by Scottish architect James Stirling.[25] Stirling was one of the young architects who first voiced their criticism of Le Corbusier's Ronchamp chapel, rejecting its pre-modern forms and revival of vernacular languages.[26] Yet a decade after popularizing a Constructivist-inspired architecture, as demonstrated by his Engineering Faculty at Leicester University (1959–63) and History Faculty at Cambridge University (1964–67), Stirling began to adopt planning strategies, proportional systems and material palettes derived from a study of Neoclassical architecture. His new reading of the importance of context and urban space found expression in the Neue Staatsgalerie in Stuttgart, where he developed a formal syntax built on unexpected juxtapositions of modernist gestures, like the Corbusian piano curve, with heavy masses of masonry and new ornamental detailing (Figures 2.7 and 2.8). Stirling employed richly textured stone cladding, against which he contrasted brightly colored industrial materials like ships' railings, metal sash windows, exposed structural steel and resilient flooring, in a unique synthesis of modern and traditional materials.

The Neue Staatsgalerie (1984) represented a sophisticated interpretation of typological precedent without the superficial adoption of historical forms. Stirling inverted the *parti* of Karl Friedrich Schinkel's Altes Museum in Berlin (1824–28), turning the central rotunda into an exterior courtyard while maintaining the Berlin precedent's enfilade of rectangular galleries for displaying art. The courtyard gathers and organizes a series of outdoor circulation spaces whose paths and terraces mediate the change in elevation across the steeply sloped site. Stirling developed a picturesque three-dimensional circuit route through the site, engendering a sense of surprise and discovery through spaces that open onto one another and onto views of the city, while connecting parallel avenues. The Neue Staatsgalerie provided a model for cultural institutions to engage and enrich the city fabric. Yet, as Anthony Vidler has remarked, while Stirling astutely re-interpreted the classical model of the Altes Museum, he avoided presenting a recognizable "face" to the street out of deference to the difficult status of monumentality in post-war Germany.[27]

The same year that Johnson designed the AT&T building, Catalan architect Ricardo Bofill began work on two large apartment complexes in France whose scale was grander than anything yet realized by the nascent Post-Modernist movement.[28] The two projects, Les Arcades du Lac in Saint Quentin-en-Yvelines, and Les Espaces d'Abraxas in Marne la Vallée, were commissioned through a French government program to relieve congestion in Paris by developing new towns outside the capital, and were completed in 1982 (Figure 2.9). Conceived at the scale of urban design, both projects employed facades articulated with classical elements inflated to the extent that "entablatures" now encompassed three stories, and columns could stretch as much as 12 stories in height. While Bofill has written of his interest in the architecture of Michelangelo and the Baroque, his work most closely recalls the inventive classicism and utopian urbanism of Claude-Nicolas

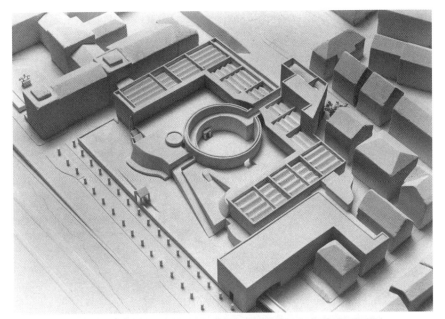

2.7   James Stirling
Michael Wilford
and Associates,
Neue Staatsgalerie,
Stuttgart, 1984

2.8   James Stirling
Michael Wilford
and Associates,
Neue Staatsgalerie,
Stuttgart, 1984

2.9   Taller Ricardo
Bofill, Les Espaces
d'Abraxas, "L'Arc"
and "Le Palacio,"
Marne la Vallée
(France), 1982

Ledoux. Bofill's cities in miniature are complete and whole within their clearly delimited borders, like Ledoux's royal saltworks in the Franche-Comté. Like its Enlightenment predecessor, Les Espaces d'Abraxas arranges some of its housing in a semi-circular plan to define a large outdoor theater. While Ledoux's "theater of industry" was a metaphorical device intended to model a relationship between management and labor, Boffil's is a literal transcription of a classical theater into the plan of the housing complex, in order to designate the space as public and to invest it with intended patterns of civic use.[29]

THE URBAN CRITIQUE OF MODERNISM

Post-modernism drew considerable energy from a diverse range of critiques of modernist urban planning practices. Jane Jacobs and Kevin Lynch offered different challenges to CIAM orthodoxy which resonated with the Post-Modern concern with traditional urban environments. Jacobs, a writer and activist, and Lynch, a professor of urban planning, influenced several generations of architects and planners who never adopted the formal attributes of Post-Modernism. In her seminal essay, *The Death and Life of Great American Cities*, Jacobs developed a critique of urban planning methods from the standpoint of civic life and the everyday experience of the city.[30] Jacobs was more interested in social participation than in aesthetic dogma. She stressed the need to preserve and amplify the traditional form of cities, and repeatedly organized successful protests against large-scale urban renewal and infrastructural projects which would have gutted thriving neighborhoods. She argued that neither the garden city movement with its emphasis on low-density urbanism, nor "Le Corbusier's Utopia," with its segregation of the city into single-use districts, could produce the vitality of life in such dense and vibrant neighborhoods as San Francisco's North Beach-Telegraph Hill, Philadelphia's Rittenhouse Square or New York's Greenwich Village.[31]

Lynch, too, offered a street-level view of urban experience that challenged post-war urban planning doctrine. In *The Image of the City*, Lynch set aside the planimetric and abstract planning categories of zoning, density and circulation in favor of a notion of "imageability"—the image of the built environment as a component of the daily life of a city's residents, based on extensive interviews with those citizens.[32] Lynch argued that exemplary cities could be read in terms of five experiential elements: paths, edges, districts, nodes and landmarks. Like Jacobs' "eyes on the street," Lynch's analytical terms changed the very vocabulary with which designers and thinkers described the built environment.

The participatory democracy Jacobs championed resonated with many architects, among whom Charles Moore emerged as a major proponent of community participation in the design process. In 1974, Moore was commissioned to design a public space in New Orleans that would commemorate the city's Italian American community and help revive a neighborhood in decline. Completed in 1978, the Piazza d'Italia featured a large fountain shaped like a map of Italy and set in front of a scenographic montage of colonnades and arched openings that turn the plaza into a urban theater (Figures 2.10 and 2.11). Moore attempted to imbue the infill development with a sense of wonder and surprise that would reward the pedestrian with rich experiences when approached from different directions. He juxtaposed traditional Italian materials and finishes, including ashlar masonry, stone paving and painted stucco, with the garish palette of a shopping mall (neon lights and reflective metal surfaces) to create an ensemble that was both recognizably Italian in its formal language and unmistakably American in its playful use of puns and ironic gestures. Moore's work is full of playful gestures that counter the disciplinary seriousness of architecture with a humor that invites engagement on the part of the viewer, implicitly eroding the coercive nature of architecture in pursuit of more democratic spatial practices.

The Piazza d'Italia commission followed the completion of Kresge College (1972–74), a residential college at the University of California at Santa Cruz whose composition gave physical form to an innovative pedagogical program that stressed student participation in academic governance. Moore and partner William Turnbull generated a sense of community through an irregular streetscape whose porches and balconies were designed to promote interaction between students and faculty, many of whom resided in the complex. The architects looked to the street life of traditional small towns as an analogue to the discourse-generating spaces of Kresge College, and referred to Italian hill towns as a precedent for the California project's response to the site's steeply sloped topography.

Léon Krier's influential critique of modernist urban planning is concerned with the legibility of architectural forms and the appropriate scale of cities. In essays dating to the mid-1970s and a series of urban plans that include the unrealized redesign of his native Luxembourg (1978) and a fantastic "completion" of Washington, DC, that replaces the city's symbolic public spaces with vast canals (1984), Krier has

2.10 Charles
Moore, Piazza
d'Italia, New
Orleans, 1978

2.11 Charles
Moore, Piazza
d'Italia, New
Orleans, 1978

2.12   Léon Krier,
Jorge M. Perez
Architecture
Center, University
of Miami, Coral
Gables, 2006

made the case that buildings must observe typological conventions in order to properly express their civic functions, and that cities and neighborhoods need both programmatic variety (e.g. housing and shops in close proximity) and a population density similar to that of traditional European cities in order to thrive. As a key proponent of the New Urbanist movement, he has attracted the patronage of the Prince of Wales (for whom he designed the Cornish town of Poundbury, 1993 to the present) and the Miami-based architects and planners Andres Duany and Elizabeth Plater-Zyberk, with whom he collaborated on the design of Seaside, Florida (1978–85).[33] In her role as dean of the School of Architecture at the University of Miami, Plater-Zyberk was instrumental in securing the commission for Krier's design of the school's new auditorium and exhibition hall (2000), in replacement of an earlier, unrealized design by Aldo Rossi.

A CONTINUING CRITIQUE

Post-Modernism found an enthusiastic reception outside western Europe and North America. Architects as diverse as Charles Correa in Mumbai, Arata Isozaki in Tokyo and Ricardo Legorreta in Mexico City have produced buildings of great narrative depth using formal languages and syntaxes of simple geometries abstracted from traditional forms. Their work reflects a broad concern with regional specificity in architecture and demonstrates a diverse range of responses to climatic, cultural and economic conditions. Such practices are not antithetical to modernism, however. Legoretta's and Correa's debts to Luis Barragan and Louis Kahn, respectively, are exemplary of Post-Modernism's roots in post-war modernism's self-criticism and the rich legacy of regionalism in modern architecture.

In Egypt, Abdel-Wahed El-Wakil, a disciple of Hassan Fathy, was awarded the 2009 Driehaus Prize for his revival of traditional Middle Eastern and Islamic architecture.[34] El-Wakil, who has twice been awarded the Aga Khan Award, shares Fathy's concern with traditional building typologies and construction methods. His architecture is driven by a strong interest in vernacular and historical form, rather than by a rejection of modern architecture. Like the Neoclassicism of Allan Greenberg (a Driehaus laureate in 2006), El-Wakil's work seems indifferent, rather than antagonistic, to modernism.

No decisive break marks the border between Modernism and Post-Modernism. Jencks's rhetorical assertion that the "death of modernism" can be dated precisely (and explained as a popular rejection of its ideology) helped legitimize a range of Post-Modern critiques, but it obscures the fact that the two "movements" are so broad that they share numerous conceptual concerns and formal attributes. For example, the search for timeless principles of design that figures so prominently in the writings of Alexander and Norberg-Schulz was also a central concern for Mies and Kahn. Many of the formal or stylistic gestures associated with Post-Modernism—such as the integration of figurative arts, the use of ornament, the adoption of symmetrical planning strategies, the interpretive adaptation of building typologies, the concern with local traditions and even the occasional interest in Expressionism—also appeared in many modernist works. What's more, Post-Modernism can lay claim to a number of practices—like those of Rem Koolhaas/OMA—whose critiques of doctrinaire Modernism nonetheless affirm many of the avant-garde concerns that shaped twentieth-century architecture. Both Modernism and Post-Modernism are too diverse to characterize as simple opposites. Post-Modern architecture's origins in the decades of modernist self-criticism and both movements' contrasting interests in narrative and social engagement, mark them as twinned expressions of a discipline constantly examining its origins and ends, rather than two movements separated by a clear rupture.

NOTES

1   Architects who looked to non-Western formal languages included Juan O'Gorman and Walter Gropius. The "native genius" group included Sibyl Moholy Nagy and Bernard Rudofsky. Those who argued for a return of ornament and figuration in order to enable architecture to fulfill its historical role as a conveyer of meaning and marker of social order included Robert Stern, Charles Jencks, Allan Greenberg, and Rob and Leon Krier.

2   Numerous architects challenged the professional codes of the discipline by pioneering new practices that stressed direct involvement of community groups in the design process (Charles Moore), or by overturning the elitist structure of the discipline through popular participation in the fabrication and transformation of buildings (Archigram, Christopher Alexander).

3   Jean-François Lyotard, *The Postmodern Condition: A Report on Knowledge*, trans. Geoffrey Bennington and Brian Massumi, Minnesota, 1984; first published as *La condition Post-Moderne: Rapport sur le savoir*. Paris: Les Éditions de Minuit, 1979.

4   Robert Venturi. *Complexity and Contradiction in Architecture* (New York: Museum of Modern Art, 1966), Aldo Rossi, *Architecture of the City* (1966), trans. Diane Ghirardo and Joan Ockman (New York: Oppositions Books, 1982). Other significant texts from this period include Christian Norberg-Schulz, *Intentions in Architecture* (Cambridge: MIT Press, 1965), Christopher Alexander, *Notes on the Synthesis of Form* (Cambridge: Harvard Univeristy Press, 1964), and Vittorio Gregotti, *Il territorio dell'architettura* (Milan: Feltrinelli, 1966).

5   Venturi roots his text in an effective reading of T.S Eliot and other literary theorists. Though neither systematic nor rigorous in its analyses, the book is nevertheless extraordinarily insightful and persuasive.

6   The importance of popular culture as an existing condition to be accommodated and a source material to be mined for architectural practice was established as early as 1956, in the work of Alison and Peter Smithson, and Team X.

7   The importance of popular culture as both an existing condition to be accommodated and a source material to be mined for architectural practice was established as early as 1956, when Alison and Peter Smithson published "But Today We Collect Ads" *ARK* (November 1957). The Smithsons were members of Team X and of the interdisciplinary Independent Group, which formed at London's Institute of Contemporary Arts in 1952 and included influential pop artists Eduardo Paolozzi and Richard Hamilton, and architectural critic and historian Reyner Banham. In collaboration with Paolozzi and photographer Nigel Henderson, the Smithsons made the case for juxtaposing high- and pop-culture forms in the space they designed as one of twelve displays in the Independent Group's "This Is Tomorrow" exhibition at the Whitechapel Gallery in 1956. Scott Brown came into contact with the Independent Group while studying at the Architectural Association in London in the 1950s, and she brought the British group's interest in integrating popular culture and modern architecture with her to Philadelphia.

8   Hannah Arendt, *The Human Condition* (Chicago: University of Chicago Press, 1958), 198.

9   Colin Rowe, "The Mathematics of the Ideal Villa," *The Architectural Review* (March 1947): 101–104.

10   Colin Rowe and Fred Koetter, *Collage City* (Cambridge: MIT Press, 1978).

11   Rowe discussed the villa in a trans-historical criticism, much as Charles Moore had in a 1960 essay that presented Hadrian's project as a heterodox alternative to the orthodox classicism of Rome in an allegorical critique of the orthodoxies of the Moore's International Style contemporaries. Charles W. Moore, "Hadrian's Villa," *Perspecta*, vol. 6 (1960): 16–27.

12   Giulio Carlo Argan and Christian Norberg-Schulz, (eds) *Roma Interrotta* (London: Architectural Design, 1979). *Roma Interrotta* included a plate by Colin Rowe and collaborators Peter Carl, Judith DiMaio and Steven Peterson. Argan had long been a proponent of a modernism that addressed social issues with a concern for the individual. By 1978, Argan admitted Modernism's inability to fulfill its mission of social transformation (a project forged in the Enlightenment), but remained committed to the transformative potential of architecture.

13   Elie Haddad, "Charles Jencks and the Historiography of Post-Modernism," *The Journal of Architecture*, vol. 14, Iss. 4, (2009): 493–510.

14   Charles Jencks, *The Language of Postmodern Architecture* (New York: Rizzoli, 1977).

15   Jencks was an important proponent of semiotics, and, along with George Baird, adapted the semiological thought of Ferdinand de Saussure and Roland Barthes to both the analysis and production of architecture. Charles Jencks and George Baird (eds), *Meaning in Architecture* (New York: Braziller, 1969).

16   Gabriella Borsano (ed.), *Architecture 1980: The Presence of the Past* (New York: Rizzoli, 1980).

17   Jürgen Habermas, "Modernity – An Incomplete Project," 1980, in Hal Foster, *The Anti-Aesthetic: Essays on Postmodern Culture* (Port Townsend, WA: Bay Press, 1983), 3–15.

18   Frederic Jameson, *Postmodernism, or the Cultural Logic of Late Capitalism* (Durham, NC: Duke University Press, 1991), 18.

19   Christian Norberg-Schulz, *Existence, Space & Architecture* (New York: Praeger, 1971).

20   Norberg-Schulz, *Genius Loci: Towards a Phenomenology of Architecture* (New York: Rizzoli, 1979). See also his *Existence, Space & Architecture*.

21   Christian Norberg-Schulz, *The Concept of Dwelling: On the Way to Figurative Architecture* (New York: Electa, 1985).

22   Christopher Alexander, Sara Ishikawa and Murray Silverstein, *A Pattern Language Which Generates Multi-Service Centers* (Berkeley: Center for Environmental Structure, 1968).

23   Christopher Alexander, *The Linz Cafe* (New York: Oxford University Press, 1981).

24   Charles Jencks, *The Language of Postmodern Architecture*.

25   Stirling was also a student of Rowe's and was one of the twelve architects who participated in the Roma Interrotta project.

26   James Stiriling, "Ronchamp: Le Corbusier's Chapel and the Crisis of Rationalism," *Architectural Review* (March 1956): 155–161.

27   Anthony Vidler, "Losing Face," in *The Architectural Uncanny* (Cambridge: MIT Press, 1992), 85–100. Vidler wrote in response to Colin Rowe's criticism of the building. Stirling and his partner Michael Wilford designed the Neue Staatsgalerie for a 1977 competition that called for both an addition to the nineteenth-century Staatsgalerie and a way to revitalize the center of Stuttgart and bring definition to a difficult site surrounded by cultural institutions.

28   1978 was a watershed year for Post-Modernism. In addition to Johnson and Bofill's projects, the year saw the completion of Piazza d'Italia, the publication of *Collage City*, the exhibition of Roma Interrotta and such unrealized projects as Léon Krier's urban plan for Luxembourg.

29   Anthony Vidler, "The Theater of Industry: Ledoux and the Factory-Village of Chaux," in *The Writing of the Walls* (New York: Princeton Architectural Press, 1987), 35–51.

30   Jane Jacobs, *The Death and Life of Great American Cities* (New York: Random House, 1961).

31   Ibid., 21.

32   Kevin Lynch, *The Image of the City* (Cambridge: MIT Press, 1960).

33   In 1993, Duany and Plater-Zyberk co-founded the Congress for the New Urbanism (CNU) with Peter Calthorpe, Elizabeth Moule, Stefanos Polyzoides and Dan Solomon.

34   The Driehaus Prize was conceived as an alternative to the Pritzker Prize, and has also been awarded to Léon Krier, Demetri Porphyrios, Quinlan Terry, Allan Greenberg, Jaquelin T. Robertson, Andrés Duany and Elizabeth Plater-Zyberk, Rafael Manzano Martos and Robert A.M. Stern.

3

High-Tech: Modernism Redux

Sarah Deyong

Out of all the movements to emerge from the ruins of May '68, it is High Tech architecture that has remained the most faithful to the ideals of the modern movement. Unlike postmodernism, High Tech still subscribes to the values of a heroic modernism: the belief in truth to materials and methods of construction and the faith in technological innovation for the social good. Its architects are the product of a modernist tradition that begins in the first machine age with the Arts and Crafts Movement and Joseph Paxton (architect of the Crystal Palace), and continues into the twentieth century with Buckminster Fuller, Frei Otto, Charles and Ray Eames, and Jean Prouvé. Drawing inspiration from earlier experiments in prototyping, for example, they work in close collaboration with engineers and manufacturers, much in the spirit of a guild. But if their ideals come from the past, their means are decidedly forward-looking, embracing the technologies of more advanced industries than building. The moniker "High Tech" therefore reflects the group's futuristic outlook, promoted foremost by the architectural historian Reyner Banham, who successively championed contemporary movements that embodied the functionalist tenets of modernism as a form of aesthetic expression, beginning with New Brutalism in the early 1950s. But while these other movements failed to make a lasting impact, High Tech was, for Banham, the one movement that had the substance to endure.[1]

EARLY WORK AND THE POMPIDOU

Continuing a modernist outlook when others were exposing the "fiction of function" risks isolation and therefore speaks to an unspoken affiliation: to common values that would spontaneously draw the major players together and to shared experiences that would shape those values into an identity.[2] These shared experiences bound them together early on in their careers. Richard Rogers and Norman Foster both studied at Yale in the Master's program and then established their first practice together, Team 4 (with Wendy Foster and Su Rogers). After Team 4, Rogers set up a brief partnership with Renzo Piano in order to build their winning competition for the Georges Pompidou Center. Rogers, Nicholas Grimshaw and Michael Hopkins all studied at the Architectural Association in London, albeit at slightly different times: Rogers in the 1950s when Team 10 was at its height, and Grimshaw and Hopkins in the 1960s when Archigram came to dominate the scene. Jan Kaplicky worked for Piano and Rogers, as well as for Foster Associates (as did Hopkins), before setting up Future Systems in 1979. These architects all went on to establish their own successful practices in London, England (with the exception of Piano, whose main office is in Genoa), and continued to learn from each other as their commissions became bigger, more prestigious and complex.

Since the professional careers of the various High Tech architects are so closely intertwined, the British context in the 1960s provides important background for the early work. Formative projects, such as Rogers's Zip Up House (1968), Piano's Italian Industry Pavilion for the Osaka World's Fair (1970), and Kaplicky's Cabin 380 (1975), for example, all reflect the pop futurism advocated by historian and critic Reyner Banham and envisaged in the fantastic architecture of Archigram, the Japanese Metabolists, Superstudio and Archizoom. These visionaries (especially Archigram) looked to popular culture for inspiration, and in the process, divined an image of technology that appealed to a burgeoning consumer culture, increasingly mobile, flexible, streamlined and fast. Banham saw this transformation anticipated in the distinctly American modernism of Charles and Ray Eames, among other Case Study architects, as well as in the industrial aesthetic of American machinery, from transistor radios to airstream trailers and jetliners.[3]

While Archigram brought a refreshing dose of fun to the concrete buildings being built at the time, High Tech turned its ultramodern imagery into a built reality. In fact they went deeper than their compatriots into the underlying motives of a genre, as their interest in advanced technology had as much to do with the perennial pursuit of speed and mobility as it did with research into new materials and construction methods that would enact that pursuit.[4] As such, early projects took their cue directly from those architect-engineers such as Frei Otto who in the 1960s led the field in light-weight structures with his innovative research on tensile structures. This research had an immediate impact on Piano who designed many a tensile structure at the beginning of his career, and anticipated High Tech's deep admiration for the engineer's sense of material and form.

High Tech is therefore not only expressive of technology, its forms are technically accomplished, as in the case of the Georges Pompidou Center in Paris (1971–77), the first High Tech building to receive worldwide recognition. An international competition for a center of contemporary art in the historic heart of Paris, the Pompidou (also known as the Beaubourg) effectively launched the careers of Rogers and Piano, as well as that of their engineering associates, Ted Happold and Peter Rice of Ove Arup. Against all odds, the team and joint venture of architect and engineer beat out 680 entries, with their design declared the winner by a blind jury of art curators and architects, including Jørn Utzon, Jean Prouvé, Oscar Niemeyer and Philip Johnson.[5] Their winning proposal was essentially a megastructure, a giant framework with flexible and mobile components, and proved that one of the most provocative images of visionary architecture, Archigram's Plug-in City (1964), could be materialized, in that it addressed the singular constraint of the fire code.

In terms of construction, the problem with a High Tech megastructure is how to express the steel framework without covering it up with fire-rated cladding (typically concrete), required for a multi-story building and in a manner befitting the gold standard set by Pierre Chareau's *Maison de Verre* (1928–32). The steel skyscrapers of Mies van der Rohe famously addressed this problem by applying steel columns on the exterior façades, but from an aesthetic-engineering standpoint, it was also a compromise, because the exposed steel was not structural but decorative and semantic (the sign of structure).[6] Rogers and Piano wanted the steel frame to be exposed on the exterior, so that the interior could be free of columns to better accommodate changing activities and flexible arrangements, but it still had to be fire-rated, and the solution Rice devised was to fill the hollow columns with water and overclad the 48-meter-long trusses that spanned the interior in aluminum. Sympathetic with the architects' desire to render transparent the inherent properties of steel, Rice designed cast-steel joints called "gerberettes" to support the long trusses (Figure 3.1).

At once beautiful and distinctive, the gerberettes are held down with slender tension members, and the frame stabilized with diagonal bracing, further lightening the external appearance of the building.[7] Following the rationale for open spans, the services (vertical circulation, ventilation ducts, lavatories and loading docks) are allocated on the perimeter of the building, where they are clipped in place, brightly color-coded, and celebrated as a major feature of the main façades.

Like the Eiffel Tower, the Pompidou has become an iconic landmark symbolizing modernity's celebration of the machine. However, also like the Eiffel Tower, it received much criticism from the academy in its day, despite its immense popularity with the public.[8] Although the design greatly benefited from the kind of technological imagery Archigram had popularized, by the time the Pompidou was

3.1   Detail of the "gerberette" designed by Peter Rice for the Pompidou Center, Paris, France, 1971–77

built, the same imagery came under fire from the radical and Marxist left. While Banham praised High Tech for its bravura, the cultural theorist Jean Baudrillard saw the Pompidou as symptomatic of a society oversaturated by technology and the media, and Alan Colquhoun faulted it for presenting an inhuman "image of total mechanization."[9] Such criticisms reflect a climate quite different from the optimistic mood of the immediate post-war years and a time when the tides had staunchly turned against the so-called "false prophets" of modernism.

Although Foster, Piano and Rogers, in their turn, have since disavowed the very term High Tech, arguing that its meaning is too narrow and even misleading, they still saw themselves as acolytes of a modernism harkening back to the heroic age of the 1920s and '30s, in opposition to the corporate modernism of SOM among others, and this persistence alone makes their contribution to architectural discourse during the postmodern years significant. As Banham wrote in 1979, "the most galling aspect of [postmodernism's] unrealized millennium must be that 'the old Modern Architecture' [has] survived as the dominant element in the new pluralism [and is being built] with its mythologies (social, economic, technological) still intact."[10] Mention has been made of High Tech's admiration of the engineer's sense of form and the desire to expose the internal logic of a building, but there are other key modernist traits that their work underscores, from prefabrication and prototyping to social programming and sustainability. Behind the technological imagery, one finds key elements of the very modernist tradition Banham tried to recuperate throughout his writings.[11]

PREFABRICATION AND PROTOTYPING

By far the most important modernist trait that High Tech promoted in the face of postmodernism was the desire to produce buildings out of prefabricated components, much the same way Joseph Paxton did in 1851 with the Crystal Palace. This tradition was carried into the mid-twentieth century in an exemplary way by the Eames couple and by Jean Prouvé, one of the jurors for the Pompidou competition. Indeed, one might even say that their experimental houses were High Tech buildings *avant la lettre*. The Eames House (1949) incorporated off-the-shelf building components (steel framing, decking and infill panels) that were composed into a compelling architectural design. And Prouvé's *Maison Tropicale* (1949), another kit-of-parts, was economically assembled out of beautifully crafted components, designed and manufactured by J. Prouvé Workshops with many operational constraints in mind: performance, manufacturing, cost, function and transportation (Figure 3.2). For example, aluminum panels were ribbed for extra strength and conformed to a specific dimension so they could be transported by cargo plane, and portal frames were made from folded, extruded steel for easy manufacturing, strength and efficiency.

The enduring interest in prefabrication was instilled in Rogers and Foster well before Archigram came on the scene. As students at Yale, they were introduced to the Case Study houses by their teacher, Vincent Scully, and after graduating from

3.2   Jean
Prouvé, *Maison
Tropicale*, 1949

Yale in 1962 and while working in California, they visited the houses designed by
the Eames couple, Ralph Soriano, Pierre Koenig and Craig Ellwood.[12] There they also
encountered Ezra Ehrenkrantz's flexible building system for school construction.
These influences are evident in the first notable project they designed together
as Team 4 (1963–67) with engineer Tony Hunt: an electronics factory for Reliance
Controls (1965). Now demolished, the Reliance Factory was a light-weight shed
consisting of standardized components, such as steel sections for the portal frame
and corrugated steel panels for both the walls and floor decking, organized on
a 12-meter structural grid (Figures 3.3 and 3.4). As such, it exhibited the same
flexibility and economy of means as the Case Study houses, but with a few non-
functional flourishes that differentiated it from its precursor and departed from a
pure engineering logic: the cross-bracing was applied to bays that did not require
stabilizing against lateral forces, and sections of projecting beams across the heads
of the perimeter columns seemed but a vestige of wood construction.[13]

Because prefabrication takes place off-site in controlled manufacturing
conditions, it allows for precision as well as for quick, on-site erection and assembly
using few wet trades in construction. It is also how Foster and Rogers quickly
built a reputation around high-quality yet cost-effective buildings to prospective
clients. Whereas formative projects such as the Reliance Incorporated standardized
components and relied on non-functional flourishes for aesthetic interest,
subsequent and more lucrative commissions facilitated one-of-a-kind buildings,
where more and more of the components were prototyped, i.e. designed and
tested by the architect in close consultation with the manufacturer, and not
just prefabricated from standardized parts into larger assemblies. Like Prouvé's
workshop or the Eameses' research into the bonding glue for laminated plywood,

3.3 Team 4, Reliance Controls Factory, Swindon, England, 1965–66, exterior

3.4 Team 4, Reliance Controls Factory, interior

High Tech integrated prefabrication techniques into the industry to the point of reinventing the way things are made. Here the experience of the Pompidou is pivotal: while the interior is unremarkable in its use of off-the-shelf components, the exterior delights with choice cast-steel details.

The focus on details like the gerberettes once again underscores the extent to which engineers were involved not only in manufacturing but in the design process. So much so that after working with engineer Tony Hunt on the Reliance, Foster kept him on as a regular consultant; Rogers did the same with Happold and Rice; and Piano even formed a brief partnership with Rice after the Pompidou. For Foster and Rogers prototyping became a logical consequence of the increasing prestige of their commissions, but for Piano, it more rigorously constituted a philosophy rooted in the Arts and Crafts tradition and in his own family history of builders. Though their *Atelier Piano and Rice* was short-lived (1977–80), their collaboration on an experimental car for FIAT impressed upon Piano a definition of craftsmanship tied to prototyping. "Craftsmanship," he said, "has no relationship with craft objects. [Rather] [t]he modern meaning of craftsmanship lies in the production stage preceding the industrial stage: the prototype."[14] The example of Prouvé is clearly seminal, but whereas Prouvé's prototyping was intended to be mass-produced, prototyping in this case was a means to create unique designs from prefabricated components.

In this respect an important project is the de Menil Museum in Houston, Texas (1981–86) by the Renzo Piano Building Workshop. A home for the modern art collection of Dominique de Menil, the museum is at first glance an inconspicuous building made of steel-frame construction with grey-clapboard siding to match the surrounding Texan bungalows.[15] Much more exciting than this grey and white box of a building, however, is the system Piano and Rice designed for sun-shading, a key requirement of the brief. The client wanted indirect, natural light, and to create a cool yet lively atmosphere, they designed and tested prototypes for sun-shading devices, which they called "leaves" because of the canopy they made (Figures 3.5 and 3.6).[16]

Suspended from a delicate, skeletal truss of ductile iron, these leaves are sinusoidal louvers whose form was mathematically based on solar angles and was built using monocoque construction in ferro-concrete, hand-polished to a luminous sheen.[17] So beautiful is the device that Piano featured it on the exterior of the museum (Figure 3.7), but it is on the interior, where it calibrates space to the circadian rhythms of the environment that its magic is revealed. And yet, for all its tranquil beauty, the de Menil is not quite pitch-perfect, for the leaves sit beneath the glazing (instead of above), trapping heat generated by the sun inside the building. Had the leaves been located above the glazing, however, their physical presence would not have been as dramatic from an aesthetic standpoint.

The Piano Workshop has experimented with top-lit galleries to the extent that these elements have become the firm's signature. With each museum, the firm has devised a novel solution to the problem of indirect, natural light, specific to client, program and context. For the Cy Twombly Gallery (1992–95), located down the road from the de Menil, they designed a sun-shading canopy made up of horizontal layers of roof and shading elements: a multilayered sandwich comprising fixed exterior louvers, roof structure and glazing, adjustable interior louvers and a fabric ceiling. The plane of exterior louvers floating above the roof line like a "flying carpet"

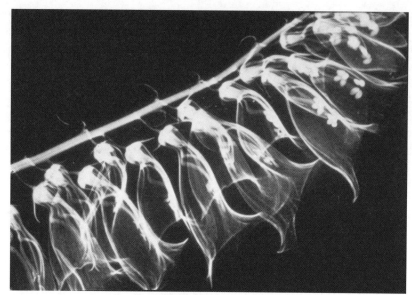

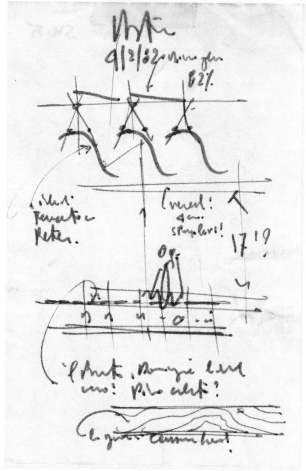

3.5 and
3.6   RPBW, The
Menil Collection
Museum,
Houston, Texas,
1981–86. Above:
Radiography of a
leaf; below: Renzo
Piano's sketch

3.7   RPBW, The Menil Collection Museum. Detail of the façade— Single bay of east colonnade

became a solution they would adapt to other projects.[18] In the Louis Kahn-inspired Nasher Sculpture Museum in Dallas's Arts District (1999–2003), the client wanted the sun-shading mechanism to be visible on the interior, and because the building housed sculptures rather than paintings, a greater amount of natural illumination was permissible. This meant that all the elements of the sandwich could be compressed and minimized. The fixed exterior shading consists of cast-aluminum panels with egg-shaped perforations, sculpted to admit only north light; the panels sit on flanges and are propped by spigots slightly above the UV laminated glazing, which in turn sits inside a thin, steel-frame structure in the shape of a shallow vault, secured from above by tensile steel members. The panels resembling egg crates are visually striking and were possibly the inspiration behind the shading device for Piano's High Museum of Art in Atlanta, Georgia (1999–2005), here blown up to a giant scale (Figures 3.8–3.9).

Another fine example of High Tech prototyping is the Renault Distribution Centre in Swindon, England, by Foster (1980–82). The building, known for its canary yellow color, is a classic kit-of-parts where nearly all the prefabricated components have been custom designed. Based on a 24-meter (78.7-foot) square module that can be infinitely added to along the axes of a virtual grid, the self-supporting structure exploits the tensile properties of steel. It consists of a central mast from which the beams and roof assembly are all hung; and where the module forms the outer envelope of the building (Figures 3.10–3.11). Glass curtain walls are hung from the beams, pin joints connect the beams to the central mast and suspension ties, and the hinge action of the joints is expressed in the canted angle of the roof assembly, creating a lively, undulating rhythm when the modules are strung together.

3.8 RPBW, High Museum of Art Expansion, Atlanta, Georgia, 1999–2005. Details of "Transition Panel."

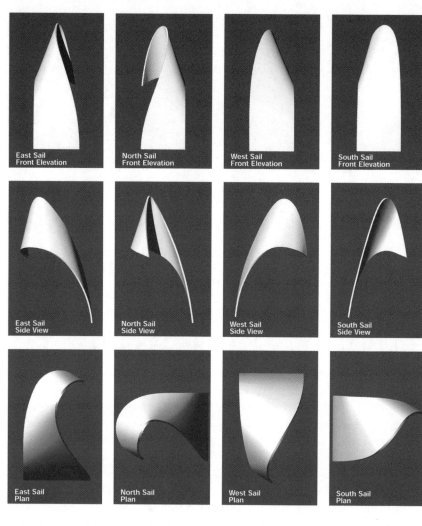

East Sail
Front Elevation

North Sail
Front Elevation

West Sail
Front Elevation

South Sail
Front Elevation

East Sail
Side View

North Sail
Side View

West Sail
Side View

South Sail
Side View

East Sail
Plan

North Sail
Plan

West Sail
Plan

South Sail
Plan

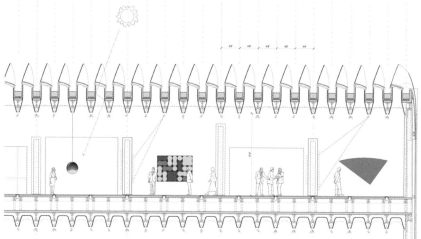

3.9 RPBW, High Museum of Art Expansion. Section

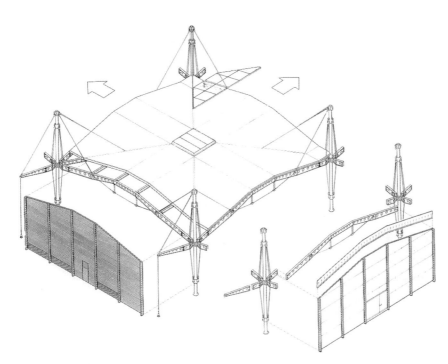

3.10   Foster + Partners, Renault Distribution Centre, Swindon, England, 1980–82. Axonometric of a structural module

3.11   Foster + Partners, Renault Distribution Centre, Swindon, England, 1980–82. Left: Axonometric of a structural module. Exterior view of the building under construction

THE PRACTICE OF INTEGRATION

Architecture as a kit-of-parts lends itself well to buildings requiring open plans, such as factories, offices and even museums, indeed, the kinds of buildings Foster, Rogers and Piano had all worked on from the beginning of their careers. But for large buildings with more complicated programs, the challenges for High Tech would prove much greater. For one, exposing the structure and internal workings of a building required that conventions be completely re-thought on a vast and complex scale. This was the case with two temples of commerce that famously extended High Tech's repertoire into the tall building realm: the Lloyd's of London (1978–86) by Rogers Partnership and the Hong Kong and Shanghai Bank (1979–86) by Foster Associates. As high-profile buildings for financial corporations, they were the two largest projects each firm had done to date, and proved that High Tech was not just about prefabricated frameworks and canopies but about integrating all aspects of design—concept, program and construction, as well as urban, social and cultural contexts—at the highest levels of design thinking and project coordination.

Fosters' Hong Kong Bank was ground breaking on many fronts, but it was especially innovative in its response to program and its approach to the building industry (Figures 3.12–3.13). In earlier projects, such as the Willis, Faber and Dumas building in Ipswich, England (1971–75), Fosters had already demonstrated boldness in taking a client's program and revising it substantially, something he had learned from his teacher Serge Chermayeff at Yale, who had favored spaces for social and communal activities. For the Willis Faber building, Fosters persuaded its clients to add recreational amenities including a swimming pool, cafe and roof garden to the requisite office space; re-prioritize the finishes used in "front of house" versus

3.12   Foster + Partners, Hong Kong and Shanghai Bank, Hong Kong, China, 1979–86. Atrium plan

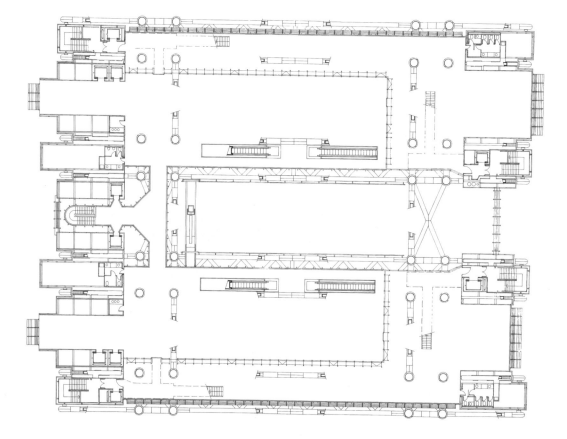

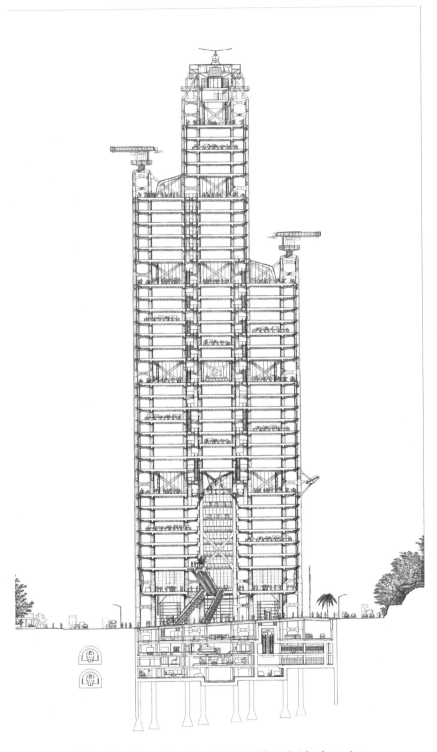

3.13   Foster Associates, Hong Kong and Shanghai Bank, section

"back of house"; and incorporate escalators in addition to elevators to encourage socialization among workers.[19] With the bank, he now took on the conventional typology of an office tower, with its central service core and skewered floor plates. But instead of the usual "shish kabob," Fosters pushed the structure and services out to the perimeter, where they could be exposed on the exterior like the Pompidou.[20]

In the Lloyd's of London, Rogers too pushed the structure and services out to the exterior, leaving the middle clear for open work space, local circulation and soaring atriums; and in both cases the rationale for this inversion was flexibility. For Rogers and Foster, flex space was important to any given program because it facilitated changes in how the building would be used over time, and for their respective clients, this made sense because of the projected growth in commerce at the time. Moreover, they anticipated the rising demand for information technology and provided flexible service space within the raised floor system (accessed by panels), an idea they both owed to Louis Kahn's separation of served and servant spaces.

The notion of flexibility was therefore pragmatic, but it was also aesthetic, since it provided a strong rationale for having the internal workings of the building, usually concealed from view, exposed and celebrated as an iconic feature of the design. While the Lloyd's of London accomplishes this feat with service towers that circumscribe a rationalized box and neatly fill in the irregular corners of the site to much picturesque effect, the Hong Kong Bank does the same though not so much with the service towers as with the imposing structure. Here the structure is a robust, steel-frame bridge from which stacks of floors are suspended. Furthermore, the building spans over an open, public plaza from which one ascends on an escalator into a spectacular glass belly.

In her book on the Hong Kong Bank, Stephanie Williams has recounted the challenges Foster faced throughout that building's design and construction.[21] What is clear from her account is the extent to which Fosters was involved in all aspects of the project. No detail was too small to be overlooked. They worked closely with the clients, engineers and manufacturers in order to realize their design ideas, as well as with the construction companies, because of the new techniques required to build them. Often these techniques did not already exist in the building industry itself and necessitated research into other industries. To this end, they looked into steel manufacturing companies that made giant steel tubes for pipelines to solve the problem of corrosion. They sought companies in Japan that made prefabricated packages (called risers) containing all the pipework for a building, as well as companies in the shipping industry that made containers to house workers on oilrigs.[22] And they designed systems entirely unique to the project, such as the prefabricated module combining lavatories, heating, ventilation and air-conditioning plant or the under-floor system for air-conditioning and sprinklers.[23] Working in this way meant that the design would change and evolve through a process of interdisciplinary exchange; that an idea would invariably morph as more information about some area of expertise came to light. In sum, they integrated the specialty knowledge of their design consultants and manufacturers in what was, by Williams's account, a dynamic and unpredictable process.

The Hong Kong Bank was a watershed for Foster (and the same is true of the Lloyd's of London for Rogers). As David Nelson said of the Fosters team: "The Hongkong Bank really changed everything for everybody. It was one of those projects where the development of building elements gave us tremendous opportunities."[24] Indeed, the Hong Kong Bank, Lloyd's and the Pompidou all proved that High Tech architects are not just specialists in one type of building, as so many firms are when projects grow complex, but specialists in a genre that creatively integrates architectural design with engineering, manufacturing and construction. That genre, as we have seen, is rooted in the modern tradition, for what compels the high level of integration can be boiled down to a fundamental desire to render the logic of how a building works transparent, light and expressive: a desire that necessitates the precision and economy of prefabrication, where all the parts of a building are designed and tested in a factory and then assembled on site.

This outlook continues to inform recent projects, which includes all kinds of buildings from airports to hospitals, concert halls and stadiums. Yet, since the 1980s, High Tech has further evolved in two significant ways: in its exploitation of digital means to create complex curvilinear shapes, and in its emphasis on sustainable design. With the popularization of NURB (non-uniform rational B-spline) software, curvilinear forms have now become commonplace, but High Tech architects had been designing complex surfaces relatively early on, even pre-dating "blob architecture." The Lord's Media Centre (1994) and the *Comme des Garçons* boutique in Paris (1998) by Future Systems—the most fashion-forward of the High Tech firms—are two such projects: the former a blob-like eyeball in the sky used by the press for viewing matches at the Lord's Cricket Ground (Figure 3.14), and the latter a renovation inspired by the topology of a Klein bottle.[25] Predisposed to High Tech images of the future, Future Systems has been experimenting with complex geometries since the late 1980s.

3.14   Future Systems, Lord's Media Centre, Marylebone Cricket Club, London, England, 1994

The interest in sustainability goes back even further to the 1970s and to Buckminster Fuller in particular, another High Tech forerunner. An early proponent of sustainable design, Fuller wrote extensively on the limits of the world's natural resources, and at that time his message inspired many young architects, including Foster, who collaborated with Fuller in 1971 on a project called the Climatroffice. While themes espoused by Fuller on lightness (he famously asked Foster, "How much does your building weigh?") and flexible building systems appear in the early work, it was not until the early 1990s that sustainability became an explicit concern of High Tech architecture in its own right, with projects such as the Inland Revenue Headquarters in Nottingham, England, by Hopkins Architects (1992–95), the winning competition for a government building that called for 100 percent natural ventilation.[26]

Consistent with their desire to express the logic of how a building works, sustainable technologies are not concealed from view but are form-drivers, sometimes inspired by biomimesis, like the biomorphic shape of the Green Building by Future Systems (1990), and other times, by vernacular forms, like the batten wind-catchers of the Centre Kanak by the Piano Workshop (1993–98). But perhaps the best example of this functionalist will-to-form (Kunstwöllen) is the British Pavilion by Nicholas Grimshaw for Expo '92 in Seville, Spain. This environmental pavilion not only gives poetic expression to the building's structure and services, but more to the point, to its sustainable mechanisms for energy efficiency. The sun-shading canopy on the roof is festive and over-scaled; a wall of recycled water greets the visitor on the east façade; the interior program is compartmentalized into climate-controlled pods; and colorful sails protect the south façade from the hot Andalusian sun.[27]

As the projects in this chapter illustrate, High Tech combines form and function in such a way that function never trumps form and form is always tempered by function. As Piano stated simply, it is not "difficult to make new shapes or invent a new form. What is difficult is to invent a new form that makes sense and that you can build."[28] This ethos, as we have seen, speaks to a functionalist tradition and what Banham called "an engineering style" that in High Tech has enjoyed a more enduring success than its modernist forbears.[29] After pivotal, high-profile projects, such as the Pompidou, the Hongkong Bank and Lloyd's, High Tech has continued to explore new forms and build them at a high level of construction by rethinking the terms of professional practice and by creatively integrating design with manufacturing and engineering.

ACKNOWLEDGEMENTS

I would like to thank my colleague, Craig Babe, for his insights, offered from the point of view of a practicing architect who once worked for Hopkins Architects. For their assistance with images, I am grateful to the offices of Foster + Partners and RPBW.

NOTES

1   Anthony Vidler makes the refined point that Reyner Banham criticized the naïve functionalism of late modernism and instead argued for an architecture that captured the expressive qualities of the second machine age. See *Histories of the Immediate Present* (Cambridge, MA: MIT, 2008).

2   The expression, "the fiction of function," is the title of Stanford Anderson's essay in *Assemblage*, no. 2 (February 1987): 19.

3   See Reyner Banham, "The Great Gizmo," *Industrial Design* (September 1965); reprinted in *Design by Choice*, ed. Penny Sparke (New York: Rizzoli, 1981), 108–14.

4   Speed and mobility are familiar tropes of modern culture explored by Paul Virilio in *Speed and Politics*, trans. Mark Polizzotti (1977; New York: Semiotext(e), 1986).

5   On the Pompidou, see Nathan Silver, *The Making of Beaubourg* (Cambridge, MA: MIT Press, 1994) and Brian Appleyard, *Richard Rogers: A Biography* (London: Faber & Faber, 1986), 159–219.

6   On the conflicting priorities of the architect and engineer, see Andrew Saint's insightful observations on High Tech architecture in *Architect and Engineer: A Study in Sibling Rivalry* (New Haven: Yale University Press, 2007), 377–94.

7   Kenneth Powell (ed.), *Richard Rogers, Complete Works*, vol. 1 (London: Phaidon Press, 1999), 112.

8   Appleyard, *Richard Rogers*, 221.

9   Jean Baudrillard, "The Beaubourg Effect," *Simulacra and Simulation* (1981; Ann Arbor: University of Michigan Press, 1994), 61–74. Alan Colquhoun, "Plateau Beaubourg," *Architectural Design*, vol. 47, no. 2 (1977); reprinted in *Essays in Architectural Criticism* (Cambridge, MA: MIT Press, 1981), 119.

10   Banham, "Foster Associates" (1979); reprinted in *On Foster … Foster On*, ed. David Jenkins (Munich: Prestel, 2000), 69.

11   See, for example, Banham's *Theory and Design in the First Machine Age* (London: Architectural Press, 1960), and *The Age of the Masters: A Personal View of Modern Architecture* (New York: Harper & Row, 1962). Banham recounts the rise and fall of visionary architecture in the 1960s in his *Megastructure, Urban Futures of the Recent Past* (London: Thames & Hudson, 1976) almost as a way of dealing with the traumas of modernism instigated by the momentous political events of the May '68 student revolution.

12   On Foster's education at Yale, see Robert A.M. Stern, "The Impact of Yale" (1999); reprinted in Jenkins, *On Foster*, 345–61.

13   What looks like projecting beams are really "head frames" welded to the steel columns. The intent behind the head frames was so that new beams could be attached to the existing frame at the point of zero moment in a beam. Because the limits of the site would not allow an extension to the building in the future, the head frames became decorative elements. See Ian Lambot (ed.), *Norman Foster, Team 4 and Foster Associates* (London: Watermark, 1991), 82.

14   "Renzo Piano Building Workshop: 1964–1988," *A+U Extra Edition*, vol. 3 (March 1989): 18.

15   Peter Buchanan, ed., *Renzo Piano Building Workshop, Complete Works*, vol. 1 (London, Phaidon Press, 1993), 140.

16   Renzo Piano, "Building Essay," *Harvard Architecture Review*, vol. 7 (1989): 80.

17   Piano learned about monocoque construction while working with Rice on the FIAT VSS Experimental Vehicle. See *A+U*, 199.

18   The metaphor of a "flying carpet" is Piano's.

19   See Norman Foster, "Social Ends, Technical Mean" (1977); reprinted in Jenkins, *On Foster*, 463–4. The famous, suspended glass wall of the Willis, Faber & Dumas building was so new that Foster had to sell the patent rights of the design to the manufacturer before the manufacturer would assume the liability to build it.

20   Saint, *Architect and Engineer*, 390.

21   Stephanie Williams, *Hongkong Bank* (Boston: Little, Brown and Company, 1989), 125. In the end, Foster was unable to expose the steel structure and clad it with aluminum.

22   Ibid., 115.

23   Ibid., 127.

24   Nelson interview with Malcolm Quantrill, *The Norman Foster Studio* (London: E & FN Spon), 56.

25   On the construction of the Lord's Media Centre, see Future Systems, *Unique Building* (London: Wiley-Academy, 2001).

26   The famous exchange between Fuller and Foster is documented in Martin Pawley, "Richard Buckminster Fuller," *Norman Foster, Foster Associates, Buildings and Projects*, ed. Ian Lambot (London: Foster Associates, 1989), 82.

27   Deyan Sudjic and Richard Bryant, *British Pavilion Expo '92, Seville. Architects Nicholas Grimshaw and Partners* (London: Wordsearch, 1992), 8.

28   "Renzo Piano Interview," *Space*, vol. 487 (2008): 133.

29   Banham, "Introduction," *Foster Associates* (London: RIBA, 1979), 5.

4

Deconstruction: The Project of Radical Self-Criticism

Elie G. Haddad

In 1988, the Museum of Modern Art in New York organized an exhibition on "Deconstructivist Architecture," curated by Philip Johnson and Mark Wigley. It coincided with another major event on the same topic, a symposium organized at the Tate Gallery in London by Andreas Papadakis, the editor of Academy Editions. These two events signaled the inauguration of "Deconstruction" or "Deconstructivism" in architecture, a movement in which a number of architects were lumped together, some of whom had no theoretical connection to the topic, which emerged originally in philosophy and literary criticism. Among those, there were some, like Frank Gehry, who declared their amusement at this association, yet found it expedient at the time to further promote their work in international circles.

Academy Editions later published a series of reviews, in addition to a concise introduction to Deconstruction, featuring two essays by Christopher Norris and Andrew Benjamin, the former an expert on Jacques Derrida, the philosopher who first coined the term "Deconstruction".[1] While Norris's essay attempted to give an overview of Derrida's thought within the context of philosophical developments from Plato to Heidegger, it was left to Benjamin to attempt an early translation of this philosophical approach into architecture. Benjamin actually saw signs of deconstruction in the work of several architects who confronted some of the established practices in architecture, especially those founded on the concept of "centrality of dwelling."[2] His interpretation of Deconstruction was illustrated by several works, from Hiromi Fuji's Ushimado Art Center and Frank Gehry's Winton House, to Bernard Tschumi's Parc de la Villette and Daniel Libeskind's City Edge project for Berlin. While the work of Eisenman was also given its due share, it was not clear why the others were included under this rubric, except as manifestations of a rather unconventional approach to design. Most of these works never had the presumption of inscribing themselves into that philosophical movement, nor of attempting to translate it architecturally. This reading by Benjamin was also disputed by others, like Mark Wigley, whose definition of "Deconstructivism" referred it back to the Russian Constructivists, intentionally severing its connection to Derrida.[3]

THE PHILOSOPHICAL FOUNDATION OF DECONSTRUCTION

In 1967, the French philosopher Jacques Derrida published three key works: *L'Ecriture et la Difference*, *De la grammatologie*, and *La Voix et le phenomene*, which ushered in a new philosophical movement, initially labeled Post-Structuralism, and later taking the distinctive designation of "Deconstruction." The main task of Derrida was to critically dismantle the foundations of the Western philosophical tradition, namely the notion of "logocentrism," i.e. the referral and privileging of the logos, the spoken word, and through it all logical structures; as well as the "metaphysics of presence," epitomized in Heidegger's *Being and Time*. The main focus of Derrida's deconstructive operations was language itself, used to uncover the hidden fault lines of certain seminal texts, from Plato to Rousseau, Freud, and Saussure. But for the French philosopher, the criticism of logocentrism itself was sustained by the very logocentrism it sought to unravel, rendering any attempt to develop a new science of meaning utterly impossible.[4] Whereas the structuralists had limited themselves to analyzing the structure of language and its operations, Derrida used language against itself, to uncover its deficiencies and contradictions, and thus to dismantle the edifice itself on which the systems of religion, logos and reason were founded. These Derridean operations were indebted somewhat to Nietzsche, although Derrida would use a different methodology in his work.

While putting under question the foundations of any systematic approach, Derrida remained vigilant and resistant to the substitution of his own concepts to those being questioned, in order to avoid lapsing into a new logocentrism. In *De la grammatologie*, he questioned the premises of the system elaborated by Ferdinand de Saussure, based on the notion of "sign," substituting for it that of "trace," since concepts and words take on meaning only in relation to others, or as he put it, through a process of *differance*, a term that he concocted to signify simultaneously a process of deferral (in time) and difference (from other signs).[5] In the same vein, Derrida launched an attack on the fundamental notion of the logos, which seemed to coincide, in the work of Levinas as well as Hegel, with divine substance, or the absolute. This metaphysical project was supported in his opinion by the oppositions of culture/nature, image/representation, sensible/intelligible; and above all by a "vulgar concept of time."

As Derrida waged this attack on the metaphysical conception of time, it would not be too difficult to infer a similar critique of the concept of space, on which modern architecture had been similarly founded. And if all the foundational premises of Western thought were to be put under examination and deconstructed, then by inference, architecture as a discipline may be subjected as well to this same operation of radical dismantling. In his *Margins of Philosophy*, Derrida explicitly questioned the notion of "origin," on which many architectural treatises had been founded, and which appears throughout language in such prefixes as *archi, telos, eskhaton*, which all refer to "presence." Thus, the *archi* in architecture, the prefix that refers the *tekton* to its primary position as a foundational element, could not escape deconstruction. Derrida specifically spoke about architecture as an inhabited *constructum*, a totality that comprehends certain invariables, and thus would be amenable to a work of deconstruction. He further defined the notion of an "architecture of architecture":

> Let us not forget that there is an architecture of architecture … This naturalized architecture is bequeathed to us: we inhabit it, it inhabits us, we think it is destined for habitation, and it is no longer an object for us at all. But we must recognize in it an artefact, a construction, a monument. It did not fall from the sky; it is not natural, even if it informs a specific scheme of relations to physis, the sky, the earth, the human, and the divine. This architecture of architecture has a history; it is historical through and through. Its heritage inaugurates the intimacy of our economy, the law of our hearth (oikos), our familial, religious and political "oikonomy", all the places of birth and death, temple, school, stadium, agora, square, sepulchre.[6]

For Derrida, therefore, architectural meaning directs the syntax of architecture according to these four elements: the law of the *oikos* (dwelling), the law of commemoration, the teleology of dwelling, and the values of beauty, harmony and totality (aesthetics). By operating in this manner, architecture not only affects itself, but also "regulates all of what is called Western culture, far beyond its architecture" and stands as the "last fortress of metaphysics."[7]

THE PROJECT OF DECONSTRUCTION OF ARCHITECTURE

Peter Eisenman was one of the few architects who took the question of Deconstruction seriously, following its developments in philosophy and literary criticism as a prelude to any attempt at elaborating a deconstructive project in architecture. Unlike his peers, Peter Eisenman was directly influenced by the writings of Derrida, and before that, by the structuralist studies of Noam Chomsky. He explored the potential of this new criticism in architecture, despite the difficulty of translating this anti-structuring and anti-foundational critique into an architectural project. This can be seen in the gradual transformation of Eisenman from a "structuralist" phase of experiments on the House series, to the House El-Even Odd (Figure 4.1) which, by its play on words as well as its play on its own rules of syntax, already expressed a shift in Eisenman's work, a process which continued in the later projects, animated by a continuous exchange and at one time a collaboration with the philosopher of Deconstruction, Jacques Derrida.

This transformation in the work of Eisenman also manifested itself in a series of writings that appeared after 1980. These writings moved from the investigations of the architectural "sign" as exemplified in his House studies,[8] to the study of Corbusier's Domino House[9] and the formal study of Terragni's work,[10] to a post-structuralist phase which started around 1982 with "The Representations of Doubt: At the Sign of the Sign"[11] and the seminal essay "The End of the Classical, the End of the Beginning, the End of the End."[12] The publications produced by Eisenman during this phase also reflected this radical shift, with Fin d'Ou T Hou S[13] a collection of loose-plate drawings that document the last project of the House series,[14] elevating the architectural document to the level of a rare and precious manuscript.

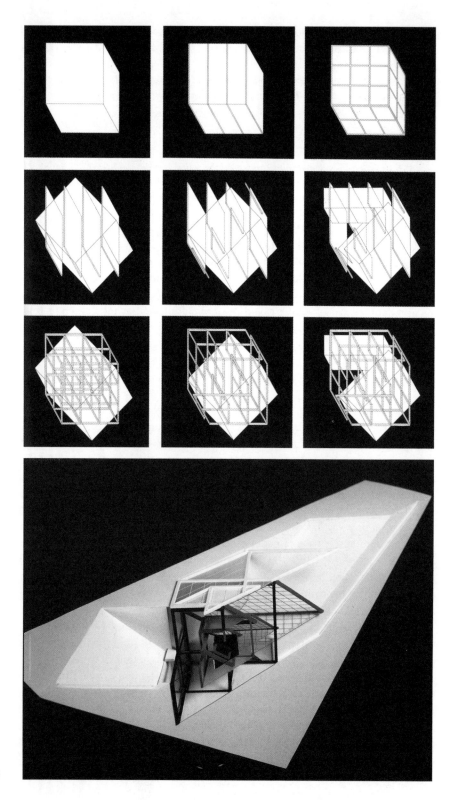

4.1a Peter Eisenman. House III, 1969–71

4.1b Peter Eisenman. House El-Even Odd, 1980

A year later, another publication came out under the title *Moving Arrows, Eros and Other Errors*, this time printed on transparent sheets, featuring the Romeo and Juliet project designed for Verona.[15]

The major essay by Eisenman, "The End of the Classical, the End of the Beginning, the End of the End," bears a striking resemblance to Derrida's title for a chapter in *De la grammatologie*,[16] although in this case he confessed his debt to an article by Franco Rella which appeared in the same issue of *Casabella* in which his winning scheme for the Wexner Center in Ohio was featured.[17] In this essay, influenced by Foucault's concept of *epistemes*, Baudrillard's concept of *simulation*, and Derrida's notion of the *trace*, Eisenman set for himself the task of critically exposing architecture as a humanist discipline, founded on the *logocentric* discourses of the Renaissance. Following Foucault, he defined the Classical as an *episteme*, a continuous period where a dominant form of knowledge reigned, since the Renaissance in this case, and marked by the three "fictions" of Representation, Reason, and History.

Eisenman later appropriated the notion of the trace from Derrida, in an attempt to overcome the predicament of architecture as an activity rooted in physical, functional or representational purposes, in order to wage an attack on its foundational certainties: origin, function, and history. These "certainties" constituted the foundations of a classical metaphysics of architecture, in which the representation of a fixed set of ideas edify a complete "body" of architecture, whether Classical or Modernist. Instead, he proposed an architecture which would negate these various "fictions" through operations in which the architect would take the role of a de-cipherer, bringing to light hidden fragments, repressed meanings or traces of other significations, transforming the site of each project into a palimpsest where architecture would be called upon to generate new fictions, multiple histories and narratives.[18] This transformation in Eisenman's work, from a practice focused on a study of "syntax" to one which resorts to strategies of "decomposition"[19] in the generation of architectural objects, that would be then read as "texts," started well before the attempted collaboration that brought together Derrida and Eisenman.[20]

Eisenman thus began to re-orient his work, after the series of experiments on the House series (1967–75), towards a form of "artificial excavation" which sought to uncover latent or hidden signs in the territory, to be subsequently subverted and turned against the original site of operation. These artificial excavations would take place in a number of "charged" urban sites, from Canareggio (1978) to Berlin (1980), to other less historically laden sites such as Long Beach California (1986).[21]

In Berlin, on a site marked by the tragic history of the city at the border of the divide between East and West, in proximity to the Checkpoint Charlie crossing (Figure 4.2), Eisenman proposed a project that developed in response to two conflicting grids: one virtual, the Mercator Grid, the other real, the grid of the city blocks, bearing the trace of the city's history. This translation, only realized partially as one building at the corner of Friedrichstrasse and Kochstrasse, did not fully express the initial proposal to radically transform that city block at the boundary between two worlds at the time. Here Eisenman, for the first time, moved from the exclusively syntactic operations to a more dissective practice, relying specifically on a horizontal layering of traces. Jean Francois Bedard explained this form of archaeology as one that does not seek to recover or illuminate the history of the site, but rather, as in the case of Canareggio in Venice, expresses "the meaninglessness of modernist rationality,"[22] in other words, an archaeology with a clear objective of uncovering the faultlines of the modernist edifice by subverting it and re-inscribing other formal operations over it.

This type of operation continued later in the Wexner Center for the Arts in Ohio (1989) (Figure 4.3), a project that effectively signaled a change in direction in the architect's work, as well as in the architectural tendencies of the time. The Wexner Center attempted to resolve the opposition of two grids, that of the university campus and of the city. In addition to this, the architect added the "recovery" of fragments of the site's history, where an armory building once stood. This significant operation not only opened new possibilities of "reading" the project as a text, but also offered a new approach to the problem of history, different from the classical post-modernist approach. And it is this difference that gave the project its winning edge, against the four other competing designs, most prominent among which were the projects of Michael Graves and Cesar Pelli, which followed a typical monumental classicism. This appears like a turning point in the history of post-modernism, while the completion of the Wexner Center in 1989, roughly coincided with the first public exhibitions on Deconstruction, mentioned above.

4.2   Peter Eisenman. Housing at Checkpoint Charlie, Berlin, 1981–85

The Wexner Center seemed to some critics to resuscitate undesirable elements in the site's history, namely the towers symbolizing the Armory building which had been located there until 1959.[23] Yet Eisenman intentionally resurrected these symbolic fragments to uncover the repressed memories of the site, not in celebration of its military history, but merely as a reminder. Again, Eisenman emphasized the opposition between the grid of the campus grid and that of the city, in order to develop the intervention, supplemented with historical elements, revived as fragments. The fragments of the Armory were thus sliced by the extension of the city grid, a white canopy steel structure running as a spine across the site. The main entry to the building was camouflaged by this collage, leading the visitor to an underground sequence of rooms which house the various functions.

This phase in Eisenman's deconstructionist work was marked by a challenging collaboration with Jacques Derrida, at the suggestion of Bernard Tschumi, on a section of the Parc de la Villette in Paris (Figure 4.4). This unrealized project was documented in a series of transcripts that appeared in book form as *Chora L Works*, idiosyncratic in its title as well as in its form,[24] as the grid of the proposal actually punctures the written text and renders the operation of reading a difficult exercise, in addition to the reversal of the traditional book organization, by relegating the introduction to the center of the book, among other things.[25] This work also revealed the limits of translating philosophical concepts into architecture, as the architect struggled

4.3   Peter Eisenman. Wexner Center, Columbus, Ohio, 1983–89

4.4   Peter
Eisenman. Parc
de la Villette,
Paris, 1987

to give forms to a discourse that does not always lend itself to formal translation. Derrida warned at the beginning of this exchange with Eisenman:

> I read your texts and examined Fin D'ou T Hou S, I recognized many things: your critique of origin, anthropocentrism and aesthetics is consistent with a general deconstruction of architecture itself. Your work seems to propose an anti-architecture, or rather an anarchitecture, but of course this is not so simple, as what I do is antiarchitectural in the traditional sense of "anti".[26]

This exchange continued over two years, through several documented dialogues[27] in addition to a set of generated drawings, culminating in a final exchange between Derrida and Eisenman, in which the philosopher posed a series of unsettling questions to the architect, putting into question his whole deconstructionist experiment in architecture.[28] Yet Eisenman's practice continued to evolve with a number of projects which shared the generative approach of the early projects of "artificial excavation," with the Guardiola House in Spain (1988), the Koizumi Sangyo Office building in Tokyo (1990), the Columbus Convention Center in Ohio (1993), the Aronoff Center in Cincinnati (Figure 4.5) (1996), and the Church of the Year 2000 in Rome (1996), all of which follow the strategy of subjecting the site to a process of computer-generated transformations of its "original" primary elements.[29] This well-assimilated "process" could lead some to question Eisenman's work in the end as another kind of formalism, or at best a continuation of the structuralist process that he had initiated in the 1970s with the House experiments, albeit using new tools, and especially after the introduction of the computer into the the design process, which offered Eisenman the opportunity to shift his theoretical explorations into another territory, prompted by the arrival of Deleuze on the architectural scene.

4.5   Peter Eisenman. Aronoff Center, Univ. of Cincinnati, 1988–96

Another major figure in "Deconstruction" was Bernard Tschumi. Tschumi started his career with a contestation of the established order in architecture, following the events of May 1968. He first advocated an interactive architecture, based on communication technology, in the form of a project titled "Do-It-Yourself-City." Seeking an alternative to the functional and formal paradigms in design, he incorporated lessons drawn from the writings of Bataille, Barthes, and Sollers, before turning to Derrida. Tschumi drew concepts derived from philosophy and literary criticism into architecture, including such notions as the "erotic," "violence", and "pleasure." In his approach to establishing a theoretical framework, Tschumi appeared closer to Rem Koolhaas than to Peter Eisenman, with his interest in establishing cross-disciplinary relations (as between film and architecture, or literature and architecture), in surrealistic juxtapositions, or in setting the stage for an opposition between the rational and the irrational.[30] One of his strategies, "cross-programming," juxtaposes programmatic uses in order to create unexpected activities, termed "events." Also, Tschumi relied on the cinematographic technique of montage as a tool for the generation of non-normative spaces that resist conventional "reading" or interpretation.

Tschumi's friendship with Derrida had probably much to do with the readings of his first major work, the Parc de la Villette, which he won in competition (Figure 4.6), as a "deconstructionist" project. The design overlaid three organizing systems with the intent to avoid endowing any of them with hierarchical importance. One of these is based on a Cartesian grid, punctuated by a series of red pavilions, designated a "follies," stripped of any functional association. The playful relationship between these follies, the formal language of which refers to early Constructivists as Iakov Chernikov, played on the Barthesian notion of the sign, showing that these "recycled" signs could be reinterpreted in a new context where their semantic dimension becomes open to different readings.

4.6   Bernard
Tschumi. Parc de la
Villette, 1982–98

The later development of Tschumi's architectural work, from his Le Fresnoy school of art in France and Lerner Hall at Columbia (1999) to his more recent Acropolis Museum in Athens (2008), showed a growing distance from the earlier "critical" agenda, as these projects no longer propose a "radical" revision of the discipline, as much as they continue to explore new ways of combining elements, subverting traditional typologies, in order to generate a stimulating, cinematographic, experience of space.

Daniel Libeskind was also associated with Deconstruction, especially after the Derrida–Eisenman debate, in which the philosopher alluded to the work of Libeskind as the one which most appropriately reflected on absence, negativity, and the void, all of which refer to the trace, to writing and the "place of deconstruction." In his letter to Eisenman, Derrida approvingly quoted at length from Libeskind's statement on the project for the Jewish addition to the Berlin Museum (Figures 4.7a and 4.7b).[31]

In his masterpiece, Libeskind was equally concerned with issues of memory, site, and narrative. And here, the weight of history in its tragic dimension added further impetus to the question of critical interpretation. Libeskind masterfully exploited the potentials of this difficult project to create an addition that defied normal conventions, while also effectively deconstructing the meanings associated with the museum as a type, and the problematic of commemorating the Jewish presence in this critical location. The work played on three separate themes: the map of Jewish presence in the city as represented through its most illustrious names, Arnold Schoenberg's incomplete opera *Moses and Aaron*, and the essay of Walter Benjamin, *One Way Street*. Drawing on these three different references, respectively geographical, musical and literary, Libeskind interpreted the addition as a separate volume, composed of two clashing elements, one straight and one broken, that cross at several intervals, creating different voids. Outside, a slanted floor garden planted with concrete pillars

4.7a and
4.7b   Daniel
Libeskind. Jewish
Museum, Berlin,
1988–99

from which sprout olive trees, symbols of hope, further accentuate the symbolic content of the project. The building's opaque appearance from the outside, without any inviting entrances, clad in zinc panels, further accentuates its idiosyncratic quality in this landscape. Its entry point, through a basement passage that originates in the lobby of the original museum, made it possible to further deny any normative physical relation to the "original" building.

The success of the Jewish Museum led to other commissions, and to the establishment of a practice which unfortunately veered into the repetition of the Jewish Museum model on other sites and programs that sometimes had a similar thematic, like the Felix Nussbaum Museum in Osnabrück, and others which had nothing in common with it, like the Denver Art Museum. What began as a potentially significant "deconstructive" practice fizzled down eventually to a master recipe that was indiscriminately applied to different projects around the world, none of which posed the problematic of the Berlin Museum.

FROM NEO CONSTRUCTIVISM TO NEO EXPRESSIONISM

The other major architects who were brought together under the rubric of "Deconstruction" had in fact other aesthetic or theoretical concerns without any direct connection to the philosophical project of Deconstruction. Yet formal similarities played a part in bringing these architects together, perhaps in order to create a critical mass that would justify the organization of a major exhibition, and the launching of a new movement.

Mark Wigley, in his introduction to the exhibition catalog on "Deconstructivist Architecture" at the MoMA, in fact postulated the relation of these works to the Russian Constructivists, whose project did not fully materialize in the 1920s, replaced on the one hand by the ascetic purity of the modern movement, and on the other by the revival of neo-classicism in Russia and Germany. Wigley saw the new architecture as negotiating the "relationship between the instability of the early Russian avant-garde and the stability of high modernism." He further defined it as an "architecture of disruption, deflection, deviation, and distortion, rather than one of demolition, dismantling, decay, decomposition, or disintegration. It displaces structure instead of destroying it."[32] Among the seven projects displayed, Wigley singled out Coop Himmelblau's office penthouse in Vienna as exemplary of this new approach.

In a slightly reworked version of the same article, Wigley was even more critical of some works placed under this label:

> Deconstruction is often misunderstood as the taking apart of constructions. Consequently, any provocative architectural design which appears to take a structure apart by the simple breaking of an object – as in James Wines or the complex dissimulation of an object into a collage of traces, as in Eisenman and Fujii – has been called Deconstructive. These strategies have produced perhaps the most formidable projects of recent years, but remain simulations of Deconstructive work in other disciplines because they do not exploit the unique condition of the architectural object.[33]

It was not until the third installment on Deconstruction, published by Architectural Design in 1990, that Wigley finally came to acknowledge the impact of Derrida on this new movement. In this essay, Wigley explored in depth the philosophical background of Deconstruction, from Kant to Heidegger and culminating with Derrida. And in parallel, he elaborated on the difficult task of translation from philosophy to architecture, and vice versa, without mentioning any specific architectural projects, simply concluding that the effort of translating Deconstruction in architecture:

> does not lead simply to a formal reconfiguration of the object. Rather, it calls into question the condition of the object, its "objecthood". It "problematises" the condition of the object without simply abandoning it … Consequently, the status of the translation of deconstruction in architecture needs to be rethought. A more aggressive reading is required, an architectural transformation of deconstruction that draws on the gaps in deconstruction that demand such an abuse, sites that already operate with a kind of architectural violence.[34]

In this essay, Wigley did not give any hints about any projects that may have explored the boundaries between philosophy and architecture, simply leaving the question suspended. Also, he did not revisit the earlier opposition between "Deconstruction" and "Deconstructivism," two terms that came to mean the same thing in the end, and which were being applied uncritically to designate projects that displayed "fragmentation" and irregular compositions, superficially challenging the formal aspects of both "modern" and "post-modern" languages.

Yet the notion of the relationship to Constructivism must also be evaluated carefully, given the scientific, systematic and economic approach that the Russian Constructivists took towards the problem of form, which distinguishes their work from the latter-day "neo-constructivists."[35] Moisei Ginzburg, one of the leaders of that movement, clearly expressed the priorities and design philosophy of Constructivism in this statement:

> There can be no question of any sort of artist losing creativity just because he knows clearly what he wants, what he is aiming for, and in what consists the meaning of his work. But subconscious, impulsive creativity must be replaced by a clear and distinctly organised method, which is economical of the architect's energy and transfers the freed surplus of it into inventiveness and the force of the creative impulse.[36]

Granted, a certain formal affinity may be present, but the technical, social and economic parameters were absent from the agenda of the "neo-constructivists," which would make it more appropriate to read their work as a manifestation of a new "Expressionism," closer in spirit to the work of the earlier Expressionists like Hans Scharoun, Hermann Finsterlin and Bruno Taut, yet this time realizable through new technologies. Zaha Hadid, for one, showed an early interest in "Suprematism," as a student at the Architectural Association. Her principal mentor, Rem Koolhaas, was at the time under the influence of the work of Ivan Leonidov, which led him to a trip to Moscow. Koolhaas, whose later work would show greater affinity to the Constructivists' experimental and scientific approaches in design, albeit stripped of

their social agendas, was almost absent from the surveys of "Deconstruction," as his
work did not really fit the "image" being propagated, despite his modest inclusion
at the MoMA exhibition with a single project that did not show much affinity to the
others displayed.[37] Hadid's fascination with "Constructivism" was in turn due to the
fact that it had never been translated before in architecture. Under Koolhaas and
Zenghelis, she explored the problem of implementing Malevitch's *Tektonik* in the
local context of London.[38] Thus began a formal tendency that Hadid masterfully
translated later into her first major work, which launched her on the international
scene, the winning proposal for the Hong Kong Peak (Figure 4.8). In this unrealized
work, slabs of different directions superpose and extend over the mountain edges,
in a gravity-defying mood, something clearly indebted to the formal language of
Malevitch, but also to Melnikov, Vesnin and Leonidov.

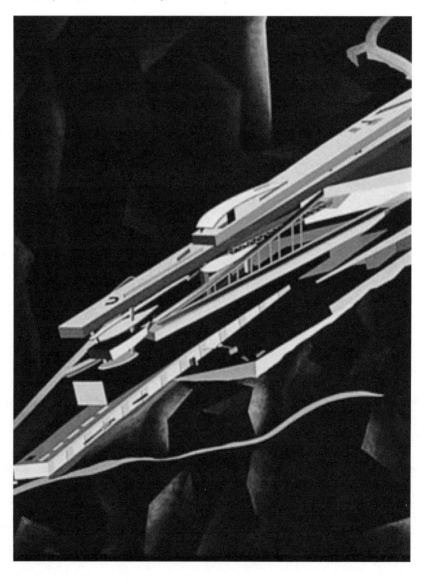

4.8   Zaha Hadid.
Project for the
Hong Kong
Peak, 1982–83

She thus explained her intervention on the Hong Kong hills in those terms:

I felt from the beginning that any intervention upon this condition could not be vertical, but had to be horizontal. It also had to have a degree of sharpness – like a blade cutting through the mountain. When you ascend the mountain away from the city the congestion lessens and the towers of the city begin to fragment across what is called the Mid-levels. The top is almost isolated – that is where the project slides in. As the object is placed on Hong Kong it begins to violate and change the city.[39]

It is noteworthy that Hadid, unlike Eisenman, never spent much time "theorizing" on her architectural projects, nor trying to reflect on any of the questions raised by Deconstruction. Her projects were not "texts" to be read or interpreted, or deconstructed for that matter, as much as experiments into gravity-defying formal collisions, that aim to produce unexpected or sublime experiences. The concepts always emerge from a provocative relation to the landscape, attempting to literally "scrape" the context, producing not objects, but a composition of elements held together in suspense. Confirming the thesis of the multiple references that her works relate to, Hadid's project for the Kurfurstendamm in Berlin (Figure 4.9), appeared in its representation as an architectural rendering of Duchamp's "Nude descending a staircase." Yet in the process of concretization, the projects lose much of their transparency and their "constructive" quality, as seen in the Vitra Fire Station (Figure 4.10) and the Contemporary Art Center in Cincinnati (Figure 4.11). From the Hong Kong Peak to the later projects done in collaboration with Patrick Schumacher,[40] Hadid gradually abandoned the earlier fascination with Malevitch and his hard-edge tectonics, moving towards "smooth" forms that emerge from a plastic modeling of curvilinear volumes, more reminiscent of the work of Erich Mendelsohn, but taken to different levels thanks to the new technological possibilities.

Frank Gehry, the other major figure who was brought into the Deconstruction camp, was even more candid about his surprise at this association. In one of his speeches at the time, he expressed his bewilderment at the linguistic discourse of Eisenman, confessing his ignorance of its theoretical foundations.[41] In many of his works, Gehry betrays more of a "bricoleur" approach, as visible for instance in the addition to his house in Venice, California (1978); or the University of Iowa

4.9   Zaha Hadid. Project for an Office Building on Kurfürstendamm, Berlin, 1986

4.10 Zaha
Hadid. Vitra Fire
Station, 1990–93

4.11 Zaha Hadid.
Contemporary Arts
Center, Cincinnati,
1997–2003

Laboratory (1992), where the design consisted of a long rectangular block, fronted by a collection of cubical elements which appear to be arbitrarily thrown around, like dice on a table. In explaining this particular project, Gehry referred to the theme of "crystals" which scientists referred to, articulating a very personal, artisanal approach to form-making:

> I looked at a lot of crystalline shapes. The shape at the top that has become boatlike or fishlike (whichever you like) is the support lab ... So I took advantage of it and started to mold the shape ... We simplified some of the pieces. And because the pipe canyon had a solid wall, I was able to make this kind of sculptural form, which I wanted to put on the street to animate it ... [42]

In his "Fred and Ginger" Office Building in Prague (1995) (Figure 4.12), Gehry resorted to a playful articulation of two elements that metaphorically re-interpret the theme of a dance, translated into a historical context that sustains a modern variation on the Baroque. Gehry's move towards the expressionist style that would mark his later phase started in fact well before the Guggenheim in Bilbao, with the Vitra Design Museum (1989) (Figure 4.13), where the building emerges as a result of a sculptural play with form, of twisting shapes that result in a composition that differs from his earlier approach. In his descriptions, Gehry invariably uses a language that is not too different from Hadid, where the decision-making process remains firmly in the hands of the architect-artist, who follows the intuitive method of an artisan, but where the tools vary from those of radical slicing through the site (as with Hadid), to those of a playful bricoleur, who often resorts to fetishes like the fish-form in order to animate his work.

CONCLUSION

Architectural historians have a tendency to assign dates for the beginning of certain movements as well as for their endings. We might in this respect put the origin of "Deconstruction" a few years before the defining events of the exhibitions of 1989, i.e. around the early 1980s, specifically with Eisenman's Canareggio project and Checkpoint Charlie, and its highpoint somewhere in the middle of the 90s decade, when it appeared to have reached its zenith. Soon afterwards, the transformations in the work of Gehry, Hadid, and even Eisenman, veered into another direction, which prompted trend-setters like Charles Jencks to re-assimilate them within a new and more inclusive phase of "post-modernism." Yet the problematic of Deconstruction lies precisely in the difficulty of its translation into architecture, which according to some critics, cannot take the form of realized "projects," no matter how self-critical those could be, but more appropriately into a form of criticism of the underlying structures of the profession as a whole, its hierarchical organization and its relation to the political and economic orders. In other words, a deconstruction of the "logos" of architecture, its principal logic of operation and the role it plays within the existing power structures. This remains an open project.

4.12   Frank Gehry. "Fred & Ginger" House, Prague, 1992–96

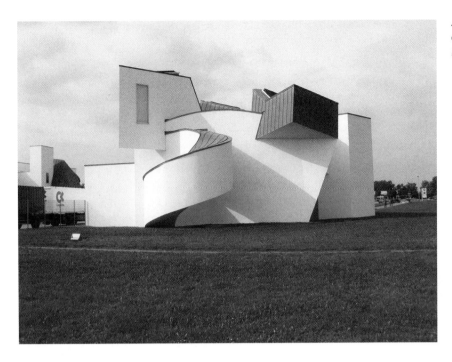

4.13 Frank Gehry. Vitra Design Museum, 1989

NOTES

1   Christopher Norris and Andrew Benjamin (eds), *What is Deconstruction?* (London: Academy Editions, 1988).

2   Ibid., 40.

3   Wigley was also the author of *Derrida's Haunt: The Architecture of Deconstruction* (Cambridge, MA: MIT Press, 1993), a work that addressed the Derridean discourse without explicitly attempting to connect it to any architectural "projects."

4   Jonathan Culler, "Jacques Derrida," in *Structuralism and Since: From Lévi Strauss to Derrida*, J. Sturrock (ed.) (Oxford: Oxford University Press, 1979), 172.

5   Jacques Derrida, *Of Grammatology*, Gayatri C. Spivak (trans.) (Baltimore: Johns Hopkins, 1976).

6   J. Derrida, "Point de Folie-Maintenant Architecture," *AA Files* 12 (Summer 1986): 65.

7   Ibid., 69.

8   Peter Eisenman, "Cardboard Architecture: House I and House II," in *Five Architects*, Arthur Drexler (ed.) (Oxford: Oxford University Press, 1972), 15–24.

9   Peter Eisenman. "Aspects of Modernism: Maison Dom-ino and the Self-Referential Sign," *Oppositions* 15/16 (1980): 119–28.

10   Peter Eisenman. "The Futility of Objects: Decomposition and the Processes of Differentiation," *Harvard Architectural Review* 3 (Winter 1984): 65–82.

11   Eisenman, "The Representations of Doubt: At the Sign of the Sign," *Rassegna* 9 (March 1982), reprinted in *Eisenman Inside Out: Selected Writings 1963–1988* (New Haven: Yale University Press, 2004), 143–51.

12   "The End of the Classical, the End of the Beginning, the End of the End," *Perspecta* 21 (1984): 154–72; reprinted in *Eisenman Inside Out*, 152–68.

13   Eisenman, *Fin d'Ou T Hou S* (London: Architectural Association, 1985).

14   Jeffrey Kipnis discussed the play on words in this title, which could alternately signify "find out house," "fine doubt house" or even the French "fin d"Aout' among other things. See Kipnis, "Architecture Unbound," in *Fin d'Ou T Hou S*, 12–23.

15   Eisenman, *Moving Arrows, Eros and Other Errors: An Architecture of Absence* (London: Architectural Association, 1986).

16   Derrida titled his chapter "The End of the Book and the Beginning of Writing."

17   See Franco Rella, "Tempo della fine e tempo dell' inizio (The Age of the End and the Age of the Beginning)," *Casabella* 498–9 (January/February 1984): 106–8; and Jeffrey Kipnis, "Eisenman/Robertson: Trasposizione di maglie urbane: un progetto per la Ohio State University," *Casabella* 498–9 (January/February 1984): 96–9.

18   Eisenman, "Misreading," in *Houses of Cards* (Oxford: Oxford University Press, 1987), 167.

19   The term used by Eisenman at that time was "decomposition." Later "deconstruction" would supplement decomposition in some of the discussions of his work.

20   Jeffrey Kipnis commented that this particular project came at a time when Eisenman's pursuit of the "elusive" goal of structuralism was faced with doubts, and as he started his readings of Derrida. See Kipnis, "Eisenman/Robertson: Trasposizione di maglie urbane", 15–21.

21   *Cities of Artificial Excavation* appeared in 1994 and covered projects that date from 1978 to 1988. Incidentally, the Wexner Center for the Arts, which is a major work in this group (completed in 1989) was not included in this collection.

22   Jean Francois Bedard, Introduction to *Cities of Artificial Excavation: The Work of Peter Eisenman, 1978–88*, Jean-Francois Bedard (ed.) (Montreal: Canadian Centre for Architecture, 1994).

23   See for instance Dianne Ghirardo's critique of Eisenman's project in "Two Institutions for the Arts," in Ghirardo, *Out of Site: A Social Criticism of Architecture* (Seattle: Bay Press, 1991). Ghirardo commented: "Here, the site's *real* political history is repressed in favor of a decorative shell, perhaps the most compelling and powerful feature of the whole project. With its delicate craftsmanship and playful slices of tower, arch, and wall, in its Disneylandish caricature of the earlier structure, it effectively realizes the gloomy prognosis of Walter Benjamin about the aestheticization of politics. The fetishized structures are wittingly emptied of their history and rendered nothing more than cheerfully manipulable images that direct attention only to formal games."

24   The previous works of Eisenman had exhibited equally word-playful titles. See above.

25   *Chora L Works: Jacques Derrida and Peter Eisenman*, Jeffrey Kipnis and Thomas Leeser (eds) (New York: Monacelli, 1997).

26   Derrida, in *Chora L Works*, 8.

27   From September 17, 1985 to October October 27, 1987.

28   Jacques Derrida, "Letter to Peter Eisenman (October 1989)," in *Chora L Works*, 161–5.

29   For more on these projects, see *Blurred Zones: Investigations of the Interstitial: Eisenman Architects, 1988–1998*, Andrew Benjamin (ed.) (New York: Monacelli, 2002).

30   For an analysis of Bernard Tschumi's theoretical project, see Louis Martin, "Transpositions: On the Intellectual Origins of Tschumi's Architectural Theory," *Assemblage* 11 (April 1990): 22–35.

31   Jacques Derrida, "Letter to Peter Eisenman," in *Assemblage* 12 (August 1990): 6–13.

32   Mark Wigley, "Deconstructivist Architecture," in *Deconstructivist Architecture*, Philip Johnson and Mark Wigley (eds) (New York: MoMA, 1988), 16–17.

33   Mark Wigley, "Deconstructivist Architecture," in *Deconstruction*, Andreas Papadakis, Catherine Cooke, Andrew Benjamin (eds) (New York: Rizzoli, 1989), 133.

34   Mark Wigley, "The Translation of Architecture: The Tower of Babel," in *Deconstruction III*, Andreas Papadakis (ed.) (London: Academy Editions, 1990), 12.

35   See Catherine Cooke, "The Development of the Constructivist Architects' Design Method," in *Deconstruction*, 21–37. Geoffrey Broadbent, in a skeptical essay on this topic, extended the sources of this new trend to include Dada and Cubism, in addition to the more recent work of the Situationists of the 1960s. See Geoffrey Broadbent, "The Architecture of Deconstruction," in *Deconstruction: A Student Guide* (London: Academy Editions, 1991), 10–30.

36   Quoted in Cooke, "The Development of the Constructivist Architects' Design Method," 22.

37   Of the three *Architectural Design* issues dedicated to this movement, Koolhaas's work figured only in the first one, with the Berlin Checkpoint Charlie project published under the umbrella of OMA, with an accompanying article by his partner at the time, Elia Zenghelis. Philip Johnson and Mark Wigley included Koolhaas in their MoMA show, with a project for an apartment building in Rotterdam, a project that does not show much affinity, neither formally nor ideologically, to what was being branded as "Deconstructivist."

38   Zaha Hadid, "Recent Work," in *Architecture in Transition: Between Deconstruction and New Modernism*, Peter Noever and Regina Haslinger (eds) (Munich: Prestel, 1991), 47–61.

39   Hadid, ibid., 48–9.

40   See for instance the Landesgartenschau in Wheil am Rhein, completed in 1999, or the BMW Plant in Leipzig, completed in 2005.

41   Frank Gehry, "Keynote Address" to the Symposium on "Postmodernism and Beyond: Architecture as the Critical Art of Contemporary Culture," held at the Beckham Center, California, October 1989. Reprinted in *Critical Architecture and Contemporary Culture*, William J. Lillyman, Marilyn F. Moriarty and David J. Neuman (eds) (Oxford: Oxford University Press, 1994), 165–86.

42   Gehry, ibid., 171.

5

Greening Architecture: The Impact of Sustainability

Phillip Tabb

INTRODUCTION

Contemporary architecture, and the culture it reflects, contributed to the cause and necessity of a burgeoning green process that emerged over the past half century. According to Julien de Smedt (JDS Architects), "There's a definition problem: 'Green' and 'Sustainability,' the terms used to name the answer to the most pressing problem of our time, have become dangerously afloat in ambiguity and indeterminacy. Sustainable architecture is everywhere and nowhere."[1] For the purpose of this discussion, sustainability is defined as the greening of architecture through accumulative reduction over time of negative environmental effects and unsustainable activities caused by buildings, urban designs and settlements.

Modern architecture focused on abstraction, standardization and serial production seeking a homogeneous international identity, and to a large extent was energy inefficient. Consequently, it added unintended adverse consequences to the environment and exposed our dependence on fossil fuels. Fortunately, early climate-responsive works by Le Corbusier, Louis Kahn, Frank Lloyd Wright, Ralph Erskine, Alvar Aalto and Hassan Fathy, emerged as modernist green precedents, as exemplified by Le Corbusier's solar oriented Chandigarh High Courts Building (1956) or Louis Kahn's daylighting in the Kimbell Art Museum (1972). From the 1960s, the ever-closing circle of a single set of universal principles was reconsidered by place-oriented intentions that initiated environmentally conscious designs. Later, green architecture became an evolving phenomenon that advanced from rationalist, performance-based and piecemeal measures in response to particular environmental concerns, to far more encompassing ecological and systemic processes cutting deep across contemporary culture.

VISIONARY BEGINNINGS AND THE 1960s

In the 1960s a growing awareness of the deleterious effects that contemporary life had on the environment became more present. Rachel Carson's *Silent Spring* was a striking wake-up call.[2] Carson, a marine biologist, documented damage caused on the environment by pesticides. She focused on the example of birds, whose populations have dwindled as a result of damage caused to their eggshells by the aerial spraying of DDT. Widespread use, she argued, harmed humans as well as other animals. The 1972 book, *Limits to Growth*, was another poignant warning that the growing world population was reaching the limits of its carrying capacity of finite planetary resource supplies.[3] The OPEC Oil Embargo of 1973 added another dimension prompting an increase in awareness of the United States' dependence upon foreign energy.

In 2006, former Vice President Al Gore brought these issues to public attention more vividly through his provocative documentary *An Inconvenient Truth*,[4] consequently, raising public awareness of environmental degradation, climate change, depletion of renewable resources, increasing global population, and the critical relationship between the natural and built environments. According to the US National Climate Data Center, the summer of 2010 recorded the highest global temperatures on record. Scientists agreed that these increased temperatures were created by trapped solar radiation due to rising anthropogenic greenhouse gasses, especially carbon dioxide, which was generated mainly through the burning of fossil fuels within the building, power and transportation sectors.

Victor Olgyay was one of the early theoreticians to propose a bio-climatic approach to architecture. His book *Design with Climate* was influential in architectural education during the 1960s and '70s.[5] His suggestions that climatic factors, such as solar radiation, variations in temperature, precipitation, wind and humidity, and on-site resources manifested regional differences and could be utilized through appropriate design were important green principles. Elemental and ambient environmental forces became potential form-givers to buildings and cities alike, as illustrated in Ralph Erskine's boreal climate image of *Arctic City* or in the design of his Villa Strom in Stocksund, Sweden (1961) whose compact form, response to the low winter sun, and wind-excluding devices responded to the severe sub-Arctic climate.

The effectiveness of green architecture depended upon the balance of on-site energy sources with building energy conservation. The more "conservative" the building envelope, insulation and the tightness of construction, the easier it was to match essential energy loads to the availability of on-site resources. The design mantra was "conservation first!" In colder climates, construction was focused on solar energy gain, heat retention using higher insulation values and double-glazing, and even movable insulation. In warmer climates attention was given to the solar control of the envelope, especially roofs and western facades, as well as to natural ventilation and daylighting. Conservation conscious design was in sharp contrast to previous modernist tendencies of spatial generosity, complexity of form, expansive glazing areas, and reliance on abundant fossil fuels and mechanical systems for heating and cooling.

The obsession for larger buildings in cities and lower densities in suburbs in the United States after WW II exacerbated the problem with increasing demands on land, infrastructure, transportation networks, building construction resources, and energy. The average American home has nearly tripled in size since the 1950s.[6]

The preference for the single-family detached residence type also contributed to sprawl. E.F. Schumacher's 1973 book, *Small is Beautiful*, challenged this version of the American Dream of a larger home and suggested, "less can be more."[7] For the emerging green approaches to architecture, it was clear that *size* mattered. Congruently, the work of R. Buckminster Fuller was innovative and inventive, especially for his shelter designs.[8] Fuller's experiments with the Dymaxion House (1929), geodesic structures, and concepts of structural and material efficiencies led to the development of another important tenet for green architecture—"synergy," which emphasized systems' components relational behavior and resulting efficiencies. The theoretical foundations of Deep Ecology, advocated in 1973 by Arne Naess, saw an ecological community of inclusive memberships where "everything was connected to everything."

The first green architectural explorations were quite radical. Alastair Gordon explained in his 2008 essay "True Green: Lessons from 1960s–70s Counterculture Architecture," that a corporate, mechanistic and monumental architecture was being replaced by young architects in search of more popular sources of inspiration—cocoons, anthills, honeycombs, nests, earth mounds, spaceships, and seedpods.[9] Buildings were constructed out of earth, recycled and scavenged materials and common building products. In 1965, a group of art students founded Drop City, a domed commune in southern Colorado, on a seven and a half acre tract of land, which they called a "dropped in work of art." It was not able to sustain itself, however, and ultimately abandoned in 1977, yet its spontaneous spirit did carry over to other emerging green utopias. Steve Baer, inspired by Fuller and Drop City, formed Zomeworks and began building polyhedral structures, which incorporated both active and passive solar energy utilization techniques as pictured in Figure 5.1.

The utopian vision of Paolo Soleri contributed to his life-long commitment at Arcosanti in the high desert of central Arizona. Planned for 5,000 residents, Arcosanti began construction in 1970 and embodied Soleri's philosophy blending

5.1   Steve Baer, Baer House, Corrales, New Mexico

architecture and ecology – what he called "arcology." Soleri's vision, as can be seen in Figure 5.2, was for the design of an urban environment within a rural setting promoting social interaction, accessibility, density, use of on-site resources and heavy mass construction, reduction of waste, and access to the natural environment. In contrast, the architectural visions of Archigram were not essentially ecological in nature, but championed the high-tech and lightweight approach towards a modular technology within the urban setting. Their urban projects, including Plug-in-City, Instant City and Tuned City, were bold propositions intended to inspire and provoke, and in some ways these early designs represented creative, innovative, and impermanent works.

The New York City-based firm SITE, established in 1970, was motivated by the social and political unrest of the 1960s and they were best known for their work with Best Products Company where portions for the "big-box" facade were precariously peeled away and served as commentary on the shopping center strip and its significance within the suburban environment. Superstudio was founded in Florence, Italy, by Adolfo Natalini and Cristiano Toraldo di Francia, in the mid-1960s and produced powerful conceptions of what they called a: "tecnomorphic" architecture and a technocratic optimism. Another noteworthy example of visionary work occurred with various projects on the 425-acre Prickly Mountain in Vermont. The experiments were the vision of David Sellers who proposed design-built projects that were "improvised into existence," including sustainable constructions. The historical significance of these works was clear as they challenged architectural discourse to consider new and more environmentally oriented architectural forms and technologies.

The relationship between the environmental movement and architecture grew as public awareness of ecological concerns and the emergence of new green technologies increased. Stewart Brand published the first issue of *The Whole Earth Catalog* in 1968, amid a wave of countercultural experimentation and a growing interest in self-built housing and intentional communities.[10] Expanding developments with alternative technologies became available to the public at large. Apple co-founder Steve Jobs described the catalog as a conceptual forerunner of the World Wide Web. During the green beginnings, concepts of environmental

5.2   Paolo Soleri and collaborators, Arcosanti, Arizona, 1970–present

health, building size, efficiency, conservation, on-site resource utilization, and emerging sustainable technologies began to influence architectural practice. The significance of projects like Drop City, Arcosanti, Superstudio, Prickly Mountain and Archigram's imaginary cities, in addition to the environmental literature, were instrumental to the free-spirited architectural forms of the 1970s, including the widespread and inceptual application of solar technologies.

SOLAR ARCHITECTURE: THE 1970s

New legislation in the United States supported the growing green movement. A series of policies were adopted in order to protect the environment, including the National Environmental Policy Act (1969), the Clean Air Act (1970), the Clean Water Act (1972), and the Endangered Species Act (1973). Subsequently, the Oil Embargo, which resulted in long queues at gasoline stations, prompted the pursuit of alternative energy sources. While techniques for passive solar heating had been practiced for thousands of years, the initial thrust after the Oil Embargo was toward active technologies that focused on solar collection panels, thermal absorption and storage mediums, heat transfer and mechanical distribution systems, and electronic monitoring and control devices.

The first examples of active solar architecture simply applied the emergent technologies unceremoniously onto buildings, usually rooftops. Solar collector arrays faced cardinal directions at optimal orientation and tilt angles often contrary to building orientations and roof forms, resulting in awkward massing. Eventually, building designs assimilated the blossoming technologies where solar collector orientation, tilt angle, and area intensiveness became more integrative. The early demonstrations of active solar architecture, especially in temperate and cold climates, revealed competition for sunlight between the area requirements of the opaque solar collector arrays and daylight needs of the users inside. Designed in 1975 by Joint Venture Architects, the Student Housing project in Boulder, Colorado addressed this issue with 70 percent of the space-heating and domestic hot-water heating requirements provided by the active solar system. The building, in Figure 5.3, responded to the systems' orientation constraints, collector area of 700 square feet, and optimal tilt angle with sloping south planes. The south facade was articulated by a "pushing and pulling" of multiple secondary forms breaking the monotony and allowing for in-between spaces for stairs, balconies, and daylight to penetrate deep into livable interior spaces.

While solar techniques have been used for millennia, the term "passive," meaning not relying on mechanical or electrical components, was popularized during the 1970s by Richard Crowther of Denver, Colorado.[11] Passive systems were designed to provide heat over a twenty-four hour period. Amory Lovins later promoted the term "soft energy" as a way of defining more benign and environmentally friendly sources of energy where production was matched in scale and quality to end use requirements.[12] The opaque systems' components of active solar technologies were replaced with more transparent conventional building elements, such as

5.3 Joint Venture
Architects,
Boulder Student
Housing, Boulder,
Colorado, 1975

greenhouses, sunrooms, atriums, windows, doors, skylights, and clerestories, and the
mass of the building for thermal storage: the building became an energy collector.
Solar tempering was the first technique used with increased fenestration areas on
southern facades, but these systems tended to overheat because of inadequate
thermal storage. The effectiveness of a passive solar system depended upon ways
in which the architecture responded to the entire solar systems' functioning parts,
including accommodating the area intensiveness of collection, adequate matching
of solar glazing to internal thermal mass for overnight storage, and efficient coupling
of solar-charged spaces with other uncharged internal spaces.

One of the most widely published projects was the Balcomb House designed
by William Lumpkins. Built in 1979, the passive design approach for this house was
accomplished with a dominant isolated-gain sunspace passive system thermally
coupled to interior adobe walls, stone floor, and in-ground remote rockbeds. The
two-story living areas adjacent to the sunspace were the beneficiary of this heat
source, and were regulated with multiple operable openings.[13] Douglas Balcomb
lived in and analyzed the house for nearly 10 years and eventually developed a
set of solar engineering design procedures for passive solar heating that enabled
architects to design with useful performance-based modeling and calculation
methods. This was especially useful for the sizing of solar collector arrays and
determining the amount of thermal storage. The integrated solar guides and
thesaurus of precedents in Edward Mazria's 1979 book *The Passive Solar Energy
Book* provided passive design strategies and details for architects worldwide.[14]

In contrast to the solar-dominant work of Lumpkins, Malcolm Wells went
underground. His unique earth-sheltered works were intended to reduce the
amount of conventional building materials, especially forest depleting products,
with more massive earth-based materials—rammed earth, green roofs, stone,
concrete block and concrete. This pioneering work would later inspire interest
in green roof projects several decades later. The Skytherm system of roof ponds,
engineered by Harold Hay, capitalized on the thermal storage capacity of water, but

5.4   William Lumpkins, Balcomb House, Santa Fe, New Mexico, 1979

5.5   Michael Reynolds, Earthships, Taos, New Mexico

proved impractical when applied to larger buildings, especially those with multiple stories or complex roof forms. The work of James Lambeth took on a different approach—one that explored delight in solar architectural form, especially with emphasis of the "solar section."[15] His projects often exaggerated form for its solar function, and were optimistic, playful and in his terms "danced with the sun."

The radical works of Michael Reynolds pushed the boundaries of residential design with his use of unconventional recycled materials, such as automobile tires, aluminum cans and recycled glass bottles. Further, his designs were completely off-grid and consequently realized the full potential of on-site resources and alternative technologies for passive and active solar heating, water harvesting, and photovoltaic electricity production. His "Earthships" were independent, free-spirited and often looked rather unusual and homegrown.[16] Single Earthships, such as the one in Figure 5.5, were built worldwide and soon grew into small communities throughout northern New Mexico often located on inexpensive land far from utilities. An important consequence of his work was the clear and visible relationship between the size of "*served*" or conditioned spaces of the residence and the various systems' area and volumetric requirements for providing completely off-grid space-heating, water harvesting and electricity production.

Ralph Knowles examined the relationship between pure form, urban density, and both seasonal and diurnal rhythms of the sun.[17] These investigations led to the development of his solar envelope concept and solar zoning guides that he tested with numerous student project insertions into the urban fabric of Los Angeles. Solar access for densities up to 50 units per acre was achievable. The works of Dean Hawkes and Stephen Greenberg in Great Britain investigated solar building positioning relative to suburban lotting schemes of varying orientations. They were able to demonstrate adequate solar siting for all buildings by relaxing the building-to-plot geometry. While the study proved it was possible, it exposed growing shortcomings in solar urban design and multiple building applications. Providing adequate solar access, while responding to flexible site designs for difficult and varying site conditions, was challenging in achieving higher density developments.

Jeffrey Cook of Arizona State University was a strong supporter of bio-climatic design, who later became critical of many solar designs. He attacked what he called the "dominant solar section" suggesting that it was too fixed and inflexible to respond to other important climatic, programmatic, aesthetic, and formal determinants. His concern was the predictable and uninteresting opacity of the north sides of these buildings and the overly angular, phototropic, and transparent southern facades that typified these early projects. In the United States growth in alternative energy industries expanded until federal and state energy tax credits expired in 1985. This coupled with the availability of cheap natural gas set back the greening of architecture in America for at least a decade as mainstream architecture engaged with new agendas exploring a variety of theoretical themes.

POSTMODERN GREEN: THE 1980s

The Postmodernism of the 1980s had an anesthetizing effect on the uninhibited solar architecture of the 1970s. Postmodernism's focus on wit, symbolism, reference and polychromatic aesthetics was in dire contrast to the fixed, overly responsible and performance-based solar predecessors. Steven Moore argued; "In the 1970s and 1980s, postmodern environmentalists in Europe and North America routinely characterize modern architecture as both inhumane and inherently anti-nature. In this reactionary view, modern architecture, like modern science and technology that enabled it, was understood be the principal source of environmental degradation, not its cure."[18] To Charles Jencks, modern architecture died in St. Louis, Missouri on July 15, 1972 when the infamous Pruit-Igoe was dynamited, thus beginning a new era.[19]

The modernist roots of early green architecture were based on the pursuit of a functional and tectonic order, yet postmodern theory released the rigid functional rules of performance-based design and resituated them to reflection, interpretation and spontaneous expression of coterminous meaning inherent to a particular place or living vernacular. North American postmodern architecture seemed to evolve in three distinct directions. First was with the appropriating of vernacular forms and their direct application to contemporary programs, such as the vernacular scaling to "big-box" buildings in commercial shopping malls. Second was the ornamentation to high-rise structures, such as Philip Johnson's AT&T Building in New York City (1978–84), and Michael Graves' Portland Municipal Services Building (1980–82). Third was the development of contemporary hybrids that focused on the environmental conditions and causes, which originally generated authentic vernacular forms. The application of indigenous greening principles to specific contexts produced hybrids drawn from cultural and environmental characteristics of a particular place and time, yet they maintained continuity with certain modernist spatial, tectonic and material concepts, such as the postmodern sun-tempered house (1980) in the Parisian suburbs, shown in Figure 5.6.

The Rural Studio, established in the early 1990s in western Alabama by Samuel Mockbee, addressed environmental concerns in a larger context of social engagement. Working with a largely impoverished clientele, Mockbee and his students at Auburn University built innovative, low-cost houses and community buildings that often incorporated reclaimed waste materials and passive solar systems. The Glass Chapel (2000), in Masons Bend, Alabama, for example, incorporated salvaged police car windshields for its roof glazing system and rammed earth walls. The work of Yestermorrow, founded in 1980 in Waitsfield, Vermont, promoted emerging renewable technologies and local materials, with self-built and low-cost building methods, and combined a design-build school with outreach projects.

5.6   Parisian House

In Australia, Glenn Murcutt was also concerned with the production of environmentally sensitive architectural works, of both residential and institutional type. His motto was, "touch the earth lightly," and connect to nature. The Magney House in New South Wales (1984) used a vaulted butterfly roof that featured water, air and light. Adapted to the hot-dry climate were wide overhangs that protected the glass from excessive sunlight and channeled breezes through the house. A trough, down the length of the house, collected rainwater, which fed to an underground cistern. The southern side of the dwelling housed service functions while the northern side was open to daylight, prevailing breezes and vistas to the Tasman Sea.

In Nova Scotia, Brian MacKay-Lyons designed with traditional vernacular forms and modernist details. While he began his practice in the mid 1980s, his seminal green designs were done a decade later. He drew inspiration from the local construction culture and regional architectural forms of the shipbuilding towns along the Nova Scotia coast. The Martin-Lancaster House, located in Prospect along the Atlantic coast, is a 3,000 square feet passive solar residential complex featuring a composition of simple gable forms including a detached garage and guesthouse, social pavilion and arrival courtyard. Passive solar building strategies were used as well as a "zero-detailed" roof in response to the freeze-thaw cycles of the marine climate. Malcolm Quantrill described his work as, "an architecture as 'instrument,' rather than as a predetermined formal or geometric entity, [that] would be open to the possibility of free interpretation or free performance."[20] The profile of the Martin-Lancaster House, pictured in Figure 5.7, illustrates the simple iconic vernacular gable roof, a more balanced form compared to the dominant solar section of the 1970s.

In San Antonio, Texas the firm Lake Flato developed a regionally driven contemporary vernacular that in their words was a "blend of sustainability and

5.7 Brian
MacKay-Lyons,
Martin-Lancaster
House, Prospect,
Nova Scotia

modesty." Their works, which generally were located in warmer climate regions, were driven by the use of a palette of regional materials, authentic forms and the natural environment. The Carraro Residence located in Kyle, Texas (1990) was designed using reassembled steel structural parts from the Alamo Cement Plant, which was being demolished and sold for scrap. The industrial vernacular shell was repurposed as an outer skin to provide sunshading and spatial definition for outdoor rooms. The success of this work was measured by the hybridity and reuse of these historic vernacular forms and their utility to contemporary architectural programs.

Collective measures such as the New Urbanism movement were largely influenced by the postmodern agenda and reacted to the rampant suburban sprawl by promoting more compact, mixed-use, and neo-traditional settlements. Places like Poundbury in Dorset, UK (Leon Krier), Seaside, Florida (Duany Plater-Zyberk), and Rio Vista West in San Diego, California (Calthorpe Associates) were among the notable examples of this new movement. Leon Krier delineated an urban design manifesto in the early 1980s that outlined a set of critiques of modern urbanism.[21] Among his counsels were the conceptual blueprints for urban growth by multiplication rather than by gross addition, promotion of integrated zoning rather than functional zoning with spatial separation of uses, and establishment of pedestrian scaled urban patterns such as blocks, streets, squares and outdoor public rooms. The "New Urbanist village," according to Ruth Durack, is by necessity a fully planned and regulated environment, fiercely resistant to change and any deviation from the rigid encyclopedic rules that govern its form and function.[22] While they embodied some sustainable planning strategies, such as densification, mixed uses, pedestrian orientation and varying transportation modes, such communities were far from being truly "green." Their architecture was largely nostalgic and referential rather than authentically responsive to climate and resource conservation.

5.8   Lake Flato Architects, Carraro Residence, Kyle, Texas

The researches of Alexander Tzonis and Liane Lefaivre into the conflicts between regional and global orders that emerged in the decades following the Second World War contributed to their concepts of design cognition and critical regionalism. They posited that problem-solving should de-empathize imported universal solutions in favor of reflective, inventive and unique qualities of a region. In his 1983 essay, "Towards a Critical Regionalism," Kenneth Frampton called for an architecture that would overcome the inherent placelessness generated by universal construction methods and planning strategies. While affirming modernism's social commitment, Frampton proposed a critical regionalism, that would draw on the topology, climate, and light conditions of its geographical context, while concurrently embracing the tectonic traditions of its cultural context.[23] He further stressed that architecture was neither a vacantly "international" exercise in modern technology nor a "sentimental" imitation of vernacular buildings, arguing for a propinquity of place cultivated between the universal and local. Steven Moore saw in Frampton's call a powerful "proto-environmentalist discourse" that helped legitimize the next green phase in architecture. Greening of architecture in the 1980s primarily focused on residential-scaled projects, with emphasis on what was referred to as "skin-dominated" and "vernacular-oriented" sustainability with corresponding technologies. This directed green measures to the energetic interaction between indoors and outdoors adopting contemporary vernacular forms and mediating envelopes or "skins" that allowed for appropriate levels of opacity, resistance, transparency and porosity.

ECO-TECHNOLOGY: THE 1990s

Green design expanded in the 1990s to encompass new and improved environmental technologies that boldly expressed and blended into contemporary architecture. The proclamation of this time was that architecture should naturally be designed sustainably and normalized within the characteristic constraints and parameters of a given project: green should become standard practice. The emerging green architecture tended towards larger and more varied building typologies that required inherent "load-dominated" energy design measures and "eco-centric" technologies for reduction of unwanted heat gains from solar radiation and internal sources, such as artificial lighting, equipment and people, mechanical ventilation, elevators, and modern air conditioning systems. For many prominent architects of this time especially in Europe (including Santiago Calatrava, Lord Norman Foster, Sir Nicholas Grimshaw, Jacques Herzog and Pierre de Meuron, Miralles, Renzo Piano, and Lord Richard Rogers), the tectonic qualities of a building's design became an opportunity for architectural integration, including the expression of the sustainable systems.

The example of the Solar House in Breisach-am-Rhein, Germany (1992) by Thomas Spiegelhalter, was a complex and sculptural arrangement of architectural volumes juxtaposing renewable energy technologies and exterior space defining elements. It expressed a complexity attributed to the deconstruction works characteristic of this time. While this project was at the residential scale, it was significant because of the architectural language and tectonic character of the design, which was largely driven by formal principles boldly expressing the photovoltaic energy, greenhouse and passive solar technologies.[24] The dynamic geometry and syncopated layering of sustainable systems can clearly be seen in Figure 5.9.

Renzo Piano's Tjibaou Cultural Center (1998) located in Nouméa, New Caledonia incorporated local Kanak traditions and vernacular forms into an ensemble of iconic shell-like structures. The 10 pavilions were positioned along a ridge in response to the tropical climate with open cup-like forms taking full advantage of lagoon breezes on the leeward side and providing protection from the stormy windward

5.9   Thomas Spiegelhalter, Breisach House, Breisach-am-Rhein, Germany, 1992

5.10   T.R. Hamzah and Ken Yeang, E DITT Tower, Singapore, 1998

side of the Pacific Ocean. The Milwaukee Art Museum Quadracci Pavilion (2001), by Santiago Calatrava, is another graceful expression of green technologies, featuring elaborate wing elements, which open and close for more accurate solar control. Constructed in a city with a strong craft tradition, the pouring of concrete into one-of-a-kind wooden forms made the structure hand-built. The blending of the powerful, harmonic and sensual form, with the shading devices, created a vibrant example of green architecture.

The London City Hall (2001) by Foster + Partners is considered one of the most sustainable new buildings built at this time. The photograph, shown in Figure 5.11, illustrates the glazed bulbous skin reducing the exterior surface area, and phototropic section of the building form with its obvious gesture toward the south creating self-shadowing. The British Pavilion in Seville, Spain, designed by Nicholas Grimshaw and Ove Arup for Expo 92, was another powerful climate-responsive building. The lightweight prefabricated structure incorporated many adaptable environmental control features and cooling devices for this extremely hot-dry climate including a large water wall on the east facade, S-shaped solar collection and roof shading devices, and translucent membranes. Another significant demonstration by Grimshaw was the Eden Project in Cornwall, UK, that featured a domed skin that could be inflated or deflated to adjust the insulation levels responding to outside temperatures. The Tropical Biome was the world's largest enclosed greenhouse, covering more than four acres of land and housing 5,000 species of plants from throughout the world.

5.11   Foster + Partners, London City Hall, London, 2001

Rather than using fixed architectural elements to control the heating of the sun, a new generation of mediating technologies emerged. The Headquarters of SAP in Newtown Square, Pennsylvania used a light sensor system, while the New York Times Company Headquarters had a draped shade system that could adjust to the movement of the sun and changing conditions of the sky. Kroon Hall (2009) at Yale University, designed by Hopkins, was elevated as a "ultra-green" building, with 50 percent reduction in energy use as compared to other comparable sized modern buildings. Its design utilized solar energy through the long slender south side of the building, earth sheltering of the lower floor, daylight illumination for most of the interior spaces, and a rooftop mounted photovoltaic array providing about 25 percent of its electrical needs. The Federal Environmental Agency, located in a former brownfield site in Dessau, Germany (2005) designed by Sauerbruch Hutton as a compact building incorporating a large rooftop solar collector array, passive solar atrium/pedestrian streets, an increased envelope insulation level for the undulating facade and most importantly a geothermal heat exchange system that ran underneath the structure.

While the majority of sustainable work at this time was directed toward ecologically oriented high technology, the literal greening of architecture provided an interesting counter point. This literal greening was exemplified by the design for the EDITT Tower in Singapore (1998), by Hamzah and Yeang, demonstrating a regeneration project with a continuous vertical landscape ecosystem spiraling around and throughout the tower to facilitate ambient cooling. In addition, the 26-story building was designed to collect rainwater and the integrated photovoltaic panels were designed to provide 40 percent of the building's energy needs.[25] Emilio Ambasz and Associates designed the ACROS Fukuoka (1995) an impressive 14-story south-facing terraced vegetative facade-roof of 35,000 plants. The mixed-use complex preserved and revitalized Tenjin Central Park. The California Academy of Sciences in San Francisco designed by Piano (2008) is another example that features multiple green venues, including an undulating living roof with 1.7 million native living plants, use of recycled materials, and large photovoltaic canopy. These works ostensibly represented a host of similar projects that took on the literal greening of a building including green roofs, green walls, greenhouses, and sky gardens. The applications were also considered living tectonics and in some instances, edible landscapes applied to both buildings and urban settings.

William McDonough and Michael Braungart, the authors of *Cradle to Cradle*, present an alternative ambit to eco-technology.[26] Their work focused on the benign effects and minimal environmental impacts of building materials, products, and equipment. Working with corporate clients, such as, Gap Inc., Herman Miller, Nike Inc., and Ford Motor Company, they designed facilities, which incorporated a blend of sustainable building products, passive solar heating and cooling, daylighting and other energy efficiency techniques. Their principal contribution to green architecture was not about formal expression of design or green technology, but rather a focus on the health and embodied energy implications of building materials.

The critical interaction between architecture and technology moved from preoccupation with Modernism's logic of mass production, functionalism and fixed tectonics to the introduction of flexible, highly interactive and mutable technologies addressing multiple engineering agendas. According to Catherine Slessor, "high-tech architecture" evolved to blend the daring feats of structural engineering and expanded the tectonic vocabulary to include sustainability.[27] And the added considerations regarding human well-being and healthy building materials, along with the advent of the merit-defining Leadership in Energy and Environmental Design (LEED) certification further propelled architecture toward a new millennium of greening processes and matriculation into ever-expanding realms and scales of application.[28]

The turn of the century brought with it growing concerns about the environment and a renewed interest in the greening of architecture, largely due to increased evidence of global warming and the rising price of crude oil. But more importantly, it brought greater awareness of the complexity and pervasive nature of the problem. Connections, relationships, interfaces and systemic processes emerged in addition to fixed notions about sustainable technology and previously focused greening efforts on single buildings. By the new millennium sustainability had accumulated a wide range of green technologies for single buildings in response to the complex contextual and ecological processes of a given place. Green architecture had taken on the blueprint of an "eco-logical" paradigm and buildings began to reflect this especially where larger and more urban applications were considered.

GREEN URBANISM AFTER 2000

Green architecture after 2000 proliferated globally with more complex, larger programs and broader reaching considerations as illustrated in James Wines' book *Green Architecture* (2000).[29] Sustainability included the focus on urbanism and communities of buildings while green architecture evolved to greater levels of integration and sophistication of renewable technologies. At the threshold of the millennium were the works exhibited at Expo 2000 in Hanover, Germany, that explored both these scales of design. The German Pavilion, designed by Josef Wund, was a lightweight and daylit structure, and the central meeting place, designed by Thomas Herzog, featured four elaborate umbrella shells erected with hybrid timber and steel construction. However, it was the new district of Kronsberg, Germany, planned by Arnaboldi, Cavadini and Hager, that was an eco-district adjacent to the Fair and was an impressive sister project to the exposition, which demonstrated a transit-driven sustainable community for 6,000 dwellings.[30] The medium-density design incorporated renewable technologies, cogeneration with district heating and cooling, super-blocks with compact mix-use building types and varying courtyard designs, and community gardens.

The sinuous Incheon Munhak Stadium (2002) in South Korea, designed by Populous Architects, was an example of the blending of infrastructure, movement systems, urban greenspace and architecture into a complex web of sustainable urbanism. The large-scale increments appear, as a dynamic layering that seemed to liberate architecture into an amalgamation and syntax of pure motion. It is reminiscent of the visionary urban designs of Michael Sorkin and his neurological insertions, such as the masterplan for Chungcheong, South Korea (2005). Another example, the remarkable New York City's High Line Park (2009) designed by James Corner, was created as an aerial greenway elevated for one mile along Manhattan's West Side.[31] Supporting these later green developments were the ideas of urban designer Nan Ellin in her book *Integral Urbanism* (2006) that shifted attention from singularity of focus and reliance on technology to sustainable urban design nuanced by hybridity, connectivity, porosity and authenticity.[32]

Between-place contexts supported a new kind of green architecture, one that had systemic fabric-oriented qualities. Sites for infrastructure architecture tended to be situated around the perimeter of dense urban centers and between defined suburban residential districts. These environments were typically linear, complex, often chaotic, and spatially fragmented with multiple land uses, functionally zoned and separated from one another. Landuses were typically designated for industrial factories, power plants, water treatment facilities, brownfields, sports and entertainment facilities, business parks, automobile dealerships, shopping malls, rail lines, watersheds, and a patchwork of residual land, and they tended to be dominated by automobile highway networks. Given the piecemeal nature of this territory, sustainable strategies tended toward increased levels of connectivity for ecological and pedestrian zones, increased mixes and integration of uses, densification, and far more sinuous forms. The new urban insertions and adaptive reuse projects for this development context typically followed linear watersheds, transportation routes, and other infrastructural systems. Designed by Jerde Partnership, Namba Parks completed in 2003 in Osaka, Japan was an example of a mixed-use infrastructural oasis within the city center. The amazing work of Teddy

5.12   Arnaboldi, Cavadini and Hager, Kronsberg District, Hanover, Germany, 2000

Cruz and Alfredo Brillembourg of Urban-Think Tank brought airborne infrastructural architecture to the informal settlements of Barrio of San Agustin, Venezuela (2010). Katrina Stoll and Scott Lloyd in *Infrastructure as Architecture*, claimed that there was an increasing demand for integrated solutions that must respond to new, complex and fragmented urban landscapes. Stoll and Lloyd further suggested infrastructure architecture created a new fluid landscape for cultural spaces connecting "spatial peaks" with stretching "regional fields."[33]

Biometrics or biomimicry developed as an interpretation of the landscape through science and the art of exemplifying nature's forms and processes in architecture and urban design. According to Michael Pawlyn, biomimicry contained sustainable principles and initiating inspirations, such as super-efficient structures, high strength biodegradable composites, self-cleaning surfaces, low-energy and waste systems, and water-retention methods. Conceptually, this was a useful green planning and design model, but taken too literally, copying nature was naïve especially as applied to complicated contemporary space programs, dense urban districts and historic contexts. The conflation of landscape and built structure was investigated within a larger context with theories of Landscape Urbanism developed in the late 1990s. The principal Post Urban themes were designed to achieved urban effects through interdisciplinarity, systemic ecology of place, adaptable territories, fluidity and spontaneous feedback of morphological development, and most importantly, through horizontal fields of urbanism (agrophilia).[34] While treating the urban environment as an ecological model had sustainable implications, Landscape Urbanism's tolerance of low-density and automobile-driven environments, promoting suburbanization, was not entirely ecological.

Agricultural Urbanism was a pragmatic green approach applicable to both architecture and urban design scales. According to Janine de la Salle and Mark Holland, it was an emerging design framework for integrating a wide range of sustainable food and agricultural systems into communities. In other words they said: "it is a way of building a place around food."[35] Examples of Agricultural Urbanism include Serenbe Community (2004), shown in Figure 5.13, located in southwest Atlanta, which was planned for 2,500 residents with 35-acres of integrated organic farming and preservation of 70 percent of the land.[36] The unique omega-shaped hamlets created a coherent community form while "containing" natural landscapes—stand of trees, lake, wetlands or stream—and creating an identity and defined sense of place. The built portions of the development employed a rural-to-urban transect and density gradient that culminated with mixes of use at the apex of the omega form. Similarly, Babcock Ranch in southwest Florida, a new development by Kitson and Partners, boasts that it would be the largest 100 percent solar city in the United States, and its design for 45,000 residents will be a network of hamlets, villages and town center with plans for an innovative in-place electrical transportation system. Included in the design are a large nature reserve with protected open space, an operating cattle ranch, and integrated agriculture. Sky, a 572 acre planned community of 624 dwellings in Florida's Panhandle, was created by principals Bruce White and Julia Starr Sanford and Florida State University. It was designed for mixes of use, pedestrians, community farming and gardens and intended to be completely off the grid with all buildings LEED certified.

The ivy hanging gardens of Ivry-sur-Seine, France (1980), were designed by Jean Renaudie, softened the concrete structure, and they provided additional insulation and dead air spaces around the exterior walls of the building. The development of garden features, such as, pergolas, wall trellis and other structures enabled climbing plants to be used on vertical surfaces. Jean Nouvel's 23-storey Residential Tower (2008) in New York was what he called a "vision machine" with forested interior. The researches of Dickson Despommier illustrated the vertical farming concept developed in 1999 that focused intense growing within high-rise structures. Arguments for vertical farming were directed toward providing necessary food for feeding future generations where population increases were projected to exceed the planet's capability of crop raising on existing arable land. Placing farms closer to actual resident populations was another sustainable measure, reducing transport costs.

Two projects designed by Foster + Partners in 2007, Moscow's Crystal Island and Masdar City in Abu Dhabi, demonstrated dramatically different approaches to ecologically responsive urbanism. Crystal Island was a proposal for a 30,000 resident spiraling tent-like city under a single roof (rising as high as 1,476 feet) whose breathable "smart skin" would insulate the interior during the severe winter months and open for natural ventilation in the summer. The building design included various solar thermal systems, daylit interiors, wind turbines and an innovative ventilation system. The helical geometry dramatically synthesizes both horizontal (urban tissue) and vertical (architectural form) spaces as the tower superstructure, with its sustainable technologies and materials, transitions to lower

5.13   Serenbe Community, Palmetto, Georgia, 2004

densities, gracefully grafted into the urban fabric and a new park of the river-formed peninsula below. While the work is clearly heroic, it does demonstrate a blending of both green architecture and sustainable urban design is clearly present in this work.

Masdar City, shown in Figure 5.14, was planned as an emerging global hub for renewable energy and clean technologies in the Middle East, in which energy will be entirely generated from renewable sources. Its regionally derived urban design for 50,000 residents incorporates integrated mixes of use, traditional narrow streets, window shading, courtyards and wind towers. Instead of the more heroic high-rise building typology, Masdar City employed horizontal, compact medium-density, interconnected streets and blocks, as well as, "thick-walled" buildings and a "clean-tech" automobile-free environment. Crystal Island was clearly an architectural approach while Masdar City demonstrated sustainability at the planning scale. To some extent the greening process has come full circle, from the early visionary works of the 1960s to these ambitious planning-scale works, that show broader and more diverse expression of sustainable measures for completely different cultural and climatic contexts.

By 2010 the greening of architecture arrived at a theoretical position that was informed by relational, multifarious and copious environmental thinking. The concept of an "ecological footprint" and the "carbon footprint" it included, gained momentum within the green movement as it expressed the measure of human

5.14   Foster + Partners, Masdar City, Abu Dhabi, United Arab Emirates, 2007–8

activity, and to a large degree the making of buildings, relative to the regenerative abilities of the Earth's ecosystems.[37] The breadth of the global environmental problems could not be ignored nor could they sustain the singularity of focus of isolated and sedentary buildings, even if they were sustainably heroic. John Ehrenfeld gives a poignant warning concerning the complacent or misdirected focus on unsustainability alone, and a well timed calling to source a new paradigm:

> Almost everything being done in the name of sustainable development addresses and attempts to reduce unsustainability. But reducing unsustainability, although critical, does not and will not create sustainability.[38]

The impact of sustainability on the greening of architecture needs to continue moving from simple remediation and formal integration of skin and load-dominated measures, to pluralistic approaches, eco-technologies and comprehensive urban designs. This includes the meta-modern concepts such as Thom Mayne's *"combinatory urbanism,"* Nan Ellin's *"integral urbanism,"* Mohsen Mostafavi's *"ecological urbanism,"* Janine de la Salle and Mark Holland's *"agricultural urbanism,"* David Grahame Shane, *"recombinant urbanism,"* and Gabriel Dupuy's *"network urbanism."*

It is no longer a simple disciplinary issue. Overcoming dystopian environments and unsustainable circumstances has become too complex, invasive and ubiquitous. The value of the greening process to contemporary architectural discourse rests on developing a plurality of inclusive thinking, systemic processes, creative and effective concrete architectural actualizations, on all levels, in time to meet future circumstances, needs and challenges.

NOTES

1.   JDS Architects, "From 'Sustain' to 'Ability,'" in Mohsen Mostafavi and Gareth Doherty (eds), *Ecological Urbanism*, (Zurich: Lars Muller Publishers, 2010), 122.

2.   Rachel Carson, *Silent Spring* (Boston: Mariner Books, 1962), 6.

3.   Donella H. Meadows, Jorgen Randers and William W. Behrens III, *The Limits to Growth* (New York: Universe Books, 1972).

4.   Al Gore, *An Inconvenient Truth* (Emmaus, PA: Rodale Books, 2006).

5.   Victor Olgyay, *Design with Climate: Bioclimatic Approach to Architectural Regionalism* (Princeton, NJ: Princeton University Press, 1963). This work illustrated single building and settlement shapes, aspect ratios, and levels of complexity relative to four general climatic zones in the United State.

6.   The average American home has nearly tripled in size since the 1950s. According to the National Association of Home Builders, the average size of a new single-family residence in 1950 was 983 square feet (91 m^2). In 2009, it was nearly 2,700 square feet (251 m^2).

7.   E.F. Schumacher, *Small is Beautiful: Economics as if People Mattered* (London: Blond and Briggs Publishers, 1973), 67–82.

8. R. Buckminster Fuller, *Operating Manual for Spaceship Earth* (New York: E.P. Dutton, 1978), 57–9.

9. Alastair Gordon, *True Green: Lessons from 1960s–70s' Counterculture Architecture* (Architectural Record, April 2008), 1–2.

10. Stewart Brand, *Whole Earth Catalog: Access to Tools* (Whole Earth Catalog Publisher, 1968). The Whole Earth Catalog was an information tool that provided green technologies and products that were available at the time of its publication.

11. Richard Crowther, *Sun Earth: How to Use Solar and Climatic Energies* (New York: Scribner Publishers, 1977).

12. Amory Lovins, *Soft Energy Paths: Towards a Durable Peace* (New York: Harper Collins Publishers, 1977).

13. "First Village, Santa Fe, NM: Living Proof," *Progressive Architecture* (April 1979), 2.

14. Edward Mazria, *The Passive Solar Energy Book* (Emmaus, PA: Rodale Press, 1979), 28–61.

15. James Lambeth, *Sundancing: The Art and Architecture of James Lambeth* (Louisville, KY: Miami Dog Press, 1993), 10–11.

16. Michael Reynolds, *Earthship, Volume 2: Systems and Components* (Taos, NM: Solar Survival Press, 1991), 45–8.

17. Ralph Knowles, *Energy and Form: An Approach to Urban Growth* (Cambridge, MA: MIT Press, 1974), 148–9.

18. Steven Moore, "Environmental Issues," in Carl Mitcham (ed.), *The Encyclopaedia of Science, Technology, and Ethics* (New York: Macmillan, 2005), 262–6.

19. Charles Jencks, *The Story of Postmodernism* (New York: John Wiley and Sons, 2011), 26.

20. Malcolm Quantrill, *Plain Modern: The Architecture of Brian MacKay-Lyons* (Princeton: Princeton Architectural Press, 2006), 28.

21. Leon Krier, *Houses, Palaces, Cities*, Architectural Design Profile (London: Edited by Demetri Porphyrios, 1980), 30–33.

22. Ruth Durack, "Village Vices: The Contradiction of New Urbanism and Sustainability," *Places* vol. 14 (Fall 2001), 64.

23. Kenneth Frampton, "Toward a Critical Regionalism: Six Points for an Architecture of Resistance," in Hal Foster (ed.), *The Anti-Aesthetic: Essays on Postmodern Culture* (Port Townsend, Washington: Bay Press, 1983), 26–7.

24. Orthmar Humm and Peter Toggweiler, *Photovoltaics in Architecture* (Berlin: Birkhauser Verlag, 1993), 50–53.

25. Kenneth Yeang and Arthur Spector, *Green Design: From Theory to Practice,*(London: Black Dog Publishing, 2011), 8–12.

26. William McDonough and Michael Braungart, *Cradle to Cradle: Remaking the Way We Make Things* (New York: North Point Press, 2002), 174–6.

27. Catherine Slessor, *Eco-Tech: Sustainable Architecture and High Technology*, (London: Thames and Hudson, 1997), 7–12. Eco-technology refers to increasing technological efficiency, reduction of negative environmental impacts, harvesting of beneficial on-site resources, and incorporation of non-toxic, permanent and effective materials and products.

28. The Leadership in Energy and Environmental Design (LEED) was an internationally recognized green building certification checklist developed by the U.S. Green Building

Council in 1998. It was a merit-defining process for a broad range of green buildings of varying architectural and aesthetic value. For example, the Cooper Union Academic Building (2009) designed by Morphois Architects incorporated an eco-tectonic undulating double-skinned facade, extensive daylighting and full height atrium, cogeneration, and it received LEED Platinum certification. At the same time a standard subdivision single-family detached home in Ontario, Canada, with no redeeming design features, received the same Platinum certification.

29. James Wines, *Green Architecture*, (Cologne: Taschen Press, 2000), 11–15.

30. The District of Kronsberg, Germany was the result of a competition in 1992 and won by the Zurich team of Arnaboldi, Cavadini and Hager. It was planned for a moderate to high density at 47 dwelling units per acre (116 dwellings per hectare). The scheme featured a density gradient that built up to the transit line, super-blocks with differentiated internal greenspaces, and a central plaza as a focal point for civic and commercial uses.

31. The High Line Park is a good example of a recycling and redesign of an urban infrastructural element along the New York Central railroad track into a viable community amenity. It has had a synergetic effect upon adjacent new development projects. This concept is reminiscent of book Christopher Swan and Chet Roaman. *YV 88: an Eco-Fiction of Tomorrow* (San Francisco: Sierra Club, (1977).

32. Nan Ellin, *Integral Urbanism*, Routledge, (London: Taylor and Francis Group, 2006), 9.

33. The interest in infrastructure is a shift away from building as object in the landscape and formal organizations to a new kind of architecture that is far more complex with disciplinary hybrids. Scott Lloyd and Katrina Stoll (Editors), *Infrastructure as Architecture*, (Berlin: Jovis Berlag Publisher, 2010).

34. Charles Waldheim (Editor), *The Landscape Urbanism Reader*, (Princeton: Princeton Architectural Press, 2006. Landscape urbanism has two primary areas of interest—the horizontal organization of space and landscape as an interdisciplinary context for contemporary cultural development.

35. Janine De la Salle and Mark Holland, *Agricultural Urbanism: Handbook for Building Sustainable Food and Agriculture Systems in twenty-first century Cities*, (Winnipeg, Canada: Green Frigate Books, 2010), 13.

36. Serenbe Community is located about 20 miles southwest of the Jackson-Hartsfield International Airport in Atlanta and was planned by Dr. Phillip Tabb in 2001 with ongoing work to the present. It is a 1,000-acre mix-use development with 70 percent undeveloped space and a constellation of omega or U-shaped hamlets. Construction of the first hamlet began in 2004. Serenbe received the Urban Land Institute Inaugural Sustainability Award in 2008.

37. Mathis Wackernagel and William Rees, *Our Ecological Footprint: Reducing Human Impact on the Earth*, (British Columbia: New Society Press, 1996). An Ecological Footprint is a measure of the demand of the amount of biologically productive land and water necessary to regenerate and provide appropriate resources for our human population. William Rees first developed it in 1992. A Carbon Footprint is the total greenhouse gas emissions produced in support of human activity.

38. John R. Ehrenfeld, *Sustainability by Design,: A Subversive Strategy for Transforming Our Consumer Culture*, (New Haven, CT: Yale University Press, 2008).

6

Postcolonial Theories in Architecture[1]

Esra Akcan

Globalization has shifted architects' attention to the world at large. Even though many architects have worked outside their home countries (or adopted lands) in the past, transnational practice has become a common routine in the architectural office today, due to the new legal arrangements, international trade agreements and advanced communication technologies. Architectural services are now designated by the World Trade Organization as globally tradable commodities. Yet, more often than not, architects find themselves unprepared for such a task due to the relative lack of theoretical sophistication and historical knowledge about architecture beyond European and North American countries. Moreover, as common as the words globalization, multinational and cross-cultural might be, the future remains unclear, since the forces of history are acting in contrary directions about opening and closing borders. Postcolonial theories aspire for an architecture better equipped for a global future, so that globalization does not unfold as a new form of imperial imagination.

This chapter gives a critical overview of authors who have contributed to postcolonial theories in architecture from the 1980s till the early 2000s. The term postcolonial may refer to both a historical period—a period that started after WWII when previously colonized countries gained their independence one by one, and were established as nation states—and a specific set of related theories. This chapter unpacks the latter meaning. While there is much to be said about postcolonial histories (architectural practices, counter-alternatives after colonization, problems of nationalism that replaced colonial rule) and how they are directly and indirectly shaped by some of the ideas explained in this chapter, such accounts are reserved for the chapters in the second part of this book.

One may start by defining postcolonial theory in architecture as the term used to refer to a new way of understanding "non-Western" contexts. It may at first seem ironic that the very definition of the geographical scope of these studies is predicated on exclusion. The word "non-West" not only refers to and simultaneously continues the ideology of an exaggerated difference between the "West" and its "other," but it also disavows the differences within these "others" themselves. The unsuccessful attempts to find alternative names for these countries, such as "third world," "underdeveloped," or "peripheral," point to the inherent unaccountability of a considerable part of the globe within the given hierarchies of the world-system. Part of the self-proclaimed task of postcolonial theory has been to allude to the insufficiency of the categories used to represent these countries, not necessarily due to the inaccuracy of the name, but because of the very process of rendering these countries as the "other" within the definition of the "Western" self. Avoiding these terms or ignoring the constructed contrast and hierarchy between the "West" and its geographical "other" does not offer an alternative, but merely disavows a fact. Therefore, I would like to discuss postcolonial theory as the quest to undo the hierarchies reflected in the term "non-West," not by avoiding the term, but by treating it in distancing and ironical quotation marks.

One of the immediate impacts of postcolonial theory on architecture has been to express the necessity to challenge the Eurocentric canon.[2] The word loosely refers to the dominance of European and North American architects (generally White and male) in the institutions that shape the canon, including architectural practice, education and publications. For a more comprehensive analysis, one might reference Immanuel Wallerstein's argument that social science as a discipline has been Eurocentric for five main reasons.[3] Its *historiography* was based on the premise that European supremacy in the history of the world in the last two centuries was something to be "proud of." Through its *universalism* one felt justified to claim that whatever happened to Europe "represented a pattern that was applicable everywhere, either because it was a progressive achievement of mankind which was irreversible or because it represented the fulfillment of humanity's basic needs."[4] The belief that modern Europe was civilized justified the interest in *colonial* conquests to "redeem" non-European people. The distortions of *Orientalist* scholarship had political consequences to secure "Europe's imperial role within the framework of the modern world-system."[5] And finally, the deeply inscribed belief that *progress* was the "underlying explanation of the history of the world"[6] became a justification imposed on all other Eurocentric practices over the world. Recent global developments in architecture, namely the facts that architects are increasingly building in places outside their country of citizenship, that more design studios and seminars in Western architecture schools focus on "non-Western" places, and that a plentiful amount of "non-Western" histories have been published in the recent years do not necessarily overturn the Eurocentric canon, because neither international practice nor curiosity about "non-Western" countries are new. They are also not values in themselves, unless their difference from previous Orientalist and colonialist attitudes can be specified. Similarly, reshaping the architecture canon in schools is not as facile as it might first appear, since bringing a few token examples from "non-Western" contexts as epilogues to a meta-narrative would hardly resolve the implications that Wallerstein, for one, discloses. According to the postcolonial theories discussed here, challenging the Eurocentric canon in architecture would ideally necessitate challenging the very conditions that have formed the canon itself. In the past 20 years, there has therefore been a growing scholarly interest in rereading the history of architecture from a perspective informed by the ideologies of colonialism and Orientalism.

Edward Said's 1978 book, *Orientalism*, laid the foundation for postcolonial theories in the humanities.[7] Criticism within the discipline of Orientalism and its post-war successor area studies had existed before,[8] but it was Said's book that generated a sea change of ideas not only in literary studies (his field) but also in visual arts and architecture. Said discussed how the "Western" representations of the "Orient," whether scholarly or artistic, constructed an imaginary border between East and West, and "Orientalized the Orient" as the exotic, fanciful, irrational, horrorful and barbarian "other" of the Western rational, progressive and civilized Self. While the roots of Orientalist knowledge date at least back to the fourteenth century, Said focused on English and French sources in the nineteenth century, as well as contemporary American representations, in order to criticize the highly mediated and ideologically distorted form of knowledge that Orientalist studies historically produced. However, *Orientalism* is more than a critique of poor scholarship. Said illustrated the severe political consequences of this knowledge in creating hierarchies and imperialist attitude. Orientalist representations have not only constructed an ideologically distorted knowledge about the "Orient", but have also created a hierarchy between the Orient and the Occident, not to mention the aim "to control, manipulate and claim hegemony" over it. Said's work inspired several architectural historians and provided a useful category for critically examining the place of the "non-West" in seminal architectural theories and histories.

Sir Banister Fletcher's broadly influential *A History of Architecture*, for one, divided world architecture into "historical" and "non-historical" styles.[9] While he discussed "historical styles" as Western ones that have continuously evolved from Ancient Egypt and Greece to the present; he introduced Indian, Chinese, Japanese, Ancient American and Saracenic architecture as "non-historical" styles without evolution or succession. Fletcher visualized his argument with *The Tree of Architecture* illustration (Figure 6.1), in which the main trunk represents Greek, Roman and Romanesque architecture that support the branches of European and American architectures. These "historical styles" are implied to be in constant progress and succession, whereas Eastern "non-historical styles" are pictured as the side branches that do not grow any longer or give life to any other style. Fletcher's representation of the "non-West" is an example of Orientalism, not because he considers it inferior, but because he presents it as non-historical. One of Said's basic objections to Orientalist knowledge was the denial of history, change and progress to the "Orient" as if these belonged exclusively to the West. Despite the manifest changes in the knowledge of the "Orient" through the centuries, a latent Orientalism which constructed the vision based on the "separateness of the Orient, its eccentricity, its backwardness, its silent indifference, its feminine penetrability, its supine malleability" nevertheless persisted, Said argued. The "very possibility of development, transformation, human movement … is denied the Orient and the Oriental."[10]

One can find similar types of Orientalism in other books of architectural history and theory. One of the most important systematic and detailed critiques of Orientalism in architecture and architectural theory is Mark Crinson's *Empire*

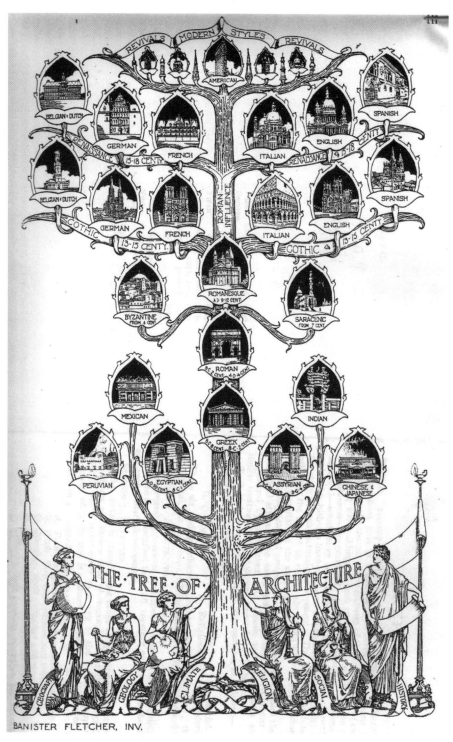

6.1   Sir Bannister Fletcher, Tree of Architecture, illustration in *A History of Architecture*.
On the Comparative Method, 1901

Building. Orientalism and Victorian Architecture, published in 1996.[11] Crinson analyzed the role of racial theory and the premise of "Western" superiority in British architectural theory during the nineteenth century. He illustrated various types of Orientalism and racism in the work of Edward Freeman, James Fergusson, John Ruskin and Owen Jones. For instance, Crinson's analysis of a debate between Ruskin and Jones proves to be quite illuminative in exposing different types of Orientalism. In *The Stones of Venice* (1851–53), Ruskin voiced his fascination with the hybrid nature of Venetian arches and celebrated the mixture of different cultures, including the "Eastern" influences that enabled this fusion (Figure 6.2). In *The Two Paths* of 1859, however, he completely adopted the dominant rhetoric of racial politics and repudiated any possible influence of the East on the West. What once enabled richness now became distant and alien "cruel persons" who produced "lower kind ornamentation" and even the "worst and cruelest nations" that took delight in it.[12] As Crinson discloses, Ruskin's "cruel and cruelest nations" were nothing but the cultures that "received the most sympathetic treatment" in Owen Jones' *The Grammar of Ornament* (1856). In this book, which was written as part of the educational reform initiated by Henry Cole after the 1851 Crystal Palace Exhibition, Jones collected examples of ornament from several parts of the world, with an unusual emphasis on "non-Western" ornament. In declaring that Islamic ornamentation was also a "rational, geometrical ordering of flat surfaces," and that its use of color was also "scientific," Jones claimed to have found the universal law of ornament based on nature (Figure 6.3). In doing this, Jones not only assimilated Islamic ornamentation within his own frames of reference, but also used the "Orient" as a legitimating ground to prove the universality of his own discovery. Crinson's reading of Ruskin and Jones exemplifies three common approaches to the "non-West" that all warrant critical attention. Ruskin separated "Orient" from Self (West) first as the alternative then as the cruel nation; while Jones sought justification for the Self's (West's) own universality by assimilating the "Other" ("Orient") into his own frame of reference.

A severe political impact of Orientalist knowledge and representations was the assumption that "non-West" needed Western help and redemption through colonization. A map prepared by Rem Koolhaas and AMO illustrating the European colonies all around the world visualizes the extent to which European colonization shaped world history throughout the nineteenth and twentieth centuries (Figure 6.4).

However, critical accounts on the impact of colonization on world architecture came late to scholarship. Only in the early 1990s did works that analyzed colonial architecture on a broad geographical scope ignite attention, beginning with the initiatives of such scholars as Brian Brace Taylor (whose early editorial article in 1984 exposed the ideological history of colonial architecture in Morocco, Tunisia, Mali, Egypt, and Indonesia), and Nezar Alsayyad, whose 1992 edited volume, *Forms of Dominance*, brought together major scholars.[13] More focused books on the history of colonial architecture in French and Italian colonies in Africa, or British colonies in Asia challenged earlier accounts of heroic modernism.[14] These studies brought forth evidence that the colonialist expansion of world powers during the rise of

6.2   Ruskin, The Orders of Venetian Arches, illustration in *Works*, 1851–53

6.3   Owen Jones, Arabian Ornament, illustration in *The Grammar of Ornament*, 1856

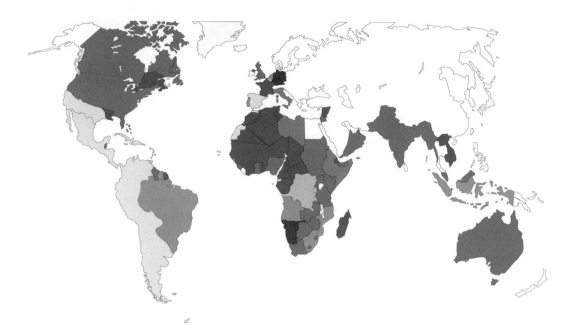

6.4   Rem
Koolhaas and
AMO, Eurocolonies
map, c.2001

capitalism in search for raw materials and new markets was coupled with layers of racism. The necessity to create controlled reorganizations in the colonies brought city planning and architecture to the fore as the main institutional setting and the crucial tool of representation in the making of colonial societies. Almost all of the master plans for the colonial cities envisioned a segregated population, reserving different zones for the colonizing and colonized populations (Figure 6.5).

In addition to spatial mechanisms of ethnic, racial and sexual segregation, the colonial architects' most common concern was their confrontation with the local building traditions and the urban fabric of the colonized city. In this regard, each place needs to be examined in relation to its own specific history. Examples of large-scale demolition of existing urban fabric, conservation according to Western values of preservation, and buildings designed as replicas of architectural styles in the mother country or imitations of local styles as a means to gain the sympathy of the colonized are too diverse to generalize in neatly fixed patterns. Nonetheless, colonial architecture is perhaps one of the best examples through which one realizes the limits of architects in sustaining critical building practice within a hegemonic setting. In her analysis of three French colonial cities in Morocco, Indochina and Madagascar, Gwendolyn Wright highlighted some colonial architects whose "good intentions" led to questionable consequences. Whether it was the proponents of *Arabisances* style in Morocco who made an effort to come to terms with local building traditions and collaborate with local craftsmen (though they ended up with a sentimental pastiche of historical styles of the region), or the proponents of *Chantiers nord-africains* who imported European modernist symbols based on the conviction that these forms would carry the indigenous people to the level of universal standards of beauty; no practice could conceal the fact that "colonialism inevitably prevented equality, no matter what kind of architecture was built."[15]

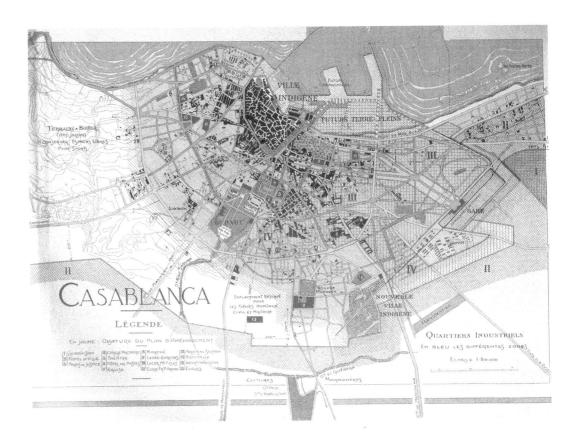

The master architects were usually no exception. As Taylor was one of the first to spell out, the assumption that "there was no connection between the work of the official architects, planners and technicians in the colonies and the so-called *avant garde*, or pioneer movement in European architecture" was simply a "myth." The most overt example, Le Corbusier's ambitious plan for rebuilding Algiers, has been critically reconsidered by historians Zeynep Çelik and Michele Lamprakos (Figure 6.6).[16]

Far from being critical, Le Corbusier often expressed his fascination with the expansionist ideologies of *la grande France*. His diagrammatic sketch of the map of France and Africa linking Paris, Algeria and Gao as the backbone of an expanded France visualizes his support for colonialism (Figure 6.7).

In his plans for the city of Algiers, Le Corbusier developed proposals that continued France's colonial policies in creating segregated spaces for different races and classes. His vision aggressively seized the whole landscape from mountain tops to the sea, and thereby turned *casbah*—where the colonized population would continue living—into a miniature imprisoned by the European city from all sides and above. The placement of the large modern office blocks at the port would cut the colonial population's access to water. In one of the versions, the 100-meter high viaduct connecting the segregated European residential and European business district contained housing cells for African workers underneath: "a poignant

6.5   Henri Prost, Master Plan for the extension of Casablanca, Morocco, published in *France Maroc*, 1917

6.6   Le Corbusier,
Obus Plan for
Algiers, 1931–42

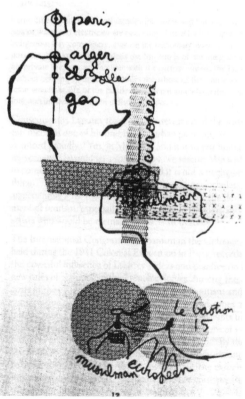

6.7   Le Corbusier,
Diagram for the
extension of
France to Africa

image of colonial infrastructure literally supported on the backs of native labor," in Lamprakos' words.[17] Le Corbusier cannot be reduced to his colonialist ambitions. Nevertheless, such demystifications help develop a more refined understanding of the relationship between architecture and ideology, as well as individual architects' abilities to transcend the hegemonic structures of their times. Apart from his colonialist ambitions for Algeria, Le Corbusier also received sound criticism for his Orientalism. The curvilinear forms of his housing blocks in the project for Algeria, and the representation of the Casbah as a veil prompted Çelik to argue that Le Corbusier gendered the "non-West" as the exotic, penetratable, feminine "other" of the masculine "West." Çelik also interpreted Le Corbusier's *Journey to the East*, where he wandered around the "delicious women" in the "exotic, distant, fanciful" streets of Istanbul, as a form of Orientalism that presumed his own superiority.[18]

While these critical accounts in the early stages of postcolonial theory rightly questioned the ideology of colonialism and Orientalism, scholars in visual arts have recently complicated the critique of Orientalism by revealing the gray zones and complexities, and by looking more closely at the Western and "non-Western" artists who took steps toward overcoming the stereotypical representations of their times.[19] Continuing with the same example, Le Corbusier's Istanbul trip was recently reevaluated by a number of scholars.[20] The architect's views of Istanbul had been formed by French Orientalists before he even reached the city, most notably by Pierre Loti, Gautier and Nerval. Le Corbusier perhaps never totally overcame this Orientalism, but he was showing signs of criticism against these writers after he lived in Istanbul for seven weeks: "The konak, the Turkish wooden house, is an architectural masterpiece. (On every page of his book Gautier wrote that it was a hen coop—proof that the dogmas of art are as immutable as those of the Holy Father!)"[21] Apart from growing to appreciate the wooden houses of Istanbul against the will of his Orientalist teachers, Le Corbusier acquired the panoramic vision as the appropriate representational mode for Istanbul after a possible acquaintance with the genres developed by local photographers, which indicates that he might have welcomed influences from not only the vernacular heritage but also the modernist contributions of "non-Western" artists.[22]

***

The rereading of modern architecture through the perspectives of colonialism and Orientalism sparked the construction of postcolonial theories in architecture, which I would like to discuss under two main approaches. The first approach—which may be called the *poststructuralist trajectory of postcolonial theory*—problematizes the very possibility of representing the "other." In her text, "Can the Subaltern Speak," Gayatri Spivak argued that the *subaltern*—just like the peasants who, according to Marx, cannot make their class interest valid without the formation of a unified class subject—cannot be represented within the received structures of the "West."[23] "It is impossible for French intellectuals to imagine the kind of Power and Desire that would inhabit the unnamed subject of the Other of Europe," Spivak wrote, "It is not only that everything they read, critical or uncritical, is caught within the debate of the production of that Other, supporting or critiquing the constitution of the Subject as Europe. It is also that, in the constitution of that Other of Europe, great care was taken to obliterate the textual ingredients with which such a subject could cathect, could occupy (invest?) its itinerary."[24] Any attempt to represent or translate the "other" into one's own system of reference would be an assimilation of the incommensurable into the familiar. Rather than the delusional attempts to "let the other(s) speak for himself,"[25] Spivak proposed Derrida's *continuous deferral* theory as a much more viable strategy in order to "resist and critique "recognition" of the Third World through "assimilation."[26] This continuous suspension theory demanded admitting the necessity of representing the "non-West," while simultaneously questioning the very possibility of this representation. Thus it meant that the confrontation with postcolonial problems necessitated a much deeper critique of the Self.

Nowhere did this argument find a better reflection in architectural theory than in Gülsüm Nalbantoğlu's "Toward Postcolonial Openings: Rereading Sir Banister Fletcher's *History of Architecture.*" Unlike the reassessment of Fletcher's book through a critique of Orientalism referred to earlier, Nalbantoğlu's critical rereading was grounded on the "recognition" of the unrepresentability of the "other," elaborated by Spivak, and the differentiation between *difference* and *diversity*, elaborated by Homi Bhabha. In "Commitment to Theory," Bhabha defined cultural *diversity* as a category of comparative studies based on the "pre-given cultural contents and customs … giv[ing] rise to liberal notions of multiculturalism, cultural exchange or the culture of humanity."[27] Cultural *difference* on the other hand, "focuses on the problem of the ambivalence of cultural authority: the attempt to dominate in the *name* of a cultural supremacy which is itself produced only in the moment of differentiation."[28] For a postcolonial critic placed in a poststructuralist background, the notion of cultural diversity gives way to the delusion that one can represent all cultures within one's own system of reference, whereas the notion of cultural difference implies the impossibility of this comparison and smooth translation. For critics who want to resist the recognition of the "non-West" simply through assimilation into the mainstream system of reference, it is *difference* not *diversity* that has to be underlined. Thus, the categories of "historical" and "non-historical" used by Fletcher to represent "Western" and "non-Western" countries assume that these cultures are *diverse* and comparable using "Western" tools. In Nalbantoğlu's words, "the underlying premise in [Fletcher's book] is that cultures can be aligned on the same plane of reference; compared and contrasted by the tools of the historian."[29] This premise of cultural diversity "covers over, however, issues of incommensurable difference and problems of representation that prevail at every cultural encounter."[30] Nevertheless, according to Nalbantoğlu, Fletcher's book is still useful, because it overtly exposes a fundamental difficulty in representing the "other." The reader realizes in the book the "other's" untranslatability. "In his analysis of non-Western architectures, Fletcher introduces his readers to such terms as non-historical and grotesque, which disturb the logos of the text. He exposes what exceeds and cannot be contained by [his own] framework."[31]

There are a number of contemporary buildings that can be better appreciated through the poststructuralist trajectory of postcolonial theory. One common misunderstanding is the assumption that the only resistance to the Eurocentric canon is radical regionalism (a term already loaded with connotations based on European developments), usually attributed to the building practice of architects such as Hassan Fathy or Abdel Wahed El'Wakil, as if they performed in a self-contained and isolated context in their countries (Figure 6.8). Postcolonial theory simultaneously seeks to challenge this preconception, and it might be worth recalling Said's own discomfort over the misuse of his book for the purposes of Arab nationalism. While regionalism might be one response among many, I would instead like to cite two authors who interpreted Jean Nouvel's and Charles

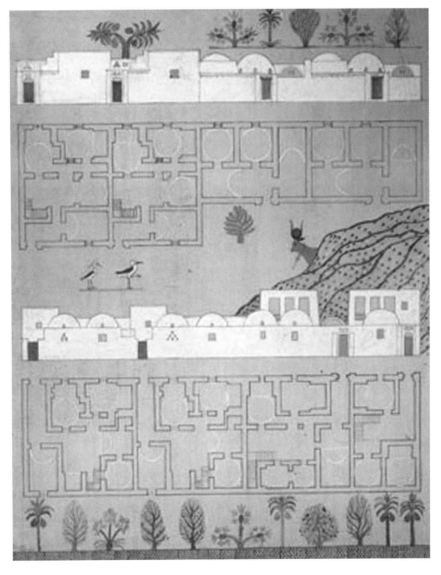

6.8   Hasan Fathy, Gouache on paper for New Gourna, Egypt, 1945–48

Correa's buildings through poststructuralist postcolonial theory. Nouvel's Arab World Institute in Paris, which was expected to represent "Arab culture" in France, exposes instead the impossibility of this task in the face of a rising consciousness of Orientalism. John Biln argued that Nouvel and more pertinently the exhibition designers successfully develop a critical strategy because they "seem resolutely self-critical, skeptical of representation but convinced of its necessity, locked in the same but in pursuit of self-difference." The designers achieve this, Biln argued, by representing the "Arab culture" always "as reflections of the West, rather than truths of the East." Deliberate distortions of the museum objects, mixed reflections and superimpositions of the references to "West" and "East" challenge conventional representation modes that presumably capture the "truth" of the exhibited object (Figure 6.9).[32]

Vikramaditya Prakash revealed a similar critical strategy in Charles Correa's Jawahar Kala Kendra project in India (Figure 6.10). A question that disturbs most "non-Western" architects, Prakash reminded, is the burden of identity, namely the expectation that a "non-Western" architect represents his/her identity in buildings, while no such requirement holds for European or North American architects. In Prakash's eyes, Correa responded to this expectation by offering an alternative, but without pretending that it does not exist: "For those of 'us' caught in the double bind of asserting a different regional identity and simultaneously preventing its normative essentialization ... I would suggest that this desire for anchoring is best left suspended." Prakash found Correa's project important because the architect

6.9   Jean Nouvel, Exhibition in Arab World Institute, Paris, France, 1981–87, photo by George Fessy

neither denies the importance of the question of identity nor seeks to represent the presumably "true" and "unchanging" Indian identity. Rather Correa "parodies the impossible stereotype 'Indian' by suspending it within distancing quotation marks."[33] The critical strategy Biln and Prakash found in Nouvel's and Correa's projects is the suspension of any definition of a particular identity despite the acknowledgment of its necessity for resisting cultural colonization.

These examples notwithstanding, poststructuralist postcolonial theory has best worked to expose the *exclusions* of Architecture, rather than offering ideas easily translatable into practice. *Postcolonial Space(s)*, edited by Gülsüm Nalbantoğlu and C.T.Wong in 1997, is a collection of articles questioning several layers of exclusion—the exclusions based on geography, gender, race and class—from historiography as well as from the profession of architecture. In this book, the word colonial is used metaphorically and the area of "postcoloniality" is broadened to include women, minorities or non-architect builders, in addition to "non-Western" and colonized subjects. In Nalbantoğlu's words:

> writing postcoloniality in architecture does not merely entail an engagement with previously colonized cultures … [but] with the boundaries that guard architecture's cultural and disciplinary presuppositions; boundaries that remain intact through certain exclusionary practices, that remain unquestioned once the institutional structure of the discipline is established. Writing postcoloniality in architecture questions architecture's intolerance to difference, to the unthought, to its outside.[34]

6.10   Charles Correa, Jawahar Kala Kendra, Jaipur, India, 1986–91

Placing the postcolonial quest in a much broader context where the basic disciplinary and professional boundaries of Architecture are problematized is the strongest contribution of this approach.

However, it may also turn out to be its weakest. Writing the history of exclusions— and only of exclusions—is actually the only appropriate step for a theory that grounds itself on the criticism that the excluded is unspeakable. In Nalbantoğlu and Wong's words, "recognizing that the repressed other can never be entirely contained in a given symbolic system—[these articles] emphasize exclusions and specific mechanisms of repression."[35] However, the logical conclusion of an assertion that the "non-Western" cannot be represented in a Western language may lead to a strategic trap. The postcolonial quest itself becomes an impossible project of speaking the unspeakable, translating the untranslatable. The representative speakers *for* the "non-West" (but not *of* the "non-West," since this is impossible according to this theory) should admit that they themselves are situated in the area of the speakable, by virtue of the very fact that they are speaking. However, they can speak about the "other"—the unspeakable—only if they contradict their own assertion that the "other" is unspeakable. It should follow that repeating the unspeakable and untranslatable nature of the "other" is all they will do, unless the given language itself within which they are also situated is deconstructed. Their approach escapes self-contradiction only if they admit—which they do—to their theory's narrow boundaries in the present and ambitious plans for the future. Continuous repetition of the same argument, the argument that the "other" cannot speak, becomes the sole (practical) strategy for the present. All attempts to let the other speak or translate the other's language are bound to be annihilated by the impossibility (or the extreme difficulty) in this attempt itself. In its constant repetition, the theory thus runs the risk of ending in self-annihilation and self-marginalization.

There are also limits in transferring Spivak's argument to architectural criticism. The content of the subaltern shifted depending on the context in Spivak's article, making it a much more layered concept than an abstraction. In the beginning of the text, one read about the unrepresentability of the "non-Western" within the reified frames of the Western thought, about the untranslatability of the "non-Western" concerns into Western languages. Later in the text, Spivak developed the argument for the subaltern, which she defined as a group that could be identified with neither the dominant foreign nor the élite indigenous groups of India. Towards the end of the text, she further specified the question as the possibility for the "subaltern (woman)" to speak. Working with the Sati story, Spivak narrated the irresolvable dilemma a widow faced in India under the pressures of the nationalist groups that demanded her to keep tradition alive by killing herself after her husband's death on one side, and the colonialist groups that claimed to be "saving brown women from brown men" on the other. The widow is left merely with the option of either supporting the nationalist groups by dying or the colonialist groups by living. Being pressed by the colonialist ideologies of the dominant foreign groups from one side, and the nationalist ideologies of the élite indigenous groups on the other, Spivak showed, the possibility of the voice of subaltern women evaporated in between. However, in the case of architectural criticism, it would be doubtful to remake this argument by dropping the class and gender issues. In their own countries at least, "non-Western" architects are not exactly like Spivak's subalterns who inherently cannot represent themselves, but they are more often than not part or catalysts of dominant groups. While the argument about the unrepresentability of the "non-West" is still relevant in the context of the Eurocentric canon, as it exposes the difficulty of a truly global architecture, it loses its convincing power when transferred to the question of representing a "non-Western" architect in his/her own city.

This leaves a theory that focuses on untranslatability with the highly expanded scope of challenging Architecture with a capital A, rather than suggesting critical strategies toward immediate practice. Concluding with a comment by Nalbantoğlu:

> I think that one of the most significant lessons that postcolonial theory offers to the architectural sphere is the identification of "architecture" with a particular trajectory of Western history … For what is at stake here is the very category of architecture, the disciplinary boundaries of which are delineated at a particular time in a particular place. Postcolonial perspectives reveal that when other architectures enter the grand narrative of the architectural discipline (i.e., the canon) they find themselves always already inscribed with the premises of the latter. The naming of other architectures with the already existing canonical tools of the discipline marks the erasure of any possibility to think the discipline differently. This is hardly surprising as the canon constitutes the very language of architecture, i.e., its symbolic identity. It sets the limits for architectural representability. Postcolonial theory, by its insistence on radical alterity, offers insights for critical openings that destabilize the very terms that the discipline takes for granted.[36]

The second approach—which may be called the *humanist trajectory of postcolonial theory*—is partly motivated by the aspiration to find an alternative to some of the uncompromising consequences of poststructuralist thought. Giving past cross-cultural encounters and intertwined histories their due acknowledgment, this approach questions the premise of untranslatability and the existence of "radical alterity" itself. One need not be imposing the Western symbolic system whenever coming to terms with the "non-West," due to the already existing shared historical values, and the promise of constructing future ones. It is better to help undo the construction of a significant part of the globe as the "other" of the Western self, than to underline difference for the sake of challenging assimilation. If its Eurocentrism can be undone, humanism is still a more productive alternative, Said argued, and aspired for the *construction* of a cosmopolitan humanism as the next step for postcolonial theory.[37] Wallerstein noted that the real objective was "a reunited, and thereby non-Eurocentric, structure of knowledge … and a more inclusively universalist vision of human possibility."[38] In the field of architecture, those who emphasize histories of cross-cultural relations and who support translations between "West" and "non-West" reinforce this approach.[39]

Returning to the question of the architectural canon, Sibel Bozdoğan challenged Bhabha's and Nalbantoğlu's emphasis on *difference* in place of *diversity*:

> But if difference is the powerful critical tool of postcolonial theory to pry open
> the western canon and to show what is wrong with it, the next step can only be
> either getting rid of the canon or trying to reconfigure it in a better way. Assuming
> that it is the second option we are after, it seems to me that an emphasis on
> both difference and diversity is necessary – an emphasis as much on what can
> be shared across cultures as on what is different. To hold these two seemingly
> contradictory impulses is our only way out if we don't want cultural difference to
> be reified into essentialist and timeless discourses of identity … [T]he fact that a
> work of art/architecture is produced by groups hitherto excluded from the canon,
> does not automatically and uncritically endorse these works … [I]it is only when
> these works reach the level of skill and sophistication commensurable with the
> western canon that they actually begin to transform the canon.[40]

Apart from suggesting an emphasis on intertwined histories, Bozdoğan argues in this passage that only when a non-Western architect "reaches the level" of Western "skill and sophistication," can s/he be appreciated and press the boundaries of the canon. This proposition can remain postcolonial only under the premise that a "non-Western" architect *can* actually reach Western standards (which to be sure are always in flux), because s/he already shares them. The main premise of the humanist postcolonial critic is that there are nevertheless globally shared criteria that are not necessarily Eurocentric. In other words, a non-Eurocentric universalism must have been possible for this approach to be theoretically consistent. However, this premise may turn out to be too fragile. What exactly are these standards? How, where and by whom have they been defined and are still getting defined? Aren't they dependent on the received hierarchies of the profession? Is taste—which seems to be the disowned yet principal criterion for inclusion and exclusion in the canon—a shared value? Such questions wait to be resolved for this position to become theoretically convincing (as Bozdoğan admits).[41]

The humanist trajectory of postcolonial theory, nonetheless, may have a much stronger chance for a practical impact in a globalizing world. As globalization continues to shape architecture, we have yet to see if the boom in transnational practice in China, the Gulf region, or ex-Soviet countries will bring a real difference. One of the most telling examples is Rem Koolhaas' own transformation from Orientalist beginnings (Figure 6.11) to what appears to be a more sincere engagement with the problems and potentials of "non-Western" contexts, or at least the acknowledgment of the necessity of a more research-based architectural practice.[42] Perhaps in a globalizing world, the viable alternative is to improve the notion of universality from below and construct a new non-Eurocentric humanism, without skipping the poststructuralist challenge (hence a third way out of the two postcolonial theories). In any event, it seems that a rejuvenated humanism can only escape some previous exclusive notions of universality if it can fruitfully come to terms with postcolonial theories.

6.11   Rem Koolhaas and AMO, Regime of the ¥€$, c.2000

The World according to AMO

NOTES

1   This chapter is an updated and condensed version of my article: Esra Akcan,"Critical Practice in the Global Era: Question Concerning "Other" Geographies," *Architectural Theory Review* 7, no. 1 (2002): 37–58.

2   Theme issues on rethinking the canon in the journals of the two major professional associations serve as examples. *Art Bulletin*, published by the College Art Association (CAA), reserved its June 1996 issue (vol. 78, no. 2), and *The Journal of Architectural Education* published by Association of Collegiate Schools of Architecture (ACSA) its May 1999 issue (vol. 52, no. 4).

3   Immanuel Wallerstein, "Eurocentrism and its Avatars: The Dilemmas of Social Science," *New Left Review* 226 (November/December 1997): 93–109.

4   Ibid., 96–7.

5   Ibid., 100.

6   Ibid.

7   Edward Said, *Orientalism* (New York, Vintage, 1978, 1994).

8   Zachary Lockman, *Contending Visions of the Middle East: The History and Politics of Orientalism*, 2nd ed. (Cambridge: Cambridge University Press, 2010).

9   Sir Banister Fletcher, *A History of Architecture: On the Comparative Method* (New York: Charles Scribner's Sons, 1901, 1943).

10   Said, *Orientalism*, 206, 208.

11   Mark Crinson, *Empire Building: Orientalism & Victorian Architecture* (London, New York: Routledge, 1996).

12   Ruskin quoted in Crinson, *Empire Building*, 60.

13   Brian Brace Taylor, "Rethinking Colonial Architecture," *Mimar* 13 (1984): 16–25; Nezar Alsayyad (ed.), *Forms of Dominance: On the Architecture and Urbanism of the Colonial Enterprise* (Aldershot, Avebury, 1992).

14   See especially: Janet Abu-Lughod, *Rabat: Urban Apartheid in Morocco* (Princeton, Princeton University Press, 1980); Paul Rabinow, *French Modern* (Cambridge, MIT Press, 1980); Thomas R. Metcalf, *An Imperial Vision: Indian Architecture and Britain's Raj* (Berkeley: University of California Press, 1989); David Prochaska, *Making Algeria French* (Paris, Editions de la Maison des Sciences de l'Homme and Cambridge University Press, 1990); Gwendolyn Wright, *The Politics of Design in French Colonial Urbanism* (Chicago, London, The University of Chicago Press, 1991); Zeynep Çelik, *Urban Forms and Colonial Confrontations* (Berkeley, University of California Press, 1997); Jean-Louis Cohen, Monique Eleb, *Casablanca: Colonial Myths and Architectural Ventures* (NY: Monacelli Press, 2002); Mark Crinson, *Modern Architecture and the End of Empire* (Burlington: Ashgate, 2003); Brian McLaren, *Architecture and Tourism in Colonial Libya* (Seattle: University of Washington Press, 2006); Mia Fuller, *Moderns Abroad: Architecture, Cities and Italian Imperialism* (NY: Routledge, 2007).

15   Wright, *The Politics of Design in French Colonial Urbanism*, 139.

16   Zeynep Çelik, "Le Corbusier, Orientalism, Colonialism," *Assemblage* 17 (April 1992): 59–77; Michele Lamprakos, "Le Corbusier and Algiers: The Plan Obus as Colonial Urbanism," in Nezar Alsayyad (ed.), *Forms of Dominance*, 183–210.

17   Lamprakos, "Le Corbusier and Algiers," 183–210.

18   See especially Çelik, "Le Corbusier, Orientalism, Colonialism," 59–77.

19   For Orientalist painting, see: Mary Roberts, *Intimate Outsiders: The Harem in Ottoman and Orientalist Art and Travel Literature* (Durham: Duke University Press, 2007). For Orientalist photography, see: Ali Behdad and Luke Gartlan (eds), *Photography's Orientalism: New Essays on Colonial Representation* (Los Angeles: Getty Publications, 2013).

20   *L'invention d'un architecte: Le voyage en Orient de Le Corbusier* (Paris: Fondation Le Corbusier, 2013).

21   Le Corbusier, *Journey to the East*, trans. Ivan Zaknic (Cambridge: MIT Press, 1987).

22   Esra Akcan, "L'héritage des photographies panoramiques d'Istanbul," (Le Corbusier and the Legacy of Istanbul's Photographic Panoramas), in *L'invention d'un architecte: Le voyage en Orient de Le Corbusier,* 240–255.

23   Gayatri C. Spivak, "Can the Subaltern Speak?" in C. Nelson and L. Grossberg (eds), *Marxism and the Interpretation of Culture* (Urbana, Chicago: University of Illinois Press, 1988), 271–313.

24   Spivak, "Can the Subaltern Speak?" 280.

25   Ibid., 294.

26   Ibid., 292.

27   Homi K. Bhabha, "The Commitment to Theory," in *The Location of Culture* (London, New York: Routledge, 1994), 34.

28   Ibid., 34.

29   Gülsüm Nalbantoğlu, "Toward Postcolonial Openings: Rereading Sir Banister Fletcher's *History of Architecture*," *Assemblage* 35 (April 1998): 13.

30   Ibid.,13.

31   Ibid.,15.

32   John Biln, "(De)forming Self and Other: Toward an Ethics of Distance," in G.B. Nalbantoğlu and C.T. Wong (eds), *Postcolonial Space(s)* (New York: Princeton Architectural Press, 1997), 30–32.

33   Vikramaditya Prakash, "Identity Production in Postcolonial Indian Architecture: Re-Covering What We Never Had," in G.B. Nalbantoğlu andd C.T. Wong (eds), *Postcolonial Space(s)*, 51–2.

34   Nalbantoğlu, "Toward Postcolonial Openings," 15.

35   G.B. Nalbantoğlu and C.T. Wong (eds), *Postcolonial Space(s)* (New York: Princeton Architectural Press, 1997), 9.

36   "Gülsüm Baydar Nalbantoğlu," Text in "e-Forum. 'Other' Geographies Under Globalization," ed. Esra Akcan, *Domus m* 9 (Feb–March 2001).

37   Edward Said, "The Relevance of Humanism to Contemporary America" Lecture at Columbia University, New York, February 16–18, 2000; Edward Said, *Humanism and Democratic Criticism* (NY: Columbia University Press, 2004).

38   Wallerstein, "Eurocentrism and its Avatars," 106.

39   New scholarship on "non-Western" architectural history is growing. In addition to recent books on modern architectures of individual countries including Turkey, Japan, China, India, Iran, Brazil and Indonesia, especially relevant among those that bring together different regions are: Sandy Isenstadt and Kishwar Rizvi (eds), *Modern Architecture and the Middle East* (Seattle: University of Washington Press, 2008); Jilly Traganou and Miodrag Mitrasinovic (eds), *Travel Space and Architecture* (Burlington: Ashgate, 2009); Duanfang Lu (ed.), *Third World Modernism: Architecture, Development and Identity* (London and New York: Routledge, 2010); J.F. Lejeune and Michelangelo Sabatino (eds), *Modern Architecture and the Mediterranean* (New York: Routledge, 2010); Mark M. Jarzombek, Vikramaditya Prakash and Francis D.K. Ching, *A Global History of Architecture*, 2nd edn (New Jersey: John Wiley and Sons, 2011).

40   Sibel Bozdoğan, "Architectural History in Professional Education: Reflections on Postcolonial Challenges to the Modern Survey," *JAE* 52, no. 4 (May 1999): 207–15. Quotation: 209, 212.

41   Ibid., 212.

42   See: Esra Akcan, "Reading the Generic City: Retroactive Manifestoes for Global Cities of the Twenty-First Century," *Perspecta Yale Architectural Journal* 41 (2008): 144–52; Esra Akcan, "World, Open City?" *Architectural Design (AD)*, Special Issue on *Islam and Architecture* (November 2004): 98–104.

PART II
Architectural Developments around the World

7

Architecture in North America since 1960

Brendan Moran

Since 1960, architecture in North America has participated in if not actually been at the forefront of a welter of global transformations concerning the built environment. Primary among these are the challenge of housing ever increasing populations and the dilemma of how to develop ever more square kilometers of the earth's surface for this particular purpose as well as others. Simultaneously, architectural designs have forcefully shaped our understanding of both the socio-cultural upheavals accompanying these changes and the technical innovations and economic realities enabling them. While the profession was the strongest force shaping a sizeable role for architects within the production, maintenance and management of the built environment, concern with the status of architecture as a discipline contributed to an increased importance for the field as a symbolically robust and dynamic cultural force. From the rise in authority of the architect-planner during the 1960s, to the bolstering of architecture as a corporate service profession and identity-fashioner during the heyday of postmodernism in the 1980s, on to the emergence of more maverick, conceptual and interdisciplinary models of practice since then (enabled largely through exploitation of advanced digital technologies), the profession has gradually encompassed wide new areas of expertise while retaining many if not most of its earlier concerns. Yet while the field has evolved to become far more carefully attuned to matters of publicity, branding and entrepreneurship than it was during the first decades of the twentieth century, its ability to reflect, enhance or even affect social progress has ebbed and flowed over the last half century.

Three constituent features of the late twentieth century landscape comprise the primary backdrop against which the architectural projects featured in this chapter arguably can best be understood. Starting in the early post-war era, a sprawling, distributed network of territorial development encompassing myriad urban centers and even more peripheral ones, usually with variegated suburban expanses in between, was produced in North America. At the same time, multinational corporations grew in size, number and importance, reconfiguring the demand for architectural services as regarded the workplace, the lower- and middle-class residential areas where most workers lived, and the retail environments granting them a stage upon which to act as consumers. Thirdly, ongoing developments in electronic and computer technologies began to generate a complex, digitized continuum of media and information systems that permeated, molded, and at times even constituted physical environs. The shifting grounds for architectural explorations framed by these three factors can best be suggested through juxtaposition of a handful of noteworthy North American projects: the late modern National Center for Atmospheric Studies (Boulder, CO; I. M. Pei, 1967); the postmodern Mississauga City Hall (Mississauga, OT, Canada; Jones and Kirkland, 1987); and the digitally enhanced Whitehall Ferry Terminal (New York City, NY; Venturi, Scott Brown and Associates, 1993 (competition)—completed by Frederic Schwartz Architects, 2008) (Figures 7.1–7.4). Pei's scientific research facility is an elegant, brusque sculptural object set off against a rugged and nearly unspoiled landscape, albeit one that like others across the continent was increasingly being encroached upon just as many others across the continent were. The Mississauga City Hall, built for an incorporated suburban expanse outside Toronto and located in an "edge city" landscape of apartment towers, office parks and suburban cul-de-sacs all but hostile to the pedestrian, is a tabula rasa collection of heterogeneous historicist forms whose meaning and organization rely heavily upon cultural associations to which they only faintly nod—and rather ambiguously so. The terminal linking Lower Manhattan to the New York City borough of Staten Island, a decade and a half in the making, sought to give a large and busy transportation hub a suitable image; with its unrealized proposal of a large wall of LED screens facing the water (and the time-pressed commuter), capable of cycling through an animated sequence of pre-programmed but also "live" visuals, it registered the expanding role within architecture for advanced digital technologies, as a powerful means to instill civic buildings with a vital cultural significance. Separated by a gap of two decades each, these projects serve as emblems demarcating the three primary eras—before 1978, from the late 1970s to the mid-1990s, and since then—through which this essay will historicize the last half-century.

7.1   I.M. Pei,
National Center
for Atmospheric
Studies, Boulder
CO, 1967

7.2 Jones and Kirkland, Mississauga City Centre, Mississauga, OT, Canada, 1987

7.3 Venturi, Scott Brown Associates, Whitehall Ferry Terminal (project), New York City, NY, 1993

7.4 Frederic Schwartz Architects, Whitehall Ferry Terminal, New York City, NY, 2008

CONTINUITY AND UPHEAVAL: 1960–1977

Compared to the decade of boom immediately preceding it, the 1960s was for architects an era that simultaneously weighed rebellion and retrenchment, due in part to a waning enthusiasm for adoption of a visionary, socially responsible architectural modernism largely of European inspiration. Though native concerns had countered and tempered this forceful tendency, the triumph of a so-called International Style was all but assured at this time. Yet while the myriad social movements endemic of the decade's upheaval—at first civil rights and anti-war protests, joined later by environmental issues as well as women's and gay liberation—shared many of modern architecture's utopian goals, they also suggested new terms for pursuing them, almost all focused on identity politics and a multicultural integration of social and spatial concerns.

By the late 1960s the large, full service "corporate" firm had become a well-established force in the profession, largely due to the post-war economic boom. Effectively this model of practice was in the process of eclipsing the earlier normative model in North America, namely the small sole practitioner.[1] Arguably the most prestigious such large entity was the firm of Skidmore Owings and Merrill (founded 1936 in Chicago), which emphasized efficacious delivery of services while also producing stylishly adventurous and efficiently executable designs. Their John Hancock Tower (Chicago, IL; SOM/Bruce Graham, 1967) maximized office floors through experimental engineering, and was the earliest of the firm's numerous skyscrapers to hold "tallest structure" records. The building's structural skeleton, realized as a tapered tube with cross bracing, was developed by the firm's partner Fazlur Khan, one of the era's leading structural engineers; it was but one among a series of innovative and milestone tower designs he realized over a nearly 30-year career at the firm.

Another form of architectural practice was prospering at this time as well; small and often known by the name of its sole principal, these offices cast architecture as solidly situated among the fine arts and as a prime venue for a designer's aesthetic self-expression. The role model (one might say patriarchal figure) for firms like these was Harvard-trained I.M. Pei, who enrolled at the University of Pennsylvania in the mid-1930s in order to study architecture in a fine arts context but ultimately transferred to MIT, absorbing that school's more technical approach to design.[2] Following graduate work at Harvard, he began designing projects for the New York developer William Zeckendorf; by the early 1960s, after nearly a decade doing so, he established a practice that quickly earned him a sizable reputation. Pei proffered dramatic works that were both geometrically austere and well-built, while also excising nearly all reference to historical styles—including modernist ones. Like the laboratory previously noted, his National Gallery of Art East Building (Washington, DC; 1978), with its angular forms, taut surfaces and minimalist detailing, was a clear expression of his signature style. Work by other designers who favored a predominantly sculptural formal language became by the early 1970s a new norm, encompassing Brutalist, expressionist and rectilinear tendencies. Buildings by East Coast architects working in this vein include the Walker Art Center (Minneapolis, MI; Edward Larabee Barnes, 1971) and the Waterside Apartments (New York City, NY;

Lewis Davis and Samuel Brody, 1974), while efforts by Midwest practitioners include Cedar Square West (now Riverside Plaza, Minneapolis, MI; Ralph Rapson, 1973). In Western Canada, Arthur Erickson's Museum of Anthropology (Vancouver, BC; 1976) was a particularly dramatic and influential example of this tendency (Figure 7.5).

In the design studios of architecture schools at this time, changes were afoot as well, with modes of studio instruction common during the mid-century increasingly undergoing examination and revision. In the 1960s, a new wave of academic figures who often also ran small firms emerged, charged with training the expanding student body generated by the post-war demographic boom. Most of these figures were not only younger when doing so than corresponding members of earlier generations had been; many were more determined to chart new directions, in the process forging new links between professional and educational experimentation.[3] In 1965 Charles W. Moore relocated from California's Bay Area to become Chair of Yale University's Department of Architecture at the age of 40, simultaneously establishing a growing practice in central Connecticut that soon was building far and wide across the continent. He followed in the footsteps of Australian John Andrews (appointed Chair of Architecture at the University of Toronto in 1962, at the age of 29!), and was followed in turn by Italian-born architect Romaldo Giurgola, who in 1966 became Chair of Columbia University's architecture department at the age of 46 while shepherding his own practice in Philadelphia. His Columbus East High School (Columbus, IN; 1972), encompassing an open classroom system that reflected recent educational developments, was an innovative product of its day; composed of sleek white metal-skinned bars elevated on pilotis, it was split in the middle to form an open courtyard for informal gathering that contributed to its rethinking of the traditional organization of educational facilities.

7.5   Arthur Erickson, Museum of Anthropology, Vancouver, BC, Canada, 1976

This design was one among many commissioned by Cummins Engine Company co-founder J. Irwin Miller, as part of a program whereby the corporation covered the fees for prestigious firms that normally would not have been enlisted to work in such a small city as Columbus. In the face of suburbanization, driven by burgeoning subdivision and commercial development that all but abandoned civic amenities and left them to be realized piecemeal or just overlooked, Miller's efforts in Indiana were anomalous, relatively unprecedented and highly productive. Beginning unceremoniously enough with a series of buildings for the Irwin Union Bank and Trust—including one by Eero Saarinen, soon followed by his North Christian Church (1964)—the city's public realm was expanded under Miller's guiding hand. Projects included the First Baptist Church (Harry Weese, 1965), Fire Station #4 (Robert Venturi, 1967), and the Cleo Rogers Memorial Library (Pei, 1969). In the 1970s, this collection was joined by the Republic Newspaper Plant (SOM/Myron Goldsmith, 1971) and Giurgola's high school, along with later projects including the Clifty Creek Elementary School (Richard Meier, 1982). By then, the town stood as a living testament to a sea change in taste and emphasis, as the mid-century modernism Irwin originally valued was augmented by successive waves of designs taking up newer concerns.

Two figures who built in Columbus—Meier and Venturi—became important figures shaping new formal directions during the 1970s. Both had growing reputations by then, and were running fledgling yet high-profile practices; Venturi (unlike Meier) had already spent nearly two decades teaching, often alongside his partner architect and planner Denise Scott Brown. Meier's designs, such as his Smith House (Darien, CT; 1966), a modest box of unassuming cedar shingles outside with blank, white surfaces inside, reveled in a geometric severity that reanimated the 1930s European work of Le Corbusier and others. In a different vein, Venturi used his formal wit and nonconformist theoretical perspectives—clearly articulated in his 1966 *Complexity and Contradiction in Architecture*—to attack the drab reductivism of much modernist design, in particular Philip Johnson's domestic work. Venturi's Brant House (Greenwich, CT; 1972), with its two-tone, green brick exterior and chevron-plan dining area, displayed an interest in formal play rivaling Meier's, yet one infused with pop art sensibilities and mannerist flourishes instead of purist austerity. Rival aesthetic platforms all but crystallized around the differences between these two designers, playing out in the pages of various professional and academic publications yet with ensuing debates due far more to the promotion of certain of their peers than to their own efforts. Meier and his cohorts Peter Eisenman, Michael Graves, Charles Gwathmey and John Hejduk were collectively christened the "Whites," as a group seen in opposition to an analogous clique spearheaded by Robert A.M. Stern and labeled the "Greys."[4] While the former were to varying degrees interested in neo-modernist investigations, the latter group explored experiments with various earlier and all-but-forgotten historic styles, ranging from the American Shingle Style and Richardson Romanesque of the 1880s on to others even farther afield in time and place.

Yet on the heels of the riots, protests and traumas of the 1960s, various forces identified as shaping and determining public space became matters upon which architects increasingly trained their sights. While the White/Grey debate had been unfolding, another important discourse about the American city had been developing as well, largely fueled by polemics penned by a few of the Greys. In 1965, Moore had published an important text in Yale's student-run architectural journal *Perspecta*; entitled "You Have Got to Pay for the Public Life," it was a contradictorily critical *and* insightfully affirmative appreciation of America's premier amusement park, Disneyland (Anaheim, CA; Walt Disney Imagineering, 1955).[5] Moore argued that Disney's commercial enterprise offered new and authentic popular experiences by replacing the shrinking urban public realms of traditional cities, then suffering the height of their de-densification through the relocation of middle-class citizenry to the suburbs. He thus presciently raised the thorny dilemma of whose interests within society architects served: theirs, their clients, or the masses of people subject to the authority and dictates of these clients?

With a brilliant series of articles published over the next few years, Venturi and Scott Brown extended Moore's gambit by initiating an in-depth examination of the communicative nature of peripheral and suburban American landscapes, as seen from the perspective of designers.[6] After taking a group of architecture students in 1968 to do "field work" in Los Angeles and Las Vegas, where they documented and studied the relatively uncluttered urban fringe landscape they found there, Venturi and Scott Brown intuited how these environs shared important similarities with traditional East Coast suburban-urban spatial continuums and the ongoing changes observable there. Their insights suggested that demand for a central agora was being surpassed by new technologies (television, as well as electronic media more generally) and new social relations, in particular the segregated, self-selective community cohesion of consumer society. By mapping out a tactical attitude toward design favoring a communicative agenda in direct opposition to the sculptural work of Pei, Paul Rudolph, and others—as well as directions the various Whites (and even some of the Greys) were taking—Moore, Venturi and Scott Brown initiated design directions that began to fragment academic architectural culture from within.

These discerning probes regarding what amounted to a new milestone in private construction of public space—the "malling" of the contemporary environment—were ultimately refracted in practice across the continent, with the repercussions reverberating far beyond the work of their originators. In the process, a new tone and scope for many subsequent architectural endeavors was revealed, and with it opportunities for novelty, variety and even excess. Already by 1965, Austrian émigré Victor Gruen had been designing and realizing suburban shopping centers for more than a decade, at first with various stores arranged around a canopy-covered outdoor area, and then subsequently within covered, climate-controlled envelopes. A decade and a half after the Ford Foundation relocated from Michigan to Manhattan in 1950, shifting its local focus to one far more national and global in scope in the process, Kevin Roche and John Dinkeloo designed the Foundation a new headquarters (Ford Foundation Building: 1968) that clearly learned from Gruen's prototype. With myriad offices wrapped around a 10-storey atrium above a lush garden, the building evinced a structural integrity capable of producing large enclosed public arenas, marking the onset of an upswing in their production as essentially privatized public spaces. Not long after, in Texas, the upscale, mixed-use development Houston Galleria (HOK/Gyo Obato, 1970) opened, constituting a heightened challenge to the traditional city center as the leading cultural and commercial district in North American cities. Initiated by local developer Gerald D. Hines, the complex alluded to its namesake the Galleria Vittorio Emanuele II in Milan through the inclusion of a barrel vaulted atrium space that also recalled Joseph Paxton's Crystal Palace. In Canada, the similar Toronto Eaton Centre (Eberhard Zeidler and Bregman + Hamann Architects, 1977) was soon completed, replete with speculative office towers, entities subsequently added at the Galleria as well.

Along with such suburban "edge city" mega-malls, two other new development typologies were ascendant at this time: corporate office parks and the adaptive reuse of disused structures as retail complexes. New headquarters for the College Life Insurance Company of America (Indianapolis, IN; Roche and Dinkeloo, 1971) epitomized the first phenomenon, while a paradigmatic example of the second can be seen in Faneuil Hall Marketplace (Boston, MA: Benjamin Thompson and Associates, 1976), where a dilapidated nineteenth-century meeting hall and its disused neighboring market structures were turned into a retail complex in time for America's bicentennial. A slew of mixed-use projects were undertaken at this time as well, which by emulating qualities found in the Ford Foundation Building produced the effect of a "city-within-the-city"; Atlanta architect and developer John Portman became the undisputed master of such projects, generating dramatic and ornate interior spaces, that in effect turned their backs on the difficult urban dynamics beyond their skin. The Hyatt Regency Atlanta (1967), located within the larger Peachtree Center and linked by glass pedestrian sky bridges to adjacent Portman-designed office towers, crystallized the parameters of such projects, with variegated open spaces, bi-axially symmetrical plans, and lush plantings hanging over floating pods. It was soon joined by the Renaissance Center (Detroit, MI; 1977), completed just as the start of the second oil crisis of 1979 marked the eclipse of North American automobile production by foreign competitors (Figures 7.6–7.7).

7.6   John Portman, Renaissance Center, Detroit, MI, 1977

7.7   John Portman, Renaissance Center, Detroit, MI, 1977

REVITALIZED MESSAGES AND URBAN REVIVAL: 1978–95

By 1976, cultural critics increasingly voiced the view that mainstream modern architecture had been largely an aesthetic and social imposition on the built environment, rather than a truly popular movement carefully attuned to the modernization processes forcefully transforming it.[7] At the same time, the almost flagrant contingency of stylistic traits displayed by the bulk of corporate, institutional and domestic projects contributed to what George Baird has characterized as a "loss of moral confidence in architectural practice and education."[8] In response to this, attempts to forge an increased authority for the field were initiated; in part this was done through experimentation with stylistics thought to be more directly communicative and accessible (historicist postmodernism), while within the academy a new vein of investigations into the terms of architecture's disciplinarity commenced (see Chapter 2, , Post-Modernism: Critique and Reaction). Equally important, by the early 1980s the so-called "Reagan Revolution" heralded an ideological shift in American mainstream politics that replaced liberalism with neoliberalism. Together, these developments produced the effect that the field all but jettisoned social responsibility in favor of catering to those private interests that were increasingly eclipsing state sponsorship of building.

Three noteworthy designs—two for buildings, one for a residential development, all from 1978—encompass most of the major issues that were to dominate the profession over the next decade and a half. In New York City Philip Johnson unveiled his iconoclastic AT&T Building, with its playfully referential Chippendale cabinetry crown that reversed the architect's earlier International Style minimalism, in effect challenging the practice of producing sleek modernist glass and steel monoliths as the necessary accoutrement of large, multinational corporations. On the west coast, in the Southern California city of Santa Monica, the Canadian-born, locally-based architect Frank Gehry remade a suburban tract home for his own use, exposing its balloon framing and wrapping it in chain link fencing. The project introduced a raw skin treatment that served to reconstitute the prototypical house's interior spaces as flayed, light-infused irregular spaces decked out in multiple clashing colors and adopting an aesthetic of angularity and disunity. In forging a formally inventive but seemingly haphazard low-key style that was contemporary but decidedly not modernist, Gehry's residential experiment—like Johnson's headquarters—raised the possibility of an antidote to the profusion of late modern design directions. While these experiments were underway on each of the two coasts, in the Florida Panhandle an upscale historicist residential development christened Seaside was envisioned by Elizabeth Plater-Zyberk and Andrés Duany. Though really a small Gulf Coast resort community consisting primarily of second homes, this "new urbanist" enclave launched a new planning ethos that subsequently built up steam by tapping into nostalgia for a traditional small-town lifestyle of holistic, integrated and intimate community that in truth had scarcely existed in the past (Figures 7.8–7.9).

Two books published that same year—*Collage City* and *Delirious New York*— took up the importance of urban dynamics within the generation of architectural form, in effect suggesting that the diverging formal concerns of Johnson and Gehry had not emerged within a vacuum. Both encompassed positions initiated by Europeans who at the time were living and teaching in North America (Colin Rowe and Rem Koolhaas, respectively); together they highlighted the intricate and conflicted relationship between an earlier development of architectural modernism in Europe and its subsequent implementation and revitalization once exported westward.[9] Rowe's book promulgated a new strategy for understanding urban fabric as a collage of elements with discreet, conflicting dispositions, and was inherently critical of those strategies implemented by "tower-in-the-parking-lot" planners and architects during the 1950s and 1960s. Pointing in a different

7.8   Frank Gehry, Gehry Residence, Santa Monica, CA, 1978

7.9   Elizabeth Plater-Zyberk and Andrés Duany, Seaside, FL, 1981

direction, Koolhaas reconsidered the inherent heroics and continued relevance of avant-garde positioning within architectural practice. Positing that New York architects between the two World Wars had proposed an unrealized, urban "culture of congestion," the book suggested this as a viable alternative to certain weaknesses endemic to mainstream modern architecture—in particular, its nearly pathological obsession with antiseptic emptiness. While Rowe's tract was increasingly adopted as a justifying assumption behind historicist postmodernism, Koolhaas' "retroactive manifesto" implied that a viable neo-modernism might well be generated out of selective reexamination of unheralded past achievements and overlooked, unrealized aspirations.

The revitalized urban vantage point these books offered architects arrived, however, at the nadir of economic disinvestment in center city neighborhoods, a process which since the 1930s had produced their marked abandonment by all but those economically unable to relocate, who often were underprivileged minorities. The bulk of North American architects sidestepped the implications of these significant changes, largely opting instead for increased concentration on the communicative potentials of form-making following Venturi and, to a lesser extent, Rowe.[10] This concern ultimately produced a "return" to earlier modes of linguistic form—heavy skins of stone or concrete with discrete windows, instead of glass and steel curtain walls; classical colonnades (at times verging on caricature), in place of rows of abstract pilotis; pediments/hip roofs, rather than flat roofs—which was meant to render postmodern historicism a "new" formal language. Emerging first as a vein of design for many relatively smaller firms such as those of Johnson, Stern and (eventually) Graves, this proclivity was soon adopted by larger firms, and increasingly adopted for the design of corporate headquarters. The firm Kohn Pederson Fox emerged as a leading practice of this type, with the completion of the imposing Procter and Gamble Headquarters office complex (Cincinnati, OH; 1986); its thin limestone veneer was offered up as a more sober and suitable replacement for the ubiquitous glass curtain walls, such as the one found in their own design for 333 Wacker Drive (Chicago, IL) completed just three years earlier.

On the heels of Gehry's project for his own residence, the domain of the private home took on a new vitality as a venue for architectural experimentation and expression, initiated by a new generation of adventuresome clients and maverick designers.[11] The economic boom of the 1980s, with its reduction of tax burdens on those in upper income brackets and its promotion of trickle-down philanthropy as a substitute for earlier public sector support of cultural production, empowered new entrepreneurial elites. The luxury home once again became a plum design commission as it had been during the Gilded Age of robber barons, while construction of project-based public housing virtually came to a standstill in America (in Canada the volume decreased but not quite as markedly).[12] In the process, domestic architecture opened a new horizon for exploring polemical design strategies and indulging in luxury (and fantasies of it). Heralding the former was the exhibition "Houses for Sale" (Leo Castelli Gallery, New York City; 1980), in which a phalanx of architects (including Eisenman and Moore) offered up representations of non-commissioned designs for public delectation, in the process treating postmodernist architecture as autonomous aesthetic production available for consumption like paintings or sculptures. Examples of the latter abound, in projects such as the Spielberg House (East Hampton, NY; Gwathmey Siegel, 1988), in which a rustic eighteenth-century New Jersey barn was disassembled and moved over 200 miles to beachfront property on the tip of Long Island, ultimately to be incorporated within a sumptuous residence for the celebrated Hollywood director.

Yet domestic architecture of the 1980s hardly adhered to any uniformity across the continent, as attention to local conditions and cultures and also to the increased pluralism initiated during previous decades freed up architects to engage in unparalleled explorations. Areas with milder climates (the American South and Southwest, as well as the West coast as far north as Vancouver) were the primary sites for projects that renewed experimentation with fanciful sculptural effects while all but dissolving the distinction between interior and exterior spaces; other more temperate locales, such as the Northeast and the Midwest, prompted investigations into the potential for adapting local building traditions. In the Pacific Northwest, the Pyrch and Appleton Residences (Victoria, British Columbia, CA; Patkau Architects, 1984 and 1986, respectively) matched their rugged, pine covered settings with brusque but elegant forms in dark stucco and other rough-hewn materials. In the South, the Spear Residence (Miami Beach, FL; Arquitectonica, 1978) riffed on the Art Deco forms of the nearby South Beach area, conjuring an almost Suprematist form of modern architecture uncannily harkening back to the 1920s. Multi-family housing was not left out of the equation, though as already noted projects earmarked for low-income residents became few and far between. A design for Scattered-Site Infill Public Housing, (Charleston, SC; Bradfield Associates, 1986) reinvented the Charleston Single, a one room wide, rectangular-plan house type native to the city, proposing that altered versions of it could be allocated in empty lots so as to constitute a viable alternative to either tower or courtyard housing blocks.

Another new direction for architectural design, labeled variously "high-tech" or structural expressionism, was emerging by the start of the 1980s (see Chapter 3, High-Tech: Modernism Redux). Following on the heels of completion of the innovative Pompidou Centre (Paris, France; Renzo Piano and Richard Rogers, 1977), an increased concern with the application of advanced technology toward both structural and symbolic ends was underway around the globe. Originally a European development, "high-tech" was an extension of modernism that in distinction to SOM's work (and that of other North American "late modernist" firms such as Saarinen's successor office Roche Dinkeloo) reveled in both spatial pyrotechnics and dynamic use of color. Early examples include Rogers' PA Technology Building (Princeton, NJ; 1982), followed soon after by his erstwhile partner's Menil Collection (Houston, TX; Renzo Piano, 1988), with its rows of scalloped louvers softly illuminating the spacious galleries below (Figures 7.10–7.11). These concerns were extended by a slightly later project, the Allen Lambert Galleria (Toronto, Ontario, CA; Santiago Calatrava, 1992), with its elegant yet overwhelming vertical trusses enclosing a spacious passage adjacent to an underground commercial concourse.

By the late 1980s, criticism of the ineffectual communicative success of much architectural postmodernism began to generate as damning a dismissal of it as had been experienced by mainstream modernism roughly two decades earlier. As expressions of postmodern urbanistic and architectural desires, projects like Mississauga City Hall, Seaside and the AT&T Building provide cases in point. Though the tower, drum and pedimented bar of the Canadian government building were meant to recall features of northern farmsteads, at their grand scale—and eventually surrounded by generic commercial buildings—they instead constituted a random and artificially hermetic formal language. Seaside's traditional balloon-frame construction, employed for its various domestic and small-scale commercial structures, was hardly a viable model for larger-scaled urban projects; moreover, the small-town ethos generated by the form-dependent building codes favored by New Urbanists—based not on zoning but on stylistics characteristics, with strict covenants for enforcing their implementation—was far more suited to peripheral subdivision development than to the urban infill that had been the focus of Rowe's *Collage City*. Furthermore, it was increasingly realized that Johnson's tower differed less from earlier glass and steel varieties than had been noted at first; rather than merely an exploration of the potential of picturesque whimsy to replace modernist dogma, his design in fact heralded the rise of the "starchitect," a designer whose visual signature secured a certain celebrity for their client and themselves, within the ever-expanding realms of media and publicity.[13] Most importantly, while Seaside took the guise of a nostalgic return, the AT&T Building heralded a revitalized avant-gardist aesthetic agenda, resuscitating a particularly problematic thread of modern architecture: iconoclastic exceptionalism.

7.10   Renzo Piano Building Workshop, Menil Collection, Houston, TX, 1988

7.11   Renzo Piano Building Workshop, Menil Collection, Houston, TX, 1988

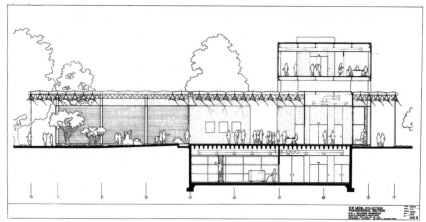

TOWARD A DIGITAL MILLENNIUM AND BEYOND: 1996–2012

As the 1980s gave way to the 1990s and the earlier decade's economic boom went bust on the shores of another recession, the discipline and the profession entered again into an era of recalibration. Though much building production was to continue following the two paths just outlined (nostalgic return and iconoclastic avant-gardism), midway through the 1990s a postmodernist "second wave" appeared, ushering in various new millennial directions. As the century came to a close, more seasoned neo-modernisms rose to the fore, promoted by a number of architects who had earlier been featured in the Museum of Modern Art's Deconstructivist Architecture exhibition held in 1988. (See Chapter 4 Deconstruction: The Project of Radical Self-Criticism) Their work, tempered by environmental issues and beefed up by the injection of an animating vitality provided by younger fingers—many of whom had trained under their tutelage—ushered in an emerging digital culture tempered by the uncertainties of an impending new millennium.

While promoting the design direction of one particular architectural clique, the 1988 exhibition also registered a rising trend within the educational context, one that only escalated over the next decade or so: interest in new architectural theories as justification for design experiments. New perspectives articulated at the time positioned the discipline of architecture in three particular ways: as the primary territory for understanding hegemonic contemporary socio-cultural practices and their limitations; as a non-traditional and often apocryphal variety of mass media; and as a disparate and free-wheeling compendium of human practices termed the "domestic project," whose role has long been the managing of humanity's desire to tame or make docile human environments, the planet, its citizenry, space itself, and even thought.[14] While these three dynamics were rather slow to produce realized (or realizable) designs, their outlines and contours had slowly been gelling within professional design instruction and among a fledgling group of younger theorist-educators for nearly a decade, in a speculative and at times tenuous manner often at odds with earlier pedagogical traditions. A noteworthy early example of this was Daniel Libeskind's experimental Chamber Works project of 1983, consisting of a suite of images testing the limits of architectural drawing and the representational imperatives inherent in their codified use professionally. A subsequent (but unfortunately unfinished) project that made good on this new direction was the Slow House (North Haven, NY; Elizabeth Diller and Richard Scofidio, 1991), a mediation on real estate that lined up a vacation home's various spaces along the curved path between an entry door and a picture window overlooking the ocean, while deploying digital technology to put exterior vistas under a self-reflexive and critical surveillance. On the campus of the Illinois Institute of Technology, the McCormick Student Center (OMA/Rem Koolhaas, 2001) extended such concerns within an educational building, one that somewhat uneasily joined Mies van der Rohe's famous post-war complex. In addition to taking the grass-worn paths already generated by student traffic across the empty site as its ready-made circulation diagram, the building parodied the formal language of Mies' earlier Commons Building—which it physically engulfed—while also extending Koolhaas' penchant for perceptually mischievous form-making.

Yet beyond these concerns central to architectural design and its varied instantiations, an additional repercussion of the Reagan Revolution was at work: urban gentrification, through accelerated re-development of those urban neighborhoods that had experienced extreme disinvestment over the last half-century. The process focused on areas thought capable of acting as magnets for upper-income urban dwellers and tourist dollars alike, leveraging them within efforts at larger economic growth at the regional scale while allowing real estate developers involved to turn a tidy profit. Examples of this process include the National Inventors Hall of Fame (Akron, OH; James Stewart Polshek, 1995), which was located near Akron's center city convention center in an effort to promote vitality for the once thriving downtown. The Seattle Art Museum opened the Olympic Sculpture Park (Seattle, WA; Weiss/Manfredi Architects, 2008) on the edge of the city's trendy Belltown neighborhood, 13 blocks northwest of its main location.[15] As part of this phenomenon, cultural institutions began to thrive during the 1990s as never before; increasingly, however, they found themselves subject to new funding formulas that often brought commerce more aggressively into the mix, in the form of extended cafe and retail areas as well as blockbuster shows with separate admission fees. In Pittsburgh, a tall warehouse building was retrofitted to house the Andy Warhol Museum (Pittsburgh, PA; Richard Gluckman, 1995), in which a minimalist aesthetic was employed in gallery, circulation and service spaces alike, to unify a series of stacked, luxuriously-large gallery spaces.

Increasingly, numerous foreign architects (many of them by now nearly household names among the profession) designed either new cultural institutions or additions to existing ones in North America. A high-profile example of this trend was the extensive Museum of Modern Art expansion, for which a short list of 10 architects was selected in 1997, over half foreign practitioners. The project was completed in 2004 by Japanese architect Yoshio Taniguchi, whose starkly neo-modernist design was chosen over two other submissions by three Swiss architects, Bernard Tschumi and the team of Jacques Herzog and Pierre de Meuron. The latter eventually had other similar opportunities in North America, completing the M.H. De Young Memorial Museum (San Francisco, CA; 2005). In the Midwest, Kazuo Sejima and Ryue Nishizawa (SAANA) designed the Toledo Art Museum's Glass Pavilion (Toledo, OH; 2007), while Toronto's native son Frank Gehry completed an addition to the Art Gallery of Ontario (2008), in which his signature curved forms wrap and infiltrate the existing gallery spaces in a tour-de-force of dynamic new spaces. Perhaps the most dramatic of all such projects, though, was the majestic J. Paul Getty Center (Los Angeles, CA, Richard Meier, 1997), a complex 15 years in the making; perched on a hill in Brentwood overlooking Los Angeles and finished in travertine and metal panels, it had the extra bonus of being free to one and all.

Inflecting the urban, institutional and domestic scales alike, the so-called "digital revolution" began to exert a strong influence on architecture during the 1990s. By the time Andy Grove, Chairman and CEO of microchip manufacturer Intel, was named TIME magazine's 1997 Person of the Year—the personal computer had already been Machine of the Year back in 1982—the processing power of affordable machines had increased at a pace that assured their central presence in both offices and schools. Within the academy, so-called "paperless studios" proliferated, amounting to a novel teaching environment in which emphasis on producing buildings was downplayed in favor of unbridled formal experimentation. Like earlier theoretical speculation, such endeavors were slow to produce innovations in realized designs; yet as software caught up with the working out of construction details, computers have all but become fixtures in offices across the continent, for communicating, managing, and drafting as well as designing.

As the millennium approached, the increased availability of sleek handheld devices gave way to ubiquitous computing, with digital components appearing in nearly every type of manufactured object—including buildings, made possible by so-called "smart building" technology. Although prior to the 1990s computers in architecture were primarily understood as drafting aids (with the exception of research labs such as those at MIT and UCLA), with advances in 3-D rendering and other software packages, especially those involving CAD-CAM capabilities, their potential as design and fabrication tools was greatly enhanced. An innovative and visionary application of this was the New York Stock Exchange's Virtual Trading Floor (New York, NY; Asymptote, 2001), in which a physical environment and an accompanying computer screen interface hybridized the virtual potential of trader's everyday activity. While the actual curvilinear physical space was equipped with LED displays continuously running market information, the accompanying screen interfaces depicted an analogous "space" in which myriad forms of market information was similarly made available for perusal (Figure 7.12).

7.12   Asymptote Architecture: Hani Rashid + Lise Anne Couture, New York Stock Exchange Virtual Trading Floor, New York City, NY, 1999

By the late 1990s, a tension between design styles referred to as the "boxes vs. blobs" rivalry appeared, as computer-generated formal experiments augmented the continued propensity for cubic, neo-modernist forms, competing with them in an effort to become the chief purveyor of "contemporary" and forward-looking explorations.[16] A testament to the vitality of box architecture was the Dominus Winery (Napa Valley, CA; Herzog and de Meuron, 1999), with its stainless steel gabions perversely arranged with the larger, heavier stones above, displaying the elegant potential of the simple cubic form (Figure 7.13). The renovation of a 1930s Art Deco factory into the Korean Presbyterian Church in Queens, NY (Garafolo, Lynn, McInturf Architects, 1998), with its computer-generated folded panels providing diffused illumination and allowing views of Manhattan from the building's sanctuary, was an early realization of so-called blob architecture. In addition, around this time a new "parametric" understanding of design emerged, encompassing both blob architecture and BIM software packages, which allowed for changes to the synthetic, "master" digital model encompassing all aspects and systems of a particular building.[17]

Following the catastrophic destruction of the World Trade Center towers in New York City on September 11, 2001, the first decade of the twenty-first century witnessed a dramatic increase in interest in architecture on the part of the general public. No doubt this was due to the emotion and excitement linked to rebuilding efforts (and building in general) in light of this shocking event, in which architecture had been both physically and symbolically attacked in such a tragic manner. Efforts to repair the ruptured physical fabric of Lower Manhattan entailed a number of high-profile competitions, with Daniel Libeskind's proposal for a master plan selected from among seven entries in 2003, and the National September 11 Memorial and Museum complex tentatively completed almost a decade to the day after the fateful event (Memorial: Michael Arad with Peter Walker, 2011; Museum: Snøhetta with Aedis Architecture and Planning, likely 2014). Over the tumultuous decade, North American was increasingly caught up in a global sweep, in which numerous much-publicized design projects were framed as endemic of a new optimism in the face of evolving conflicts and struggles.

7.13   Herzog and de Meuron, Dominus Winery, Napa Valley, CA, 1999

Yet if architectural objects experienced a newfound visibility, the construction of viable and successful public spaces has lagged behind, despite a few noteworthy exceptions. While a fully reconstituted "Ground Zero" at the World Trade Center still awaits completion as of early 2014, the new TKTS Booth (Choi Ropiha/Perkins Eastman, 2008) for the non-profit Theater Development Fund sits within a recently pedestrianized Times Square that is so heavily illuminated by animated electrical signage as to experience 24/7 daylight. The kiosk incorporates red illuminated steps surmounting a modest, angular form; in replacing a temporary scaffold structure initiated nearly 40 years earlier, it allows a nearly ten-block stretch of open space to function as outdoor stage and auditorium within the relentless city grid. In a high-tech vein, the Susan and Raymond Brochstein Pavilion at Rice University (Houston, TX; Thomas Phifer Partners/James Burnett, 2010) introduced a glass enclosed, un-programmed public space within a previously underutilized and irregularly shaped campus quad, in the process reinvigorating campus life with its white steel and aluminum trellis roof providing shaded terrace areas around an indoor cafe (Figures 7.14–7.15).

The global financial crisis commencing in the fall of 2008, initiated by the bursting of a North American housing bubble fed on subprime mortgages, was the third significant instance since 1965 in which a considerable number of architects were rendered unemployed in North America. While it remains to be seen whether the profession will experience a strong enough upswing in the near future to accept the swelling ranks of recent graduates, it is likely that an increasing population and ongoing territorial development will continue to promote demand for entire panoplies of architectural services, including some new and unprecedented ones. While the realization of buildings is still the profession's central aim, varied

7.14   Thomas Phifer Partners/ James Burnett, Susan and Raymond Brochstein Pavilion at Rice University, Houston, TX, 2010

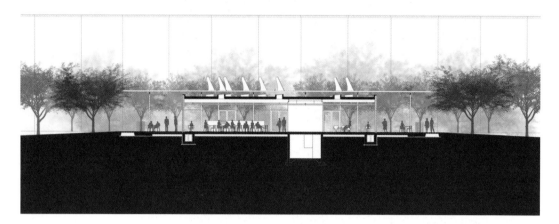

7.15 Thomas Phifer Partners/ James Burnett, Susan and Raymond Brochstein Pavilion at Rice University, Houston, TX, 2010

activities such as corporate and product identity (especially place-making as branding) and event architecture (the designing of temporary environments for spectacles such as the release of new commercial products) are transforming the breadth of professional involvement in contemporary life. The sophistication of advanced computer technologies also holds potential for architectural imagination and professional competence to contribute future innovations. Together these developments may be mapping out distinct new models of practice, as well as additional disciplinary horizons.

Many practitioners have by necessity passed up the full service model, embodied by behemoths like SOM (now with 13 offices around the world) and the global architecture, design and engineering firm Gensler, instead opting for new provisional modes of practice in which experimentation with digital fabrication and software programs round out concentration on design deliverables.[18] Yet the phenomena of a continually shrinking public realm in the face of rampant territorial development and ubiquitous computing imply that new ways to frame collective interactions and communal encounters will still be necessary, with architects being the best poised professionals to generate and deliver them. Recent buildings such as the Seattle Public Library (Seattle WA; OMA/Rem Koolhaas, 2005), in which a bold, seemingly arbitrary form brusquely but benevolently houses a wide variety of disparate public programs, ranging from reading and researching, DVD and book loaning, websurfing, small-scale retail and even old-fashioned people-watching, suggest that architecture still has a valuable role in contemporary life (Figure 7.16).

Recently, the turn at many architecture schools to a new interdisciplinary understanding of building, termed "landscape urbanism" for its integration of large scope with innovative outdoor public spaces, implies that augmentation of an architectural understanding with those of parallel professions could lead to a newfound vitality. Moreover, as past moments have shown, times of economic downturn often produce inventive focus on pressing problems, with budding ventures only reaching fruition after an initial phase of speculation. No doubt environmental concerns will shape much of this exploration, as the pressing concern of how to augment the built milieu while not further overburdening

7.16   OMA/Rem Koolhaas, Seattle Public Library, Seattle, WA, 2005

the planet's ecosystem is brought to bear on new challenges. Yet, much as has already occurred over the past five decades, emphasis on formal invention and experimentation will likely remain a primary force shaping public perceptions of the significant role of architecture in society.

NOTES

1   Over 90 percent of American architects worked in firms of 20 people or less as of 1972, while nearly 25 percent of the nation's architectural work was handled by large, corporate firms, constituting less than 2 percent of the offices. Robert Gutman, *Architectural Practice: A Critical View* (Princeton: Princeton Architectural Press, 1986), 5.

2   Eero Saarinen, an equally significant architect of this variety who was seven years older than Pei, died suddenly in 1961 of a brain tumor, while at his professional prime and the height of his firm's prestige. Numerous projects initiated prior to his untimely death were completed by former associates Kevin Roche, John Dinkeloo, and Cesar Pelli over the next half decade; while this assured that his immediate influence was felt well into the 1970s, the office initiated arguably no new designs under his direction during the historical era that constitutes this essay.

3   Leadings schools where such links were forged during the 1960s included Harvard University's Graduate School of Design, Yale University's School of Architecture, the University of Pennsylvania's Graduate School of Fine Arts and the University of California Berkeley's College of Environmental Design, as well as others.

4   This group proved a far looser counterpart to the Whites, encompassing variously Giurgola, Moore and on the fringes, Venturi, among others. It is important to note that Stern, who had earlier been a student of Johnson's at Yale, was a far more vocal and polemical proponent vis-à-vis the "Greys" position than Venturi ever was.

5   Charles W. Moore, "You Have Got to Pay for the Public Life," *Perspecta* 9/10 (1965): 57–87.

6   A list of the most important pieces should include: "A Significance for A&P Parking Lots, or Learning from Las Vegas," *Architectural Forum* 128 (March 1968): 37–43; "Mass Communications on the People Freeway, or Piranesi is Too Easy," *Perspecta* 12 (1969):

49–56; "Co-op City: Learning to Like it," *Progressive Architecture* 51/2 (Feb. 1971): 64–73; "Ugly and Ordinary Architecture, or the Decorated Shed," Parts 1 & 2, *Architectural Forum* (November 1971): 64–7 & (December 1971): 48–53.

7   Before 1968, Venturi's aforementioned *Complexity and Contradiction* joined Jane Jacobs' *The Death and Life of Great American Cities* (1961) as the two primary English-language publications challenging the unwritten principles that undergirded modern architecture and modern planning respectively. These were later joined by: Oscar Newman, *Defensible Space* (1972); Robert Sommer, *Tight Spaces: Hard Architecture and How to Humanize It* (1974); Brent C. Brolin, *The Failure of Modern Architecture* (1976), and others. Charles Jencks, an American critic who moved to Britain in the mid-1960s, ran a veritable cottage industry writing about the demise of modernism; among his books are: *Modern Movements in Architecture* (1973); *The Language of Post-Modern Architecture* (1977); and *Late Modern Architecture and Other Essays* (1980).

8   George Baird, "1968 and its Aftermath: The Loss of Moral Confidence in Architectural Practice and Education," *Reflections on Architectural Practice in the Nineties*, William Saunders, ed. (New York: Princeton Architectural Press, 1996), 64–70.

9   Both volumes quickly became central to future training regimens for architects and urban designers, primarily because they clearly encapsulated those dilemmas faced by contemporary architects. Colin Rowe, with Fred Koetter, *Collage City* (Cambridge: MIT Press, 1978); Rem Koolhaas, *Delirious New York* (Oxford: Oxford University Press, 1978).

10   Another important influence in this regard was Aldo Rossi's *The Architecture of the City*; though it was published in Italian the same year Venturi's *Complexity and Contradiction in Architecture* appeared, it was not translated into English for over a decade and a half.

11   Though over the previous three decades numerous iconic houses had been realized, architectural modernism in North America trafficked most heavily in institutional and corporate commissions, in addition to public, collective housing projects. Significantly, postmodern proselytizer Jencks dated the death of architectural modernism with the 1972 destruction of the abandoned government-funded Pruitt-Igoe public housing complex (St. Louis, MO; Leinweber, Yamasaki & Hellmuth, 1956); see Jencks, *The Language of Postmodern Architecture*, 9.

12   In addition to project-based public housing, through which multi-unit complexes were generated, a new form was initiated under President Richard Nixon in 1974; entitled the Section 8 Housing Program, it was based on landlord subsidies (through vouchers) and continues to the present day. See Jason Hackworth, *The Neoliberal City: Governance, Ideology, and Development in American Urbanism* (Ithaca: Cornell University Press, 2006).

13   Although Google's Books Ngram Viewer cites fewer than two dozen instances of the term's use before 2000, by then it had been applied to Frank Gehry and Michael Graves, among others.

14   Heavily influenced by new investigations into the production of knowledge and its management then being developed within (and in relation to) universities, this concern asked whether architecture was merely a domain of realized buildings and unrealized designs, as opposed to the much larger sphere of overall sociopolitical organization. Linked back to university unrest from the late 1960s and the rise of discourse about race, class and gender that followed it, this discourse played out not in mainstream professional magazines, but instead in what were primarily academic publications and journals, among them *Oppositions* (1973–84), *Assemblage* (1985–2001) and *ANY: Architecture New York* (1993–2000).

15 These types of projects, often funded in America through sizable public subsidy, have on the whole failed to deliver the types of economic growth (in the form of jobs and business opportunities) that their advocates have projected.

16 The terms "box" and "blob" were used to describe much of the work included in an exhibition held at the Museum of Modern Art in 1999, The Un-Private House. See Nina Rappaport, "Box and Blob: The Un-Private House," *MoMA* 2:7 (Sept., 1999): 2–5, as well as Anthony Vidler, "Diagrams of Diagrams," *Representations* 72 (Autumn, 2000): 1–20.

17 As Antoine Picon has noted, concern with control of complex parameters is intrinsically anti-tectonic; without the necessity to understand a design's structure (or skin) as an aggregate, the spatial implications of structural systems are often repressed within designs that have employed computer software to develop their formal integrities. See Antoine Picon, *Digital Culture in Architecture: An Introduction for the Design Professions* (Boston: Birkhauser, 2010), 136-38.

18 Innovative technological systems increasingly offered the possibility that a small firm could greatly extend its manpower and its control of design processes through CAD-CAM (computer-aided drafting—computer-aided manufacturing) and other digital capacities. On this particular possibility, see *Provisional: Emerging Modes of Architectural Practice*, Elite Kedan, Jon Dreyfous and Craig Mutter, eds. (New York: Princeton Architectural Press, 2010).

8

Architectural Developments in Latin America: 1960–2010

Zeuler R.M. de A. Lima

AN ELUSIVE CONSTRUCT

In 1985, during the First Architecture Biennale of Buenos Aires, an international group of architects launched the first of a series of periodical seminars to promote debate about architecture produced south of the Mexican–United States border. Until then, their contacts had been informal and sparse. The period of unfettered modernization, nation building, and political and cultural prestige that gave architects from Latin America international exposure in the second quarter of the twentieth century was long gone. So was the time when critics and leading cultural institutions in the United States and Europe had turned their eyes to the region. They no longer sanctioned and analyzed it in books, magazines, and exhibitions as they had done in the decades that preceded and followed World War II. Architectural production and experimentation slowed down and remained isolated in Latin America between the late 1960s and 1980s, but activities and dialogues had gradually increased since then. Work circumstances were different from the ones found by early modernists. Economic, social, and political adversities called for the reevaluation of previous practices and the creation of new ones. The time had come to organize a collective discussion as a means for overcoming isolation and the lack of visibility.

The proliferation of conferences, publications, prizes, and exhibitions about architecture in Latin America since the mid 1980s has been an important attempt to address new conceptual and professional challenges. Architects face issues ranging from the modern cultural legacy to citizenship and climate change. Their efforts have contributed to re-inscribe the region in international architectural discourse, even though this geographic framework faces an ambivalent if not elusive undertaking: to embrace the idea of a shared continental identity while recognizing the multiple realities and profound historic, physical, demographic, and cultural differences in an enormous area that stretches throughout South, Central, and part of North America, and the Caribbean. For the first time, architects from different countries adhered as a group to a continental cause paradoxically born outside the confines of their profession and their own land.

The genealogy of Latin America as a place shows a fluid, complex, and contested construct. The idea was French in origin, serving colonial interests in the middle of the nineteenth century. Influenced by French liberalism, writers and politicians on both sides of the Atlantic were persuaded that the establishment of a Catholic and Latin America in the New World could counter the growing ascendancy of a Protestant and Anglo-Saxon America. After France's failed involvement, the term Latin America was absorbed into the geopolitical divide between the United States and the southern section of the continent. This dubious notion was appropriated into uneven power relations throughout the twentieth century, appearing in collective continental struggles and disappearing in the individual affirmation of national identities. More than the term Iberian America proposed by some contemporary scholars, the term Latin America has prevailed in the debate about the subcontinent, being sometimes embraced, sometimes co-opted, and sometimes disputed by those who live under its designation, including architecture practitioners and critics.

In this context, the idea of a shared or unified language of architecture in or from Latin America stands on even more unstable ground than the region's geographic and political definition. This is why this essay does not talk about Latin American architecture and instead presents different architectural practices in Latin America. While singling it out as a region helps to give most recent productions long-due recognition, this continental clustering requires some caution, because it is at odds with the multiplicity and scale of its cultural production as well as with the changing geopolitical constituency of the contemporary world. Concision requires an assortment of dispersed and varied examples to cover such heterogeneous production and territory, and they do not represent either a single image or a compendium of canonic buildings and designers with a consciously shared continental identity. The examples in this chapter suggest a provisional mosaic of works produced in the decades since the 1960s in countries and cities south of the United States and of how different architects articulated responses to realities permeated by a recent convoluted history, fast development and urbanization, and uneven distribution of resources.

Scholars generally agree that architecture in this vast territory is heterogeneous and should not be reduced to the manifestation of a regional or peripheral production dependent on norms established in Europe and the United States.[1] They suggest it should rather be seen as architecture of divergence, responding to specific conditions and realities.[2] This approach also suggests that architecture is part of cultural exchanges in complex historical and international cultural networks. It provides less stable interpretive frameworks and denotes contemporary uncertainties, but it also avoids fixed hierarchies while valuing the otherness of countries and urban centers in Latin American in the broader context of a changing world.

INHERITED MODERNITIES

The period that followed the Cuban Revolution in 1959 and the inauguration of Brasília in 1960 was paradoxically marked by hope and crisis with significant changes to the conditions that framed modern architectural production and debate in Latin America. Both events symbolized the inflection into two decades of political, economic, and social instability in the region, turning from progressive nation state projects into authoritarian regimes supported by the superpowers of the Cold War. Despite such difficulties, a second generation of modern architects emerged in Latin America in the 1950s producing significant works that took root in the international revision of functionalism.[3] They worked in booming metropolitan areas, which concentrated economic development as well as major schools of architecture and renowned cultural institutions. Though constrained to national boundaries, they absorbed and transformed international ideas. They also explored the use of local and traditional construction materials, employed exposed concrete structures, and were concerned with place making amidst booming urbanization. They advanced some of the formal, technical, and conceptual approaches of their predecessors in Latin America but also faced the gradual emptying out of the modern social discourse in architecture. Their trajectories were sometimes interrupted or delayed for political and economic reasons. International or regional audiences may not have noticed many of them until much later, but they were not forgotten locally.

Between the 1960s and 1980s, Mexico saw significant architectural developments in a diverse range of scales, materials, and forms.[4] The intimate, poetic, and hybrid works designed by Luís Barragán as well as with Spanish-born Félix Candela's wide-spanning thin shells for churches, the Bacardi Plant (1960), and the Olympic

8.1   Pedro Ramírez Vázquez, Museum of Anthropology, canopy and patio, Mexico City, Mexico, 1963–65

Gymnasium (1968) coexisted with monumental reinforced concrete buildings such as health, sports public facilities and the monumental and ceremonial Museum of Anthropology (1963–65) designed by Pedro Ramírez Vázquez and his collaborators. Among Barragán's unorthodox rationalism were the many cloister-like houses he designed in Mexico City, the Riding Club in San Cristóbal (1968), and the organicist plans for El Pedregal (1940s–1960s), the celebrated subdivision that served as experimental ground for Demonstration Houses by architects such as Max Cetto and Enrique Yáñez. The continuity between modernity and tradition endured in Mexico as in other places in Latin America. Ramirez Vázquez's museum dedicated to indigenous peoples and located at the leafy Chapultepect Park in the federal capital has a simple rectangular layout with a ceremonial glazed entrance leading into a large central patio emulating the Nunnery Quadrangle in the Mayan city of Uxmal. The patio contains a large reflecting pool and a large square canopy supported by a single column surrounded by a circular skylight through which splashes an artificial cascade welcoming visitors.

Cuba and its capital, Havana, like other locations in the Caribbean, had, until the late 1950s, seen its horizontal landscape change with the development of luxury high-rises by international architects serving the tourist industry of the United States. However, the island's architectural culture dramatically changed after the 1959 Revolution. During the first years of Fidel Castro's regime, Cuban architects embraced the notion that architecture should satisfy the needs of common people as a goal to overcome underdevelopment. Architect Fernando Salinas headed those efforts by organizing public building programs and promoting the work of other Cuban architects. Their focus was to improve social infrastructure and mass housing adapted to site and climate conditions. Among the structures produced during this period are several multifamily buildings with experimental

8.2   Ricardo Porro, Vittorio Garatti, and Roberto Gottardi, National Art Schools, Havana, Cuba, 1960–65

prefabrication such as the ones by Antonio Quintana and Josefina Rebellón, and the organic buildings combining modern and traditional construction techniques and open and enclosed spaces for the National Art Schools (1960–65), built on the site of a former country club.

Reflecting the Cuban Revolution's utopian optimism, the schools educated a new generation of artists, designers, and performers on the island until falling out of favor with the imposition of Soviet educational standards.[5] Among them are the School of Modern Dance and School of Fine Arts designed by Ricardo Porro, the Drama School designed by Roberto Gottardi, and the Music School and Ballet School designed by Vittorio Garatti using innovative Catalan-vaulted brick and terracotta structures.[6] Though shaped differently to accommodate varying programs on diverse sites, the school buildings each attempt to create the experience of collective spaces. While independent, the building complexes share the notion of architectural promenades with interstitial and inward-looking spaces evoking streets, plazas, and small-scale urban open spaces.

Countries along the varying latitudes of the Andes also produced significant architecture during this period, some of which denoted sensitivity to urban and material conditions as well as to social programs. In Bogotá, for example, architect Germán Samper Gnecco and his associates designed large and refined buildings in reinforced concrete such as the Luis Arango Library Concert Hall (1962), the Avianca Headquarters (1968), and the Gold Museum (1968), but also low-cost housing incorporating vernacular traditions. In the meantime, Rogelio Salmona, who had a professional sojourn in Le Corbusier's office, synthesized modernist vocabularies with brick construction techniques to produce houses, public buildings, and low- and high-income apartment blocks carefully built into the complex topography of the capital and other Colombian cities. Salmona's elaborate brickwork and organic siting, which is exemplified by his San Cristóbal housing project (1962) and the complex El Parque tower complex (1968–71), opened his early rationalist affiliation to include more locally available construction techniques.

In Chile, several projects in exposed reinforced concrete ranging from housing to public buildings marked the country's architectural landscape particularly around the growing capital, Santiago. Among them were housing projects such as the horizontal blocks in various scales of the Portales Complex (1963) carefully designed by the Bresciani, Valdés, Castillo, Huidobro partnership, and the Presidente Frei Housing Complex and Valparaíso Naval School (1960–75) designed by Sergio Larraín García-Moreno and associates. Emilio Duhart was among the most prominent architects in Chile and the project he and his collaborators designed for the United Nations' Latin American Economic Committee (CEPAL) building (1966) at the edge of Mapocho River remains an outstanding example of both the lasting influence of Le Corbusier's ideas among his generation and of changing international political and economic interests in Latin America. The large horizontal square volume lifted above the ground is laid out around a courtyard, making reference to Spanish colonial houses, containing thoughtfully crafted sculptural volumes connected by ramps and stairs.

8.3   Emilio Duhart and collaborators, CEPAL Complex, Santiago, Chile, 1966

In Uruguay, the technical and formal experiments of engineer Eladio Dieste stand out for his rigorous knowledge and creative use of reinforced concrete and reinforced brick techniques, attention to details, and insightful spatial qualities. He designed churches such as Atlántida (1958) and San Pedro (1967–71), houses, warehouses, public markets, and even rural buildings in several towns ranging from the coast of Uruguay to southern Brazil. Associating architecture with the engineering logic of machines and with the warehouses containing them, Dieste combined programmatic clarity, building inventiveness, and phenomenological intent. Through laminate surfaces with various formal, structural, and spatial qualities, he mastered the rational and economic use of mainstream construction materials for the creation of what he considered to be equipment for human use.

Besides Dieste, several architects who graduated from the school of architecture of Montevideo gave continuity to the work in reinforced concrete initiated decades earlier by Júlio Vilamajó. Among them was Nelson Bayardo, whose Columbarium (1961) in Montevideo rearticulated some of Le Corbusier's use of raw concrete, elevated volume, and spatial promenade into a semi-open courtyard typology like in Emilio Duhart's CEPAL project. While the solid exterior of the gray building contrasts the verdant landscape of Cementerio del Norte, it is internally lit by large openings facing the courtyard garden and water pool and by small slits on the walls and ceilings. Visitors gradually gain access to the upper floors by passing under the building and taking a stepped ramp along a mural cast on the concrete wall, establishing close continuity among architecture, art, and landscape design. This comprehensive approach to design could also be found in Paraguay, where Beatriz Chase and Carlos Colombino operated in the fields of architecture, fine arts, and literature, and collaborated with several artists such as Jenaro Pindú, and community residents to design public art projects for urban spaces. They translated those experiences into architecture through abstract compositions in

8.4   Eladio Dieste, Atlántida Church, Montevideo, Uruguay, 1958

concrete, brick, and white stucco which they perfected in residential projects such as the Cabará and the Mulder Houses (1966–68) built into the rolling landscape of the capital, Asunción.

In Argentina, Italian-born architect Clorindo Testa and his collaborators initiated the experimentation with brutalist use of reinforced concrete.[7] Among Testa's most prominent early works is the Bank of London and South America (1959–66) in the heart of the financial center of Buenos Aires. Compressed at a narrow street corner, the distinctively perforated concrete shell frames the hollow building, while maintaining continuity with the urban block. During the construction of the bank, in 1961, Testa also co-designed the new National Library building with Francisco Bullrich and Alicia Cazzaniga. The structure was finally completed in 1992 after convoluted bureaucratic and political obstacles and followed by both architectural praise and controversy. A cantilevered volume containing the panoramic reading rooms and main offices rises as an acropolis from a plinth containing the buried stacks and creates a covered plaza spatially and visually open to the surrounding park slopes that descend toward the city and the estuary. The building's apparent symmetry and monumental scale are complemented by details and smaller sculptural elements that negotiate the different scales and uses of the project.

Another example of the use of wide-spanning raw concrete structures by Testa's team is the Civic Center for Santa Rosa in La Pampa central province. The first phase of the project, completed in 1963 with later additions, reinterpreted Le Corbusier's scheme for the Secretariat Building in Chandigarh, adjusting it to the existing scale and surroundings. Similar references can be found in the Normal School (1961) designed by architects Mario Soto and Raúl Rivarola in Leandro Alem. Aside from such manifestations, the experimental work of Claudio Caveri provided a differentiated critique of Rationalism through the use of local building materials. In the late 1950s, he founded Comunidad Tierra (Earth Community) in Moreno, outside of Buenos Aires, merging Utopian Socialism and liberal Christian thinking. The tent-like concrete shells of the community houses and church translated Caveri's concerns with collective living, respectful use of natural resources, and the incorporation of underqualified labor in reaction to industrial production systems.

As in other areas of Latin America, contrasting positions could also be observed in Brazil, among different cities and different generations. As the self-gratifying sculptural forms of Oscar Niemeyer crowned the country's collective imagination with the construction of Brasília, other architects took more austere positions. São Paulo emerged as a new center of architectural innovation, where professional education was more closely connected to technical and engineering programs

8.5 Clorindo Testa, Francisco Bullrich, and Alicia Cazzaniga, National Library, Buenos Aires, Argentina, 1961–92

than the Beaux-Arts lineage among architects in Rio de Janeiro. In the context and in tune with concurrent developments in Europe, a strong interest in brutalism emerged in São Paulo, especially around the charismatic and politically engaged figure of João Vilanova Artigas. After flirting with Le Corbusier's early vocabularies and Frank Lloyd Wright's organic architecture, Artigas adopted raw concrete as a formal language in the late 1950s and early 1960s, as did many other architects in Latin America. Also, as the dean of the School of Architecture and Urbanism at the University of São Paulo (1961–68), he conducted a professional curriculum reform, while designing the wide-spanning and hollow concrete structure that houses the school, which bears resemblance to Nelson Bayardo's Columbarium in Montevideo. Designed as a large concrete volume lifted from the ground by sculptural columns with generous internal ramps, open spaces, and zenithal lighting, Vilanova Artigas' School of Architecture is one of the many projects he designed for public facilities such as schools and even a bus station, representing his ambition to create shelters combining technical innovation and collective purpose.

Vilanova Artigas' militant leadership led many younger architects to adopt his formal vocabulary and his discourse in many residential projects in affluent neighborhoods around the growing metropolis. Despite his wide influence, a few of his disciples took a more critical route as they strived to reconsider and reinvigorate modern social utopias. Among them were Rodrigo Lefèvre, Sérgio Ferro, and Flávio Império, who questioned conventional office practice as politically disengaged and aimed at developing alternative building solutions. The three young men opted for experimental projects with vaulted concrete and brick shells directly produced on the site and with special attention to technical and labor conditions, which depended mostly on unskilled workers and simple building materials and

8.6   João Vilanova Artigas, School of Architecture and Urbanism, University of São Paulo, São Paulo, Brazil, 1961–68

techniques. They aspired to transform the production of social housing, a recurrent problem in cities such as São Paulo, with self-governed sweat-equity projects. For all their socialist idealism and desire to use the techniques for creating public buildings, their experiments remained mostly constrained to the experimental houses they designed for progressive intellectuals and upper middle-class clients. Above all, their architectural investigation was not met by the structural social and economic transformations they envisioned as part of their broader aspirations.

As in Europe and the United States, architects in Latin America were attuned to the critical revision of the premises of modern architecture and functionalism.[8] However, in neither case could architects reverse the emptying out of the social discourse which had sustained early twentieth-century avant-gardes. This challenge was especially true during the unstable economic and political context between the 1960s and 1980s, when Latin America experienced the exhaustion of populist development policies and of the symbolic role architecture played in the collective imagination of nation building. The establishment of authoritarian military regimes and export economies in the context of Cold War tensions in several of those countries redirected public investments and programs with significant changes to the material and symbolic conditions of architectural production.

The conservative and economically dependent modernization model that took over most of Latin America during that period stimulated fast urbanization and led to a building boom that was more focused on the profit of its promoters than on social reform. In Cuba, private development was abolished, but architectural developments initiated by the state were short-lived and restricted by rigid construction rules after the country's submission to Soviet ideology. Conversely, intense building activity associated with international capitalism and with technocratic and ineffective urban planning in leading Latin American nations continually empowered a short-sighted real estate market and a mediocre construction industry. Many cities in the region began to see the long-lasting sprawl of banal high-rises and neighborhoods catering to an emerging middle class paralleled by rapidly disappearing colonial and pre-modernist architectural heritage that would spur preservation efforts after the 1990s.

While some architects in Latin America embraced revisionist and revolutionary ideas after the 1960s, such as abandoning practice, moving into public and academic positions, and even leaving their countries, others continued to pursue private and government-sponsored commissions.[9] The professional situation became more challenging between the mid 1970s and 1980s, when the region was harshly affected by the international economic crises that escalated foreign debts and aggravated internal social and political problems, destabilizing authoritarian regimes. Economic hardship limited the quantity but not the quality of architecture production. Increased openness and communication enabled some of the second generation of modernist architects in Latin America to gain international visibility, following the example of Luis Barragán.

FROM MONOLOGUES TO DIALOGUES

Since Barragán's conversations with Louis Kahn about the design of a paved plaza with water open to the sky and to the ocean helped shape the Salk Institute in California in the mid 1960s, he gained great admiration from the Philadelphia architect and his collaborators. In 1976, his work in Mexico garnered a retrospective at the Museum of Modern Art of New York, through the initiative of Emilio Ambasz, the museum's Argentinean-born design curator. One year later, UNESCO published a long overdue series of interviews with selected architects from Latin America.[10] Those events were followed by awarding the Pritzker Prize to Barragán in 1980 and by an exhibition of Colombian architecture at the Pompidou Art Center in Paris, highlighting the work of Rogelio Salmona. Still, those isolated choices were more in tune with emerging postmodern sensibilities in Europe and the United States than the desire to portray the complex changing panorama of architecture and cities in Latin America.

Still, increased visibility and new international relations created new opportunities for exchanges. The influence of architects from the United States grew in Latin America between the 1970s and 1990s, especially in Spanish-speaking countries that had not been dominated by nationalist authoritarian regimes. As architects from the South tightened their contact with those from the North, they developed interest in Louis Kahn's monumental vocabulary as well as in Colin Rowe's urban theories. Some of Barragán's contemporaries incorporated and disseminated those values among older and younger generations. Diverse projects such as Oscar Tenreiro Degwitz's vast Bicentennial Plaza complex (1981–83) in Caracas, Venezuela, Salmona's classicizing National Historical Archive (1989–97) in Bogotá, Colombia, and Abraham Zabludovsky's massive National Auditorium (1990) in Mexico City, Mexico, provide varying evidence of the interest in simple, regular, and large scale architectural shapes and patterns. This influence was enhanced by the collaboration of August Komendant, Kahn's structural engineer, on various projects with architects from Latin America. These included Jesús Tenreiro Degwitz, whose archetypical geometries and centripetal courtyard layout for Saint Joseph's Benedictine Abbey (1984–89) in the small town of Güigüe in Venezuela stands as an original interpretation of those principles. The building complex, built in reinforced concrete structure with brick cladding, is centered on a small courtyard core atop a hill overlooking a verdant rural landscape a few kilometers south of Valencia Lake. This square diagram sets up the general geometry and spatial relations of the horizontal building complex with four centripetal wings that house the living quarters, everyday activities, and the chapel. While the communal wings and paved platforms stretch between south and north along the crest of the hill, the volumes with the cells supported by large piers seem to cantilever out of sculpted slopes, creating a sharp contrast between natural and artificial shapes.

Another approach to architecture, based on an articulated geometry of platonic volumes, can be traced in the work of a younger generation of architects, such as Mexican architect Ricardo Legorreta, who drew heavily on Barragán's work, and Argentinean architect Miguel Ángel Roca, who studied and worked with

8.7a　Oscar Tenreiro Degwitz, Saint Joseph's Benedictine Abbey, general
view of the chapel and main access, Güigüe, Venezuela, 1984–89

8.7b　Oscar Tenreiro Degwitz, Saint Joseph's Benedictine Abbey, view of one
of the wings with residential quarters, Guigue, Venezuela, 1984–89

Kahn in Philadelphia. Aside from Legorreta's earlier interest in geometric plays of light and color with more intense tones and monumental scale, his project for the New Cathedral in Managua, capital of Nicaragua, is exemplary of the legacy of his Mexican predecessor. Built in 1990 after an earthquake destroyed the old cathedral and at the end of 1980s civil war, the project opened up the possibility for creating new public spaces in the city. Located on a new site at the top of a hill, the cathedral designed by Legorreta established a new referential center to the city and the building staged more participatory religious rituals. The dome is located above the center of the congregation breaking the traditional hierarchy between priests and congregation. More grandiose than ostentatious, the main dome is structurally supported by several smaller buttressing domes allow for natural light and ventilation and for the accommodation to different scales.

In the meantime, in Argentina, Roca explored complex orthogonal and circular compositions with large public spaces and also became involved in urban design and planning. He developed a large number of projects in Córdoba, at the foothills of Sierras Chicas and beginning in the late 1970s, which gave him exposure both nationally and internationally.[11] While some of his projects have included public parks and plazas with architectural mosaics from the 1979 Plaza de Armas in Córdoba to the redesign of 1998 study for Avenida Corrientes in Buenos Aires, several public and private housing projects such as and public buildings ranging from several branches of Banco de la Provincia de Córdoba, others involved the creation of community centers in peripheral urban areas such as the 1991 cylindrical project for Monseñor Pablo Cabrera Community Center as part of an effort to decentralize public investments. In an analogous way but with different vocabulary and materials, Brazilian architect Jaime Lerner organized a design team as long-time mayor of the city Curitiba, whose proposals came to symbolize a significant shift from the abstract functionalist model of city planning to a methodology that aimed at improving urban life and integrated projects. His team worked for almost two decades on the revitalization of the city's historic center, new buildings such as the Wire Opera House, the implementation of a park network, and an integrated mass transit system, which included iconic tube-shaped bus shelters and multi-functional neighborhood stations connecting social, commercial, and transportation facilities. The system, nicknamed Ligeirinho (The Fast One) and widely advertised, included the innovative redesign of main urban thoroughfares with dedicated bus lanes, the creation of compact and modular stations, and intermodal terminals connected to commercial and social service facilities with pre-fabricated steel structure.

In spite of a significant shift from European to United States design models between the 1970s and 1990s, architectural production in Latin America was much more diverse than the examples promoted by international critics.[12] In the context of economic, political, and social tensions and uneven modernization, the formalist frenzy that crowned the ideological crisis of functionalism drew attention but had limited repercussion among architects and critics in Latin America. Many of them saw the pursuit of simplified historicism and playful formalism as a form of cultural and political alienation, even though such manifestations can be found in some of the work produced during the 1980s and early 1990s by architects such as Teodoro González de León and Abraham Zabludovsky in Mexico, Eólo Maia and Jô Vasconcelos in Brazil, and even by Miguel Ángel Roca and Clorindo Testa, especially in their later projects in Argentina. Among those experiments are Roca's public buildings, employing purist geometries that sometimes leap into abstract historicist citations, and Testa's team project for the Buenos Aires' Recoleta Cultural and Commercial Center (1979–84), which proposed the adaptive reuse of the Recoletos Franciscan monastery built in the early 1700s and later used as a school and an asylum. Their project associates colonial fragments with small new structures and architectural elements such as steel staircases, lighting fixtures, and mosaic pavements in addition to new bold exterior ochre and auburn colors.

Similar conceptual uneasiness can be detected with regard to deconstructivism, which appeared in limited projects in Latin America such as the Xul Solar Museum in Buenos Aires (1987–93) designed by Pablo Tomás Beitía. The museum project is based on the adaptive reuse of the artist's former residence into a cultural center that interpreted his pictorial world. Beitía kept the façade intact, but transformed the interior into a versatile set of rooms in different levels separated and united by a set of fixed and moveable partitions that seem to float within the interior of the building. Old bearing walls, new concrete structure and walls along with the slits among them allow for different spatial, light, and scale arrangements.

Beyond looking at formal experiments, the first Seminar on Architecture in Latin America (SAL) that took place in Buenos Aires in 1985 proposed to investigate the conceptual notions of identity and modernity as a way of assessing the crisis of functionalism in the subcontinent. Not only did it expect to offset international tendencies and the sentiment of cultural dependency, it also intended to reinvigorate the discourse about architecture throughout the continent. One of the fruitful results of that first encounter—and the following ones—was the increased awareness of issues and opportunities that had remained at the margins of established international discourses. The manifestation of different voices was a sign of the postmodernist sensitivity to cultural diversity, though not of historicist, classicizing, or anti-modern positions. While architects in the West called the modernist legacy into question—functionalism in Europe and the International Style in the United States—many architects continued to follow the legacy of early modern architecture while addressing specific situations with new interpretations.[13] For all its predicaments, the idea of modernization remained central to the architectural discourse in Latin America as an ambiguous double to the efforts of cultural socialization, the fight against underdevelopment, and the growing awareness about environmental problems.

One of the examples of how architects in Latin America continued to subscribe to a modern mindset under transformed historical conditions is the consolidation, in the mid 1980s, of the idealist Open City project at the School of Architecture of the Catholic University of Valparaíso in Chile. Originally created by architect Alberto Cruz Covarrubias in the 1960s, this collective pedagogical, ecological, and cultural project associated Le Corbusier's theories with poetry, literature, and the desire for Latin American integration. The school-community focused on design-build projects, some of which are formally refined while others approach the spontaneity of buildings on the outskirts of metropolitan areas. Another example of this differentiated design sensitivity was the practice carried out by Severiano Mário Porto, Mário Emílio Ribeiro, and other architects working along the Amazon River basin between the 1970s and 1990s. Based on the study of vernacular architecture, they designed hotels, houses, clubs, and university facilities which responded to climatic conditions, merging modern and traditional construction techniques with the desire to maximize natural light and ventilation, attempting to carefully insert the buildings into their delicate ecosystems.

8.8   Pablo Tomás Beitía, Xul Solar Museum, Buenos Aires, Argentina, 1987–93

A third example of a design sensitivity that creatively questioned functionalism can be found in the work of Lina Bo Bardi, one of the few women architects whose work stands out in the Latin American context, if not in the world. She arrived in Brazil, like Clorindo Testa in Argentina, as an Italian émigrée, and her work, ranged from theoretical writing to exhibition design and from furniture to architecture. In addition to her early project for the Museum of Art of São Paulo (1957–68), the SESC Pompéia Cultural and Leisure Center (1977–86), also located in São Paulo, stands out among her projects, along with the restoration of the historic buildings in the city center of Salvador, Bahia (1986–89). These three projects summarize her life-long search to combine elements of rationalism, brutalism, and everyday and popular culture in her design work. The large SESC Pompéia project includes the

8.9   Lina Bo Bardi, SESC Pompéia Leisure Center, São Paulo, Brazil, 1977–86

revitalization of modular concrete and brick industrial sheds organized along a central alley with the inclusion of a few new architectural elements in rough concrete that allow the generic spaces to flexibly accommodate cultural and pedagogical activities. Next to the old factory, three rough concrete towers with idiosyncratic windows and details contain sports facilities separated by a channeled creek at the ground level and united by four dramatic sets of skywalks above. For the Salvador projects, her team devised a pre-fabricated system in ferrocement with architect João Filgueiras Lima and engineer Frederico Schiel to allow for the recovery of ruined historic buildings. Such experiences offered new references to the adaptive reuse of old buildings—which she described as industrial archeology—and the revitalization of historic downtowns, coupled with a growing interest in cultural memory, particularly since the late 1980s.

CONTRACTING DISTANCES, EXPANDING REPERTOIRES

While conceptual and formal experimentation expanded and shifted direction since the 1990s, the restructuring of capitalism at a global level had an ambivalent outcome with significant implications to cultural exchange and to architectural production and discourse in Latin America.[14] The economic downturn of the previous decade destabilized the power of authoritarian governments and it also yielded growing intervention from the international monetary system. This increasingly dominant world order imposed neoliberal reforms in several countries in the region. The competitive free-market model reinvigorated pockets of economic activity with its share of new investments in architectural production and particularly in the first decade of the twenty-first century. In spite of increased real estate speculation along with being unconcerned with advancing urbanistic and architectural standards, this economic model opened the way to new production and closer contact among architectural elites within Latin America as well as exposure and participation within international professional and academic circles.

At the same time, international practitioners and scholars—especially in the former colonial metropoles of Spain and Portugal—began to play an important role in promoting architects from Latin America, through awards and exhibitions, such as the Iberian-American Architecture and Urbanism Biennale shown in different cities across the north and south Atlantic. The worldwide activities of the DoCoMoMo organization (International Working Party for Documentation and Conservation of the Modern Movement) also took strong roots in Latin America, promoting the study, protection, and dissemination of the legacy of modern architecture in those countries.

Neoliberalism allowed for greater circulation and exchange of goods, information, and cultural repertoires, but it also led to significant cuts in social investments and continued uneven wealth accumulation. In this context, the association between nation-building projects in Latin America yielded the fluctuating logic of market operations, often reducing architectural practice to service provision and further undermining modernist tenets of social responsibility and collective purpose. Still, it is possible to affirm that architects working with conventional commissions have been able to expand, revise, and refine their production. Among them, those whose works easily adhere to mainstream discourses have gained more international recognition than their preceding generation, which was active between the 1960s and 1980s but more connected to local realities and cultural discourses.

The work of recipients of international prizes and recognitions coming from Latin America, such as Enrique Norten from Mexico, Paulo Mendes da Rocha in Brazil, and Solano Benítez in Paraguay, may help illustrate this changing scenario. Norten, principal of TEN Arquitectos, started his career in the 1980s, and maintains offices in both Mexico City and New York City, operating within the sphere of international business. His project for the Mexican multi-media conglomerate Televisa (1993–95) placed him on par with high-tech European architects. Not only did a familiar vocabulary facilitate his contentious selection as the first architect in Latin America to receive the Mies van der Rohe award in 1998, it also led to the recognition of similar work by other practitioners in the region. For example, the Chilean architect Enrique Browne combines the use of high-tech steel construction and natural climate-control systems as in his Consorcio Building projects (1990–2004) in Santiago and Concepción.

Other examples that have helped to re-inscribe Latin America within international architectural discourse can be found in the work of the veteran Mendes da Rocha and the young Benitez, among others. Their formal and material vocabularies offer innovation, while containing strong references to the original work of predecessors who remained ironically invisible to international critics. The studio Gabinete de Arquitectura led by Benítez, who was one of the finalists in the Mies van der Rohe award in 2001, received the first BSI Bank Foundation award granted by the Swiss banking group in 2008. Interested in the history of technique as part of social development, he combines references to other architects in Latin America such as the austere and poetic structural forms of Mendes da Rocha and the simple materials and techniques of Dieste. Examples of his interest in the investigation of building systems range from his own horizontal studio built with exposed cinder blocks and lined with wood boards to private residences in artisanal brickwork such as the Abu Font house (2005–2006) with both programmatic and building ingenuity, and the industrial building for Unilever (2000–2001) with lateral perforated concrete frames combining structural clarity, aesthetic appeal and adequate climate performance.

Mendes da Rocha started on a long and mostly introverted career in the late 1950s, designing remarkable concrete and steel structures. He received the Mies van der Rohe award in 2000 and the Pritzker Prize in 2006. His carefully composed projects advance and, to a certain extent, dematerialize the idea of orthogonal structures conceived by Artigas, with less political commitment but more international recognition than his mentor. While Artigas professed structural prowess with large reinforced concrete frame at the service of collective and social programs, Mendes da Rocha invests in the aesthetic and topographical features of his wide-spanning structures. Among his early works there are several private houses. More recently, he has designed several cultural institutions such as the

Brazilian Sculpture Museum in São Paulo (1986–95) with its extensive pre-stressed concrete portico; the rehabilitation of the São Paulo State Gallery (Pinacoteca, 1993–98) with the juxtaposition of large steel frames against the traditional brick walls; and the National Coach Museum in Lisbon (construction initiated in 2009), which proposes wide-spanning steel and concrete volumes to replace old warehouses facing Afonso de Albuquerque square and completing the museum complex of Belém district. His work has served as an imperative reference to an emerging generation of architects (such as the MMBB and SPBR architectural studios in São Paulo, and Benitez in Paraguay) who have advanced Mendes da Rocha's and Artigas's interest in the structural performance of architecture.

While some contemporary architects in Latin America have dedicated their careers to technological innovation and experimentation, others have placed their efforts in cultural and programmatic issues. Among those dedicated to cultural programs, the work of Brasil Arquitetura Studio stands out. The team's pluralistic work departed from earlier collaborations with Lina Bo Bardi, merging local and international references, adaptive reuse, and traditional and contemporary

8.10   Paulo Mendes da Rocha, Brazilian Sculpture Museum, São Paulo, Brazil, 1986–95

techniques with keen attention to the social and environmental specificities of each design situation. Among their varied work is the research center and lodging for the Social-Environmental Institute (1994–95) in the Amazon region, which combines simple geometries in masonry reinforced concrete with a large thatched canopy built according to local construction techniques. Another example is the Bread Museum (2004–2005) in the southern town of Ilópolis, which includes the conversion of a small historical building into a restaurant related to two new buildings in rough concrete and glass containing a pedagogical museum and baking school. This project is part of a larger initiative to preserve a series of historical mills built by Italian immigrants in the south of Brazil.

ARCHITECTURAL DESIGN AS CIVIC PRACTICE

In addition to single commissions, many architects working for private practices, not-for-profit organizations, and governmental offices have dedicated themselves to problems that affect large metropolitan areas, including the provision of low-income housing and public infrastructure in informal areas of urbanization. Pioneering transformative grass-roots efforts in Latin America—as, for example, the ones pursued by Brazilian architect and anthropologist Carlos Nelson Ferreira dos Santos—flourished in the late 1970s and thrived after the end of authoritarian regimes with increased attention since the 1990s. Such initiatives have grown in the shadow of the global expansion of neoliberal policies, but have also received international attention through exhibitions, awards, and publications. Several of those projects rely on the work of interdisciplinary teams bridging urban and architectural scales and technical and social concerns, as in the housing projects by Elemental S.A., a design-build team directed by Alejandro Aravena and sponsored by a partnership between the Catholic University of Chile and COPEC, the national oil company, in Santiago. Their small-scale and participatory design projects aim to counter bureaucratic projects developed in the 1960s and 1970s throughout Latin America, such as seen in the pioneering Quinta Monroy project (2003) on the outskirts of the port town of Iquique, which saved over 90 families from relocation, providing them with expandable units and basic public infrastructure.

Another team that has gained considerable visibility at the turn of the twenty-first century is the Atelier Metropolitano coordinated by Argentinean architect Jorge Mario Jáuregui in Brazil. Their most renowned work is the Favela-Bairro project developed in several shantytowns in Rio de Janeiro. Like other similar projects by different teams throughout Brazil, their initiatives propose to avoid eradicating informal settlements from metropolitan areas. These projects are multidisciplinary and their scope ranges from in-depth research and community organization and the legalization of informal land occupation to the design and construction of urban infrastructure and social service facilities, aiming to promote safe and thriving places and to integrate those urban areas with regular adjacent neighborhoods.

8.11   Elemental S.A., Quinta Monroy expandable housing project, Iquique, Chile, 2003

8.12a FJorge Mario Jauregui and collaborators, Favela-Bairro project, Morro do Alemão cable car and public facilities, Rio de Janeiro, Brazil, 2009

8.12b Jorge Mario Jauregui and collaborators, Favela-Bairro project, Morro dos Macacos housing project, Rio de Janeiro, Brazil, 2010

The relationship between architecture and urbanization remains a central topic in the architectural discourse and practice in Latin America, manifesting itself in regular and irregular settlements as well as in different scales. For example, the Colombian City of Medellín passed legislation in the early 2000s—after years of struggle with low human development indicators—to promote Integral Urban Projects (PUI), improving the living and social conditions of irregular urban areas. As it expanded other experiments with integrated public transit systems in Latin American cities such as Curitiba (Ligeirinho) and Bogotá (TransMilenio), the intervention plans for Medellín emphasized collective institutions and urban spaces.[15] Such projects range from the improvement of pedestrian transportation as, for example, sidewalks and bridges in informal settlements, to neighborhood libraries associated with public plazas, giving designers the opportunity to foreground the social dimension of buildings and public spaces. Examples of those projects can be seen in the works of Carlos Pardo, Felipe Uribe de Bedout, and Giancarlo Mazzanti, who designed referential schools, libraries, and plazas in peripheral neighborhoods of Medellín, mediating the relationship between buildings and landscape and providing open and safe collective spaces.

An analogous initiative can be found in São Paulo, Brazil, in the work coordinated by Alexandre Delijaicov through the city's Departments of Public Works and Education. In 2001, his team established the Unified Educational Centers (CEU) program, which includes school, sports and community facilities in underserved neighborhoods and uses pre-fabricated concrete structural components and is open to local architects through public competitions. These park-schools stand out in the urban landscape because of their size, regular forms, strong colors, and height. However, they are carefully placed on each site, allowing for multiple uses on the ground level and serving as social and physical references in areas where informal urbanization and material scarcity predominate. Architect João Filgueiras Lima has carried out analogous design proposals in a number of Brazilian cities. After starting his career collaborating with Oscar Niemeyer in the construction of several buildings in Brasília, he dedicated himself to low-cost prefabrication techniques. His remarkable contributions, particularly since the late 1980s, include the creation of infrastructural elements, the reurbanization of informal urban areas, and the federal SARAH hospital network, in which he and his team combine formal and technical experimentation, programmatic innovation in health treatment, and natural climate-control systems.

Aside from architects' participation in public programs and policies and the creation of non-governmental organizations, a few academic programs dedicated to problematic urban areas in Latin America have emerged at the turn of the twenty-first century, including design and research initiatives outside the region, especially in the United States. One of their most broadly advertised examples is the Urban Think Tank and the S.L.U.M. Lab centered at Columbia University in New York, directed by Alfredo Brillembourg and Hubert Klumpner. This multidisciplinary design practice has established international collaboration between academic, professional, and governmental institutions aiming to carry out projects such as the Metro Cable (2009), a cable car and social service facilities for shantytowns in Caracas. Another example of the expansion of design scope can be found in the practice of Teddy Cruz, a Guatemalan-born architect based in San Diego, California. His team operates in several border towns between the United States and Mexico and works with immigrant communities, undertaking the revision of repetitive suburban communities along the north side of that border based on observations of spontaneous constructions and urbanization patterns to the south.

OPEN DIALOGUES, NEW ASSOCIATIONS

Though such recent international initiatives have limited impact on complex local problems or on the weakening social and political content of the mainstream architectural discourse, they have helped promote dialogue and exposure among different professional design cultures. As architects expand their practices beyond their national boundaries both within and outside Latin America, they reveal the limitations of an artificially constructed continental divide. This constraint seems particularly tangible when economic and population exchanges produce increasingly complex cultural relationships that reorganize the world and large metropolitan areas into a mosaic of enclaves of overlapping symbolic repertoires, ethnic groups, wealth and poverty throughout the whole American continent. Such changes also propel the revision of established architectural discourses and their geographic, political, and symbolic criteria, revealing that architectural production is, in reality, part of a process of cultural exchange and mutual transformation and not in a naturalized hierarchical division between primary centers and derivative regional manifestations.

To continue to isolate Latin America as a geographic cluster and to attribute a unified identity to the architecture produced in it would mean to contradict its dynamism, multiplicity, and permeability. It would mean to favor the persistence of a hegemonic discourse that remains largely centered in the experiences and in the intellectual exchange among wealthy industrialized nations, especially between the two sides of the northern Atlantic Ocean. As international relationships are rearranged, it seems less certain that architectural discourse can or should continue to subscribe to the same cultural and geographic divisions and hierarchies defined by scientific and political bureaucracies that were pervasive in the second half of the twentieth century and that framed the construction of modern architecture. A survey of the architectural developments in such a vast territory in the turn of the twentieth century cannot do without the understanding that the idea of Latin America stands for a fluid and complex construct always open to new relations and new meanings. The same is true in regard to the architecture produced within such tangible and intangible boundaries. And this dilemma can be both intriguing and fascinating.

NOTES

1   Hugo Segawa, *Arquitectura Latinoamericana Contemporánea*, Barcelona: GG, 2005.

2   Marina Waisman, "Introduction," in Malcolm Quantrill (ed.), *Latin American Architecture: Six Voices*, College Station: Texas A&M University Press, 2000, 17–19.

3   Roberto Segre (ed.), *Latin America in Its Architecture*, New York, London: Holmes & Meier, 1981.

4   Enrique X. Anda, *Historia de la Arquitectura Mexicana*, Barcelona: GG, 2008.

5   Roberto Segre, *Arquitetura da Revolução Cubana*, São Paulo: Nobel, 1987.

6   John Loomis, *Revolution of Forms, Cuba's Forgotten Art Schools*, New York: Princeton Architectural Press, 1999.

7   Francisco Bullrich, *Arquitectura Latinoamericana 1930/1970*, Buenos Aires: Editorial Sudamericana, 1969.

8   Francisco Bullrich, *New Directions in Latin American Architecture*, New York: Braziller, 1969.

9   Michael Quantrill (ed.), *Latin American Architecture: Six Voices*, College Station: Texas A&M University Press, 2000.

10   Damián Bayón and Paolo Gasparini (eds), *The changing shape of Latin American Architecture: Conversations with Ten Leading Architects*, New York: UNESCO/ John Wiley & Sons, 1977.

11   Miguel Angel Roca (ed.), *The Architecture of Latin America*, London: Academy Editions, 1995.

12   Jorge Liernur, *Amérique Latine: 1965–1990*, Paris: Moniteur, 1991.

13   Roberto Segre, *América Latina: Fim de Milênio*, São Paulo: Nobel, 1991.

14   Felipe Hernández, *Beyond Modernist Masters: Contemporary Architecture in Latin America*, Basel: Birkhäuser, 2010.

15   "Medellín, 2015, "Enduring Development through Culture and Education," in Marco Brizzi and Paola Giaconia, *Visions*, Florence: Image Publishing, 2009, 194–7.

9

The Place of Commonplace: The Ordinary as Alternative Architectural Lens in Western Europe

Tom Avermaete

In Western Europe the regional and the global are no opposite categories. The global seems to realize itself through the regional and the regional is articulated in close connection with the global. A good example of this last perspective is the role that Dutch architecture started to play in the 1980s. As a small country (capitalizing on the strong reputation of Dutch modernist architecture and carried by strong state sponsorship) a handful of architectural offices managed to position themselves on a global map and – more importantly – to define themselves as recognizable regional entity on the global architectural scene. The architectural practices that thrived within this logic are too well known by now.

This chapter looks at a different point of encounter between the regional and the global in Western European architecture. Due to the structure of the book, I will address here the general area of Western Europe, excluding developments in Spain, Portugal, Switzerland, and Holland, which will be covered in other chapters. My main argument is that, though building culture in Europe is increasingly typified by unification and sameness – echoing the transnational character of real estate investment, product development and distinct architectural practices – it is simultaneously strongly characterized by regional conditions that depend upon particular construction and dwelling practices, local attitudes and building cultures and the specific availability of materials. In a lot of instances these regional particularities are neglected. Under the banners of 'globalization' and 'branding' regional conditions are exchanged for transnational forms and styles. Simultaneously, however, a range of architectural practices have developed another strategy that relies on a new engagement with ordinary local conditions, with the commonplace, and offers as such an alternative perspective for contemporary architecture. This last category of architectural practices I will address in this chapter.

REALISM AND EVERYDAY SOBRIETY IN THE UK

In Britain it was Tony Fretton with his design for the Lisson Gallery in London, who in the mid 1980s introduced a different set of minds.[1] Within a context dominated by the internationalist high-tech expression of Norman Foster and Richard Rogers, as well as by the neo-traditionalist architectural politics of the Prince of Wales and the neoclassical revival of the Krier brothers, Fretton proposed to return to the realism of the everyday:

> The buildings in British cities have been made mainly not by designers, but by builders and functionaries … The dimension they add is populist and homogenized because they are building what people like and in this way they are masters of the art of communication. From time to time, developments in building technology get incorporated in their language; steel framing, cladding, etc. … Art-architecture has a relationship to this area of building, because it is copied and turned into a generalized style, its ideas being emptied out and its forms used for other purposes.[2]

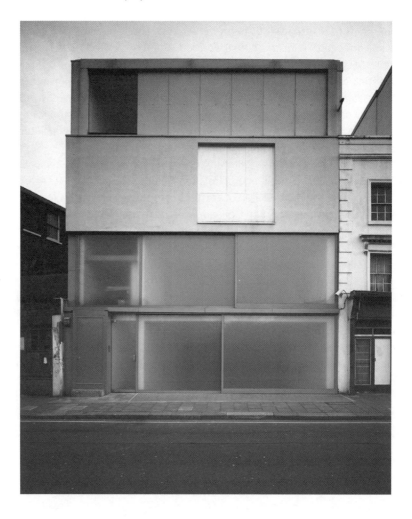

9.1   Tony Fretton,
Lisson Gallery,
London, 1986
and 1990

Fretton echoed the vision of his notable British predecessors Alison and Peter Smithson who coined the 'everyday' as a full-fledged architectural theme. Hence, not the purified forms transmitted by architectural history, but the everydayness of the anonymous architecture of the London suburbs –with its terraced houses, but also with its shops and restaurants – became the raw material for the Lisson Gallery. Within the limited programme of an art gallery, Fretton illustrated how the everyday sobriety of the London suburb could be turned into a poetic space for the arts. A simple entrance façade of which proportions and materials seamlessly integrated in the adjacent row houses, interior spaces that followed the sheer size of the plot and openings that had the sheer task to allow for light and view, formed the rudimentary recipe for the first building of the Lisson Gallery in 1986. The second part (1990) was largely conceived in the same fashion. Though the façade was somewhat more abstracted and outspoken, the aim was mainly to provide a space that would acculturate art pieces, as well as the urban context. Fretton brought the everydayness of the urban condition in the gallery and vice versa the specificity of the gallery into the urban space of the street. Materiality plays a prime role in this inversion: the façade seems constructed virtually without details and thus allows exchange between the public and the semi-public realm. The conventionality of the material of the shop windows is used to obtain this exchange: 'Materials are heavily conventional for people so in looking at a project, the prosperities of the materials will come from the idea of the project. This is what I have been thinking for a long time and I achieved it at the Lisson Gallery, which was insubstantial, intentionally insubstantial.'[3]

The dismissive attitude towards contemporary architecture in 1980s Britain, as well as the pseudo-deterministic approach of Foster and Rogers, brought also David Chipperfield towards a detailed engagement with everydayness. In his first assignments he was especially interested in engaging with the complexity of the ordinary – too often banned in the name of focus in the design process or clarity of aesthetics. Chipperfield stated: 'I am not obsessed with the idea of a clean sheet. In think that we are in a continuum and that our responsibility is to find clues in memory and context. That is what for me is potent about European architects we admire – such as Siza. There is a familiarity and yet there is a shock, and I find that jolt very interesting.'[4]

In early projects like the Mews Studio (London, 1987) and the Knight House (Richmond Surrey, 1987) Chipperfield acted as a designer that intervenes in a historically pre-established and charged context. Though strongly informed by a modernist idiom, Chipperfield's architecture is never sterile; it rather applies a method in which he uses a number of materials in a kind of assembly. The dynamic of the composition is a function of the way that the different materials react to the existing context of an industrial building (Mews Studio) or a terraced house (Knight House), as well as towards each other. Central in this composition is the consideration of the multiplicity of ordinary spaces. Chipperfield's early projects are sober but layered; they are abstract and multifaceted compositions of space, form, light and material that resonate with the complexity of everyday life.

Tony Fretton and David Chipperfield acted as important sources of inspiration for the work of their younger colleagues Adam Caruso and Peter St John, who also cultivated an approach of 'seeing things as they are'.[5] Accordingly, there is for them no good or bad site: 'No matter how unpromising a situation there is no such thing as an uninteresting site: you just add … I find it difficult to justify demolition today'.[6] Realism is a very important characteristic of the approach of Caruso-St John, but especially the idea that architecture is always about adding to existing constructions and meanings would become a main attitude. In their work, the site is conceived as a 'ground', in both a physical and a painterly sense, upon which building takes place.

9.2a, b   Caruso St. John Architects, One-family house, Lincolnshire, 1993

The one-family house that they designed in Lincolnshire (UK, 1993) offers a good example of this attitude. Located on a small plot at the edge of a village, the simple house was rendered in brick, black roof tiles and wooden panelling. The typology and outlook of the house was designed to complement the English village, and is carefully positioned in relation to an old brick barn and some mature trees. However, in this house the form and material articulation are not the only means that are activated to create a meaningful relationship with the surrounding agricultural landscape. The interior also participates in relating the house to its typical English context.

The interior composition of the house refers to traditional English manor houses with various living spaces organized around a central hall. This dramatic tall space generates frames views into the various living spaces and out into the landscape. The varied sizes and seemingly random placement of the window openings lend the house scale and a sense of whimsy. The reveal of the brick wall around the window openings is covered with galvanized steel frames so that the thickness of the wall disappears and the attention is drawn to the matter and texture of the brick façade.

MITIGATED MODERNISM IN BELGIUM

In Belgium it was not a grand rhetoric of historical form or the supremacy of high-tech expression, but rather a lack of large-scale assignments that fostered an interest in the ordinary. In contradistinction with neighbouring countries like France or the Netherlands, Belgium politicians had never allied with modern architecture –in the form of large housing projects or innovative institutional buildings – as a way to promote the post-war welfare state.[8] Rather they promoted private initiative, and as a result, the building culture of the 1970s and 1980s in Belgium was characterized by two tendencies: large-scale projects designed by commercial offices with little sense for innovation, and small-scale (private housing) projects produced by real estate developers in neo-traditionalist styles that were equally innovative.

Within this particular landscape avant-garde architects were drawn to small-scale assignments like one-family houses or even small renovations and alterations in the realm of housing. Out of this condition emerged a very unique sensibility for everyday practices of inhabitation. In the region of Flanders there were several architects who started to work with this sensibility. They referred to the basic compositional and formal moves of modernism, but mitigated the abstract character of some of the modern forms through a detailed interest in everyday practices.

The work of Juliaan Lampens set – in radical terms – the tone for a series of small-scale experiments with the everyday realm of dwelling.[9] In his House Vandenhaute – Kiebooms in Ghent (1967), Lampens started a meticulous investigation into the organizational elements of the private house: Lampens coupled his search for an architecture of inhabitation and experience, with an investigation into the basic elements of architecture. In the footsteps of modern masters as Mies van der Rohe, he defined the house as a few walls and a continuous roof, but the rich palette of Miesian materials is substituted here with the reticence of rough-cast concrete. The result is an impressive landscape of natural and cultural elements that offers a rough frame for the everyday practices of dwelling.

9.3a   Juliaan Lampens, House Vandenhaute – Kiebooms, Ghent, 1967

A reinvestigation of the basic elements of architecture seems also to inform the work of Christian Kieckens.[10] In his essay 'Timeless Space beyond Conception and Perception', Kieckens reacted to the architectural culture of the 1970s: 'concepts such as participation, monuments care, semiology, ecology … disguise or excuse the lack of architecture'. Instead Kieckens proposed a return to the essence of architecture:

> Architecture – as a myth – stripped of all its technology and reduced to her
> basis, or better to her geometrical purity, always falls down on the same basic
> principles. History itself shows us a range of timeless architecture such as
> the Pyramids, the villas of Palladio, the Cenotaph by Boullée, etc. A historical
> analysis proves that constant values as 'timelessness" and "geometry" are to be
> understood as a synthesis between the avant-garde of the past and the maniera
> moderna of the future.[11]

Kieckens' architecture is indeed a *recherche patiente* into a possible synthesis between timelessness and zeitgeist. In the Van Hover-De Pus house in Baardegem (1991), there are references to a modernist aesthetic, but these are balanced with a precise attention for more perennial architectural qualities such as proportion, rhythm, light and view. Through an enormous sense for detail and a high degree of control, Kieckens managed to create a house that seems close to the everyday practices of dwelling – because of the attention for small-scale details – and at the same time distanced from it – because of its pristine precision and finished character. The house is for Kieckens indeed an architecture beyond conception and perception, beyond the temporary authorship of as well architects as inhabitants. It is a contribution to, and inscription in, a discipline that has long-lasting principles.

The work of Marie-José van Hee aims also at a re-assembly of the basic elements of architecture and illustrates some affinity with the approach of Adolf Loos in its meticulous attention for the character and scale of transition spaces, its attention for the interlocking of rooms and for the thresholds between inside and outside,

9.3b   Christian Kieckens, House Van Hover-De Pus, Baardegem, 1991

between the private and the public sphere, between day and night zones.[12] However, Van Hee is not applying this modern sensibility to a mansion or villa that is located on a larger plot, but rather using it for one-family houses within an urban context – acculturating the principles of Loos to an ordinary Belgian situation. The architect shares Loos's concern with the house's ability to project the qualities of physical and psychological shelter, and hence avoids radical formal gestures in favour of a basic, almost archaic expression.

A good example of her approach is a courtyard house in Prinsenhof, in an old quarter of the city of Ghent that Van Hee designed for herself. The house is built around an L-shaped gallery and a covered patio. In between the living spaces and the outside city garden are multiple larger and smaller mediating places. But also in between the

9.4a, b, c   Marie-José Van Hee, House Prinsenhof, Ghent, 1990–1998

public sphere of the street and the privacy of the domestic sphere a nuanced play of architectural elements is at stake: the high windows in the front facade deprive every look towards the street, but nevertheless bring the roofs of the houses across even closer. Stairs that are positioned at different points in the house provide an infinite circulation. The architecture of Marie-José van Hee encompasses a sort of layering that is articulated with great but rudimentary detail, continuously arousing surprise.

Paul Robbrecht and Hilde Daem were fellow students of Marie-José van Hee and Christian Kieckens.[13] They share an interest in the autonomous qualities of architecture, focusing on basic elements as materiality and detail and basing themselves on the modern tradition but also on more historical predecessors. With the 'Interventions-Inventions' project for the existing medieval Mys House (1983, together with Christiaan Kieckens), they investigated the architect's position as a latecomer in the work of centuries – an important lesson – adding here, cutting away there. Through additions and cuts they created ambivalent views, sharp communications and floods of light. Not only are their spatial interventions the last in a long line of transformations, they cede the foreground to discreet art works by Juan Muñoz and Thierry De Cordier.

This attitude of continuously relating to the existing while projecting the new plays an important role throughout the work of Paul Robbrecht and Hilde Daem. It is most convincingly illustrated in their design for a concert hall in Bruges (1999) – in one of Belgium's immaculately preserved medieval city centres. The design criteria for the concert building referred to openness, innovation and a modern image but also to the existing and the ordinary. The result is a building that is reminiscent in its composition of the work of Hans Scharoun and Hugo Haring. The enormous amorphous volume of the concert hall is at odds with the city of Bruges because of its sheer scale, but simultaneously it is strongly attuned due to its terracotta tiling which refers to the red

9.5   Paul Robbrecht and Hilde Daem, Concert hall, Bruges, 1999

roofs of Bruges urban landscape. The Lantern Tower, slightly separate from the main volume, refers to the many tower buildings in the historical centre of Bruges while given it a new function (chamber music hall for 300 people) and expression.

For the Mariaplaats in Utrecht (1994), Belgian architect Bob Van Reeth relied on ordinary urban typologies as a way to mediate between the open form of the modernist city and the closed morphology of the urban block in the historical European city.[14] In this project Van Reeth conceived of an urban configuration that was composed by apartment buildings that are positioned in the middle of the block and single-family row houses forming the perimeter. The lower massing of the row houses opens the complex to the surrounding city.

The architect uses the combination of different building types to generate an engaging and varied urban experience. The diverse spaces achieve continuity by sharing an urban logic and material palette. The ground-level passage through the block forms a lovely public domain for the residents, and is accessible to other city dwellers. As such, Mariaplaats receives is meaning as a fragment of the ordinary urban pattern and its web of secondary public spaces.

FIGURES OF LANDSCAPE AND TACTILITY IN SCANDINAVIA

In Scandinavia the context for a renewed interest in the ordinary can be regarded as a reaction to an existing tradition of mass design for the everyday, as well as to a large post-war interest in prefabrication. The different Scandinavian governments had been relying on construction methods of prefabrication to fulfil the ambitions of the welfare state to provide housing for the greatest number. This resulted in large housing estates that arose mostly on the outskirts of cities. Surprisingly also the private sector of contractors and developers shared the state interest in prefabrication and started to develop prefabricated single-family houses, called *parcelhus*, throughout the different Scandinavian countries, soon provoking widespread criticism from architects and urban planners, who condemned the monotonous neighbourhoods of single-family dwellings as well as the high-rises estates for their sense of isolation and anonymity.[15]

As a reaction to this criticism several architects started to focus again on the qualities of ordinary materiality and everyday landscapes. One of the earliest proponents of this approach was the Danish architect Jørn Utzon. His Terrasserne project designed in 1963 and located on the outskirts of the small town of Fredensborg is designed as an alternative to the suburban house on its often under-sized plot of land.[16] The design's underlying principle is simple: extremely compact private houses with a limited amount of outdoor space, which Utzon compensates for with collective facilities and a common landscape. In Fredensborg house and site are one: 165 square meters defined by the materiality of a yellow brick wall, featuring living areas, garage, storage and a small patio. These patio houses are arranged side by side, like stone chains in the landscape.

Utzon uses the savings in budget and space to develop a community centre that features all the functions that could not be accommodated in the houses themselves: guest rooms, work rooms and a party room with a professional kitchen. The space saved by the small patios is used for a large collective green space which adjoins the community centre and is accessible only to pedestrians. It not only facilitates residents' communal activities, but also serves as an extension of the private garden via apertures in the walls around the houses. In 1965 the prominent critic Sigfried Giedion described this feature of Terrasserne as follows: 'The relation between the individual and the collective spheres is a problem which has preoccupied generations but whose solution becomes increasingly urgent. Very few have succeeded in expressing this as an architectural form. In Utzon's project … instead of a small scale landscape of minuscule gardens the site displays a spacious generosity.'[17]

Also the Finish architect Reima Pietilä was simultaneously investigating the possibilities of landscape and materiality as elements of an alternative approach to the monotony and anonymity of mass housing.[18] In his Suvikumpu project in Tapiola (1967), Pietilä attempted to combine modularity with variety, with typical apartment units linked in long, staggered lines, forming terraces of varied height across the forested landscape. The elevations of the single buildings are articulated as a patchwork of small material surfaces, as a way of breaking down the building's external surface, of fragmenting the rational whole into a skin that echoes the chiaroscuro of the forested site.

In his St Peter's Church in Klippan (Sweden, 1966) he illustrates how the use of this ordinary material offers the possibility for a new architectural presence. The designs of Lewerentz are marked with a continuous investigation into the latent meaning that is embedded in the materiality of buildings. In order to activate this meaning Lewerentz dissociated material from technique and held that it was possible to conceive of architectural form directly from a material basis. In Klippan all of the design attention is directed toward the materiality of the wall: the presence of brick supersedes all other concerns.

9.6   Reima Pietilä, Suvikumpu housing, Tapiola, 1967

9.7   Sigurd
Lewerentz, St
Peter's Church in
Klippan, 1966

In order to achieve this presence a specific detailing is required: bricks are composed according to a particular bond and joints are flushed in a rough fashion so as to underline the material qualities surfaces. As a result, the brick surfaces present themselves as an envelope that entails walls, ceilings and floors. It forms a tactile surrounding that encloses the user and embeds him in an atmosphere of textures, patterns and materials.

Utzon, Pietilä and Lewerentz drew – with their focus on everyday landscapes, tactility and materiality – the thematic horizon for the work of a new generation of Nordic architects in the last decades of the twentieth century. A good example is the Danish architectural office Vandkunsten that turned perspectives on the ordinariness of materials and landscapes into a productive field for architectural design. The Blue Corner housing project (Copenhagen, 1989) demonstrated how strikingly modern buildings can complement older neighbourhoods with historical character through particular material choices.

Vandkunsten's choice of materials such as corrugated steel made the project different from the ordinary stucco facades of the adjacent nineteenth-century buildings, while referring to everyday construction methods of the twentieth century. A similar Janus-faced approach can be found on the level of the building typologies, in which the building roofs are turned at right angles to those of their neighbours. The Blue Corner housing project illustrates how careful attention to mass and form, combined with particular awareness of materiality, allows for nuanced attitudes of modern building in an existing context.

9.8   Vandkunsten,
Housing project
Blue Corner,
Copenhagen, 1989

QUOTIDIAN MATERIALS AND PRINCIPLES OF CONSTRUCTION IN FRANCE

Architectural culture in France had since the middle of the 1970s been characterized by an openness to new European and American experiences.[19] The ideas of Carlo Aymonino and Aldo Rossi on the urban dimension, as well as the reflections on architectural history made by Louis Kahn and Robert Venturi would have important influence on French architectural culture, as evidenced in the main architectural periodical *L'Architecture d'Aujourd'hui*, as well as in the curricula of the new architecture schools which came after the transformation of the École des

Beaux Arts. As a result, as Jean-Louis Cohen noted, 'French architecture set out on a course of conceptual and formal diversification.'[20]

It is against the background of the strong re-capturing of historical forms and narrativity, as of a particularly French continuing belief in Corbusian modernism, that an interest in the ordinary developed within French architectural culture. In the 1980s several French architects started to engage with ordinary forms and especially materials and principles of construction. These practices engaged from a variety of angles with typologies and construction methods that can be found in ordinary built environments and use these to devise innovative architectural approaches.

One of the key moments in this tendency was the design for the social housing complex called Nemausus (Nimes, France, 1986) by French architect Jean Nouvel (1945), who employed materials and techniques normally associated with industrial buildings[21] The project attempted to harness the benefits of industrial building methods – such as standardization and mass production – to provide more affordable dwellings. Nemausus was built in the south-west of Nimes as part of a larger programme of revitalizing public housing neighborhoods built in the 1960s. Nouvel raised the two seven-storey buildings on piltois, providing parking underneath and framing an existing public space shaded by two rows of trees. Continuous balconies cantilevered along both sides of each slab provide gallery access to the apartments on the north side and spacious terraces on the south side.

As a housing project Nemausus stands out for its material characteristics. The balustrades' inclined panels are made from galvanized industrial grating whose perforated forms strongly marks the outside appearance of the buildings. The roof ends are made up of PVC louvers that are normally used for agricultural applications. In this repetitiveness of materials and elevations a variety of flats, duplexes and triplexes are created. For the division of the concrete structural frame into different apartments Nouvel uses simple corrugated aluminum panels, aluminum windows and white-painted bi-fold doors that offer not only a variety of dwelling typologies, but also a complete new expression of mass housing.

9.9   Jean Nouvel, Nemausus housing, Nimes, France, 1986

Dominique Perrault, a graduate of the École des Beaux Arts and a first-hand witness of the rise of postmodernism in France, was also a proponent in this

reaction against an architecture of exaggerated effect and explicit narrative quality.[22] Perrault's approach encompassed a reliance on pure geometry, more specifically the geometry found in the ordinary industrial typologies that appear as the most common denominators of towns and urban landscapes. In his design for the Hotel Berlier (1986–90) – a project containing industrial premises and offices – he illustrated how the *esprit de géométrie* of quotidian industrial architecture, combined with an *esprit de finesse* could offer a new-fangled expression of exquisite roughness. Between the transit roads, train tracks and fluvial passages of the Parisian *boulevard périphérique* Perrault positioned his rectangular block with a completely glazed skin, characterized by a simple geometry and meticulous constructive rigour.

Perrault does not endorse his building with recognizable details or elements. Instead he his giving it the neutrality of a warehouse; strips of perforated industrial metal grating is placed along the inside of the glass façade. These continuous louvers do not only play a role in the climatization of the glass building, but – as shelves – also offer the possibility to display some of the artefacts that are made or used within the industrial premises and offices. As a result the plain glass box gets a texture. This approach of the façade is also recognizable on the level of the plans, where only a very limited amount of elements is defined and the rest is left to the user. Perrault initiates with his Hotel Berlier an open architecture in which space is multiplied in impermanent definitions and locales, an operational architecture of territories privileging mobility and interactivity in the definition of space.

Other French architects that take ordinary materiality and construction methods as their point of departure are Anne Lacaton and Jean-Philipppe Vassal. The work

9.10   Dominique Perrault, Hotel Berlier, Paris, 1986–1990

of Lacaton and Vassal openly proclaims to be a reflection about and a search for architectural economy:

> *The question of economy seems particularly important to us. In the relationship between construction and materials, economy today constitutes that material – it is no longer concrete, steel or stone, as it used to be. In that sense, manipulating and organising the economic aspect becomes very interesting, so that it can then offer the maximum of possibilities … Taking account of the real, the everyday, in a positive way, transforms situations so that generous designs can then be created that the inhabitants will appropriate. Luxury does not cost much.*[23]

Maison Latapie in Floriac (1993) is a good example of this economical approach. Situated in the inner suburbs of Bordeaux, the house fits into the contour of the street with its simple volume on a square base. The house is divided into two halves – one opaque and the other transparent – by the contrasting claddings (fibre cement and PVC) hung on its metal structural skeleton. Inside the fibre cement portion of the house, wood panelling defines the heated winter zone. It opens onto a greenhouse and the outside world, on the street side. The house can thus switch from being very enclosed to very open, depending on the family's requirements and their desire for light, privacy, protection and ventilation. The house's living

9.11   Anne Lacaton and Jean-Philipppe Vassal, Maison Latapie, Floriac, 1993

spaces vary with the season, expanding to embrace the garden in summer and contracting into smaller rooms in colder months. The house becomes not only a receptacle of everyday living practices, but – more importantly – accommodates their continuous redefinition.

THE COMMONPLACE

Engaging in particular ways with ordinary materials, construction methods, building typologies and landscapes has become a commonly held strategy amongst several architectural offices in Europe during the last decades of the twentieth century. The conditions and drivers from which this interest in the ordinary emerges, as well as the architectural approaches that result from it differ. Nevertheless, this survey starts to delineate regions of sensibilities within this more generally held attention for the ordinary. It illustrates the possibility of defining resonance, kinships and affinities in those architectural practices that actively engage with these ordinary conditions –well-knowing that the ordinary is always a function of specific cultures of building, dwelling and thinking.

One of these affinities is most prominent: the choice of these different architects to regard architecture as field of expertise that is not only related to the exclusive domain of professional norms and forms, but also to everyday meanings and 9.s. With this search for a balance between specialized and generalized architectural knowledge, the discussed architectural practices distance themselves from more globalizing architectural tendencies that retrieve both in sheer exclusivity or flat commonness. This is what binds the different discussed approaches: they take a critical position vis-à-vis globalizing processes by redefining architecture through an engaged encounter with the commonplace.

NOTES

1   For a general introduction to the work of Tony Fretton see Tony Fretton and Kunstcentrum deSingel (Antwerp Belgium), *Op Zoek Naar Openbare Ruimte: Vier Architecten Uit Londen = in Search of Public Space: Four Architects from London* (Antwerp: deSingel, 1997), Sophie Parry et al., *Home/Away: 5 British Architects Build Housing in Europe: British Pavilion: De Rijke Marsh Morgan, Maccreanor Lavington, Sergison Bates Architects, Tony Fretton Architects, Witherford Watson Mann* (London: British Council, 2008).

2   Fretton and deSingel (Antwerp Belgium), *Op Zoek Naar Openbare Ruimte*, 78.

3   Interview with Tony Fretton at: http://www.floornature.com/architetto_intervista. php?id=5159&sez=5. Consulted on 25 July 2011.

4   Interview with David Chipperfield by Adam Caruso and Peter St John, theme issue 'David Chipperfield 1991–1997', *El Croquis*, no. 87 (1998), 8.

5   An introduction to the work of Caruso St John can be found in Philip Ursprung (ed.), *Caruso St John: Almost Everything* (Barcelona: Ediciones Poligrafa, 2008), and Adam Caruso, 'You Choose the Language in Accordance with the Context', *ORIS Year*, no. 51 (January 2008), 34–53.

6   Irenee Scalbert, 'On the Edge of Ordinary: Two Houses by Caruso St John', *Archis* (March 1995), 50–61.

7   See Theme issue 'Sergison Bates', *2G: International Architecture Review*, no. 34 (2005) and Sophie Parry et al., *Home/Away*.

8   Bruno De Meulder, Jan Schreurs and Bruno Notteboom, 'Patching up the Belgian Urban Landscape', *OASE Architectural Journal*, no. 52 (1999), 78–113.

9   An introduction to the work of Lampens can be found in Angelique Campens (ed.), *Juliaan Lampens* (Brussels: ASA Publishers, 2010) and Paul Vermeulen et al., *Juliaan Lampens* (Antwerp: DeSingel, 1991).

10   The work of Chistian Kieckens is well introduced in Christian Kieckens et al., *Searching, Thinking, Building* (Ghent-Amsterdam: Ludion, 2001) and William Mann, 'Between Memling and Descartes: Two Buildings by Christian Kieckens', *Archis*, no. 1 (1997), 8–15.

11   Christian Kieckens, 'Timeless Space Beyond Conception and Perception', *GA Houses*, no. 14 (Tokyo, 1984), 45–7.

12   A discussion of the work of Van Hee is given in André Loeckx, Marie-José van Hee, William Mann, *Marie-José Van Hee Architect* (Ludion, 2002).

13   The projects of Robbrecht and Daem are discussed in Steven Jacobs, Paul Robbrecht and Hilde Daem, *Works in Architecture: Paul Robbrecht and Hilde Daem* (Ghent: Ludion, 1998) and Maarten Delbeke, Paul Robbrecht and Stefan Devoldere, *Robbrecht en Daem: Pacing through Architecture* (Cologne: Walther König, 2009).

14   Geert Bekaert, *A.W.G. bOb Van Reeth Architects* (Antwerp: Ludion, 2000).

15   A summary of this criticism can for instance be found in Ingrid Gehl, *Bo-miljø (Dwelling Environment)* (Copenhagen: Teknisk Forlag, 1971) and Jan Gehl, *Life between Buildings: Using Public Space* (New York: Van Nostrand Reinhold Publishers, 1995 (original title: *Livet mellem husene* (Copenhagen: Arkitektens Forlag, 1971)).

16   An introduction to the Terrasserne project can be found in, amongst others, Henrik Sten Moller, Vibe Udsen and Per Nagel (eds), *Jørn Utzon: Houses* (Copenhagen: Living Architecture, 2006) and in Michael Juul Holm, Kjeld Kjeldsen and Mette Marcus (eds), *Jørn Utzon: The Architect's Universe* (Copenhagen: Louisiana Museum of Modern Art, 2008).

17   Siegfried Giedion, 'Jørn Utzon and the Third Generation: A New Chapter of Space, Time and Architecture', in *Zodiac: A Review for Contemporary Architecture*, no. 14 (1965), 46–7.

18   For a discussion of the work of Pietilä see Malcolm Quantrill, *Reima Pietilä: Architecture, Context and Modernism* (New York: Rizzoli, 1985).

19   See Jean-Louis Cohen, 'New Directions in French Architecture and the Showcase of the Paris City Edge (1965–90)', in Alexander Tzonis and Liane Lefaivre, *Architecture in Europe since 1968: Memory and Invention* (New York: Rizzoli, 1992), 32–3.

20   See Jean-Louis Cohen, 'New Directions in French Architecture and the Showcase of the Paris City Edge (1965–90)', in ibid., 33.

21   Philip Jodido and Jean Nouvel, *Jean Nouvel: Complete Works 1970–2008* (Stuttgart: Taschen, 2009) and Olivier Boissiere, *Jean Nouvel* (Basel : Birkhauser, 1996).

22   A good introduction to the work can be found in Dominique Perrault, *Dominique Perrault Architecture* (Basel: Birkhauser, 1999).

23   Tom Avermaete, 'The Spaces of the Everyday: A Dialogue between Monique Eleb en Jean-Philippe Vassal', *OASE Architectural Journal* (81), 79.

10

Dutch Modern Architecture: From an Architecture of Consensus to the Culture of Congestion

Frances Hsu

This chapter links the social concerns associated with Dutch Structuralism, led by Aldo Van Eyck, to the vision of metropolitan dynamics advocated by Rem Koolhaas and the Office for Metropolitan Architecture (OMA). It examines how structuralist critiques of the modern movement evolved into an architecture founded on the values of consensus, and the rise of SuperDutch as a new international movement with Koolhaas and OMA taking pivotal roles in debates on the relationship of built form to social interaction.

DUTCH STRUCTURALISM

The Dutch structuralist movement in architecture developed from dissatisfaction with CIAM. During preparations for the 10th meeting at Dubrovnik in 1955, Aldo van Eyck, Alison and Peter Smithson, Jacob Bakema, Shadrach Woods, William Howell, and others who formed Team X challenged the technocratic, social unresponsiveness of the older generation of mainstream modernists (mainly Jose Luis Sert, Walter Gropius, and Sigfried Giedion). Broadly speaking, the positions separated the pragmatism of the younger generation from the idealism of the older one. Team X developed principles on the organization of urban growth through "deep structures," a term transposed from French anthropologist Claude Lévi-Strauss's work on systems of kinship and language.[1] An ideological split within Team X occurred when Van Eyck attacked the abstraction of modern architecture in the work of Smithson and Bakema, who used mega-structure-like housing blocks and elevated pedestrian decks to address individual space and identity. Van Eyck rejected functionalism, replacing "space" and "time" with "place" and "occasion" as the ontological categories of architecture. He became the editor of *Forum* magazine and presented the journal at CIAM 1959 in Otterlo as a platform for his ideas to place the human point-of-view at the center of the design process and to create an architecture of memorable situations and activities.[2]

10.1   Collage, left: Aldo Van Eyck, Sonsbeek Pavilion, Arnhem, 1966. Right: OMA (Rem Koolhaas, Elia Zenghelis, Kees Christiaanse, Stefano de Martino, Ruurd Roorda, Ron Steiner, Alex Wall, Jan Voorberg), Parc de la Villette, Paris, France, 1982–83

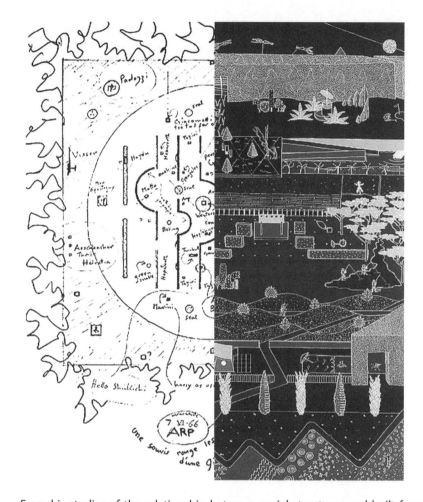

From his studies of the relationship between social structures and built form in African Dogon settlements Van Eyck asserted the importance of vernacular values and building form for psychological well-being. The constructions of the indigenous culture were additive in nature and used a limited range of related components arranged in a limited range of variations according to a particular set of rules based on the social patterns of the inhabitants. Van Eyck's empirical research translated loosely into an architecture that rejected composition and monumentality in favor of more or less flexible arrangements of interchangeable but generally clearly defined spatial units, categorized and then systematically combined to reflect social structures. He viewed the dwelling as a microcosm of the city and the city as an analogy for the dwelling, corridors were analogous to streets and urban squares were analogous to living rooms. The Amsterdam Orphanage (1957–60) is his paradigmatic work of this period that correlates built form to social structure. His "tree-leaf" diagram explained the principle of reciprocity between part and whole, and offered an alternative approach to the architectural theories of other groups drawing on structuralism, such as the New York Five, who referred to structural linguistics and treated the building envelope as a formal language.

The Structuralist emphasis on a bottom-up design approach was based on user agency. It contributed to the evolution of two new building types: aggregated forms or "mat-buildings," often modeled on the traditional North African form of settlement known as the casbah; and constructions in which architects controlled a framework within which others could find freedom to develop user-friendly forms. Systematic treatment of structural and functional demands, and opportunities for growth are seen in examples such as Van Eyck's Sonsbeek Sculpture Pavilion (1966) and Piet Blom's project for the Prix de Rome, SOS Village (1962). The Centraal Beheer Office building (1968–72) in Apeldoorn by Herman Hertzberger, consists of a number of equal spatial units, building blocks, which due to size and arrangement are adaptable to varying programmatic requirements. It is a poeticized version of mat-building, sacrificing compositional ideas for provision of individual place-making.[3]

The social motivations of post-war Dutch architecture were identified as Populist, associated with the international architectural debates that viewed the architect as a facilitator rather than as an autonomous designer.[4] This group included Ralph Erskine and Lucien Kroll, whose buildings were the product of participatory design processes, as well as authors including Christopher Alexander, who developed systems of form, or grammars, for a range of urban configurations and architectural types. Bernard Rudofsky, in *Architecture without Architects*, examined global indigenous and vernacular solutions for building.[5] The Populists were one of the more politicized positions that redefined the role of the architect and the architectural project. They did not impose an elitist architectural tradition but rather focused on programmatic, participatory needs and issues like flexible design. In certain circles they were overtly anti-intellectual.

PARTICIPATORY DESIGN

Western European architecture had developed from 1910 to the 1930s with a strong social orientation, maturing in the Netherlands without the difficulties faced by some other European countries during the First World War due to Dutch neutrality. After World War II, during the '50s and '60s, participatory design processes were put in place by Dutch government agencies to assist in reconstruction. For example, the Alexanderpolder (Rotterdam, 1956) by Jacob Bakema, was designed according to the "Neighbourhood Concept": green space in the district, organized hierarchically, consists of small private gardens, somewhat larger communal gardens, and parks for sport and recreation. Maintenance is a collective responsibility—the residents care for the green space as communal property.[6] Municipal "building for the neighbourhood" initiatives enabled community committees to be instrumental in the selection of projects to be constructed. Large-scale urban renewal projects for the Kop van Zuid, an abandoned shipping port on the south bank of the Maas River adjacent to the city centre of Rotterdam, span from plans of the late 1970s for transportation infrastructure and low-income social housing to more recent development of public spaces and buildings driven by public-private partnership.

Public participatory activity was intensified by a parliamentary political system that strove for broad consensus as a whole. Post-war public protests in favor of construction and/or renovation of housing led to higher living standards. Social innovation addressed inclusive models of living other than the nuclear family, such as singles, elderly, and two-person households. Cost-effective construction techniques based on pre-fabrication and replication methods were developed and widely used for housing and other communal building types including schools, libraries, and community centers.[7] Generally speaking, citizens were considered as individuals rather than members of the anonymous masses. Projects that were varied in massing with "humane" scale such as the Amsterdam Nieuwmarkt residential complex (1970–1975) by Van Eyck and T.J.J. Bosch were built in contrast to the monolithic high-rise developments that represented the failed promises of the modern movement. Ultimately, the rhetorical appeal made by the Forum group, including Van Eyck's abstract notion of the "city as a village" was replaced by a focus on concerns (such as sensory deprivation and "flat neurosis") drawn from the social sciences. Architects viewed the decade of the 1970s as a period of "consensus terrorism" … in which the goal was "to make architecture and urbanism disappear as a monumentally visible presence … the massive repression of architectural ambition … and (buildings were) made to blend in with existing neighborhoods formally and politically as well as socially."[8]

POSTMODERNISM

In their late phase, the the Dutch branch of CIAM produced works removed from their earlier ideas about the structure of space, yet criticized postmodern architecture for its lack of logic. Van Eyck argued for his own humanist interpretation of the modernist tradition, defending functionalism in his 1981 RIBA lecture "Rats Posts and Pests" even though he had criticized the modern movement for its rationality at the 1947 CIAM VI meeting in Bridgewater.[9] As architects born in the thirties who came of age during CIAM founded offices in the postmodern period they developed pluralist design approaches. A range of cultural, institutional, and civic building based on modernist compositional, geometric, and tectonic idioms includes the work of Wim Quist (Kröller-Müller Museum extension, Otterlo, 1969–77 and Schouwburg Municipal Theater in Rotterdam, 1988), Carel Weeber (*De Peperklip* housing, Den Haag, 1982), and Cees Dam (Amsterdam City Hall and Opera, with Wilhelm Holzbauer, 1979–87).

TRANSITION TO A NEW MOVEMENT IN THE MAKING: OMA AND THE RISE OF METROPOLITAN DYNAMICS

The earliest projects in the Netherlands by Koolhaas, Madelon Vriesendorp, Elia Zenghelis, and Zoe Zenghelis, the original partners of OMA, were designed following the publication of Delirious New York (1978). As such, they addressed the "culture of congestion" and "programmatic instability," ideas in Koolhaas's his first book with antecedents in the work of Le Corbusier and Sant'Elia as well as cities such as Manhattan. The 1979 competition entry for Extension to the Dutch Parliament in The Hague is a collage of monumental Suprematist and Constructivist forms in extreme contrast with the existing medieval complex. The Netherlands Dance Theater (1980–87) is an assemblage of everyday materials and motifs.[10] (Figure 10.2) The three areas of the program are individually expressed and juxtaposed: Volumes for a stage and auditorium, rehearsal studio, and complex of offices and dressing rooms are stacked loosely together with an off-balance, non-Platonic collage aesthetic composed with a deft touch. The auditorium volume displays a mural designed by Madelon Vriesendorp. On the interior, the underside of the auditorium seating above slopes diagonally downward towards the back of the deep lobby space to create an exaggerated perspectival view.

The emergence of the OMA office in Rotterdam as an international voice coincided with a number of factors set in place in the 1980s. During this decade, the waning influence of architectural activity in Amsterdam, the spatial center of Structuralist activity, allowed Rotterdam to evolve into an incubator with strong ties between academia and professional practice. The city, known for its modern architecture, offered inexpensive office space compared to Amsterdam (the historical city) and The Hague (the government seat). The density was such that architects often not only shared an office building but sometimes also the same office space within buildings. Rotterdam was the site of new institutional infrastructure including the Netherlands Architecture Fund, the Netherlands Architecture Institute (whose new headquarters building designed by Jo Coenen opened five years after its founding in 1988) and 010, an independent publishing house established in 1983 by Hans Oldewarris and Peter de Winter, architect and urban designer, trained at Delft University.[11]

10.2   OMA/ Rem Koolhaas, Netherlands Dance Theater, The Hague, 1980–87

The decade also witnessed the growth of an extensive system of national grants and competitions offering building opportunities to younger as well as foreign architects who adapted modernist conventions to new ends. Delft University architecture students Francine Houben, Henk Döll, and Roelf Steenhuis won the competition for young people's social housing on Rotterdam's Kruisplein (1981–85), part of a government initiative to accommodate communal living quarters and a flexible apartment types that could be aggregated to allow for various use options. For two low-cost housing blocks in the district of Schilderswijk West (1983–93) in The Hague, Portuguese architect Alvaro Siza adapted "international style" architecture by borrowing materials, building heights, and typical entry conditions from the area, and adapting floor plans to suit the customs of the Muslim residents. The international invited competition to design The Hague City Hall resulted in the construction of Richard Meier's City Hall and Library (1986–95) even though the entry by OMA won the jury's vote. In contrast to Meier's formalist composition of carefully articulated elements clad in gleaming white porcelain panels enclosing a multi-story atrium, OMA's scheme is configured as a collection of towers informally assembled to suggest the outline of an urban skyline. The concept is based on planning for the generic office building with adaptable flexibility on the office floors that allow for user appropriation. The project explores principles of the "open city" and functional indeterminacy put forth by the Allison and Peter Smithson.

A primary characteristic of almost all OMA buildings, from small to extra large, is the concern with networks of circulation. Multiple, interwoven spatial experiences traversing public and private realms--occurring both within the building and linking outside and inside--often involve ramps and elevators. OMA's Souterrain Tram Tunnel (1990–2004) in The Hague was conceived as a multilevel complex of underground tunnels and ramps connecting Metro stations. For the apartment building Amsterdam Nord (IJ-Plein, 1981–88), zig-zag stairs running along both the longitudinal center of the building and in the transverse direction connected to the exterior circulation gallery are the major feature of two public housing slabs. Glass is used for roofs, exterior wind walls, and on the interior to separate kitchen from living room. A public street that runs underneath the slab raised on pilotis with market and retail on the ground floor urbanizes the ground plane.

The design strategy of overlaying a series of formal and programmatic layers onto the site was introduced in the masterplan of IJ-Plein (1981–88), a residential complex located on the Bijlmermeer polder opposite the city center of Amsterdam. The layers, each with autonomous geometric and functional logic, ideally allow for chance encounters and unexpected behaviors. They are a counterpoint to the mono-functional planning of the housing complex built in the late 1960s following CIAM principles for strict zoning and separation of traffic. The first layer of parking brings cars into the development, the next layers are a linear arrangement of marketplaces along a boulevard, a patchwork of greenery, and a confetti of informally placed buildings, for the school, community center, and two housing blocks, connected by pedestrian pathways. The last layer assigns open spaces for various sports and leisure activities. The strategy of programmatic layers has a hybrid origin in the New York skyscraper and the Constructivist social condenser.

Its purest form is found at Parc de La Villette (1982), OMA's design for a vast cultural park, situated on the former site of the central slaughterhouse of Paris from the nineteenth century to the 1960s. (Figure 10.1). This territorial re-imagination of the public realm based on the organization of fields and bands of programmatic flux engages citizens in its ongoing process of formal and programmatic definition.[12]

SUPERDUTCH: THE ASCENT OF THE NEO-MODERN

Koolhaas conceived the 1990 symposium held at Delft University entitled "How Modern is Dutch Architecture" as part of his preoccupation with the social aspects of modernism. He argued that current day architects were increasingly unable to effect change in contrast to the Russian Constructivists, Manhattan's architects, and Ludwig Hilberseimer, whose works proposed alterations of how people lived and catalyzed events that "happened and continue to happen on more that just visual levels." A year later, the Dutch entry to the 1991 Venice Biennale encapsulated contemporary Dutch architecture as "Modernism without Dogma." The view of architecture in the Netherlands as modernist form without content, style without substance, was presented to an international audience by Neutelings Reidijk Architects, the firm of former OMA collaborator Jan Willem Neutelings.

The influence of Koolhaas over a whole new generation was seen at the exhibition *Reference OMA: The Sublime Start of a New Generation* (Netherlands Architecture Institute, 1996), which attributed a new architectural landscape to former OMA collaborators. Essays by curator Bernard Colenbrander and historian Jos Bosman addressed the work of OMA, MVRDV, and Neutelings as the inventive reworking of mat-building and "street in the air" typologies, Team Ten's reactions to and extensions of the work of Van Eyck. In the late 1980s and early 1990s, it was *de rigueur* for international professional periodicals such as *Archithèse*, *l'Architecture d'aujourd'hui*, and *A+V* to devote special issues to architecture in the Netherlands and to OMA. Terms such as *fresh conservatism* were coined as "a means of understanding what is going on in the current landscape of the "avant-garde" … not something purely Dutch."[13] *Supermodernism* denoted the "superficiality and neutrality" held in common by the work of Koolhaas, Toyo Ito, Jean Nouvel, Dominique Perrault et al.[14] In the words of Dutch historian, critic, curator, and architect Bart Lootsma, *SuperDutch* signaled a "Second Modernity" determined by internationalization, global economy, and rapidly developing information technology.[15] These terminologies conflated architecture in the Netherlands with the next "ism" following postmodernism.

SuperDutch: New Architecture in the Netherlands (2000) (Figure 10.3) based the notion of a new international architecture on national identity. The eponymous term branded Dutch architecture of the nineties as part of a kind of second Golden Age surpassing both the strenuous national social objectives of building for the neighborhood in the seventies and the play on formal idioms of the eighties. According to Loostma, Dutch architects freed themselves from the conventions of architectural modernity in order to respond to "global economies and information technologies" through large-scale projects that, encouraged by private investors who filled the void left by the withdrawal of state subsidies, differed from the government-driven piecemeal approach to urban renewal prevalent in previous decades. The autonomy of the architect and of design resulting from the loosening of intertwined relationships between architect and planners was demonstrated by the inventive work of 12 firms, including Wiel Arets, UN Studio, Nox/Lars Spuybroek, OMA, MVRDV, Neutelings Reidijk, Kas Oosterhuis, Kees Christiaanse, Koen van Velsen, Eric van Egerrat, Atelier van Lieshout, and Mecanoo.

The SuperDutch were identified with the search for design processes that question conventions, new ways of interrogating context, and innovative means for the analysis of program. They also developed formalist approaches to design. The headquarters for Karbouw (1990–92) building contractors in Amersfoort were the first buildings by Ben van Berkel and Caroline Bos, founders of UNStudio, an interdisciplinary practice for architecture, urbanism, and infrastructure in Amsterdam. The building is a horizontal slice of concrete and metal panels with horizontal and vertical shifts in slightly angled non-orthogonal planes producing a dynamic, sculptural quality. The concrete and glass planes of the Mobius House (1993–98) follow the lines of the loop that traces the 24-hour living and working cycle of the client family. Surface treatments are seen in the NMR Facility (Nuclear Magnetic Resonance) at the University of Utrecht (Figure 10.4). The austere and

10.3 *SuperDutch*, by Bart Lootsma (Princeton Architectural Press), with cover image showing Wozoco Housing for the Elderly, Amsterdam, by MVRDV, 1994–97

10.4   UNStudio, NMR Facility (Nuclear Magnetic Resonance), University of Utrecht, 1996–2000

pristine volumes of the Academy of Art and Architecture in Maastricht (1989–93), one of the earliest buildings by Wiel Arets Architects, are constructed with translucent glass block panels held by a concrete frame structure.

The Minnaert Building (1994–97) for the University of Utrecht Faculty of Mathematics, Information Technology, and Geophysics by Willem Jan Neutelings and Michiel Riedijk contains classrooms, laboratories, and restaurant (Figure 10.7). In the vast interior gathering hall, the result of efficient space planning, a pool captures rainwater streaming in from openings in the ceiling. The water is pumped daily through grills on the lower floor to cool the computer laboratories then flows back into the pond where it cools at night. The water level rises and lowers according to the seasons and in the winter may freeze. A series of seating compartments on the perimeter of the hall are used for study and meeting areas. The volume is faced in red-pigmented concrete graphically patterned with a large-scale ripple effect.

The work of Mecanoo, founded by Francine Houben and Erik van Egeraat in 1984, is noted not only for attention to detail and juxtaposition of materials and color but also for the social life of interior and exterior spaces. The Faculty for Economics and Management (1991–95) on the Utrecht University campus masterplanned by OMA is based on the casbah, a model used by Van Eyck (Figures 10.6 and 10.7). Mecanoo's three-storey, shallow bar building is enveloped with a neutral facade enclosing a sheltered interior of rooms, halls, footbridges, stairs and leisure places. Three large patios with different layouts allow light to enter the building. In the largest patio luxuriant bamboo suggests a jungle, while the other two are more calm—a Zen garden and a 'water' patio provide a glimpse of the charming landscapes. The facade has various forms—sometimes exposed and sometimes

10.5   Neutelings Riedijk Architecten, Minnaert Building, University of Utrecht, 1994–97

10.6   Mecanoo, F aculty for Economics and Management, University of Utrecht, 1991–95

10.7   Mecanoo, F aculty for Economics and Management, University of Utrecht, 1991–95

with a veil or skin. Facades of cement slabs are concealed behind steel grids and wooden lattices in seemingly random trellis patterns. Other parts of the facade have their entire breadth covered with gigantic blinds, a series of moveable aluminum lamellas."[16]

The work of West 8 exemplifies strategic thinking that crosses boundaries between architecture, urban design, and landscape design. Founded by Adrian Geuze, the office designs frameworks within which urban dwellers act and interact. Situated in the city centre of Rotterdam, Schouwburgplein (1990– 97) is surrounded by the city theatre and a cinema complex. The surface of the urban square, suspended above an existing underground parking garage and made of wood and metal with a pattern reflecting the former harbour of the city, acts as a stage for and leisure activities. Lights for night-time illumination and fixtures to accommodate temporary structures are incorporated into the floor thickness. West 8 designed the furniture and crane-like lights, operable by users, that line the square. The firm was master planner of Borneo Sporenburg (1993–98), a development on two narrow islands located a short distance from the city center of Amsterdam, marketed to offer suburban living in the city. The designers created a high density and variety of architect-designed 3-story residences with private terraces and gardens organized in rows that exploited the concept of life on the water's edge. A wide variety of Dutch and international architects participated in this project, a few are Stéphane Beel, Kees Christiannse, Ben van Berkel, Herzog de Meuron, Steven Holl, Jose Luis Mateo, MVRDV, Neutelings Riedijk, and Koen van Velsen.

Lars Spuybroek and his office, NOX, research the relationship between art, architecture, and computing. Their work links continuous geometries to the Gothic, Picturesque, and Art Nouveau traditions. D-Tower (1999–2004), is an interactive urban monument that changes colors with the emotions of its town's citizens, a hybrid of media in which architecture is part of a larger interactive system of relationships. The intensive (feelings, *qualia*) and the extensive (space, quantities) exchange roles where human action, color, money, value, and emotions all become networked entities. The project consists of a physical building (the tower), a questionnaire and a website (www.d-toren.nl). The tower is a 12-meter high structure where standard and non-standard geometries together make up a complex surface, made of epoxy formed by a computer generated molding technique (CNC milled Styrofoam). This surface is very similar to a Gothic vault structure, where columns and surface share the same continuum. HtwoOexpo (1994–97) is a water museum equipped with real time electronics to activate the senses and emotions (Figure 10.8). Spuybroek's aesthetic exploration diverges from the egalitarian tradition of "flexible" programmatic design that has sustained Dutch modern architecture.

The work of MVRDV (an acronym of founders and ex-OMA collaborators Winy Maas and Jacob van Rijs, and Nathalie de Vries) exploits the urban, programmatic, or commercial forces of a project. Their publication Metacity/Datatown (1999) contrasts consumption and thrift in Holland. The divisive and humorous Pig City (2001) is a project for optimizing the production of pork through a series of 76 towers. The architects extrapolate and expand upon programmatic requirements, building codes, and urban conditions as creative tools to generate datascapes that inform their designs.

Their approach opposes the social models that support modern movement ideology: the deployment of "scientific" data to objectify functional concerns and identify "loopholes" in logics contests the idea of consensus as the driver for design decisions.[17] The client for the Wozoco (1994–97) slab in Amsterdam was a large housing corporation who wished for gallery circulation and a high density of units. The elderly housing buildings were designed

10.8   Lars
Spuybroek/NOX,
HtwoOexpo,
Neetlje Jans, the
Netherlands,
1994–97

to economically and spatially optimize unit depth and width and to maximize outdoor space, with 13 of its apartments cantilevering from the main volume. Variations on window positions, balcony sizes and materials give units their own identity within the collective. Silodam (1994–97) is a housing slab built on the site of a former dam with a sunken parking machine and renovated silo buildings (Figure 10.9). The program of offices, commercial, public, and semi-public spaces as well as over 150 units, clustered into "neighborhoods" for a mix of different social groups, of various size, cost, daylight requirements, facade treatment, and organization (single- or double-height, harbor or side views, patio) resulting from market trends and community discussion.

The Kunsthal (1992) by OMA, a gallery for temporary installations, refutes the role of an elite art institution. (Figure 10.10) A ramped public passageway dissects the building and connects the front of the building along the highway to the back, facing the garden. The entry is located midway along the passageway. Galleries are organized around a circuit of pedestrian ramps from the garden to the roof that traverses the exhibition halls, auditorium, cafe, and bookstore. The building further disrupts the monolithic representation of culture with media that refer to both high and low culture, everyday, often inexpensive materials—such as plastic, metal grids, a retaining wall made of a special black stone used for building dykes and a rhythm of the tree-trunk columns in the ground floor gallery that continues in the garden beyond—as well as materials of mass production, steel, glass, asphalt, and concrete. Perception of the Kunsthal changes depending on the position of the viewer. The street facade is photographed to recall the portico of the *Neue Nationalegalerie* in Berlin, Mies van der Rohe's temple to high art. On the west elevation, concrete columns emerge at right angles from the inclined ground plane of the auditorium to introduce the reality of parking garage construction to this cultural building.[18] The garden facade resembles the elevation of Le Corbusier's unbuilt project for a Congress Center in Strasbourg.

10.9   MVRDV, Silodam, Amsterdam, 1994– 2007

10.10   OMA/ Rem Koolhaas, Kunsthal, Rotterdam, 1992.

THE OMA PHENOMENON

Koolhaas and OMA continue to explore design strategies that optimize the interplay of circulation and program. The continuous folded floor slab was conceived as a folded urban void in the competition project for the Jussieu Library (1992) at the University of Paris. It is realized in the Educatorium (1997) at the University of Utrecht (Figures 10.11 and 10.12) where the ramp engenders chance encounters.

10.11   OMA/Rem Koolhaas, Educatorium, University of Utrecht, 1997

10.12   OMA/Rem Koolhaas, Educatorium, University of Utrecht, 1997

Each project is an argument for social infrastructure as the last remaining task for the modern architect.[19]

OMA projects often rethink the core assumptions of a given program. In a competition entry for the extension to MoMA (1997) in New York, for example, the entire ground floor level of the renowned art institution is radically given over to the public, ironically reintroducing the street to the "revolutionary experience" of modern art isolated above. Historian John Summerson stated in the late 1950s that, "The source of unity in modern architecture is in the social sphere, in other words in the architect's program."[20] OMA sets up various relationships to institutions in which programming is crucial. Working from the ground up, through a series of "small" statements, a critique is created through the accumulation of work that indexes the shifting spatial, political, and social conditions of program.

The irreverent attitude of OMA work, which at times deliberately ignores conventional criteria or sensibilities, can be seen as another way to create critical form. Despite Koolhaas's rhetoric, which ostensibly accepts and even celebrates the practical limits of change through architecture, the designs themselves evidence a critical position vis-à-vis the discipline. The modernist mat-building typology derives from a structuralist conception of architecture as a framework for circumstantial or idiosyncratic factors rather than the reflection of an overall rationalizing process. In OMA work, this typology transforms into a metropolitan culture of congestion and field of programmatic flux and flow. Koolhaas (and to an extent the SuperDutch, particularly MVRDV) opposes Dutch culture's consensus-driven ethos and its repression of architectural ambition. Instead, the arc of his forbearer's trajectory is redirected, away from consensus and towards the radicalization and reframing of problems, with implications for the agencies and freedoms of users that renew the debates of Dutch Structuralism.

NOTES

1   Claude Lévi-Strauss, *The Elementary Structures of Kinship*, 1949, and *Structural Anthropology*, 1963.

2   From 1959 to 1963 and in 1967 other editors included Bakema, Herman Hertzberger, Dick Apon, Gert Boon, Joop Hardy, and Jurriaan Schrofer.

3   Herman Hertzberger, "Structuralism: A New Trend in Architecture," *Bauen + Wohnen* 30/1 (1976): 23. See also *Structuralism in Dutch Architecture*, W.J. van Heuvel, 1992.

4   Alexander Tzonis and Liane LeFaivre, "The Populist Movement in *Architecture*," *Forum* 3 (1976).

5   Ralph Erskine, Byker Wall Housing at Newcastle-upon-Tyne, England, 1973 to 1978; Lucien Kroll, Medical Facility Housing, Leuven, Belgium, 1970–76. Christopher Alexander, *A Pattern Language: Towns, Buildings, Constuction* (Oxford University Press, 1977); Bernard Rudofsky, *Architecture without Architects: A Short Introduction to Non-Pedigreed Architecture* (MoMA, 1965).

6   See Jaap Bakema. Presentation sheets for Alexanderpolder, Rotterdam, 1956. Collection NAi, BAKE t134.

7   "The Engagé 70s, Acquisition Plan 1968–1979," http://en.nai.nl/collection/about_the_collection/item/_rp_kolom2-1_elementId/1_341754; "Conversation Pits and Cul-de-Sacs: Dutch Architecture in the 1970s" (NAI, 2010).

8   Wouter Vanstiphout, "Consensus Terrorism: The Dutch 70s," *Harvard Design Magazine*, Summer 1997, number 2. Vanstiphout is founder of Crimson, a Rotterdam-based group of architectural historians that connect contemporary Dutch architecture directly back to ideologies of the 1930s. Scholarship states that "No other decade was shaped to such an extent by conflict and contrasts as the 1970s and no other period in the history of Dutch architecture arouses so much passion, resistance and revulsion." Martien de Vletter, *The Critical Seventies: Architecture and Urban Planning in the Netherlands 1968–1982* (NAi, 2004).

9   Aldo van Eyck, "Rats Posts and Pests," *RIBA Journal* 88/4 (April 1981): 47–50. Aldo van Eyck, "Statement against Rationalism," in *Aldo van Eyck Writings*, Amsterdam, 2008.

10   Robert Venturi, the Smithsons, and others considered the everyday elements of contemporary life critical to modern art and architecture. Bernard Tschumi shares Koolhaas's interest in Surrealist shock and provocation through the unplanned or unexpected juxtaposition of those elements.

11   See "The Battle for the Netherlands Architecture Institute," in Patricia van Ulzen, *Imagine a Metropolis: Rotterdam's Creative Class, 1970–2000* (Rotterdam, 010, 2007), 10.

12   Caroline Constant, *The Modern Architectural Landscape* (University of Minnesota, 2012).

13   "Fresh Conservatism: Landscapes of Normality," Roemer van Toorn, *Quaderns*, 1997. "Fresh Conservatism is a conceptual frame, a means of understanding what is going on in the current landscape of the 'avant-garde' in architecture, art and film … The Dutch do perhaps form a vanguard in the domains of architecture, industrial design and graphic design."

14   Hans Ibeling, *Supermodernism: Architecture in the Age of Globalization* (NAi, 1998).

15   Bart Lootsma, *Superdutch* (Princeton Architectural Press, 2000).

16   www.mecanoo.nl.

17   Ibid.

18   Kathy Battista and Florian Migsch, *The Netherlands: A: A Guide to Recent Architecture* ((Ellipsis, 1998).

19   From an unpublished book of competition texts compiled by OMA for its employees.

20   John Summerson Summerson, "The Case for a Theory of Modern Architecture," in Joan Ockman (ed.), *Architecture Culture 1943–1968*, (Rizzoli, 1996), 226–36.

11

Metaphorical Peripheries: Architecture in Spain and Portugal

Xavier Costa

MODERNITY AS A CONTEXT

Spanish and Portuguese architecture of the twentieth century should be interpreted within a wider context that is first and foremost European and has in the last few decades been on a global scale. Iberian architects have struggled throughout this century with the dual condition of finding themselves stranded on the geographic and cultural periphery of the continent and, at the same time, of upholding a tradition and a set of ideas that are recognizably their own. Although the course of the countries' histories during the twentieth century have been marked by periods of political and cultural isolation, the best Portuguese and Spanish architecture has managed to maintain an ambitious curiosity and the intellectual stature that fully entitles it to be interpreted and appraised from an international perspective.

SPAIN

The architecture in Spain produced during the first three decades of the century was clearly indebted to that of the nineteenth century. Both Madrid and Barcelona developed and implemented their plans for urban expansion, conceived by Castro and Cerdà, respectively, and approved in the mid-nineteenth century. Leading architects of the early years of the twentieth century worked with ideas and vocabularies that originated in the previous century, which fused a variety of romantic and historicist influences. They imbued generally Beaux-Arts practices with local, traditionalist and neo-colonial elements, derived from the academicism dominant in the architecture schools of Madrid and Barcelona, themselves founded during the second-half of the nineteenth century. Certain Catalan architects such as Domènech i Muntaner and Puig i Cadafalch combined their architectural work with an active political sensibility, while in Madrid Antonio Palacios imposed an essentially monumental architecture that coexisted with more forward-looking works such as those by Secundino Zuazo, and with the urbanism of Arturo Soria for the "Linear City" and of Rafael Bergamín and others in the development of the *colonias* or residential suburbs.[1]

The architecture of a historicist and monumental stamp was to achieve its supreme expression in the two great events of 1929: the Ibero-American Exhibition in Seville dominated by the contribution of Aníbal Álvarez, and the International Exhibition in Barcelona with its general plan conceived by Puig i Cadafalch. In contrast to these operations governed by conceptions of architecture rooted in the nineteenth century, that same year of 1929 saw the construction of Josep Lluís Sert's first work, the Casa Duclós in Seville, and the German Pavilion in Barcelona, by the German architect Ludwig Mies van der Rohe. These two architects marked the first steps in the introduction into Spain of the architecture of the Modern Movement then emerging in central and northern Europe. Sert, together with other architects of his generation such as Fernando García Mercadal, José Torres Clavé, Joan Baptista Subirana, Germán Rodríguez Arias, Sixto Illescas, and Ricardo Churruca, had already invited Le Corbusier to lecture in Barcelona and Madrid, and had helped organize the exhibition in the Galerías Dalmau that resulted in the creation of the GATEPAC (Group of Spanish Architects and Technicians for the Progress of Contemporary Architecture).

The Interwar Period

As in other parts of Europe, the Modern Movement in Spain sought to publicize and disseminate a particular architectural culture. Spanish architects engaged their foreign peers by means of exhibitions, publications, new magazines such as *AC*, participation in CIAM (Congrès International d'Architecture Moderne) and a very active range of contacts with such European architects as Le Corbusier and with some of the leading politicians of those years. Sert and GATEPAC attained significant expression in the Spanish Republican Pavilion for the Paris International Exhibition in 1937. This pavilion, in which Luis Lacasa was also involved, was in effect a cooperative undertaking between architects and artists, and included artworks by Alexander Calder, Joan Miró, Julio González and Pablo Picasso, who painted *Guernica* for the occasion.

Many of the architects who were most active during the Republic, and to a greater or lesser extent sympathetic to its political principles, were subsequently forced into exile abroad or subjected to a form of internal exile which severely curtailed their chances of receiving commissions. Antoni Bonet Castellana went to Argentina, where he designed the splendid residential development of Punta Ballena in Maldonado (Uruguay), while Félix Candela worked in Mexico, Germán Rodríguez Arias in Chile, and Luis Lacasa in the Soviet Union. Sert himself took refuge in New York in 1939, where he commenced a series of urban projects for various countries in Latin America, in addition to succeeding Walter Gropius as head of the Graduate School of Design at Harvard University. In due course Sert was again able to build (albeit sporadically) in Spain, notably with two works for Joan Miró: the artist's studio in Palma de Mallorca and the Fundació Miró in Barcelona.[2]

11.1   Antoni Bonet Castellana, Villa La Ricarda, El Prat de Llobregat, 1949–1961

11.2   Josep Lluís Sert, Joan Miró Studio, Palma de Mallorca, 1953–1957

The Fifties and Sixties

One of the consequences of the Spanish Civil War was to attenuate the continuity between the GATEPAC generation of architects and the generations that followed them, who were in effect obliged to rediscover Modern architecture. This second generation in Spain can be characterized by its extensive and important work in the field of housing, directly linked to large-scale movements of population and urban expansion, and also to new styles of living that reflected the progressive modernization of the country and the emergence of a new culture of the habitat which came to be associated in the sixties with new forms of leisure and the impact of mass tourism.

The years immediately after the Civil War provided a number of opportunities to test out new models of urbanism, particularly in the new settlement towns that had to rationalize the distribution of the rural population, followed by the satellite towns built to accommodate the new migratory movements on the outskirts of the great cities, above all Madrid. Other similar initiatives were referred to as new towns or experimental towns, and all together they constituted a highly important area of activity. Other key works from this period are the Gobierno Civil building in Tarragona and the Maravillas gymnasium in Madrid, both by Alejandro de la Sota. With the sixties came further new examples of residential architecture, such as the Torres Blancas complex by Francisco Javier Sáenz de Oiza, and the work being done in the Basque Country at the same time by Luis Peña Ganchegui, whose housing projects in the sixties sought to combine Modern architecture with local elements drawn from the Basque building tradition.

11.3   Francisco Javier Sáenz de Oíza, Torres Blancas, Madrid, 1961–1968

Meanwhile, in Barcelona the Group R set out to redefine the legacy of the Republic, combined with a manifest interest in the subsequent evolution of architecture in other countries. Led by Oriol Bohigas, Josep Maria Sostres, Antoni de Moragas, and José Antonio Coderch, the group's members were responsible for some of the most influential ideas and works to appear in the whole course of the century, such as the Ugalde house and the apartment building in Barceloneta by Coderch, both from 1951, and the MMI and Iranzo houses by Sostres, which date from the latter half of the fifties. These were years when housing assumed an indisputable importance, exemplified in a series of key works by Francesc Mitjans, Oriol Bohigas and Josep Maria Martorell, who in collaboration with other architects developed such residential and urban schemes as the Escorial Street and Maragall complexes in Barcelona. These complexes brought a new urban perspective as well as an innovative approach to collective housing.[3]

Once again, throughout these years the relationship, however tenuous, with the European context was decisive. Coderch was present at the meetings of Team 10 at which that group set out to redefine Modern architecture in the late fifties. In addition to this contact with British and Dutch architects, Coderch established strong links with leading Italian architects, particularly with Gio Ponti, a relationship he cultivated to significant effect from Barcelona during the following period. European design and architecture in the sixties owed a great deal to the leading role of Italy, and in particular to the Milan–Barcelona axis.

The Prodigious Decades

The relative opulence that the economic boom and the first waves of tourism generated on certain sectors of Spanish society was reflected in more refined, more cosmopolitan, and more expressive architecture as a manifestation of the comfort that was also extending into other design fields. A certain continuity with the work of Coderch can be seen in practices such as that of the Federico Correa and Alfonso Milà team, who created a highly sophisticated architecture that embraced various aspects of design, ranging from industrial to interior design, incorporating

11.4   Luis Peña Ganchegui and Eduardo Chillida, Peine del Viento ('Comb of the Wind'), San Sebastián, 1975–1976

11.5   José Antonio Coderch de Setmenat, Casa Ugalde, Caldes d'Estrac, 1951–1952)

the new languages derived from pop culture, media and advertising—as in the Flash-Flash restaurant in Barcelona. Their legacy is present in the ironic stance of Studio PER (Tusquets, Clotet, Bonet, Cirici), who also produced their own exclusive lighting and furniture designs, or in Carlos Ferrater's more personal interpretation of Coderch's legacy.

Other expressions of the cosmopolitanism of the sixties can be seen in the early works of Ricardo Bofill, whose residential blocks on carrer Nicaragua and in the Barri Gaudí in Reus were to lead to the incomplete apotheosis of the great Walden 7 housing complex in Sant Just Desvern, in the 1970s. As one of the few architects of his generation with a substantial European education and experience, Bofill introduced a new interest in megastructures and an Italianized blend of architecture, landscape and interior design. Later, Bofill moved towards a more eclectic mixture of stylistic moves that progressively tended towards a grand neoclassicism founded on a vague political argument that the new collective architecture deserved the monumentality of historic structures.

The optimism and explosion of ideas of the sixties and seventies is reflected in other highly significant figures, such as Rafael Moneo, who developed an early interest in Scandinavian architecture and worked with the Danish architect Jørn Utzon. Moneo, one of the most influential architects of the last quarter century, is outstanding for his contributions to both professional practice and teaching, first in Madrid and Barcelona and since the mid-eighties at Harvard University, where he taught and chaired its Department of Architecture. Moneo made his name in the seventies as a provocative theorist and author of some of the most stimulating texts of the last decades, being actively involved in journals like *Arquitecturas Bis* and *Oppositions*. As a fellow at the New York Institute for Architecture and Urban Studies, he built a rich connection between the Iberian tradition and the emerging North American debate. He also promoted the work of the Portuguese architect Alvaro Siza, securing his international stature. Among his built works, the Banesto office building on Madrid's Paseo de la Castellana comprised a powerful statement that became the basis for his later trajectory. The National Museum of Roman Art in Mérida (1980–93) marked a decisive inflection in which he combined a cultured and rigorous appreciation of his region's history with a thoroughly contemporary response to a museum program.

The Merida museum represented turning point in Modern architecture's relationship to the built heritage, and by extension to historical references, a major concern during the 1980s, when the museum was designed. The museum is located in the heart of the Roman colony, so its lower levels reveal an archaeological excavation of the ancient town. Whereas Modern design applied to existing structures had always emphasized the need for a strong contrast between the new elements and the historical ones, so that any confusion could be avoided in a quasi-pedagogical way, Moneo introduced a more subtle and complex concept of analogy in architectural design. The new museum is inspired by the materiality, tectonics and spatial organization of classical design. The use of brick, arches, and massive walls illuminate the visitor's understanding of Roman construction, yet it clearly defines a contemporary building. The geometry of its parallel walls cuts through the existing, irregular geometries of the archaeological site.

Merida exemplifies a strategy of letting history impregnate contemporary design that became an effective alternative to the ubiquitous banalities of post-Modern historic revivals, based solely on stylistic and formal quotations from historical references. It thus served as a built manifesto for another understanding of how the past could be readable in the present, a hermeneutical problem that gained special weight in the architectural debate of the time. Within Moneo's personal trajectory, it also represented a turning point that allowed him to instill a classical sense of space and structure in his otherwise Modern designs.

Moneo followed the National Museum of Roman Arts with a wide–ranging output of structures of great coherence and continuity, including works in the United States (the Davis Museum, the Museum of Houston) and more recently in Sweden (the Museum of Art and Architecture in Stockholm). As an educator, writer, and practicing architect, Moneo represents the fullness of contemporary architecture in Spain, only surpassed in the twentieth century by the figure of Sert.

In Barcelona, the extraordinary blossoming of architectural culture has largely been due to the decisive contribution of Bohigas, who after spearheading Group

11.6   Rafael Moneo, Kursaal Auditorium, San Sebastián, 1990–1999

11.7   Rafael Moneo, Kursaal Auditorium, San Sebastián, 1990–1999

R went on to direct the ETSAB Architecture School during its most brilliant period, before becoming city councilor for urbanism and culture, successively. Bohigas orchestrated the ambitious architectural, cultural and media operation that culminated in the 1992 Olympic Games, the zenith and end point of these prodigious decades in Catalan architecture. Under the guidance of Bohigas, Barcelona was the catalyst that revitalized the architecture of the rest of Spain, which achieved moments of extraordinary synergy in the works of a series of architects of note: Juan Navarro Baldeweg, Antonio Cruz and Antonio Ortiz, and Guillermo Vázquez Consuegra; and, in Barcelona, Josep Llinàs, EliasTorres, Carlos Ferrater, Jordi Garcés and Enric Sòria, Helio Piñón and Albert Viaplana, Eduard Bru and Josep Lluís Mateo.

In partnership with Josep Maria Martorell and David Mackay, Bohigas also designed the outstanding low-income housing at Pallars Street, investigated new typologies for school architecture for institutions such as Garbi and Tau in Barcelona, and promoted a social approach to contemporary architecture in combination with a Team 10 sensibility for public space, and an emerging attention to local traditions that would later be named as critical regionalism by Kenneth Frampton.

11.8   Elias Torres and Martínez Lapeña. Restoration of City Walls. Palma de Mallorca, 1983–1992

11.9   Elias Torres and Martínez Lapeña. Restoration of City Walls. Palma de Mallorca, 1983–1992

11.10 Oriol Bohigas, Josep Martorell and David Mackay, Thau School, Barcelona, 1971–1975

This body of work has coincided with a steadily increasing interest in Spanish architecture at the international level. The quality of so many of the Spanish magazines (*Arquitecturas Bis, Quaderns d'arquitectura i urbanisme, El Croquis, Arquitectura Viva*); the organization of exhibitions devoted to the work being produced (such as *Contemporary Spanish Architecture*, which travelled to Chicago and New York),[4] and the inviting of leading foreign architects to take part in this ambitious project of generating a new Spanish architecture—from Alvaro Siza to Norman Foster, from Arata Isozaki to Frank Gehry—have awakened a global interest in Spanish architecture.

Towards the Twenty-First Century

The whole range of architectural production stimulated directly or indirectly by the climate of the 1992 Olympic Games of Barcelona has marked the conclusion of a phase in which discourses and built work have coincided under the aegis of public-sector policies that have greatly favored Spanish architecture. Since the late nineties, however, this situation has given way to a profound inflection that heralded the emergence of new ideas in a markedly different environment. The generation that started working during these years has highlighted still further the need to think Spanish architecture on the global scale, at the same time defining the channels that serve to guarantee and communicate this presence. A particularly eloquent example of this is the recent and tragically curtailed trajectory of Enric Miralles, who in addition to his extensive body of work in various parts of Spain designed major new projects in Holland (the City Hall in Utrecht) and in Scotland (the Scottish Parliament in Edinburgh). Another key architect in these years is Alejandro Zaera, who in tandem with his former teaching at the Architectural Association in London has produced a highly significant body of writing and won a major competition for the Passenger Terminal in Yokohama.[5]

Other influential architects of the turn of the century have been Inaki Abalos and Juan Herreros, who worked together until recently. Their joint work was developed in the field of architectural design as well as in a rich compendium of writings,

11.11   Enric
Miralles and
Benedetta
Tagliabue, Town
Hall Extension,
Utrecht, The
Netherlands,
1997–2000

11.12   Enric
Miralles and
Benedetta
Tagliabue, Town
Hall Extension,
Utrecht, The
Netherlands,
1997–2000

coupled with significant academic activity both in Spain and North America. At another level, the work of Spanish architects has been greatly promoted by publishers like Gustavo Gili, El Croquis and ACTAR. The latter is a group that has been effectively innovating in the publishing fields of architecture, design, and the arts, becoming a powerful platform from where new work could be internationally presented and disseminated.

The emergence of new schools, of new groups, of new architectural imprints and magazines, of new forms of support from various institutions for programs in favor of architecture, together with an effective change-over of generations, all usher in a change of century with an intense and innovative panorama ahead, and with the impetus of the significantly high level of activity that has characterized Spanish architecture over the course of the last decade. The phenomenon of recent Spanish architecture at the turn of the century, and its robust international projection needs to be understood in the context of a professional community solidly supported by the structure of the professional organizations (Colegios), as well as dependant on an abundance of public commissions and public competitions that have fairly offered opportunities to younger generations and to designers with a more experimental or conceptual twist in their trajectory. Other parameters to be included in this phenomenon are the aforementioned publishing groups, which have promoted and disseminated the work of Iberian designers equating them to the main international names. One should also include the influential work of institutions such as the Mies van der Rohe Foundation and the early period of the Museum of Contemporary Art (MACBA) in Barcelona, or the exhibition space of the Arquerias de Nuevos Ministerios in Madrid, among others, that have consistently promoted the public presentation of contemporary practice from a critical perspective. At the international level, the Museum of Modern Art's exhibition *Spain Builds* effectively summarized a few years ago the vitality of this period, discovering powerful emerging figures, such as Enric Ruiz Geli, Nieto and Sobejano, RCR Arquitectes, Mansilla and Tunon, Francisco Mangado, or Jose Morales.

PORTUGAL

Portuguese architecture shared with Spain a progressive transition into Modernism. The critical time, however, was the decade of the 1950s, when the early works of architects such as Fernando Tavora and Alvaro Siza started to develop, leading to the role of the Porto school as one of the most influential and admired in contemporary times. Tavora has been an exceptional figure in the twentieth century, defining the direction of the profession and its values. Several generations of architects have seen him as a fatherly character, owing to him the course that Portuguese architecture took in the second-half of the century. His participation in the famous "Survey of Portuguese Architecture" (Inquerito a arquitectura regional portuguesa) documented thoroughly the legacy of popular buildings in the country, and defined a political compromise for the professional community.

Tavora's main works were modest buildings like the Barrio de Ramalde in Porto, or the Municipal market at Santa Maria da Feira, both designed in the early 1950s. His work as an educator at Porto was equally influential, and decisive for the future course of the school. Siza completed a series of structures in the small town of Matosinhos, near Porto, in the fifties as well, such as the Piscinas das Mares pools, several houses, and the Casa de Cha Boa Nova restaurant. Later in his career, some of the main designs are the new school of architecture at the University of Porto, the Serralves Museum of Contemporay Art in the same city, or the Expo'98 flagship pavilion in Lisbon.

As it happened in Spain as well, the production of the last decades of the twentieth century in Portugal has been interpreted as a paradigm of critical regionalism by Kenneth Frampton, a phenomenon seen as emerging in peripheral countries that nonetheless achieved a singular blend of Modernism and local traditions that translated into an architectural production of outstanding quality. Alvaro Siza became the major figure of Portuguese design and one of the highest exponents of "critical regionalism", his work managed to blend the tradition of radical modernist design with a powerful sense of relating to the place and to some local ways to express materiality, tectonics and space.[6]

Siza's public pools in Matosinhos, near Porto, constitute a paradigm of this approach. The building combines a careful landscape design for the pools that takes advantage of and reshapes the rocky topography of the natural waterfront, yet at the same time introduces a sharp geometry of concrete construction. The interior spaces of the facility, providing changing rooms and other services, create a horizontal slab that also plays with the horizon as perceived from the street and generates some carefully planned promenades that frame the visual and sensorial experience of the place. The rich and complex dialogue between natural and built elements unfolds for its visitors with a mastery that manages to stay away from any cliche of "organicism." A modest structure in size and in use of resources, the Matosinhos pools encapsulate the spirit of the new Portuguese architecture and became an ever-present model for the next generations of designers.

A different approach can be seen in the case of the Fundação Calouste Gulbenkian, built in 1960s in Lisbon, and designed by Rui Atouguia, Pedro Cid and Alberto Pessoa. This is an example of international tendencies having a resonance in Portuguese production, especially in the brutalist, massive use of reinforced concrete, yet it constitutes an isolated case when compared to influential development of the Porto school, and its capacity to engage different generations of architects.

Shortly after the Revolution of April 25,1974, an organization called Servicio de Apoio Ambulatorio Local (SAAL) was formed to seek state aid to alleviate poor housing conditions in Portugal. Siza and others worked for SAAL. Its power was sharply reduced after the right wing coup of 1975, and its activities virtually suppressed by the end of 1976. Siza, together with Rafael Moneo, was responsible for the Portuguese-Spanish Encounters that took place in 1997 and 1998. In these encounters, an extensive group of younger architects presented their work, and promoted a closer link between the Iberian countries. In 2001, the Catalan Order of Architects sponsored an exhibition titled Panorama Portugal, and the Barcelona-based FAD (Design Centre) included Portuguese architectural works in their annual award, previously limited to the Spanish territories.

The New Generations

Eduardo Souto de Moura has continued the Porto's school tradition with some careful renovations of the special inns named Pousadas, housing projects, and recently some singular structures like the Braga Stadium of 2003, the University of Aveiro, or the Burgo tower in Porto. At the level of combining architectural and urban design and planning, Gonçalo Byrne in Lisbon and Nuno Portas in Porto also deserve to be mentioned. They have also combined education and professional practice, a common trait among the most influential Portuguese architects. The recent award of the Pritzker Prize to Souto is an indication of the international weight of the younger architects that can shine independently of the father figures of Tavora and Siza.

Other architects among the prolific younger generations include João Luís Carrilho da Graça, based in Lisbon, with recent works such as the Poitiers Theatre and Auditorium, completed in 2008. Carrilho has taken the minimalist impulse of some of his Portuguese colleagues to a highly elegant extreme, radicalizing the sharpness and geometrical expression of its design to a very personal level. Francisco and Manuel Aires Mateus have continued this minimalist tendency with special paradigms such as the buildings at the Coimbra University campus, or the Universidade Nova de Lisboa rector's office. Carrilho and Aires Mateus have embodied the new white, radically Modern architecture to emerge after Siza, characterized by a refreshing new approach based on a more radical minimalism of form and a departure from the "critical regionalism" blend of Modernism and local tradition, as well as on a special elegance in its refrain from any formal complications.

Among the younger architects one could mention teams like Atelier Bugio, with work in the island of Madeira, Cristina Guedes and Francisco Vieira de Campos, whose Faculty of Fine Arts in Porto has received a special acclaim, or Ines Lobo and Pedro Domingos, authors of the Portuguese Embassy buildings in Berlin.

In all these cases, Portuguese architecture has shown a special capacity to continue a "school," that is, sharing some common traits that tie today's designers to their recent tradition and identity, while actively pursuing an innovative approach to the profession. This is a commendable effort given the many limitations the profession suffers, ranging from a lack of exclusivity when it comes to building, or the high competition given the high proportion of schools and graduates in the country. Yet the profession enjoys a very high social recognition given the role it has played in recent decades, politically and socially, uniquely in the international scenario of contemporary practice. To quote the architecture scholar and historian Ana Tostoes, the best Portuguese architecture of recent decades has been characterized by its "tradition of pragmatism and austere innovation."[7]

CONCLUSION

Modern Iberian architecture constitutes an eloquent testimony to the recent history of Europe. Based on a well-grounded tradition, both Spanish and Portuguese architecture experienced a powerful renaissance in the second half of the twentieth century. There are strong parallels in the political evolution of both countries, an evolution in which the architectural community played a substantial and leading role in the transition to democracy. Later, the integration with a unified Europe became an extraordinary social and cultural stimulus that provided additional resonance to this architectural work. The professional figure of the architect also benefited from a high reputation in society, often seen as a model, leading intellectual that provided a much needed inspiration.

The challenges that the architectural culture and the profession are facing nowadays have to do with the previous success. Architects greatly rely on a structure of small offices and on a system of public competitions and public commissions. This combination has translated into an architecture of great quality, crafted in the special environment of competition-based micro studios. The present time is calling for a profound revision of the construction industry, its technologies and management, of the real estate markets, and consequently of the role of the architectural profession. As the European community is also facing its own political and economic challenges, the role of the periphery is also being revised, and the historic dichotomy between the core states and the fringe ones seems to reappear in a way that could be damaging for phenomena like the Iberian design.

On the other hand, the architectural production of recent decades in Portugal and Spain are the proof that architecture can be a powerful cultural engine of our society, creating the quality of civic space that is needed for a true public sphere. It also proved architecture's resilience to dominating forces, as it developed a special domain of intellectual debate, of cultural development, and of aesthetic enjoyment. Iberian design has contributed to the extraordinary quality of contemporary European architecture, and therefore has constituted a source of great cultural pride in the consolidation of a unified Europe that needed to integrate its geographical, as well as its metaphorical peripheries.

NOTES

1   Carlos Flores, *Arquitectura Española Contemporánea* (Madrid: Aguilar, 1961).

2   Oriol Bohigas, *Arquitectura Española de la Segunda República* (Barcelona: Tusquets, 1970).

3   Xavier Costa and Susana Landrove (eds), *Architecture of the Modern Movement in Spain and Portugal: Iberian Docomomo Register* (Barcelona: Fundacio Mies van der Rohe, 1996).

4   Ignasi de Solà-Morales, *Contemporary Spanish Architecture: An Eclectic Panorama* (New York: Rizzoli, 1986).

5   Xavier Costa (ed.), *Habitats, Tectónicas, Paisajes: Arquitectura Española Contemporánea* (Articles by Michael Speaks, Ole Bouman, and Ignasi de Solà-Morales) (Madrid: Ministerio de Fomento, 2002).

6   Kenneth Frampton, "Towards a Critical Regionalism: Six Points for an Architecture of Resistance," in Hal Foster (ed.), *The Anti-Aesthetic* (Port Townsend: Bay Press, 1983).

7   Ana Tostões, "Arquitectura Portuguesa: Una Nueva Generación," *2G* 20 (2001).

12

Architecture in Switzerland: A Natural History[*]

Laurent Stalder

The last comprehensive review of Swiss architecture took place probably in the 1970s. As a matter of fact, the Confederation launched a competition for the campus of the Swiss Institute of Technology in Lausanne (EPFL) at that time, in which seven firms, representing the seven greater regions of Switzerland – from Geneva to Zurich, and from Basel to Ticino – took part.[1] The design approach pursued by the seven firms was surprisingly similar, from the winning project submitted by the Zurich team around Jakob Zweifel, with its generic grid, to that of Haller / Barth / Zaugg (Soleure), who conceived the campus as a matrix, through to that of the team led by Paul Waltenspühl (Geneva), which foresaw variable and successive phases of expansion. All these projects were based, not on a plastic approach but on a diagrammatic one that allowed them to be extended more or less flexibly, in their horizontal and vertical planes. What unified these megastructural projects was a conception of the university as a centre of production, a centre for the production of knowledge, which – thanks to its flexible and evolutionary structure – would be able to adapt to changing needs just like any other industrial centre. The Ticino Group's entry, whose genealogy could be followed back to projects such as Le Corbusier's Venice Hospital, Louis Kahn's proposal for the centre of Philadelphia, or Candilis, Josic & Woods' building for the Free University of Berlin, might conceivably – given its horizontal expanse, evolutionary aspect and superimposed circulation systems – be ranked with them as an example of megastructural endeavour.[2]

Such historical references allow the EPFL proposal to be read in the light of a precise architectural tradition yet they do not explain the ways in which the Ticino Group set a new architectural benchmark, one that was to catapult its members – Mario Botta, Tita Carloni, Aurelio Galfetti, Flora Ruchat and Luigi Snozzi – onto the national and international architectural scenes of the 1970s (Figure 12.1).

What became apparent in the EPFL project, with a clarity unique in that period, was an epistemological shift in the design approach, which was to fundamentally

---

[*]   This chapter is a revised and expanded version of my article 'Das Haus als Bild', published in *Neue Zürcher Zeitung*, 27 February 2010. A shorter version as been published also as: 'For the Museums', in: Marc Angélil / Jørg Himmelreich (eds.), *Architecture dialogues: positions – concepts visions* (Sulgen: Niggli, 2011), 132–143.

12.1 Ticino
Group: Swiss
Institute of
Technology,
Lausanne
(EPFL), 1970

redefine architectural production in Switzerland in the following years. The concept of architecture illustrated by the majority of the projects for the EPFL, as an adaptable, extendable and transformable environment, was to cede eventually to a concept of architecture, whether in relation to the isolated object or to the city, as a formal problem. From that point on, the physical reality of either a selected territory or a city would be taken as the point of departure for any analysis, and as the context against which any intervention should be evaluated.[3] Indeed, the grid of the Ticino Group draws not on a programmatic approach but on a spatial one, for its square shape is derived not solely from an organizational problem but from a formal intent; its dimensions are no longer explained as the outcome of programmatic constraints but as a response to a territorial problem.

The Ticino project obviously owed a great deal to the Italian *Tendenza* and its discourse, and it demonstrated how successfully the Italians' theoretical models might be adapted to Swiss circumstances. Nonetheless, as proposals for the restoration of the Castelgrande in Bellinzona exemplify only too well, the way these theoretical models were to be interpreted was to prove highly controversial. In 1974, Bruno Reichlin and Bruno Reinhart, then assistants of Rossi at the ETH, devised a concept for the restoration of the castle (Figure 12.2). It proposed a dual strategy: firstly, to expose the original parts of the building and, secondly, to build a modern concrete and steel structure above it, and thus facilitate visits to the archaeological site. The first step corresponds to the methods applied in the same period by archaeologists, i.e. to expose any layers concealing the original structure. For, just as it is necessary to remove the earth that covers remains in order to understand them, so too, it would be necessary to clear the eclectic and historicist additions to the castle in order to allow its original structure and any architectural remnants to re-emerge. The new structures proposed in the second step – a concrete porticus and an observation deck in ironwork – were designed to add a contemporary layer, in striking contrast to the castle's original features. This proposal for Castelgrande was determined thus neither by original construction methods nor by historical motifs. On the contrary, the architects sought to highlight through a structural reading of the castle the different strata in the history of the site, and thereby embed their intervention in an ongoing historical narrative. This reading of the Castelgrande as an archaeological museum stood in marked contrast to the proposal made by Aurelio Galfetti, who took over the project in 1981, in the wake of some political controversy (Figure 12.3).

Instead of exposing the castle's remains, Galfetti simply cleared the hilltop of vegetation in order to emphasize its gneiss stone, created by glaciers in the Neolithic era. Instead of Reichlin and Reinharts' historic promenade over archaeological remains, he designed a panoramic walkway that linked the town's main square to the foot of the rocky mountain to the castle's courtyard via an elevator. Hence, the castle was set to become, not an archaeological site relating Helvetian history by exposing and reconstituting its signifiers, but a site of entertainment; it no longer stood in relation to traces of a reconstituted past, but in direct relation to the territory.[4] The shift from the first to the second project is of importance in two respects: on the one hand, it marks the transition from a typological approach to a spatial one and, on the

12.2   Bruno Reichlin, Fabio Reinhart: Castelgrande, Bellinzona, 1974

12.3   Aurelio
Galfetti:
Castelgrande,
Bellinzona, 1981–88

other, from a historic reading of the site to its interpretation in formal terms. It is on
the basis of this dual shift that the architecture of the 1980s in Switzerland was to
emancipate itself definitively from that of its Italian *Tendenza* precursors.[5]

This shift was to be precisely described also for German-speaking Switzerland a
few years later by architect Marcel Meili, in his survey of contemporary architecture,
'A Few Buildings: Many Plans' (1989). Meili echoed a common viewpoint of the day,
in that he ascribed the re-orientation in architecture to the influence of Aldo Rossi,
who had taught at the Swiss Institute of Technology in Zurich (ETHZ) in the 1970s,
where Jacques Herzog, Pierre de Meuron, Miroslav Šik, Meili himself and other
major protagonists of contemporary architecture numbered among his students.
Meili's description of the enthusiasm provoked by Rossi's architectural approach
was accurate. Yet he also emphatically pinpointed the difficulties inherent to
transposing the Italians' teachings to the specific Swiss situation. According to
Meili, this is why, from the outset, Rossi's students sought their identity less in their
local legacy of building types, and all the more pointedly in the everyday rituals
of contemporary modes of living in Switzerland. This confrontation with Helvetian
reality – the non-urban character of the cities, the faceless modernity of the
service economy, and its commonplace rationality – allowed them to emancipate

themselves from the historical pathos of Latin rationalism. Meili logically concluded his excursus on Rossi with the remark that the young Swiss architects were better able to deal with the term 'ambiente' in Rossi's teachings than they were with the term 'tipo'.[6] With the exception of Rossi's closest collaborators – Bruno Reichlin and Fabio Reinhart, for instance, who were to pursue the Rossian theses, and to add a linguistic dimension to them in certain major projects such as the Casa Tonini in the Ticino (1972–74); or Max Bosshard, Eduard Imhof, Christoph Luchsinger and Karl Lustenberger, who, some 10 years later, were to borrow several Rossian motifs and elements such as the access gallery, the vertical order, or the volumetry of the Gallaratese for their competition entry for the Klösterli development in 1981 – the architecture of the late 1980s[7] did ultimately come to define itself around the notion of 'ambiente' or, to cite the two German terms used synonymously in the architectural debate of the period, 'Stimmung' or 'Atmosphäre'.

There is no attribute more vague, in the literal and figurative sense, than that of 'atmosphere'.[8] In fact, etymologically speaking, atmosphere signifies a gas surrounding a body. In architecture therefore, atmosphere begins where the building and its construction ends. It concerns that which emanates, in the real sense of that term, from the surface of a building, its colour, light, odour, scents, temperature and humidity. It inscribes itself therefore in an architectural tradition defined by the art of illusion, from the trompe-l'oeil of the Baroque, to the subconscious alphabet of Aldo Rossi's metaphysical architecture, expressed in his drawings, through to the atmospheres carefully collated in the images of the periphery and in 'second-rate architecture' – a certain provincial modernism – by Swiss architects of the period. However, the terminological shift from the Italian 'ambiente' to the German 'Stimmung' or 'Atmosphäre' is revealing: it translates a shift, away from an interest in the environment in terms of its social and historic dimensions towards the individual object in terms of its geographic context and materiality. As trivial as this may seem, it was to be of importance to Swiss architecture, as it would make it possible to understand the built environment, not only in its historical dimension but in a diachronic way, and hence to replace the abstract logic of typology in the reading of the city by a material logic such as is inscribed and constructed in everyday life. It allowed Rossi's successors to steer the focus away from the great Italian classical tradition to the architecture of the Swiss periphery; away from an architectural language coded by architectural history to the language of common habitus. In the process, the interest in embedding architecture in its historical context was transferred to the object, to the process of its making, and to its effect. This is the manner in which Miroslav Šik – a student of Rossi who, together with Fabio Reinhart founded the movement, 'Analogical Architecture' at the Swiss Institute of Technology at Zurich in the late 1980s (Figure 12.4) – and also Peter Zumthor understand the notion of 'atmosphere'. For example, when Šik demands that his students represent the 'dirt of the roads' in their chalk perspective drawings, or to think even about the 'heat of asphalt' in the sunshine, he encourages them not to limit themselves to the exigencies of the quotidian, but both to capture and, most importantly, to represent the 'atmosphere'.[9] 'What moves me the most?' Peter Zumthor asks himself in his book *Atmospheres*: 'anything, anythings, the things, the people, the air, noises, tone, colors, material presence, textures, forms, too … My mood, my feelings, my expectations then.'[10]

Indeed, the title of Meili's essay – 'A Few Buildings: Many Plans' (1989) – is symptomatic. It does of course describe the precarious condition of young architects short on commissions and obliged thus to practice their profession through architectural competitions; but above all, it puts the finger explicitly on a working technique – the architectural drawing, as opposed to the diagram or text – as a primary mode of reflection. This pictorial intent, which is associated with the notion of 'Stimmung' manifest in the work of Šik, Meili or later, Zumthor, is accordingly more than a simple and detailed representation of a building on its site; it testifies also to a desire to use architecture to reconstruct a new, coherent,

HERAUSGEGEBEN   VON   MIROSLAV   ŠIK

ANALOGE ARCHITEKTUR

BOGA

12.4   Miroslav
Šik: Analogue
Architektur, 1987

and distinctive ensemble, be it an urban or rural landscape, or even an interior one with its particular 'Stimmung' – the authenticity that is constituent of any landscape.[11]

To understand architecture through its atmosphere is first and foremost to define it through its surfaces – and perspective drawings attest to that. What is realized in a radical manner in the academic context – in the Analogues' immense perspective drawings made at the ETHZ, or in competition drawings – found its resonance in the same period in various projects realized by the young avant-garde. At the semantic level (and in the wake of Swiss architectural journals' interest in this period in the work of Venturi), this translates into a reflection on the signs of the periphery – aesthetic, legal and cultural, among others – made manifest in certain motifs such as a window, a chimney or eaves, as in Marques and Zurkirchens' Hodel House (1986–87). At the technical level, it comes down to a quest for a grammar of construction as manifest in projects by Christian Sumi and Marianne Burkhalter, namely the expression of different modes of construction through joints, texture and colours, or the use of planks, beams and plywood as signifiers of a building's different functions – the entrance, the main body, the pedestal or even the roof, as in their house in Langnau (1985–87).[12] In the early works of Herzog & de Meuron, this shift translates into a new reading of the everyday conventions of the site, manifest in its materials, motifs, geometry or even in its colours, as in the Blue House (Oberwil, 1979–80) situated in an anonymous suburb with restrictive codes of construction; or in the Frei photographic studio near Basel (Weil am Rhein, 1981–82), a true collage of motifs and materials such as the skylights of a factory building or the inclined wooden roof of a garden shed, which reflect the banality of the peripheral zones; or finally, on the urban scale, in the projects of Diener & Diener, one of the few firms to be given large projects since the 1980s. In their two housing blocks on the banks of the Rhine (Basel, 1984–86), Diener & Diener reinterpretated the modern grammar – horizontal window, structural grid and flat roof – and its formal potential to conceive the building as a reflection of the site's different images – industrial, rural or urban. A similar collage is present at the level of the plan and its contradictory grammar, which exploits different modes of spatial and functional organization through typological play – enfilade and corridor, open space and individual rooms (Figure 12.5).

Despite these divergent expressions, there was a similarity in the methodology employed. Jacques Herzog, when talking about his own work of the 1980s, aptly summarized this architectural approach as collage,[13] and thereby underscored not only the formal and pictorial interests of his generation, but also – through the asynchrony provoked by the collage of disparate motifs – its review of a historical logic.[14] In fact, the fragmentation of extant elements is a fundamental prerequisite of any collage. This technique presents reality as a succession of isolated fragments (as in painting) or of successive sequences (as in film), which are added together to create a temporal sequence or to articulate different narratives. The significance of each image selected in isolation is subordinated to the principle of their assemblage. The import of any signifier is thereby transposed from its content to its construction. This shift has rightly been described by Bruno Reichlin as the

12.5   Diener &
Diener: Residential
Building St Alban
Tal, Basel, 1984–86

movement from a semantic grammar to a grammar of construction.[15] The latter's roots can be traced back to an architectural tradition firmly anchored in a still vibrant local heritage of craftsmanship, as well as in a polytechnical – or at least technical – tradition in Swiss architectural education and training.

This shift from a historic understanding of architecture towards a constructive principle goes beyond technical aspects, however. It is no coincidence that Herzog & de Meuron organized their retrospective exhibition at the CCA in Montreal around the theme of 'Natural History', in reference to the large collections held by nineteenth-century museums of natural history.[16] The historical order ceded here to a new order, one that consciously displayed objects – models, materials, samples – in various states of aggregation or disintegration. To think about architecture from this perspective is to challenge not only dialectical relations – as did the Analogues' postulate, 'neither old, nor new' – but also the distinction between that which is 'natural' or 'artificial'.

This new relationship between architecture and its environment has been particularly evident in recent decades in the work of Herzog & de Meuron, Peter Zumthor, Valerio Olgiati and other Swiss firms. In a number of projects it is limited to analogy, and attests to research into visual concerns. The relationship of the Ricola Storage Building in Laufon (1986–87) to the limestone quarry in which it is located thus remains formal, even if the stratification of the building transforms our perception of the site. What is achieved through visual structure in Laufon finds its geometric echo in Valerio Olgiati's School at Paspels (1996–98), a deformed paralleliped, the pitched roof of which traces the inclination of the site. As Bruno Reichlin has noted, to pursue the topography in this way accentuates the object's abstract character, and makes us overlook the obvious analogical association with its essentially traditional form of roof.[17]

At Laufon and Paspels, the relation to the environment is above all a formal one. By contrast, in Herzog & de Meuron's small project in Tavole in the north of Italy, the Stone House (1982–89; Figure 12.6), the relationship between the building and the site acquires a conceptual dimension (in the artistic sense of the term), first and foremost by refuting any distinction between old and new. The house is built of local ferruginous dry stone, recycled from nearby ruins. In Tavole, therefore, ruins precede the edifice. This interest in different moments in history, to which the house attests, has a material correlation, for the dry ferrous stone walls are contained within a pre-stressed concrete structure. Thus one finds here a combination of two materials whose components are the same but in different aggregate states. Valerio Olgiati's Yellow House in Flims (1995–99), likewise demonstrates the history of the building not through academic reconstruction but through a genuinely archaeological project. It not only reveals various successive phases of transformation, but unifies them also, both at the structural level and – given the coat of white paint applied uniformly to the stone substructure, the timber construction, the concrete window frames and even the concrete belt en attique (Figure 12.7) – at the visual level. At the structural level, the concrete belt retains the four walls of the hollowed structure, and yet is simultaneously supported by them. Here too, the historical logic of the building cedes to a material and constructive logic, and the relationship between cause and effect is erased accordingly not only at the formal level, but also at the constructive, material and static levels. A similar approach can be found also in Christian Kerez's apartment building in Zurich, in which space and structure are no longer separate but interdependent (Figure 12.8).

12.6   Herzog & de Meuron: Stone House, Tavole, Italy, 1982–88

12.7   Valerio Olgiati: Museum Yellow House Flims, 1995–99

12.8   Christian Kerez: Apartment Building, Forsterstrasse, 1998–2003

The morphogenesis hinted at in Flims or Tavole – in an implicit or metaphorical way – finally becomes an integral part of the construction process, for instance in Herzog & de Meuron's Schaulager (Basel-Münchenstein, 1998–2002), which is simultaneously a museum and the archive of the Basel Kunstmuseum's art collection, or in Devanthéry & Lamunière's psychiatric clinic in Yverdon (2000–03), and again, in Peter Zumthor's small Brother Claus Chapel (Mechernich-Wachendorf, 2006–07) and, at the territorial level, in his Thermal Bath in Vals (1993–96). In Basel, the constructive approach perpetuates the conceptual approach pursued at Tavole, given that the gravel extracted from the excavation pit is integrated in the concrete of the façade. At Yverdon, the striped facade attests to the layers of poured concrete applied successively in varying shades of red and purple. At Mechernich-Wachendorf, within the concrete structure of Zumthor's chapel, the internal formwork – a tipee built from 120 slender tree trunks – is set alight and left to smoulder until only its charred shell remains, creating a potent place of worship with a unique patina (Figure 12.9).

At Vals finally, as Akos Moravánsky has suggested, the distinction between matter and materials – between matter that participates in the domain of nature, and materials that participate in the realm of the artificial – becomes irrelevant.[18] Constructed from quartz stone, a stone characterized by its layered structure, the Thermal Bath at Vals can be understood in a general sense as a stratified (re) construction of an artificial landscape – i.e. of a stone quarry – or conversely, as Zumthor has put it, as an edifice that creates the impression it has been in existence far longer than its neighbours, and is a natural part of the landscape.[19]

This development mirrors an endeavour currently evident in Switzerland, namely to provide an adequate response to the increasingly complex relationship of architecture to its environment. Bruno Latour has aptly described the poles of this situation:[20] on the one hand, a metascience of nature that encompasses all complexity, all organic and inorganic processes in an energetic, overflowing and prolific whole and, on the other, a concept of nature that regards the environment as a human construction. The first seems predominant in projects such as the Tenerife Harbour by Herzog & de Meuron (since 1998) or Christophe Girot's proposal for the Rhône Valley (since 2009) while the second is more palpable in the autonomous and Latin tradition as interpreted since the 1970s in the work of the Ticino Group, and as represented by the Thermal Bath at Vals, and in the work of Valerio Olgiati, Christian Kerez and Made in (Figure 12.10). For, while Swiss architecture appears contemporary with regard to its concept of landscape, its themes must be understood nonetheless as an updated version of a much older debate about Swiss topography, one that dates back to the early eighteenth century. Since that time, scientists, artists, tourists and cartographers, the military, and civil engineers have participated in the physical and imaginary construction of this landscape, which remains the most important model Switzerland has ever been able to formulate.

12.9   Peter Zumthor: Saint Nicolas Chapel, Mechernich-Wachendorf, 2006–07

12.10   Made in: Villa Chardonne, Chardonne, 2006–08

NOTES

1   'Sieben Projekte für die ETH-L in Dorigny', *Werk* 57 (October 1970), 646–71.

2   See for example: 'Architekturgespräche der Nachkriegszeit' on: http://www.stalder. arch.ethz.ch/videoarchiv/luigi-snozzi-16112010 (22.09.2011)

3   Ignasi Sola Morales, 'Neo-rationalism & Figuration', *Architectural Design* 54 (Mai/June 1984), 17.

4   For the history of the projects for the Castelgrande, cf.: Stanislaus von Moos, 'Castello Propositivo', in Jacques Lucan, *Matière d'art: architecture contemporaine en Suisse – A matter of Art: Contemporary Architecture in Switzerland* (Basel: Birkhäuser, 2001), 165. Bruno Reichlin, Bruno Reinhard, 'Progetto di restauro di Castel Grande', *Casabella* 41 (November 1977), 51–8.

5   One of the most differentiated studies on Swiss Architecture of the period 1980–98 is: Martin Tschanz, 'Tendenzen und Konstruktionen: Von 1968 bis heute', in: Anna Meseure / Martin Tschanz / Wilfried Wang (eds), *Schweiz* (*Architektur im 20. Jahrhundert*, vol. 5) (Munich / London / New York: Prestel 1998), 45–52. On Rossi's stay at the ETHZ, see: Ákos Moravánszky / Judith Hopfengärtner (eds), *Aldo Rossi und die Schweiz: Architektonische Wechselwirkungen* (Zurich: gta Verlag 2011), Jacques Lucan / Bruno Marchand / Martin Steinmann (eds), *Aldo Rossi: Autobiographies partagées* (*Cahiers de théorie*, vol. 1) (Lausanne: Presses Polytechniques et Universitaires Romandes 2000).

6   Marcel Meili, 'Ein paar Bauten, viele Pläne', *Werk, Bauen + Wohnen* 76 (December 1989), 26–31, 26–7.

A number of representative of the Ticino *Tendenza* were to teach at the ETH. It is significant for instance, that the teaching work of Aldo Rossi (guest lectureship 1972–74, full lectureship 1976–78) and Luigi Snozzi (full lectureship 1973–75) at the ETH Zurich coincided in 1973. Cf.: Roger Diener, 'Architektur jenseits von Design: Adam

Szymczyk im Gespräch mit Roger Diener', in: Bundesamt für Kultur (ed.), *Prix Meret Oppenheim 2009*, Bern: Bundesamt für Kultur 2010), 38–61, p. 42. Among Snozzi's students numbered Roger Diener, Pierre de Meuron, Jacques Herzog, Stephan Mäder, Daniele Marques, Luca Merlini, Wolfgang Schett and Heinz Wirz. Mario Campi and Flora Ruchat-Roncati, who held guest lectureships in 1975–77 respectively 1979–81, before both being appointed to full professorships in 1985, were likewise proponents of the Ticino *Tendenza* at the ETH Zurich in the 1970s.

7   On this issue, see: 'Ein Rückblick auf einen Ausblick (*Werk, Bauen & Wohnen* in discussion with Jacques Herzog and Pierre de Meuron, Roger Diener, Marianne Burkhalter and Christian Sumi, Marie-Claude Bétrix and Eraldo Consolascio)', *Werk, Bauen & Wohnen* 76 (September 1989, 28–31.

8   Mark Wigley, 'The Architecture of Atmosphere', *Daidalos* 68 (1988), 18–27. On the notion of atmosphere in Swiss architecture see: Ákos Moravánszky, 'My Blue Heaven: The Architecture of Atmospheres', *AA Files* 61 (2010), 18–22; Jacques Lucan (ed.), *Matière d'art: Architecture contemporaine en Suisse / A Matter of Art: Contemporary Architecture in Switzerland* (Basel / Boston / Berlin: Birkhäuser 2001), 49.

9   'Die Stimmung ist die SIA-Norm [Axel Simon und Hendrik Tieben im Gespräch mit Miroslav Šik]', in: Miroslav Šik: *Altneue Gedanken. Texte und Gespräche 1987–2001* (Lucerne: Quart Verlag), 143 [first published in: *Transreal* (2000), 66–71]. Cf. also: 'Building conflicts. Interview with Miroslav Šik', *Daidalos* 68 (1988), 102–11.

10   Peter Zumthor, *Atmospheres: Architectural Environments – Surrounding Objects* (Basel / Boston / Berlin: Birkhäuser 2006), 17.

11   Cf. Georg Simmel, 'Philosophie der Landschaft', in: Rüdiger Kramme et al. (eds), *Georg Simmel: Aufsätze und Abhandlungen 1909–1918*, vol. 1 (*Georg Simmel Gesamtausgabe*, vol. 12) (Frankfurt a. M.: Suhrkamp 2000), 471–82, p. 477. First published in: *Die Güldenkammer: Eine bremische Monatsschrift* 3 (2/1913), 635–44.

12   This revival of Swiss tradition in wood construction is to be read against the background of important archival and historical work, as well as related publications by the young Swiss avant-garde. Cf. for example, the book series *Dokumente zur modernen Schweizer Architektur* published at the gta (Institute for the History and Theory of Architecture) at ETHZ since 1985.

13   'Gespräch: Jacques Herzog und Theodora Vischer', in: Architekturmuseum Basel (ed.), *Architektur Denkform; Herzog & de Meuron. Eine Ausstellung im Architekturmuseum vom 1. Oktober bis 20. November 1988* (Basel: Wiese 1988), 4.

14   Peter Bürger, *Theorie der Avantgarde* (Frankfurt a. M.: Suhrkamp 1974), 98–111.

15   'Ein Wohnhaus aus der Werkstatt (Bruno Reichlin in conversation with Marcel Meili and Markus Peter)', in: *Werk, Bauen + Wohnen* 80 (November 1993), 16–27, here 18. Also, Martin Steinmann, 'Die Gegenwärtigkeit der Dinge: Bemerkungen zur neueren Architektur in der Deutschen Schweiz', in: Mark Gilbert / Kevin Alter (eds), *Construction, Intention, Detail: Five Projects from Five Swiss Architects / Fünf Projekte von fünf Schweizer Architekten* (Zurich: Artemis 1994), 9.

16   On the exhibition in Montréal, see Marc Grignon, 'Weiche Vitrinen, Archive und Architektur', in: *werk, bauen + wohnen* 90 (July / August 2003), 58–61. For a critical discussion of the term 'Natural History' used by Herzog & de Meuron, see Hans Frei, 'Poetik statt Fortschritt', *NZZ* (June 26, 2004), 69.

17   Bruno Reichlin, 'Réponse à Martin Steinmann', in: *Matières* 6 (2003), 41.

18   Ákos Moravánszky, 'Die sich selbst erzählende Welt. Peter Zumthors Thermalbad in Vals und die Phänomenologie des Sehens', in: Anna Meseure, Martin Tschanz und Wilfried Wang (eds): *Schweiz (Architektur im 20. Jahrhundert, Bd. 5)* (Munich / London / New York: Prestel, 1998), 110.

19   Peter Zumthor, 'Thermal Bath Vals', in: *Peter Zumthor* (Tokyo: A+U Publishing 1998), 138.

20   Bruno Latour: *Politiques de la nature: comment faire entrer les sciences en démocratie*, Paris: Editions La Découverte, 1999.

13

Architecture in Eastern Europe and the Former Soviet Union since 1960

Kimberly Elman Zarecor

Eastern Europe and the former Soviet Union are often associated with grey, anonymous, and poorly constructed post-war buildings. Despite this reputation, the regional architectural developments that produced these buildings are critical to understanding global paradigm shifts in architectural theory and practice in the last 50 years. The vast territory of Eastern Europe and the former Soviet Union covers about one-sixth of the world's landmass and currently contains all or part of 30 countries.[1] Since 1960 other national boundaries have existed in this space, including East Germany, Czechoslovakia, Yugoslavia, and the Soviet Union. Given the region's large size, numerous languages, and tumultuous recent history—communist and authoritarian regimes, democratic revolutions, civil war and ethnic strife, political corruption, prosperity, EU accession, and economic instability—a comprehensive summary of 50 years of architectural developments cannot be achieved in one chapter. Rather than survey individual architects or projects in depth, this chapter instead explores the shared transformation in architectural discourse and practice that resulted from the region's political and economic shift to communism after World War II, and the changes that followed the fall of communism in the 1990s.[2]

ARCHITECTURAL PRACTICE DURING COMMUNISM

After World War II and the rise of Communist parties across the region, architects living in Eastern Europe and the new territories of the Soviet Union found themselves in a novel position. Unlike the lean years of the Great Depression in the 1930s, when most architects were left without work, they now had guaranteed employment and their services were in high demand for post-war reconstruction. Many were politically leftwing and supported the social agenda of the Communist Party, such as providing a minimum standard of housing for all citizens, whether or not they were party members. In territories that had been part of the Soviet Union before the war, architects also prospered due to the growth of the Soviet economy, a benefit of the expansion into Eastern Europe and the Baltics, and new investment in industrial infrastructure. Soon, however, the initial enthusiasm was tempered in Eastern Europe by the realization of the authoritarian nature of the regimes and the lack of professional freedom.

The professional lives of architects in communist economies differed significantly from the experiences of architects in capitalist countries. In this system, architects worked directly for the state or for state-owned enterprises; private practice was abolished.[3] These changes first occurred in the Soviet Union in the 1920s and after World War II in Eastern Europe and the new Soviet territories. Communist economics relied on planning—the prediction of future input and output needs for all sectors, typically in a five-year increment called "the five-year plan." This system relied on quantifiable targets and quotas, which forced architects to evaluate building projects in terms of material and labor costs—quantities of concrete and steel, number of units, volume of skilled and unskilled labor, and so forth. The experiential and formal aspects of architecture had no measurable value, and therefore had little relevance to design decision-making, except for one-off projects with political significance to the various regimes. As a result, architects across the region became technicians producing an industrial commodity, rather than creative artists executing an individual vision.[4]

At the same time, and perhaps as a result, the social status of the architect diminished. Architects had once been at the center of the avant-garde (one can think of the Russian Constructivists and the Yugoslav Zenitists, as well as other groups such as Devětsil in Czechoslovakia and Blok and Praesens in Poland), but during the communist period architects typically worked anonymously at state design offices where they functioned as engineers and managers more than designers. Those unwilling to accept new working conditions or unsuited to the professional environment took less visible positions at universities, historic preservation offices, archives, or consumer product enterprises such as furniture and industrial design companies. By the late 1960s, few practicing architects had any personal memory of architectural practice before World War II.

Because of this shared set of priorities emphasizing typification, standardization, and mass production, architectural practice across the Soviet Union and the Eastern Bloc shared more similarities than differences among the various countries by the 1950s. This represented a significant shift since Eastern Bloc countries like Czechoslovakia, East Germany, and Hungary had sophisticated building industries before World War II, while the construction sector in the Soviet Union had been underdeveloped and largely unmechanized. New methods and processes for design, finance, and building construction were developed and shared between professionals in the various countries, often through travel exchanges and research visits. These architects also shared the everyday economic realities of communism: unyielding labor and material shortages; the push toward faster and cheaper construction methods; and the lack of long-term investment in public space and building maintenance. As János Kornai and others have noted, shortage was the system's defining characteristic.[5] Therefore, as in other sectors, architects focused on strategies to address the problems including prefabricated building elements, lightweight building materials, and the mechanization of work on building sites.

The consistency of architectural strategies across the region was remarkable both for the discipline that the economic model imposed on production and for the scale of construction (over 50 million standardized housing units were constructed in the Soviet Union alone from 1957 to 1984).[6] Manufacturing and distribution were streamlined to such a degree that one was likely to find the same building and hardware components across large swathes of the region. Stephen Kotkin, author of two books on the Soviet steel city of Magnitogorsk, writes this about the general conditions:

> The Soviet phenomenon created a deeply unified material culture. I am thinking
> not just of the cheap track suits worn by seemingly every male in Uzbekistan
> or Bulgaria, Ukraine or Mongolia. Consider the children's playgrounds in those
> places, erected over the same cracked concrete panel surfaces and with the same
> twisted metal piping—all made at the same factories, to uniform codes. This was
> also true of apartment buildings (outside and inside), schools, indeed entire cities,
> even villages. Despite some folk ornamentation here and there (Islamic flourishes
> on prefab concrete panels for a few apartment complexes in Kazan or Baku) a
> traveler encounters identical designs and materials.[7]

R.A. French and F.E. Ian Hamilton made similar observations in their 1979 book, *The Socialist City: Spatial Structure and Urban Policy*, writing that "if one were transported into any residential area built since the Second World War in the socialist countries, it would be easier at first glance to tell when it was constructed than to determine in which country it was."[8]

This stress on sameness was also ideological, since the communist ethos of a minimum standard for all was integral to thinking about designing cities with undifferentiated class structures. Housing was the most indicative of this approach as a homogeneous housing stock of mainly two- and three-room apartments was built from East Germany to the Soviet Far East. The resulting buildings were not valued as architectural objects, but rather as indicators of production performance. Meeting quantitative targets was more important than evaluating what had been produced, thus removing any incentive to improve architecture on aesthetic or functional grounds. Mark B. Smith writes that "to some extent, this [mass-produced similitude] was the end of architecture" and "the final takeover of the profession by construction experts."[9] After decades of conforming to this system, Polish architect Maciej Krasiński had this to say in 1988, "the Polish architecture of the present is bad … The idea of "maintaining a building" both as regards its function and its technological state practically is non-existent, and if here we add, to put it gently— the hopeless quality of the work—then the general picture provides us with no reason for optimism."[10]

This sentiment was widespread in the Communist Bloc, particularly in the 1980s, when economic and political crises led to even more acute material and labor shortages and worsening construction quality. The building technologies and construction practices developed for prefabrication and panel construction in the

1960s had not changed much by 1989. Economic planning in multi-year increments slowed down processes of change and innovation. Given the myriad architectural developments in the capitalist West in the same decades, this stagnation and failure to keep up with international standards became more apparent with each passing year.

DESIGN CULTURE IN COMMUNIST EUROPE

From the perspective of architectural form making, the buildings of the 1960s, 1970s, and 1980s, have their origins in earlier struggles to find an appropriate architectural language for the "ideal" communist society. The Russian avant-garde provided the first images of the potential for communist architecture in the 1920s, but the style was later denounced as "bourgeois formalism," and replaced in the Soviet Union by historicist Socialist Realism after 1933. Eastern European architects, many of whom had been trained and practiced as modernists in the interwar period, faced a similar crisis when pressure mounted in the late 1940s to embrace the principles of Socialist Realism to symbolize their countries' new affiliations with the Soviet Union. The necessity to work in a Socialist Realist style was short-lived, however. After Stalin's death in 1953 and Khrushchev's 1954 call to reject Stalinist aesthetics and "useless things in architecture," Socialist Realism quickly receded.[11]

Khrushchev's "thaw" followed—the liberalization of the most repressive policies of Stalinism in politics, culture, and everyday life. With this change to official discourse, architects were able to return to avant-garde forms from the 1920s and re-embrace the Constructivist legacy. A highlight from this period was Expo '58 in Brussels when the Soviet, Czechoslovak, Hungarian, and Yugoslav pavilions showcased an unexpected new communist style expressed in glass, concrete, and steel. The change was striking to many given how recently the region had been associated with Socialist Realism with its monumental scale and opaque materiality. This new version of modernism was not a reimagining of post-war practice as something akin to the interwar years, but rather a revival of forms and concepts that had figured prominently in avant-garde circles such as functionalism, mass production, and prefabrication, now deployed in support of the communist system by architects working for state design institutes. (Figure 13.1)

In these years, architects once again adopted an internationalist perspective that sought out universal, rather than regional or national, principles for modern architecture including standardized building types and industrial building methods. This transformation occurred in many countries outside the Soviet Bloc, notably in Western Europe, but on a much more limited scale. Virág Molnár writes that by the early 1960s, Hungarian "architects were ready to accept their subjugation to industrialized mass production because they envisaged state socialism as an alternative route to modernity."[12] In fact, Western ideas about architecture and urban planning, particularly those derived from CIAM and Le Corbusier, were widely promoted and implemented by architects and planners working in communist countries. Exemplary manifestations of tower in the park urbanism and zoned cities can be found throughout the region. (Figure 13.2) As James Scott discusses in his book, *Seeing like a State*, this was part of the global phenomenon of post-war high-modernist city building, examples of which were found in capitalist and communist countries, and in developed and developing economies.[13]

Architects in communist countries, however, had no choice about the direction of their work. The generation whose careers started around 1960 had few opportunities to challenge a consistent and systemic preference for typified, standardized, and mass-produced buildings. Prefabricated concrete—used for structural elements,

13.1   Vjenceslav Richter, Pavilion of Yugoslavia at EXPO '58, Brussels, 1958

13.2   Tower in the Park Urbanism in Bucharest, Romania

facade panels, and exterior landscaping—was the primary building material available for the majority of projects, forcing architects to find creative ways to work with its limitations. Other components, such as windows, doors, and fixtures, were industrially produced in mass quantities, and in limited sizes and finishes, adding to the repetitive and uniform nature of the environment. Concrete facades were often left grey and undecorated, although better examples incorporated colored panels or carefully detailed window assemblies. For new housing developments in many countries, a portion of the budget had to be spent on public art, thus fountains, sculptures, and murals, often made of concrete and tile, were common elements in public spaces.[14] Unfortunately these attempts to beautify neighborhoods were undermined in many cases by poor workmanship during construction and a total lack of maintenance in subsequent years that hastened deterioration.

Despite these challenges, there are many examples of good design work executed in communist Europe, although the architects themselves remain largely unknown. Rather than radically departing from conventions or expectations, these projects succeeded by using a restricted palette of building elements and materials in exciting and novel ways. Noteworthy examples in the Soviet Union include the Palace of Sports in Minsk by Sergey Filimonov and Valentin Malyshev from 1966; the Lenin Museum (now the Museum of the History of Uzbekistan) by V. Muratov in Tashkent from 1970; the Cinema Hall "Rossia" in Yerevan, Armenia by Artur Tarkhanyan, Grachya Pogosyan, and Spartak Khachikyan from 1975; as well as the venues built for the 1980 Moscow Olympic Games which included the Dynamo Sports Palace and the Druzhba Multipurpose Arena (Figures 13.3–13.4).

In Eastern Europe, the reliance on prefabricated and standard elements was just as fundamental. A few representative examples are the Spodek Stadium in

13.3   Sergey
Filimonov
and Valentin
Malyshev, Palace
of Sports, Minsk,
Belarus, 1966

13.4   V. Muratov,
Lenin Museum
(now the Museum
of the History
of Uzbekistan),
Tashkent,
Uzbekistan, 1970

Katowice, Poland by Maciej Gintowt and Maciej Krasiński from 1960; Przyczółek Grochowski housing estate in Warsaw by Oskar Hansen from 1963; the Federal Assembly of Czechoslovakia in Prague by Karel Prager from 1966; the Czechoslovak Radio Building (now the Slovak Radio Building) in Bratislava by Štefan Svetko, Štefan Ďurkovič and Barnabáš Kissling from 1967; the National Gallery in Bratislava by Vladimír Dědeček from 1969; the Palace of Culture in Dresden by Wolfgang Hänsch and Herbert Löschau from 1969; and Republic Square in Ljubljana by Edvard Ravnikar from 1977 (Figures 13.5–13.6).

In terms of square meters, the design of housing and community buildings in new neighborhoods dominated architectural practice in this period. The planned economy fundamentally changed approaches to housing design and construction as repeated apartment buildings organized in large districts replaced virtually all other residential types in most countries.[15] Starting in the early 1970s, when the regimes finally acknowledged their collective failure to adequately raise living standards for the majority of residents, these new methods were deployed on a massive scale. In cities and towns across the region, low-cost prefabricated apartment towers sprung up creating whole new urban districts, and even new cities (Figure 13.7). In Bratislava, for example, more than 90 percent of the city's 430,000 residents lived in post-war industrialized housing by the late 1980s.[16] In the Soviet case, whole post-war cities, such as the 1960s-era car-manufacturing city of Togliatti, were built with prefabricated concrete.[17]

A small intellectual class of architects rebelled against this standardization, and instead turned toward postmodernism and High-Tech in the 1970s and 1980s. They knew of these developments through architectural journals, either smuggled into the countries or available in the libraries of the state design institutes. The work of the Czechoslovak SIAL group (The Association of Engineers and Architects of Liberec) is one example. Following the Prague Spring in 1968, Karel Hubáček and Miroslav

13.5   Spodek Multipurpose Sports Arena, Katowice, Poland, 1960

13.6   Štefan Svetko, Štefan Ďurkovič and Barnabáš Kissling, Czechoslovak Radio
        Building (now the Slovak Radio Building), Bratislava, Slovakia, 1967

13.7   Petržalka
Housing Estate in
Bratislava, Slovakia

Masák, from the state-run design office in Liberec, established an independent
design studio and began to train young architects. They called their operation
the SIAL Kindergarten (SIAL-Školka). The studio's work coupled the legacy of the
avant-garde in central Europe with an interest in contemporary British High-Tech
and engineered buildings. Hubáček's own science-fiction-inspired Ještěd Hotel
and Television Transmitter won the 1969 Perret Prize, awarded by the International
Union of Architects (UIA) for its application of architectural technology (Figure
13.8). In the aftermath of the Soviet invasion in 1968 and the "normalization" period
that followed, SIAL lost its independence and again became part of the state-run
system in Liberec in 1971. But its architects continued working and a group from
the SIAL Kindergarten won the competition for the now iconic Máj Department
Store in the center of Prague in the early 1970s.[18]

Unlike SIAL, which operated publicly and with state consent, many architects who
wanted to challenge the official discourse were forced into secrecy. Ines Weizman
writes about East German and Soviet architects who gathered in private apartments
to discuss magazines illicitly brought into the country and to prepare competition
designs that would then be smuggled to the West or sent to international architecture
competitions, such as those sponsored by the Japanese journals, *Japan Architect* and
Architecture and Urbanism (A + U).[19] She positions these practices within the culture
of dissidence, more often associated with literature and music, which was a critical
development in establishing a theoretical basis for intellectuals' opposition to the
regimes in the 1970s and 1980s. Depending on the local political situation in their
respective countries, these "dissident" architects were subject to various levels of
retribution for their lack of cooperation. Some like John Eisler from SIAL went into
exile in the West, while others, like Imre Makovec in Hungary, were forced to live in
rural isolation. In extreme cases, architects, including Maks Velo from Albania, and

13.8   Karel Hubáček, Hotel and Television Transmitter, Ještěd Mountain near Liberec, Czech Republic

13.9   Maks Velo, Apartment Building, Tirana, Albania, 1971

Christian Enzmann and Bernd Ettel in East Germany, were imprisoned for their perceived architectural actions against the regime (Figure 13.9).[20]

ARCHITECTURE AFTER COMMUNISM

This was the state of things in the late 1980s when the various regimes began to fall. By the early 1990s, the European communist experiment was over and countries went through a period of turbulent change, including the dissolution of Czechoslovakia, Yugoslavia, and the Soviet Union, as well as vast transfers of state wealth into the hands of individuals through privatization programs. The architectural profession, centered for more than 40 years around a system of state-run design offices, had to be reinvented.

The transition was both conceptual and practical. Architects went from salaried employment in large public offices with regimented cultures to the capitalist model of private practice. Architects now had to find clients and financial backing for projects on their own, but they gained creative and conceptual freedom. The lack of intellectual rigor that characterized the state design system also had to be overcome. A high level of architectural discourse emerged into this void, particularly in Eastern Europe where many theorists and designers had continued writing in the communist period. Professional organizations and cultural institutions continued, active galleries and ambitious publishers dedicated to architecture appeared and numerous online venues for disseminating information sprung up in regional languages. All of which created a fertile intellectual context for the profession to make the difficult transition into the capitalist system.

Once the political and professional situation stabilized in the early 1990s, domestic and foreign investors were eager to tap into the region's appetite for new buildings, especially in large cities like Budapest, Moscow, Prague, and Warsaw. By the early 2000s, this demand even reached smaller cities in less developed regions, like Baku in Azerbaijan, Bucharest in Romania, and Kiev in Ukraine, making this a truly region-wide phenomenon, except perhaps east of Moscow where the financial and social situation remained difficult.

In terms of building typologies, production since the early 1990s has focused on types neglected in the communist period or which never existed at all in the region—commercial skyscrapers, office parks, luxury apartments, suburban houses, boutique hotels, high-end commercial properties, and shopping malls. Such buildings fulfill residents' yearnings to have what they missed during communism, not only the physical presence of new, colorful, and well-made buildings, but also architecture practiced as a creative act by a known author. Financing for these projects came from multiple sources, both legal and illegal. Some were spurred by the concentrated wealth, influence, and political power that the privatization process generated, including money gained through criminal, deceptive, and corrupt means. This includes villas and vacation homes for rich oligarchs and ex-Communist officials, and office buildings, condominiums, and cultural centers financed with suspicious funds.

Investors in legitimate projects were often large international real estate companies, many headquartered in Western Europe, looking to take advantage of pent-up demand in the region. The real estate arm of the Dutch Bank ING was typical. In 1992, ING commissioned Frank Gehry's Dancing House in Prague and then two years later hired the Dutch architect Erick van Egeraat from Mecanoo to renovate a nineteenth-century palace in Budapest for its Hungarian offices (Figure 13.10). In 2001, ING went back to Van Egeraat for the design of a newer 41,000-square-meter (441,000-square-foot) headquarters in Budapest. In the last 10 years, ING has funded a number of large mixed-use urban developments in cities such as Warsaw, and Liberec and Olomouc in the Czech Republic. Local entrepreneurs were also rich enough as the global building boom started in the early 2000s to commission commercial and residential projects, on their own or with international partners.

Rather than hire the local architects trained in the communist system, many large developers hired Western "starchitects" for their speculative projects, such as Norman Foster, Frank Gehry, Jean Nouvel and Renzo Piano. Their work in the region included Nouvel's Galeries Lafayette (1996) and the Potsdamerplatz redevelopment (2000) by Renzo Piano and others in the former East Berlin, Gehry's Dancing House (1996) and Nouvel's Zlatý Anděl/Golden Angel Building (2000) in Prague, and Foster's Metropolitan Building (2003) in Warsaw (Figure 13.11).

Successful émigrés such as the Czechs Eva Jiřícná and Jan Kaplický, and Polish-born Daniel Libeskind, also returned to the region and built successful practices using their knowledge of the region's languages and building culture. More recently, specialist architects such as American retail designers Jerde Partnership and Austrian housing designers Baumschlager and Eberle, have also been brought in to raise the notoriety and technical level of new projects. Other developers, like the Dutch Multi Corporation, have stopped hiring outside architects altogether,

13.10   Frank Gehry with Vlado Milunić, Dancing House, Prague, Czech Republic, 1996

and rely, instead, on an in-house team of unnamed designers to spread its global brand of commercial modernism (Figure 13.12).

A continuing interest in international architects can certainly be seen as a reaction against decades of anonymous design culture, but it is also reflects a desire to have some global status and proof of economic viability in the post-communist era. Not surprisingly, some starchitect proposals remain unbuilt because of inexperienced developers with overly ambitious designs. For example, Norman Foster had at least seven large Russian projects cancelled during the recent economic crisis, including the Crystal Island (2006) in Moscow, which would have been the world's largest building with 2.5 million square meters (27 million square feet) of floor area and

13.11 Jean
Nouvel, Zlatý
Anděl/Golden
Angel Building,
Prague, Czech
Republic, 2000

13.12 Construction
of Forum Nová
Karolina by Multi
Corporation, Ostrava,
Czech Republic, 2011

the Russia Tower (2006), designed to be the world's tallest naturally ventilated building with 118 floors. There is also a scarcity of highly qualified workers in the construction industry and a lack of government transparency and corruption in some countries. Recently this pattern—the preference for starchitects, corrupt politics, labor shortages, and a high rate of failed projects—has been repeated in Asia and the Middle East on an even larger scale.

Local architects have started to prove their potential to do work equal to their international peers. Some trained in the 1970s and 1980s have been able to adapt to the new conditions successfully, such as Vinko Penezić and Krešimir Rogina in Croatia and Josef Pleskot in the Czech Republic. There are also young practitioners, many educated both at home and in Western Europe or the United States, who are building reputations through small commissions and architectural competitions. One standout is the Slovene firm, Ofis Arhitekti, who started by designing innovative low-income housing in Slovenia and now have a global practice. Those looking to sample the region's young talent can often encounter their work at the national pavilions of the Venice Biennale where the small size of the region's countries allows for the work of many of the best designers to be exhibited. The ubiquity of English-language skills and the digitization of architectural practice mean that young Eastern European and Russian designers can now compete for projects outside their own countries, but so far few have made a name internationally.

Not surprisingly, the recent economic downturn has slowed the pace of development across the region and stopped the progress of young practitioners who are now struggling to find work. Some countries, including Latvia and Hungary, were especially hard hit by the 2008 collapse of the financial markets and subsequent crash of real estate prices. Cities and towns across the region were overconfident in the demand for new residential construction and currently have thousands of unsold units on the market. In many countries, residents have stayed in their communist-era apartments, spending money to renovate kitchens and bathrooms, instead of investing in costly new construction. The current situation is by far the worst in the former Soviet Union. Unlike countries that have joined the European Union, or the former Yugoslavia which has finally recovered from the destructive 1990s, much of Russia and its former territories suffer from poverty and severe social problems. Little investment has reached beyond the large Russian cities on the Western side of the country or the oil-rich nations in the Caucasus Region like Azerbaijan and Kazakhstan. Most Russians still live in unrenovated communist-era housing that continues to deteriorate with few options for financing improvements.

CONTEMPORARY PRACTICE

Two examples suggest the diversity and complexity of contemporary practice in the region. The Jerde Partnership's Złote Tarasy/Golden Terraces (2007), next to the Main Train Station in Warsaw's central business district, is a mixed-use development with 232,000 square meters (2.4 million square feet) of office, retail, entertainment, and hotel space and 1,400 underground parking spaces. The complex brought an

American-style mall experience to Warsaw with brands like Victoria's Secret, The
Body Shop, and Levi's, as well as a multiplex cinema, Burger King, the Hard Rock
Cafe, and two food courts. Its signature architectural feature is an undulating glass
roof, one of the largest in the world, which emerges amoeba-like from among
the complex's more traditional office and hotel towers to enclose the retail space
(Figure 13.13).

Like many similar mixed-use projects in the region, including Jerde's own
WestEnd City Center (1999) in Budapest, it was designed to enhance the commercial
infrastructure of a city that had previously relied on networks of small, poorly
stocked shops and dismal office spaces. The city and ING Real Estate jointly financed
the project, which was led by Chicago-based Epstein in consultation with Jerde
Partnership. Epstein opened a Warsaw office in the 1980s and helped shepherd the
project through the complexities of local building codes and contractors. Like other
large cities in the region, new construction is a point of pride for the city's image.
Złote Tarasy is just one of many new projects by international architects in Warsaw
including an office building by Norman Foster, residential towers by Helmut Jahn
and Daniel Libeskind, a museum by Finnish architect Rainer Mahlemaeki, and the
German Embassy by Kleine Metz Architekten. In speaking about the boom in new
buildings, and reflective of a general regional attitude, Tomasz Zemla, Deputy
Director of Warsaw's Department of Architecture and City Planning, recently said,
"we intend to build skyscrapers, yes … to be honest, we want to show off."[21]

A different view of contemporary practice comes through in a Russian example
that shows the challenges of working in the region, especially when a building
has national cultural significance. The new stage for the Mariinsky Theater in St.
Petersburg finally opened in May 2013 after 11 years of planning and construction. In

2002, Los Angeles-based architect Eric Owen Moss was hired to expand the theater by adding a second stage to the existing historical complex. His proposal, which included an exuberant glass façade that appeared to explode out of a rectangular volume, drew ire from the citizens of St. Petersburg and theater professionals and worried the Ministry of Culture who had to pay the bill. The ministry decided to fire Moss and then announced an international design competition for the same site. Moss was invited to submit a new design, but did not prevail. Instead, French architect Dominique Perrault won with his vision for a new theater volume encased in a web of gold filigree. Construction started on the project and work continued for five years, but by then only the foundations were complete. At that point, the government abandoned the design due to cost and scheduling concerns.

Finally in 2009, a second competition was held and the commission awarded to Toronto-based Diamond and Schmitt Architects who had to partner with local architects, KB ViPS, who had been working on the foundations of the Perrault proposal. The new design, which had to be adjusted slightly to incorporate some already-built foundation walls, is a contextual and comparatively conservative project with a masonry facade that matches the existing streetscape. According to the architects, its curved metal roof with a glass canopy "gives the building a contemporary identity rooted within the context of St. Petersburg's exceptional architectural heritage."[22] Unhappy with its less ambitious design, some locals have likened it to a "supermarket."[23] Even so, it is notable that the theater actually opened in 2013 after such a protracted design process.

CONCLUSION

The history of architecture in Eastern Europe and the former Soviet Union in the last 50 years offers instructive lessons about the relationships between models of architectural practice and design culture. Communist economic planning imposed a set of priorities and restrictions on architects that were not formal, or even material, but rather established a professional culture through which a set of practices and standards emerged. This building culture operated for more than 70 years in the Soviet Union and 40 years in Eastern Europe. In this period, cities were created, expanded, and remade. Millions of modern apartments were built that still house the majority of the region's citizens. However these environments were left to deteriorate without proper maintenance or investment. The last 20 years have been a period of reinvigoration and stabilization of these degraded spaces. For the most part, this has been a massive rehabilitation project, rather than the widespread demolition that some predicted. Thus Eastern Europe and the former Soviet Union have an imprint of their communist years that will not easily be erased, even as new building types and international architectural trends become the norm.

NOTES

1   Countries include Albania, Armenia, Azerbaijan, Belarus, Bosnia and Herzegovina, Bulgaria, Croatia, Czech Republic, East Germany (now considered Western European as part of a unified Germany), Estonia, Georgia, Hungary, Kazakhstan, Kosovo, Kyrgyzstan, Latvia, Lithuania, Macedonia, Moldova, Montenegro, Poland, Romania, Russia, Serbia, Slovakia, Slovenia, Tajikistan, Turkmenistan, Ukraine, and Uzbekistan.

2   Scholars use the terms communism, socialism, and state socialism to refer to the systems in these countries. For clarity, communism will be used here. Political scientist Andrew Roberts describes communist countries as "ruled by a single mass party that placed severe restrictions on all forms of civil society and free expression … [had] almost complete prohibition of private ownership of the means of production and a high degree of central planning … [and] were committed to revolution and the massive transformation of existing society." Andrew Roberts, "The State of Socialism: A Note on Terminology," *Slavic Review* 63/2 (Summer 2004): 359.

3   The only exception was Yugoslavia where private practice was initially ended, but returned as the economy became more open to independent enterprises in the 1960s.

4   For a discussion of the nature of this shift, see Kimberly Elman Zarecor, *Manufacturing a Socialist Modernity: Housing in Czechoslovakia, 1945–1960*, Pitt Series in Russian and East European Studies (Pittsburgh: University of Pittsburgh Press, 2011).

5   See for example, János Kornai, *The Socialist System: The Political Economy of Communism* (Princeton: Princeton University Press, 1992).

6   Henry W. Morton, "Housing in the Soviet Union," *Proceedings of the Academy of Political Science* 35/3 (1984): 72.

7   Stephen Kotkin, "Mongol Commonwealth? Exchange and Governance across the Post-Mongol Space," *Kritika: Explorations in Russian and Eurasian History* 8/3 (2007): 520.

8   R.A. French and F.E. Ian Hamilton, *The Socialist City: Spatial Structure and Urban Policy* (Chichester and New York: Wiley, 1979), 14–15.

9   Mark B. Smith, *Property of Communists: The Urban Housing Program from Stalin to Khrushchev* (DeKalb: Northern Illinois University Press, 2010), 113.

10 Przemyslaw Szafer, *Współczesna architektura polska/Contemporary Polish Architecture* (Warsaw: Arkady, 1988), 157.

11 Thomas P. Whitney (ed.), *Khrushchev Speaks: Selected Speeches, Articles, and Press Conferences, 1949–1961* (Ann Arbor: University of Michigan Press, 1963), 153–92.

12 Virág Molnár, "Cultural Politics and Modernist Architecture: The Tulip Debate in Postwar Hungary," *American Sociological Review* 70/1 (Feb. 2005): 118.

13 James C. Scott, *Seeing Like a State: How Certain Schemes to Improve the Human Condition Have Failed* (New Haven: Yale University Press, 1999).

14 See for example, Marie Šťastná, *Socha ve městě: vztah architektury a plastiky v Ostravě ve 20.století* (Ostrava: Ostrava University, 2008).

15 Hungary was the exception in the region, since only about 30 per cent of the new housing construction was large state-sponsored projects. This compares to East Germany 63 per cent, Czechoslovakia 83 per cent, Romania 92 per cent, and the Soviet Union 62 per cent. See Virág Molnár, "In Search of the Ideal Socialist Home in Post-Stalinist Hungary: Prefabricated Mass Housing or Do-It-Yourself Family Home?," *Journal of Design History*, 23/1 (2010): 61–81.

16   Henrieta Moravčíková (ed.) *Bratislava: Atlas Sídlisk 1950–1995 / Bratislava: Atlas of Mass Housing 1950–1995* (Bratislava: Slovart, 2011), 33.

17   See Lewis H. Siegelbaum, *Cars for Comrades: The Life of the Soviet Automobile* (Ithaca: Cornell University Press, 2008) 80–124.

18   Rostislav Švácha (ed.), *SIAL Liberec Association of Engineers and Architects, 1958–1990: Czech Architecture against the Stream* (Prague: Arbor Vitae, 2012).

19   Ines Weizman, "Citizenship," in C. Greig Crysler, Stephen Cairns and Hilde Heynen (eds), *Sage Handbook of Architectural Theory* (London: SAGE Publications, 2012), 107–20.

20   Thanks to Elidor Mëhilli for information on Maks Velo who spent eight years in prison in Albania after being accused of exhibiting foreign influences and modernist tendencies in the apartment building design shown in Figure 13.9.

21   Rudoplh Chelminski, "Warsaw on the Rise," *Smithsonian* 41/10 (February 2011): 32.

22   "New Mariinsky Theater," Diamond & Schmitt Architects, http://www.dsai.ca/projects/new-mariinsky-theatre-russia, accessed: February 1, 2013.

23   Anisia Boroznova, "The Mariinsky Faces New Challenges," *Russia beyond the Headlines*, December 2, 2011, http://rbth.ru/articles/2011/12/02/the_mariinsky_theater_faces_new_challenges_13888.html, accessed: February 1, 2013.

14

Finland: Architecture and Cultural Identity

Taisto H. Mäkelä

INTRODUCTION[1]

Finland was under Swedish rule for some 600 years until 1809 when it became an autonomous Grand Duchy under Russian rule and remained so until 1917 when Finland became an independent republic. The debate concerning the arts and architecture, nationalism, and what exactly constituted Finnish cultural identity in distinct contrast to Swedish or Russian had been ongoing since the mid nineteenth century. By coincidence, Finnish independence coincided with the advent of the modern movement that was international in scope and one of the consequences was that Finnish architecture became identified as a strand of modern architecture but adapted to its specific cultural context. The formal principles and social goals of the modern movement provided a framework for a newly independent nation seeking recognition as a distinct identity on the world stage. These modern principles and goals, along with regional traditions, continue to provide general reference points for Finnish architecture today. In 1990, architect Georg Grotenfelt stated: "In the 1910s the great change began with the breakthrough of modernism. Subsequently this has been developed in Finland in an unbelievably fine way right up to the fifties and sixties. Here modernism has acquired a more unique, more organic and local form than elsewhere."[2]

After the Winter War of 1939–40 and the Continuation War of 1941–42 with the USSR, reconstruction became Finland's major concern with architecture being considered an agent of social change as it generally was for the advocates of modern architecture in Europe.[3] This objective continued through the 1950s as part of the agenda of the *Congrès International d'Architecture Moderne* (1929–59) and Team 10 (1953–81). These organizations provided critical sources for architectural discourse in Finland, as well as Europe.[4] Of particular significance was the founding in 1959 in Helsinki of the modest but influential international quarterly architectural journal *Le Carré Bleu* by Finns associated with CIAM: Aulis Blomstedt, Reima Pietilä, Keijo Petäjä, Kyösti Alander.[5]

THE POST-WAR PERIOD AND THE 1960S

Aulis Blomstedt believed in universal laws of beauty and harmonics and developed a proportional system that he called "Canon 60" (and served as the title for his thematic article in *Le Carré Bleu* Volume 4, 1961). Based on the number "60" and on the human body and musical harmonies, this rationalist system was designed to produce simple and clear design and reflected a general interest in principles governing standardized production. Kristian Gullichsen and Juhani Pallasmaa used their *Moduli 225* system for experimental wooden summerhouses in Naantali in 1969 and Noormarkku in 1973.[6] These works were related to Blomstedt's "Canon 60" system but took the next step in exploring prefabricated serial production.

Histories of modern architecture in Finland often focus on Alvar Aalto. After all, he had been an internationally recognized figure since the early 1930s when he explored functionalism—but always mediated by humanism—in the Paimio Sanatorium (1932). His career blossomed in the 1950s with numerous famous works including the Municipal Center in Säynätsalo (1953), the Experimental House (1953), the Vuoksenniska Church in Imatra (1958), and the House of Culture in Helsinki (1958). Aalto's design for the Helsinki University of Technology in Otaniemi (1961–64) reflected an interest in creating a new educational environment appropriate to the twentieth century. The auditorium in the Main Building (completed 1964) explores a ribbed structural system (Figure 14.1) with innovative indirect day lighting and a steep angle for the seating to provide unhampered views of the stage.

As with Finnish architects for the most part, Aalto never lost sight of the value of the past for the present. For him, history provided a touchstone for practice in the present and believed that "Our ancestors will continue to be our masters."[7] As confirmed in both his writings and buildings, Aalto espoused humanist values as providing a core agenda for modern architecture.

There is, however, much more to Finnish architecture than Aalto. Kaija and Heikki Sirén's Student Chapel (1957, competition 1954, Figures 14.2 and 14.3) on the Helsinki University of Technology campus is hidden from view from the road but accessible by a narrow, dirt path rising through the trees. This building references the "forest" which holds a primordial sacredness for Finns. Even the cross is placed outside the glass wall of the altar.[8] The focus is not so much on the cross as on the forest in which it is placed. The materials throughout are simple with minimalist detailing.

Pre-cast and cast-in-place concrete became a central interest for many Finnish architects in the 1960s. A notable example is Pekka Pitkänen's Chapel of the Holy Cross, a crematorium complex in Turku (1967, Figures 14.4 and 14.5). Set back on a rise of a large grassy site framed by juniper bushes, the building itself is not visible from the parking lot upon approach. Only a tall, simple cross is visible from the foot of the steps and hints at the direction to take. It is an elegant design creating a harmonious formal composition of low volumes with circulation paths taking advantage of its site. The interior is equally thoughtful in terms of scale, proportion, textures, details and lighting. Pitkänen handles concrete in a precise and even delicate manner taking full advantage of the play of light to create surface texture and overall atmosphere. The focus here is on sensitive material expression rather than earlier modernist interests such as metaphors about the machine or the building's function as was the emphasis with 1970s Constructivism in Finland.[9]

The 1960s witnessed the emergence of a significant, even controversial, duo of architects after Aalto: Reima and Raili Pietilä. Together they produced a relatively small body of internationally recognized works of which most were built in Finland and generally defy standard architectural categories. Perhaps for this reason, their work stood as distinct from their compatriots and was marginalized for much of their careers.[10] Reima Pietilä published a number of thematic essays in *Le Carré Bleu*

14.1   Alvar Aalto. Helsinki University of Technology, Otaniemi, 1961– 64. Auditorium interior

14.2   Kaija and
Heikki Sirén.
Student Chapel,
Otaniemi, 1957.
Exterior

14.3   Kaija and
Heikki Sirén.
Student Chapel,
Otaniemi, 1957.
Interior

beginning with "Morphologie de l'Expression Plastique" in Volume 1 1958. Central, however, to his mature period was a belief in the existence of a *genius loci* at each specific building site. The architect's role, acting as a shaman of sorts, was simply to commune with these spirits to reveal authentic architectural form. Besides his commitment to the notion of *genius loci*, Reima Pietilä also stood out for his ideas about the relationship between language and the design process. He explained that "I talk whilst I draw—the rhythm and intonation of Finnish govern the movements of my pencil. Do I draw in Finnish? My language rhythm influences my

14.4   Pekka Pitkänen. Chapel of the Holy Cross, Turku, 1967. Exterior

14.5   Pekka Pitkänen. Chapel of the Holy Cross, Turku, 1967. Interior

drawing shapes, phrases my lines, outlines my surfaces."[11] Instead of the standard references driving architectural design, Pietilä had his own.

Their popular *Dipoli* student union building on the Helsinki University of Technology campus (1966, competition 1961, Figure 14.6) was, and is, a controversial and idiosyncratic work that juxtaposes rectilinear and curvilinear elements in plan and section. As Reima explained, "*Dipoli* has no definite demarcation at its base, or even at the top. It sinks into its terrain ... *Dipoli* breaks the boundaries of good functionalist aesthetics by aiming at nature's own way of making architecture. Smooth rocks, primeval shores, erratic boulders, rhombic shapes broken by ice."[12] The ground floor space was created by excavating the granite on the site with the resulting large boulders then carefully distributed inside and outside of the building.

14.6　Reima
and Raili Pietilä.
Dipoli, Otaniemi,
1966. Exterior

Variety in scale and form dominate the interior experience of *Dipoli*. Metaphors abound. Reima himself referred to the interior as evoking the experience of being in a cave or even inside a huge ancient beast such as a dinosaur. In this manner, the *genius loci* manifested as architectural form.

THE 1970S AND 1980S

Aalto's *Finlandia Hall* in Helsinki (1971–75) is a relatively monumental work in white Italian Carrara marble—hardly a local material—stretched out along the shore of Helsinki's Töölö Bay. It is the only part of an extended civic complex that Aalto had designed between 1959 and 1964. Rather than deferring to the existing context, Aalto intended to introduce a new type of urban model based on the automobile. Such approaches have never been popular in Finland and fortunately Aalto's plan was never carried out except for the fragment that is *Finlandia Hall*.

Georg Grotenfelt has a distinct agenda for architecture as a strategy for preserving the specifics of traditional cultural values in the face of universal mass culture with its alienation and contradictions. He suggests taking a different path that "gently follows an animal trail with the smell of sand and clay. It leads to the distant Wilds, the depths of the Forest and unvisited Islands—to our subconscious, conjured up by longing memory, deeper and deeper into our innermost world, back Home."[13] Grotenfelt also believes that it is only from this authentic, primordial path that it is possible to "self-confidently walk on the other path … without compromising ourselves."[14] His *Huitukka Sauna* of 1982 in Juva, Sääksjärvi (Figure 14.7) uses salvaged logs blackened from being in an old smoke sauna as a way of expressing this continuity between the past and the present.[15]

For Grotenfelt, tradition is the ground and source of meaning for architecture in the present.

One of the most respected and significant senior architects in Finland today is Juha Leiviskä. His well-known Church and Parish Hall in Myyrmäki (1984, competition 1980, Figure 14.8) is an extremely clever response to a very difficult site nestled up against a commuter railway track and station. The building is organized in a linear manner with tall walls along the side along the railway track sheltering the daily internal functions of the church from the ruckus just outside. Given the extreme dichotomy of daylight in a far northern country–in the summer there is very little darkness while in the winter there is very little light—light is a critical design component. Leiviskä is a master of manipulating it and refers to architecture as "an instrument played by light."[16] The interior congregational seating space registers the shifting qualities of external light that varies from season to season, from sunny to cloudy days, from the morning to the evening. Within just five minutes of sitting in the pews, it is possible to experience a significant change in interior atmosphere as the exterior light conditions change.

14.7 Georg Grotenfelt. Huitukka Sauna, Juva, Sääksjärvi, 1982. Exterior

14.8 Juha Leiviskä. Church and Parish Hall, Myyrmäki, 1984. Interior

Along with many other Finnish architects, Leiviskä is not interested in novelty but in preserving cultural continuity and coherence in a physical environment that is more and more fragmented: "If the environment is incoherent and includes contradictory elements, how with the help of new buildings, do you create the missing coherence? With really simple means, which may be thousands of years old, a rich and living environment can be created ... a milieu which is articulated and which contains highlights and nuances, changes in light values and intensity" and, moreover, "Within the framework of new architecture we must try to create the same spirituality and immateriality which can be quietly breathed in the interiors of old buildings."[17] According to Leiviskä, he has designed only one building over and over again trying to get it right.[18]

Another aspect of recent tendencies in Finnish architecture is manifested in Kristian Gullichsen's Poleeni Cultural Center in Pieksämäki of (1989, competition 1982, in collaboration with Timo Vormala, Eeva Kilpiö, and Aulikki Jylhä). This project employs an eclectic assortment of cultural metaphors and historical references and was designed for a small town in south central Finland. Gullichsen explains that Poleeni integrates traditional, regional references with pre-war functionalism, of which there are also examples in Pieksämäki. Functionalism was part of a faith in the future which appeared in independent Finland had in the 1930s and, consequently, became part of the country's national identity.[19] Again, it is the historical context of modernism in Finland that provides the most significant source of meaning as Gullichsen confirms, "At a deeper level lies the tradition of some 65 years of the modern movement which we are trying to interpret. It is my conviction that this intellectual and artistic base contains an inexhaustible source of architectural concepts, rich in meaning and history."[20]

THE 1990S AND 2000S

Mäntyniemi, the official Residence of the President in Helsinki, was completed by the Pietiläs in 1993 (Figure 14.9). It is definitely not an exercise in standardized production but rather a unique *Gesamtkunstwerk* in which all of the interior elements including, textiles, furnishings, tableware and lighting were designed by the Pietiläs. The exterior entry side of Mäntyniemi presents a defensive façade with a multifaceted, angled, massive granite base and walls that shield the waterfront walls of fenestration looking out onto a garden terrace. It is distinct as is each work by the Pietiläs and confirms again that they have never done the same building twice.

Lusto, the Finnish Forest Museum and Information Center (Figure 14.10) by Rainer Mahlamäki, Ilmari Lahdelma, and Juha Mäki-Jullilä opened in 1994 in the small eastern town of Punkkaharju. The forest industry (including pulp and paper) is central to the Finnish economy.[21] Lusto is a cast concrete building with its curvilinear external walls wrapped in wood siding. It celebrates not just the commercial value of wood but also the cultural myths of the Finnish forest.[22] As a visitor pamphlet states: "For a Finn the forest is a basic element of existence. Life has been agrarian for so long and urbanization is so recent that any Finn would feel a closeness and familiarity with the surrounding forest. For a Finn the forest is a multidimensional entity which includes ancient beliefs, folklore and modern life as well as industry."[23]

Among significant recent works outside of Finland, the Finnish Embassy in Washington, D.C., by Mikko Heikkinen and Markku Komonen with Sarlotta Narjus (Figure 14.11) deserves special attention. It has received much praise since it opened in 1994.[24] The architects successfully dealt with an awkward, steeply sloped and cramped site. Despite its simple external appearance, carefully detailed high-quality materials are used throughout. Main meeting rooms appear as floating

14.9 Reima
and Raili Pietilä.
Mäntyniemi,
Helsinki, 1993.
Exterior

14.10 Rainer
Mahlamäki, Ilmari
Lahdelma, Juha
Mäki-Jullilä. Lusto,
Punkkaharju,
1994. Exterior

cubes clad in shiny copper placed in a network of vertical and horizontal circulation. Complementing the contemporary aspects of the embassy, in the basement one finds a cliché of Finnish culture—a carefully crafted timber framed sauna. Again, a critical contemporary program is grounded by a primordial cultural reference.

The 2008 competition for a new library in Seinäjoki was won by JKMM architects (Asmo Jaaksi, Teemu Kurkela, Samuli Miettinen, Juha Mäki- Jullilä) opened in 2012 (Figure 14.12).[25] The Seinäjoki Library sits next to the Alvar Aalto-designed library of 1965 that was one of six buildings he designed for the Seinäjoki Administrative and Cultural Center that were built over a lengthy period, 1951–1988.[26] Apparently this

14.11   Mikko Heikkinen and Markku Komonen. Finnish Embassy, Washington, D.C., 1994 Interior

14.12   JKMM, Seinäjoki Library, Seinäjoki, Competition 2008, opened 2012. Exterior. Photo by Mika Huisman

old library had become too small to adequately serve the community. The JKMM design asserts itself in a respectful manner given its context. It stands separate from the Aalto's library but is connected by an underground passageway. Copper, a material that Aalto used mainly for roofs and details, serves as an external skin for the new library. It has been pre-treated to give it an aged green patina that respectfully connects it to the existing Aalto buildings. Again, careful attention is paid to materials, details, and lighting.

CURRENT AGENDAS

The reflection of cultural values and traditions with the use of specific materials carefully crafted and detailed along with the strategic use of light continues in four recent exemplary works with religious affiliations. Anssi Lassila's Kärsämäki Shingle Church (2004) is dramatic in its deference to traditional wood building, particularly shingles. Located by a river in Kärsämäki some 80 miles south of Oulu, the church was Lassila's master's degree thesis project. Not only are traditional materials used but also traditional building techniques. The inner log structure is wrapped in a pine-tarred shingle exterior shell. Daylight is provided by a lantern at the peak of the roof with only candles and lanterns used when it is dark.

Viikki Church of 2005 by Asmo Jaaksi, Teemu Kurkela, Samuli Miettinen and Juha Mäki- Jullilä (JKMM Architects) (Figures 14.13 and 14.14) is located in the new sustainable community in Helsinki. It also is sheathed in traditional shingles with the interior completely of wood (including the organ keyboard). St. Henry's Ecumenical Art Chapel, Turku (2005) by Matti and Pirjo Sanaksenaho of Sanaksenaho Architects (Figures 14.15 and 14.16) is a modest but exquisitely designed work that has become a very popular building for the public to visit. The exterior form reminds some of an upturned boat hull sheathed in copper. The simple, minimalist interior is completely of wood with indirect lighting strategically placed at the altar end to great effect. The final work to mention is the Kamppi Chapel of Silence in Helsinki (2012) by Kimmo Lintula, Niko Sirola, Mikko Summanen of K2S Architects (Figures 14.17 and 14.18). In the form of a large bowl with indirect interior light from the ceiling above, wood again is the dominant material and is used to isolate an interior experience from the hustle and bustle of the busy urban commercial center of Kamppi.

14.13 Asmo Jaaksi, Teemu Kurkela, Samuli Miettinen and Juha Mäki- Jullilä (JKMM). Viikki Church, Helsinki, 2005. Exterior

14.14 Asmo Jaaksi, Teemu Kurkela, Samuli Miettinen and Juha Mäki- Jullilä (JKMM). Viikki Church, Helsinki, 2005. Interior

14.15 Matti and Pirjo Sanaksenaho. St. Henry's Ecumenical Art Chapel, Turku 2005. Exterior

Finnish architects continue to explore tectonic principles including material, structure, and details, within specific cultural contexts. The Kärsämäki Shingle Church, the Viikki Church, St. Henry's Ecumenical Art Chapel, and the Kamppi Chapel of Silence are part of a historical continuum of Finnish architecture that can be seen as paying homage to the Petäjävesi Church of 1763–65, the paradigm of traditional wooden church building in Finland (Figure 14.19).

These four contemporary works constitute a tempering of the universal agenda of modern architecture with the regional specifics. As Alan Colquhoun incisively explained, "the acceptance of tradition, *in some form*, is the condition of architectural meaning,"[27] and that "Clearly, the doctrine of regionalism is based on an ideal social model—one might call it the "essentialist model." According to this model, all societies contain a core, or essence, which must be discovered and preserved. One aspect of this essence lies in local geography, climate, and customs involving the use and transformation of local, "natural" materials.'"[28]

The history of architecture in Finland is a series of evolutionary debates against a backdrop of traditional cultural references. The architectural historian Riitta Nikula has explained on behalf of her fellow Finns that, "Because we are on the periphery, we feel free to adopt innovations from the main cultural centers via many different routes, and to mix and match them as we see fit to suit our own unique requirements."[29] Architects in Finland continue to reference their cultural traditions in the attempt to create a relevant architectural identity in a global present.

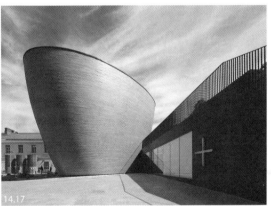

14.16   Matti and Pirjo Sanaksenaho. St. Henry's Ecumenical Art Chapel, Turku 2005. Interior

14.17   Kimmo Lintula, Niko Sirola, Mikko Summanen (K2S). Kamppi Chapel of Silence, Helsinki, 2012. Photo by Marko Huttunen. Exterior

14.18   Kimmo Lintula, Niko Sirola, Mikko Summanen (K2S). Kamppi Chapel of Silence, Helsinki, 2012. Interior. Photo by Tuomas Uusheimo

14.19   Jaakko Klemetinpoika Leppänen . Petäjävesi Church, Petäjävesi, 1763–65. Interior

NOTES

1   This chapter is based in part on the author's "Architecture and Modern Identity in Finland," *Finnish Modern Design: Utopian Ideals and Everyday Realities 1930–97*, ed. Marianne Aav and Nina Stritzler-Levine (New Haven: Yale University Press, 1998), 52–81.

2   Georg Grotenfelt, "Interview," *An Architectural Present—7 Approaches* (Helsinki: Museum of Finnish Architecture, 1990), pp. 184–5. He also states "I see no reason to re-evaluate this development. There is no reason to look elsewhere to invent something new—the world created by the great radical architects of modernism is a fathomless source of inspiration and theoretical rejuvenation."

3   An important example of this approach is Yrjö Lindegren's (1900–1952) *Snake House* apartment block of 1951 in Helsinki. Containing 190 state-financed apartments, its curving forms adapt themselves to the irregular terrain of the site. Another later example is Aulis Blomstedt's *Ketju* row houses and *Kolmirinne* apartment blocks of 1954 are located in the new garden suburb of Tapiola (begun in 1953), itself a symbol of post war social ideals.

    See also *Heroism and the Everyday*, ed. Riitta Nikula and Kristiina Paatero (Helsinki: Museum of Finnish Architecture, 1994).

4   Eric Mumford, *The CIAM Discourse on Urbanism—1928–1960* (Cambridge, MA: MIT Press, 2002).

    Max Risselada and Dirk van den Heuvel (eds), *TEAM 10: In Search of a Utopia of the Present 1953–1981* (Rotterdam: NAi Publishers, 2005).

5   Joining them was the Romanian André Schimmerling. Each volume had a theme and after the first volume numbered "0" and titled "Introduction du Débat – par le groupe C.I.A.M. de Helsinki," the main thematic essay in each of following seven volumes was written by a Finn. Having *Le Carré Bleu* in Helsinki imbedded Finnish architects and their collaborators in the broader debates about modern architecture.

6   For a discussion of the history of residential wooden construction systems, see Pekka Korvenmaa, "Talotehtailusta Universaalijärjestelmin: Teollinen Esivalmistus, Modernismin Utopiat ja Puukulttuurin Ehdot," ("From House Manufacture to Universal Systems: Industrial prefabrication, the utopias of modernism and the conditions of wood culture"), *Rakennettu Puusta: Timber Construction in Finland*, Marja-Riitta Norri and Kristiina Paatero (eds) (Helsinki: Museum of Finnish Architecture, 1996), 62–75.

7   Aalto, "Motifs from Times Past," *Sketches*, 1–2.

8   Tadao Ando's Church on the Water in Hokkaido (near Tomamu), Japan of 1985–1988 also has the cross outside but in a pool of water. Ando was familiar with the Chapel in Otaniemi and apparently had visited it.

9   Another example of sacred architecture during this period is the *Tapiola Church* of 1965 by Aarno Ruusuvuori in Espoo is often referred to as an example of Brutalism but more appropriately it should be described simply as an exercise in concrete minimalism. Ruusuvuori used modular concrete block and pre-cast panels create an interior sheltered from the exterior. Indirect day lighting combined with candles and the delicate sound of a small fountain facilitates withdrawal into a spiritual realm. Erkki Elomaa shared Ruusuvuori's interest in tectonic expression in concrete. Elomaa is not a well-known architect and his main work is the *Church* in Järvenpää of 1967 (competition 1963). It has always been a controversial building generating strong reactions for and against, particularly the bell tower. In any case, Elomaa successfully

combined pure volumes with carefully detailed cast in place concrete surfaces. Again, day lighting plays a crucial role in creating an appropriate interior atmosphere for a spiritual building.

10   Pietilä, "Concept of Visual Entity in Environmental Design (1971)," *Pietilä: Intermediate Zones in Modern Architecture*, 137, explained the predicament thus: "My colleagues say that I am not communicating in the way that common people could understand, or that my image is language only for myself having not much to do with current practice. My answer to the critics is that my subject is so unpopular because visual design is wrongly identified with architectural aesthetics. When one is trying to conceive [of] the wider context than the usual functional and technological forms of [the] physical environment, the subject is hard to discuss even in professional circles."

11   Pietilä, "Architecture and Cultural Regionality," 8.

12   Reima Pietilä, "Architecture and Cultural Regionality: Interview with Reima Pietilä," *Pietilä: Intermediate Zones in Modern Architecture* (Helsinki: Museum of Finnish Architecture, 1985), 12–13. Pietilä, ibid., also explains how the windows play a critical role in the interconnection between the forest outside and the forest inside: "*Dipoli* contains over 300 different windows or sets of windows all at varying angles ... When the vertical frames of the windows stand like trees in nature, the spaces in between them increase and diminish naturally ... The visual impression created is of the forest extending through the windows into the interior."

13   Georg Grotenfelt, *Arkkitehti* 2 (1993), 17. Translation modified by author.

14   Ibid.

15   *An Architectural Present—7 Approaches*, Marja-Riitta Norri and Maija Kärkkäinen (eds), (Helsinki: Museum of Finnish Architecture, 1990), 151: "*Huitukka Sauna* has been built from old barn timbers. There is the date 1861 carved on the door jamb, but as the timber was moved before this, it is obviously even older." This author understands that the logs were taken not from a barn but from an old *savu sauna* (smoke sauna) and that's why they are black.

16   Leiviskä, "The Lasting Values of Architecture," *New Finnish Architecture*, 12. It also should be noted that he is a talented pianist.

17   Leiviskä, "The Lasting Values of Architecture," 12.

18   Leiviskä, quoted in a lecture given at the Helsinki University of Technology in 1995.

19   Kristian Gullichsen, "Kulttuurikeskus Poleeni," *Arkkitehti* 8 (1989), 3 (offprint).

20   Gullichsen, "Civic Centre Poleeni," *An Architectural Present—7 Approaches*, 34.

21   Forests are treated as sustainable resources. "National Forest Inventories" that estimated the total number of trees in Finland were begun as early as 1921.

22   Two fairly recent exhibitions at the Finnish Museum of Architecture reflect the ongoing interest in a mythical forest culture: *The Language of Wood: Wood in Finnish Sculpture, Design, and Architecture* (Helsinki: Museum of Finnish Architecture, 1987) and *Timber Construction in Finland* (Helsinki: Museum of Finnish Architecture, 1996).

23   *Discovering the Forest* (Punkaharju: The Finnish Forest Museum, 1994), 8. *Lusto* is a successful amalgam of corporate interests and cultural references.

24   The website for the Finnish Embassy (www.finland.org) provides a virtual tour of the building and lists quotes from various commentators: "Critic William Morgan of the *Architectural Review* (United Kingdom) said the Finnish Embassy was 'the U.S. political capital's best building in 50 years'. Benjamin Forgey of *The Washington Post* said it was

'a breath of fresh architecture in Washington'. And Herbert Muschamp of *The New York Times* especially noted the spatial complexity of the building and concluded: 'Once you are inside, it may occur to you that Finland's space program is light–years ahead of ours.'"

25   The firm earlier had won the 1998 competition for the *Turku Central Library*. This very successful and much praised design opened in 2007.

26   The other five buildings are the "Cross of the Plains Church" of 1951–60, the "Parish Centre" of 1951–66, the "Town Hall" of 1958–60, the "Office Building" of 1964–68, and the "City Theatre" of 1961–87. These were built by a town with a population of around 30,000.

27   Alan Colquhoun, "Three Kinds of Historicism," *Modernity and the Classical Tradition: Architectural Essays 1980–87* (Cambridge, MA: The MIT Press, 1989), 15. In addition, Colquhoun, "Introduction: Modern Architecture and Historicity," *Essays in Architectural Criticism: Modern Architecture and Historical Change* (Cambridge, MA: The MIT Press, 1981), 19: "If criticism is to carry out its function of making judgments, it must have at its disposal norms which belong to the architectural tradition—a ground against which to measure and evaluate the contingencies of the present" and Colquhoun in "Postmodernism and Structuralism: A Retrospective Glance," *Assemblage 5*, February 1988, 10: "Just as language always preexists a group or individual speaker, the system of architecture preexists a particular period or architect. It is precisely through the persistence of earlier forms that the system can convey meaning. These forms, or *types*, interact with the tasks presented to architecture, in any moment in history, to form the entire system."

28   Alan Colquhoun, "The Concept of Regionalism," *Arquitectura* 291, March 1992, 16.

29   Riitta Nikula, "Great Men from Little Finland," *Arkkitehti* 2 (1993), 35.

15

Architecture in Africa: Situated Modern and the Production of Locality

Iain Low

INTRODUCTION

As a construct, Africa has always been defined in the interest of outsiders. Predominantly conceived of as a resource base for its mineral wealth and cheap labour, the continent has been historically reduced to a commodity. This 'othering' was exemplified by colonial practice which overwrote all in its path, effectively embarking on a project of cultural genocide. 'Whiteness' in the shape of Western value and its limited Cartesian and perspectival vision became the measure of all things 'good'. This marginalisation of the local had profound effect on spatial practice. Under colonial rule, indigenous architecture and the vernacular were subject to 'arrested development' with Western modernism supplanting the local. Indeed with modernity underpinning the colonial project, modernism became the logical handmaiden of the colonial project. Consequently, it is possible to travel the entire continent and be confronted with exceptional examples of modern architecture and urbanism.[1] 'Colonial Modern' as Tom Avermaete and others have chosen to term it, reflects the persistence of the colonial project in a context of the creative experimentation with local conditions, which ultimately contested the colonial imperative, evolving to more nuanced and negotiated moderns.[2] This is not unlike other colonial peripheries such as India, Brazil and Turkey where the contradictions of climate, technique and cultural imperative have been critically incorporated by designers in countering the hegemony of colonial imposition.[3]

The half-century period from 1960 through 2010 is marked by numerous events that have impacted on global change and development. Whilst for architecture the closing meeting of CIAM signified an important transition for the Modern Movement, it was the advent of independence for African countries during the second half of the twentieth century that has presented the opportunity for democracy and enabled the possibility of real change across the continent.[4] This moment signified the promise of regime change and the advent of the new, including transformed spatialities. Initially architectural responses to political change were uncritical and predominantly mimicked the approach of the colonial powers. This is particularly evident in early nationalistic projects such as Ghana's Independence Arch (1957) and Nigeria's National Assembly (1999), that sought to establish an identity for liberation movements.[5] However, the [re-]surfacing of local cultural bias very soon introduced tension into the struggle for the representation of new national identities in their struggle of formation. Ali Al'Amin Mazrui and Nnamdi Elleh refer to a triple heritage project for African architecture, locating it within a competitive dialogue between African, Arab and European cultural imperatives.[6] This historicist interpretation might have been the basis for early post-independence architectural and spatial production, but world events such as the advent of globalisation and the collapse of the Cold War combined with the benefit of 50 years of independence has enabled a more complex production on the continent.

PRECONDITIONS

Independence in Africa brought with it not only a transfer of power to liberation movements, but, and perhaps more importantly, a desire for a return to 'origins,' to those cultural conditions shared by indigenous people.[7] It was unrealistic and impractical to eradicate the imposition of modern architecture. Whilst the period up until the commencement of independence had been characterised by wholesale modernism, it had never been embraced by ordinary citizens. Contestation came in various forms, however, most obviously through physical amendments to the architectural fabric. Whereas the work of Maxwell Fry and Jane Drew in West Africa adapted modernism to local conditions, this was predominantly reflected in innovative responses to climate.[8] Local cultural practices were inaccessible and largely misunderstood by outsiders. At this time most architectural design in Africa was still being undertaken by colonists whose education and cultural bias was grounded in Western modernism. The few local architects, such as Olowole Olumuyiwa in Nigeria, were educated overseas in a euro-centric paradigm, only to return as masters of modernism.[9]

It was inevitable that the clash between cultures should have its effect on spatial production. This is obvious in two primary manifestations; the adaptation of

15.1   Pierre Fakhoury, Basilica of Our Lady of Peace, Yamasoukra, Ivory Coast, 1985–89

buildings by users, to suit specific cultural needs, and the adaptation of architects in interpreting local factors in the design of buildings. This is evident in modernist projects across the continent, in 'French Morocco', 'Belgian Congo' and 'British South Africa;' most notably where colonial powers had imposed housing solutions for local inhabitants who had become rapidly urbanised in response to the colonisers' need for cheap labour. In each these cases modernism remains the measure of architectural authenticity.

The '60s saw not only the advent of independence, but also a new wave of local colonial architects; those who had been born and raised, and possibly even educated in Africa, and consequently had a better respect and appreciation for the pre-existent. The work produced by this generation demonstrates a more nuanced approached to design, whereby the local has been negotiated. Considerations of climate and technique predominate over cultural concerns, and the projects persist in reflecting the European modern base. The projects of Jean-François Zevaco in Morocco, Roland Simounet in Algeria, Henri Chomette in Ivory Coast and Congo, Richard Hughes in Kenya, Anthony Almeida in Tanzania, Julian Elliott in Zambia, and Amancio ('Pancho') Guedes in Mozambique reflect the early commencement of not simply more a located modernism, but also a certain freedom of expression. In a certain sense this early period displays 'mannerist' tendencies and previews post modernism yet to come.

The oeuvre of Roelof Uytenbogaardt reflects this tendency. Born and educated in Cape Town, he subsequently sojourned at the British School in Rome before proceeding to Philadelphia to undertake graduate studies through an Urban Design degree in architecture and planning under Louis Kahn and David Crane.[10] Returning to Cape Town his projects bear witness to an evolving sensibility that demonstrates the ability of design to mediate difference and offer open representations. All of these projects originate in the latter part of the twentieth century and are firmly based in the modernist tradition. However, they are each permeated by an idea of what it might mean to dwell under a specific set of conditions, in this case

15.2   Antoni Almeida, Joint Christian Chapel, University of Dar es Salaam, Tanzania, 1976

apartheid Cape Town. Embracing contemporary complexity, these projects have all been contentious, yet also generally each capable of transcending the singular and connecting with the needs of disadvantaged and politically excluded communities. Whilst modern referents are clearly discernible in this body of work, for the first time the specificity of place as a socio-spatial construct becomes evident. Each project is discernibly different, yet obviously emerges from the same author, evoking a contradictory autonomy in work that has been contextually produced.

Despite the granting of independence, colonial powers maintained significant political and economic influence over their former colonies. Toward the end of the twentieth century, the fall of the Berlin Wall and the end of the Cold War, and the subsequent advent of globalisation, have been paralleled with the struggle for democracy in Africa. The result has been in a more localised production where the agency of authorship has come to creatively mediate between complex determinants of form.[11]

Change on the continent is historically slow. This is predominantly accountable to power relations between coloniser and colonised and has inhibited the production of 'other' architectures and contemporary responses to global problems. Nevertheless Africa is increasingly faced with similar problems and demands as the rest of the world.[12]

SITUATED MODERN: THE PRODUCTION OF LOCALITY IN AFRICA

Today one might discern an emerging body of work and concomitant architectural condition that could be considered as an *African architecture-in-progress*.[13] Located at an intersection between competing rationalities of colonial modern and indigenous traditional, the work is predicated on critical authorship. Mediating

15.3   A typical project of this tendency; Uytenbogaardt et al., Werdmuller Centre, Cape Town, South Africa, 1973

the design of 'site, enclosure and materiality' with the specificity of local cultural imperative, the agency of architectural design and its capacity for speculative interpretation is becoming a primary basis for a conscious renegotiation of the modern project.[14]

Identifiable as 'situated modernism', it is recognisable in the manner by which local culture and practices are [re-]incorporated into respective projects. Of these, it is the creative inclusion of participatory processes that appear to be capable of providing stronger direction for an African architecture. Running counter to modernistic modes of production, these processes contest a number of fundamental attributes of modernism, such as its economic and technical rationalisation and the reductive abstraction of the socius.[15]

Multiple positions of architecture have recently been projected by Duanfang Lu and colleagues.[16] The benefit of hindsight enables better clarity in identifying the emergence of a critical capacity within the discipline on the continent in the post-Fathy to early twenty-first century period. Intersections between design, practice, materials and use have facilitated a participatory practice predicated more in principles of *ubuntu* than economic utilitarianism and material consumption, through a tension that gives both character and valence, situating projects as critically different.[17]

Whilst the earlier work of architects such as Zevaco, Simounet, Chomette, Hughes, Almeida, Elliott, Guedes[18] and Uytenbogaardt[19] initiated this trope of architectural identity, its subsequent pluralisation is accountable to gradual political stability associated with developing democracy and the concomitant absence of a limiting meta-narrative, such as modernism under colonialism. Such projects are comparatively uncommon and, unlike in the case of the West, they do not present us with any clear evolutionary trajectory, but rather, they exist on disparate sites across the continent.[20] Unlike in developed contexts, these do not present a discrete body of work, but simply represent a situated production resulting from highly specific and temporally determined set of influences. In the absence of a particular set of meta-references it becomes impossible to classify them, except perhaps through an expanded lens of the local, or what has become termed by Appadurai's 'production of locality'.[21]

15.4 'from outside to inside' illustration from Antoni Folkers, *Modern Architecture in Africa*, 2010

Spatial order is one of the most striking means by which we recognise the
existence of the cultural differences between one social formation and another.
Bill Hillier and Julienne Hanson, The Social Logic of Space.[22]

In the book *From Outdoor to Indoor Living*, Anita Larsson reflects on her research and experience of living and working in Botswana.[23] Her primary observation is directed at a critique of the effects of modernisation in the radically shifting patterns of human settlement and the configuration of sites within those terrains. She identifies the move "from outdoor to indoor" as the spatial consequence of this shift. Where traditional settlement and vernacular building types privilege outdoor space, the exterior becomes productively engaged in the life of buildings and their occupants, with fundamental benefit for sustaining the extended traditional family.

The weak urbanism that modernism spawned has been a consequence of the rising autonomy of the architectural object and the alienation of the human being in both the production of space and its subsequent use. Many of the underlying disputes at CIAM and Team 10 can be related to conflicts over interpretations of the architectural project as a social or an abstract material one, and its consequence for human environment. It is not surprising that 'dissidents' such as Aldo van Eyck and Jacob Bakema owe their difference to embodied experiences of otherness on the African continent, where, as Larsson has encountered, indigenous social systems still find their physical representation within the built environment.[24]

Hassan Fathy's work in Egypt, exemplified by the village of New Gourna (1945–48), was emblematic of a sensibility toward the coexistence of difference and the production of locality, and encouraged a vein of architectural innovation across the continent.[25] Through this approach there emerged a genuine possibility to restore traditional practices within the framework of the colonisers' project. Bureaucratic failure and infighting within the Egyptian government rendered Fathy's efforts mute. The potential of this approach was further eroded by co-option and fake revivalism of Islamic architecture in the Gulf.[26]

However, the unevenness that characterises post-independence architectural production in individual states renders it impossible to identify specific strains of a 'non-Western modernism' across the African continent. The dearth of architectural schools for the training of professionals, the absence of a progressive and advanced construction industry, the relative prominence of geography, climate and culture as conditions impacting on the design of human settlement, and the absolute imperative for progressive development in the face of the bitter void left by colonial occupation all contribute toward local resistance to Western modernism. Nevertheless, at the same time, the legacy of colonialism, and its failure to either transfer or develop local knowledge, has ensured an ambivalent inheritance that enables innovative transgressions. Homi Bhabha expanded on Albert Memmi's 1957 treatise on the colonised to identify these as 'colonial mimicry, hybridity or social liminality'.[27] Underlying this ongoing struggle is a quest for an authentic African identity, of ridding oneself of the shackles of colonialism and offering new models for contemporary life on the continent. The project of architecture in Africa must therefore be construed as necessarily one of de-colonisation.[28]

PRODUCTION OF LOCALITY: THE SPATIO-TECTONIC-MATERIAL IMPERATIVE

Four related projects, by different architects, in different countries, produced at different times, across the length of the continent, demonstrate a consistent approach to the contemporary project of architecture on the African continent.[29] What binds these projects is a reliance on spatio-tectonic-material translations that have been produced through substantial and evident reliance on the interpretation of local cultural practice. In each instance this has been construed through re-imagining both human and material processes into architectural production. By embedding local skill and community effort it is possible to effect contemporary architectures which, whilst separated by the specificity of particular place and time, are intimately connected in an identity making that is authentically African.

01. Diébédo Francis Kere, Primary School, Gando, Burkino Faso

Gando is a small village of 3,000 in the southern plains of Burkino Faso, some 200 km from the capital, Ouagadougou. Diebedo Francis Kere is the first person from Gando to study abroad. Believing in the primacy of education for development he promoted the design and construction of a school for his home village. As an architectural student at TU Berlin he initiated 'Bricks for Gando School' to raise funds for the project. Working with a government agency, LOCOMAT, and the local community, he designed and built a primary school for 150 children.[30]

Three rectangular classrooms blocks joined by a plinth and a double roof make for the structure. Each classroom accommodates 50 learners. Both walls and ceiling are fabricated from compressed stabilised earth, strengthened by the addition of a small percentage of cement. Thirty thousand 6-cm-long bricks were manufactured on site by the villagers. A 'floating' zinc sheet roof on steel trusses permits free air movement, reducing heat gain by virtue of the space and its overhang. The trusses are manufactured from lightweight reinforcement steel. Villagers cut with a handsaw and assembled them by welding, obviating the necessity to import large material and equipment to site. The simple hand-operable shutters promote cross-ventilation and the ability to modulate light.

Whilst the linear configuration of classrooms reflects a modern rational organisation of space, it is also a necessary quality for the functioning of a modern school and the education of pupils who want to enter the formal economic system. Where the project excels is in Kere's identification and design appropriation of

15.5   Diébédo Francis Kéré, Secondary School, Dano, Burkino Faso, 1999–2001

local materials and construction methods for villager inclusion. The resultant architectural form substantially engages the local in innovative ways. The creative interpretation of traditional spatial practices, of local materials and construction techniques has reasserted the role of tradition in design and propelled an unknown designer from remote rural village into the global imagination.[31]

Not only has Kere achieved a first for his village through his acquiring professional expertise, he has imaginatively reflected on that education and projected a new architectural approach to the problem of rural development. In attending to the dualities between indoor and outdoor space he has also managed to suggest spatial configurations that re-engage productive outdoor space that is appropriate to the African rural context.

02. Fabrizio Carola, Community Projects in West Africa

Kaedi is located in a remote sector in the South of Mauritania, close to the border with Senegal. Its hospital serves a large rural community. An extention to the complex has added 120 beds, an operating theatre complex, paediatric, surgical and ophthalmic departments, a maternity and general medical unit, a laundry, kitchens, store rooms, a garage and workshop. The architects' brief was to develop new low-cost construction techniques employing local materials and skills that could also be applicable to other building types in the region. All labour was locally sourced and trained on site. Whilst brick was not in the local vernacular, a good clay source enabled the production of handmade, in-situ fired bricks. The design evolved through experimentation, developing a vocabulary of half domes, pod-shaped spaces and self-supporting pointed arches for connecting corridors. An overall plan for the extention was derived from deploying these forms in relation to the new functions. The incorporation of glass blocks enabled adequate natural

15.6 Fabrizio Carola and Birahim Niang, Regional Hospital, Kaedi, Mauritania, 1987–89

light at interstices without hygienic or structural compromise. Despite reliance on natural locally produced materials and techniques the hospital is both sanitary and spatially pleasurable for all users, whilst predominantly built with site sourced materials and local labour.

In the case of architect Fabrizio Carola's expanded ouevre, innovation resides in technical instrumentation. The adaptive invention of his offset "radial formwork" mechanism has provided a simple tool through which to mass-produce, yet spatially manipulate, forms. The adjustable radius enables units of space, of different dimension, to be easily constructed by semi-skilled workers, whilst unskilled labour produces the necessary building blocks. The composite layouts, whilst geometrically organised, are capable of being ordered to different scales and configurations depending on the complexity and specificity of programmes. It includes numerous innovations around appropriate technology and energy conservation. Carola's production straddles multiple countries and sites throughout western Africa. Three decades of persistent investigation through the same approach has evolved a grounded modernism. A productive tension between mass production and differentiation has been creatively resolved on local terms against a wide variety of site and social conditions. In this sense he is perhaps an inheritor of Fathy's legacy, having interpreted it through both technical and spatial advances.

03. Training for Self-Reliance Project – TSRP Architects: National Schools Upgrade Program, Lesotho

The task of upgrading education throughout a small mountainous kingdom poses a compelling task for architectural innovation. However, funding by the International Development Agency division of the World Bank opened the project to tendering by contractors from all of the bank's member countries. How, then, to rapidly deploy across difficult rural and urban contexts without rendering the project to the economically utilitarian and rationality of mass production and prefabrication that Western modernisation has evolved?

The solution lay in a systemised approach to rapid in-situ production. Relying on a symbiotic relation between skilled and unskilled labour with local materials and site conditions, the project promotes the local. Clear differentiation was established

15.7   Iain Low – TSRP Architects, Training for Self-Reliance Project, Kingdom of Lesotho, 1982–87

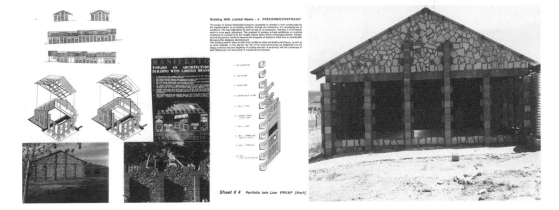

Sheet # 4   Portfolio Iain Low PRVAP [Arch]

between minimal skilled construction and maximising local participation in an iterative, yet adaptive process. Whilst contextually derived, the system is capable of replication across multiple sites throughout a geographically diverse country.

Massification is dependent upon the design of a single apparently simple structural columnar system. However, it has an inherent valency that encourages for multiple combinations and spatial permutations, thereby rendering it capable of responding to changing demands. As an enabling structure, the system is open to achieving different functional and technical possibilities, whilst simultaneously affording unique aesthetic resolutions between opposing modes of production.

Tradition and modernity have been creatively reconciled by responding to multiple informants comprising competing rationalities of urban-rural, identity making-utilitarianism and the possibility to effect different spatial-functional types. This open-ended approach encourages participatory practice in both its construction and its everyday use. The possibility of double storey permits both densification and the potential for doubling accommodation with minimal effort and cost. Energy efficiency has been promoted through the utilisation of passive systems that deploy the plentiful solar energy and wind. This is evident in the incorporation of *trombe* walls, overhead rooflights, ample cross-ventilation and related passive strategies such as orientation and siting to maximise the use of outdoor areas.

04. Cohen Judin Architects, Nelson Mandela Museums, South Africa

The design and implementation of a new museum in the Eastern Cape, home of Nelson Mandela, presented a compelling challenge for design. Initiated at the outset of post-independence South Africa, it is located in a poverty stricken rural province where traditional livelihoods are still barely intact. The response has reconfigured the museum as a conventional type by reconceptualising both its siting and its programming. Three sites associated with Nelson Mandela's history

15.8   Cohen Judin & Department of Public Works, Government of Republic of S.A., Nelson Mandela Museums, Eastern Cape, South Africa, 1999

were chosen: Mvezo, his birthplace, Qunu, where he spent his early childhood, and Mthata the capital of the Eastern Cape.

Movement is essential to rural life. These historical sites have become reconnected along a national highway, placing them within the domain of the everyday and tourist experience. A series of routes and interventions establishes links between rural places, whilst built interventions have been programmed to accommodate both everyday rural needs, as well as those of ceremonial and tourist interests. Shading and water points provide a utilitarian layer catering to the basic needs of ordinary poor people, whilst visibility and legacy information speak directly to the needs of tourism and local visitors to the historic sites.

The built interventions are pavilions, comfortable in their rural outdoor contexts. Simple steel structures with flat iron roofs, combined with infill of traditional materials, constructed by local women, thereby introducing a hybrid architecture that straddles the rural hut and the farm shed. Evoking Mies' Barcelona Pavilion, they do not enclose space, but rather embrace traditional spatial syntax to engage their context. This understanding represents a provocative interpretation of modernism, and suggests a unique transcendence of colonial modernism by virtue of its resonance as a contemporary rural or vernacular construct. In interpreting both local spatial and tectonic practice, it has brought architecture into confrontation with integrated development and poverty alleviation.

PRODUCTION OF LOCALITY: THE SPATIO-TECTONIC-FORMAL IMPERATIVE

At the other end of the spectrum there exists a body of African work that, whilst locally produced, participates in contemporary global discourses.[32] Whilst representing architectural responses to the plethora of contemporary issues of

15.9   OMM Design Workshop, Constitutional Court, Johannesburg, South Africa. 2001–2004

space and transformation, such as sustainability and climate change, technological advancement, movement and mobility, the densification of living environments and the privatisation of the public realm, the identities of individual buildings seem more closely associated with authorship than with a new modernism or specific architectural genre.[33]

Within this paradigm a new contradiction has emerged. It appears that there is heightened competition between the multiple rationalities that inform architectural form. Authorship, building type and the plurality of underlying architectural projects have become increasingly difficult to reconcile. It would be easy to dismiss this tendency within the generalised trope of hyper-modernism, but the increasing evidence of exemplary architectural projects on the African continent suggests otherwise.

The 'situated modernism' that arises from producing our own locality is not necessarily confined to low-income projects in rural areas that employ local skill and materials. Globalisation has ensured that marginal territories need more than ever to strategically compete within the socioeconomic and political realities of a rapidly emerging world culture. The advantage of the African continent lays in its less developed status. This infers the possibility of producing localities that are primarily rooted in relational and contextual exigencies, as opposed to simply the spatial and the scalar.[34] Consequently, new forms of collaborative practice between foreign and local firms, between economic empowerment of black and previously advantaged white forms, between local authorities, communities and consultants, as well as site-specific practices such as upgrading facilitated by composite NGOs. Similarly, contemporary post-colonial forces across the region have contributed to informing the production of new building types that are either specifically African, or demonstrative of a peculiar local interpretation of a global trend.

Altered power relations and rising democratic governance has necessitated new institutions in support thereof. The Constitutional Court of South Africa is emblematic of this tendency. Its spatial configuration and architectural representation attempt to counter the neoclassical 'Temple' format that has come to indicate power and authority the Western world. The new building is approachable, urbanistically integrated into an old inner city environment and imaginatively composed as an open representation somewhat reflective of the so-called 'rainbow nation' South Africa aspires toward.

After power, the re-presentation of history, memory and traditional heritage has proven a fertile site for architectural exploration. The number of museums and monuments being implemented in Africa reflects both the need to recover lost memory, to preserve current history and to encapture contemporary events as they unfold. This is highly contested terrain. Not only does it rupture healing wounds regarding the injustices of the past, but more so it temporally concretises memory with highly specific interpretations of events of collective memory.

In Rwanda, the genocide has been commemorated in a series of site-specific museums. These have been locally generated by communities to reflect popular representations of past events. Here African tradition, in the form of community practice, supersedes the singular vision of Western architectural authorship, raising crucial issues regarding the contradictions between the measures that inform local and global values.

The Apartheid Museum, located on old mining ground between Johannesburg and Soweto, is a constructed landscape where design has been deployed to interpret and evoke spatial relations of the past, as a means of engaging and enhancing experience. Designed by a consortium of architects, it is sited adjacent to a mining theme park and a new casino. Adopting a linear but contorted trajectory, viewers are taken on an intense journey where the interrelationship between architecture, curatorial installation and site have been choreographed in such a manner so as to empower user experience of people from all backgrounds. The dialogue between information and its spatial organisation provide a context for multiple experiences. The production of space is countered by the space of production, thereby continually affording new experiences for visitors, who frequently return, simply on account of this heightened and temporally adjusting architectural experience.

North Africa is often classified as Mediterranean and yet, culturally more connected to Europe than Africa. Morocco, Algeria, Tunisia, Libya and Egypt each enjoy attention from outside. Not dissimilar to the Middle East, the region is suffering an onslaught of 'starchitecture' with projects by Snøhetta (Alexandria Library, 2002), Zaha Hadid (Grand Theatre, Rabat, 2010) and Norman Foster and Partners (BMCE Bank Branches in Rabat, Casablanca and Fez, 2009–10). Not only has this projected these countries onto the global stage, but more significant is the profound effect on the contestation of traditional architecture and local culture. The twin faces of tourist infrastructure and gentrification are consequently rapidly shifting the practice and perception of architecture in a region that is becoming even more destabilised by the contemporary events of liberation. To some extent warfare and the commercialisation of heritage practice may be viewed as similar in their destructive force.

In Sudan, David Chipperfield has implemented a new excavation museum at the ancient site of Naga (2008-present). Attempts to interpret the local are apparent and the intervention borrows and interprets from locally materials and forms. It makes strong reference to Kahn's proposal for the USA embassy in Luanda Angola, and evolves an innovative roofing solution. However, the result ultimately introduces an alien object into an ancient landscape. Its size and autonomy of siting suggest a predilection toward formal qualities of the scalar and spatial attributes of intervention, rather than being attentive to the experiential dimensions that emerge from attention to the integrative contextual and relational. Regardless of its architectural potency, the overwhelming evidence is of a foreign modernist at work in an unfamiliar terrain.

The architecture of new embassies is the subject of significant architectural polemic throughout the world. In post-independence Africa it presents opportunity for identity making, particularly in relation to the ambiguity afforded by the insertion of a 'foreign' imbued by diplomatic status, within sovereign state. The new British Embassy in Algiers (John McAslan and Partners, 2007) presents a modest modernist intervention within an existing neo-Moorish complex dating from the 1900s, where landscape and topography have acted as spatial unifiers.

At the outset of the twenty-first century the Dutch government embarked on a project of embassy building around the world, among which figured three projects in Africa. Of these the Royal Netherlands Embassy in Addis Ababa (2005) warrants particuar attention. A collaboration between Dutch architects Dick van Gameren and Bjarne Mastenbroek and the Ethiopian firm ABBA Architects, this project represents probably the most profound work to have been implemented in Africa's recent past. Here, locality has been produced to engage a contemporary reading of site, enclosure and materials through acute interpretation of socioeconomic relations of local building and architectural production.[35] The contour datum and the combination of concrete with the rich coloured local earth have affected a counter ambiguity whereby the building approximates the political. Translation through landscape tectonic has brought foreign and local spatial practice into intimate encounter, producing a new building type that transcends typological function and contributing toward new architectural knowledge out of Africa.[36]

BUILDING DWELLING SURVIVING: AFRICAN CITIES IN THE TWENTY-FIRST CENTURY

The year 2010 marks another significant date on the African calendar: 50 per cent of its population was registered as 'urbanised'.[37] This statistic is complemented by the prediction of a rapid and sustained rate of urbanisation, reaching up to 75 per cent by 2050.[38] The implication of this prediction for space and resource management is enormous, not to mention the need for increased economic growth necessary to maintain an increasing levels of development. Health provision, service delivery, education and cultural imperatives, not to mention the need for shelter and human settlement and associated levels of consumption, all have radical implication for the organisation of land and built form for 'orderly' development.

15.10   Savage + Dodd, Brickfields Social Housing, Johannesburg, South Africa, 2005

One of the contentious issues confronting the architectural community at present on the continent is the nature of African Urbanism.[39] The African Centre for Cities (ACC) at the University of Cape Town (UCT) is a research centre focused on this issue.[40] On its agenda is to theoretically identify African Urbanism and to

provoke debate in respect of related practical and policy knowledge production. Throughout Africa informal settlements have become a definer of African Urbanism. This is evident in similar contexts in the 'global South' of Asia and South America and reflective of the colonial rule. The capacity of new states to address; the complex phenomenon of colonial legacy, and its skewed spatial construct; the lack of cultural continuity and the consequent clash of modernity and tradition; the crisis of globalisation and population growth, and the economic implications thereof; become highly questionable when framed within the trajectory of Western capitalism and its imperative for growth through exploitation.

Conversely, where communities have embarked on the practice of rapid occupation of strategic land, they have demonstrated exceptional innovation in attending to immediate needs of shelter. The larger order imperatives of movement and mobility, of public open space, institutions and services, of safety and security and of future growth and sustainability, have been radically compromised. Yet this has become the predominant form of development that characterises urban growth on the continent. In responding to this we have witnessed countless interventions by local authorities, by government ministries, by NGO's and research institutes, yet all have been 'piecemeal' and none have yet engaged the scale and pace required to contribute toward the radical transformation of this African urban phenomenon.

In Lagos, Rem Koolhaas, through his 'Harvard – Project on the City' experiments, has recognised distinctive urban qualities that emanate out of Africa. Lacking in conventional urban infrastructure, a city of over 15 million manages to 'self-regulate' itself through organisational systems that do not correlate with Western concepts of planning. The conventional logic of 'rational' order, regulation and connectedness have been replaced by the local, contingent upon a material reality of necessity informed by the here and now. Nevertheless despite real and demonstrable capacity to grow and sustain within its own hybridised systems, African Urbanism is historically ignored and marginalised.[41]

In his publication 'For the City Yet to Come'[42] Maliq Simone has sought to validate the latent potential embedded within the African city and its capacity for contributing toward the new spatialities that are necessary to initiate a radical shift in city making. This attitude is profoundly developmental and unashamedly predicated on identifying means, other than the accepted, toward engaging with urbanism. Ultimately it is in the production of local hybridities, grounded in cultural practices, that 'African' cities of the global South will find alternative forms of expression; local production is capable of contesting the hyper-modern hegemony of globalisation.

Land invasion might be the most obvious and common response, but it also the most unsustainable model. The 'city yet to come' will need to mediate the immediate need of urban migrants with the long-term necessity of orderly urbanisation that is capable of upgrade and growth, not to mention accommodating socioeconomic functions. The location of contemporary urbanism will be at the interface of the competing rationalities of formal and the informal cultures, and encourages new thinking that provokes imaginative speculation from [African][43] designers.

The project of architecture on the continent of Africa is confronted with a significantly challenging moment in its history. Complex and contradictory demands confront its future; competing rationalities that characterise future growth provide opportunity for design innovation. The coexistence of modernism with deeply vested traditional interests provides a unique confrontation for producing localities that straddle the imperative of the globalising economy with the friction of a unique African pre-existent. Disparities in income levels across the continent where Gini coefficients are some of the worst in the world, the continent's lag in technological advancement and its capacity for self-reliance present further platforms for design insight. From a Western modernist perspective these may be construed as impediments to advancement, yet we have already begun to

15.11 Ivor Prinsloo, Competing rationalities of post-colonial African urban context, *SAIA – Architecture SA*, 1982

experience its positive attributes, especially when interpreted through the lens of development. Half a century is a short time in the life of any country. The prospect for Africa in the next 50 years is to produce its own design locality by attending to the exigencies of an exceptional condition and projecting a situated modernism that is uniquely of Africa, whilst simultaneously participating in global discourse. However, lest we forget, political emancipation without economic transformation is meaningless, particularly in Africa.

NOTES

1   Antoni Folkers, *Modern Architecture in Africa* (Amsterdam: Uitgeverij Boom/SUN, 2010). Folkers demonstrates this and identifies particular tropes of African modernism by differentiating between the imposition of colonial power and the alliance of local rulers with external power as a consequence of the Cold War; e.g. Eastern Block modernism on the African east coast.

2   Tom Avermaete, Serhat Karakayali and Marion von Osten, *Colonial Modern: Aesthetics of the Past – Rebellions for the Future* (London: Black Dog, 2010).

3   Zeynep Celik, Sibel Bodzogan and others have established a strong case for this position as opposed to the critical regionalist approach of Kenneth Frampton, Alexander Tzonis, Liane Lefaivre and others. See also Leon van Schaik, 'Against Regionalism', *Architecture SA* (March/April 1986): 19–23. Much of Kahn's and Le Corbusier's work in India and Dacca demonstrates critical interpretations of local climate, technique and social practice, thereby provoking spatio-technical interpretations of their readings of these environments. In this sense a negotiated modernism seems to be more advanced in these contexts. Maxwell Fry and Jane Drew, *Tropical Architecture in the Dry and Humid Zones* (London: Batsford, 1964), demonstrate a British sensibility through a 'scientific' approach to interpreting climate.

4   Gold Coast (Ghana) was the first in 1957, and South Africa the most recent in 1994, whilst following the referendum of 2011, Southern Sudan is imminently due to become the 54th African state. Despite that both Ghana and South Africa were British colonies; the difference in post-independence architectural response is vast due to extreme temporal and cultural differences.

5   Albert Memmi, *The Colonizer and the Colonized* (London: Earthscan, 1990).

6   Ali Al'Amin Mazrui, *The Africans: A Triple Heritage* (London: BBC Publications, 1986); Nnamdi Elleh, *African Architecture: Evolution and Transformation* (New York: McGraw-Hill, 1997); Elleh, 'Architecture and Power in Africa', *Digest of SA Architecture* vol. 11 (2006/07): 68–72.

7   Western built form is extraneous to the majority of indigenous people in Africa. The necessity of contesting and negotiating space by local people is a daily phenomenon. The inappropriateness of modern life, particularly when imposed from above, necessarily reveals tensions and unproductive relations between the extremes of modernity and tradition. One of the early and abiding characteristics of life is the conflict between competing interests; however, in Africa, difference has been exacerbated by the racialisation of class that colonialism produced. Consequently, as much as racial prejudice is the founding base of colonial rule, spatial segregation and the imposition of alien norms remains its indelible legacy on the continent.

8   Fry and Drew, *Tropical Architecture in the Dry and Humid Zones*.

9   Udo Kultermann, *New Directions in African Architecture* (Studio Vista: London, 1969).

10   Crane and Kahn were the 'studiomasters' for a new joint degree that sought to promote the value of urban design as a co-producer in architecture and planning projects. This was an early contribution toward disciplinary collaboration that is common at Penn, most recently in the development of James Corner's Landscape Urbanism during the '90s.

11   For a more in depth argument for the rewriting of type and the agency of architectural authorship see Iain Low, 'Space and Transformation: Architecture and Identity', *Digest of South African Architecture* vol. 7 (2003): 34–8.

12   Memmi, *The Colonizer and the Colonized*.

13   This chapter draws on a paper, 'The Production of Locality', delivered by the author at the Non West Modern conference organised by AAAsia and Singapore Institute of Architects [SIA] and held in Singapore in January 2011. Iain Low; 'Situated Modernism: The Production of Locality in Africa', in *Non West Modern Past: On Architecture and Modernities*, W.S.W. Lim and J.-H. Chang (eds) (Singapore: World Scientific Publishing Co., 2012), 127–142.

14   David Leatherbarrow, *The Roots of Architectural Invention: Site, Enclosure, Materials* (Cambridge: Cambridge University Press, 1993), This is a term offered by Leatherbarrow in his projection of a basis for engaging the contemporary project of architecture.

15   Ari Graafland, *The Socius of Architecture: Amsterdam. Tokyo. New York* (Rotterdam: 010, 2000.) This term refers to the socio-cultural phenomenon that emerges from particular relationships between urban form and lived experience of communities in a society.

16   Duanfang Lu (ed.), *Third World Modernism: Architecture, Development and Identity* (London: Routledge, 2011).

17   This derives from an African term that has come to represent a local interpretation of democratic practice. It refers to a mode of being in the world whereby one's existence is interdependent on others: I am because of others – '*Umuntu ngu muntu nga Bantu*': a person is a person though other persons, and hence; 'batho pele' – people first.

18   Pancho Guedes, 'Architects as Magicians', *SAM: Swiss Architecture Museum* no. 3 (2007): 8–23.

19   Giovanni Vio, *Roelof Uytenbogaardt: Senza tempo / Timeless* (Padua: il Poligrafo, 2006).

20   In attempting to gauge this emergent production, it is necessary to recall that one of the primary tensions between tradition and modernity is located at the site of material and spatial reproduction. The abstract rationalisation in modernism has served to marginalise both local social organisation and its techniques of making. Modernism rationalised the interface between labour and production in that technocratic advancement has worked progressively toward removing labour from the site of construction. Specialisation, prefabrication and massification have colluded in alienating labour from participating in site work. In Africa, the rate of urbanisation combined with the endemic levels of poverty mean that most citizens have had to build for themselves. Relying predominantly on 'found materials' these people apply incredible ingenuity to establish instantaneous human settlements, maintaining the claim for Africa's prodigious building culture [Rudofsky: 1977]. For architects working on the African continent this presents the universal human conundrum of reconciling extremes whilst simultaneously contributing toward progress and participating in the modern globalising project. How to become modern without losing contact with sources [Ricouer: 1985] is a critical question that has both social implications and

material impact for the architectural project. Ultimately each project must subscribe to both universal and individual conditions, thereby demanding the production of its own locality.

21   Arjun Appadurai, *Modernity at Large: Cultural Dimensions of Globalization* (Minneapolis: University of Minnesota, 1996): 178–99.

22   Bill Hillier and Julienne Hansen, *The Social Logic of Space* (Cambridge: Cambridge University Press, 1984).

23   Anita Larsson, *From Outdoor to Indoor Living: The Transition from Traditional to Modern Low-cost Housing in Botswana* (Lund, Sweden: Lund University Press, 1988).

24   As early as in 1945 the African architect, Hassan Fathy confronted this dilemma in Egypt. His task of establishing the settlement of New Gourna represents the quintessential modernist project, involving the forced removal of a community to make way for infrastructural development in the national interest. See H, Fathy, *Gourna: A Tale of Two Villages* (Guizeh: Ministry of Culture, 1989). The apparent failure of New Gourna is convincingly ascribed by Fathy to petty politic-ing by state bureaucrats, and therefore not to the underlying conceptualisation or execution of the settlement project.

25   Fathy, *Gourna*.

26   The work of Abdel Wahed al Wakil is notable for promoting this reductionist tendency.

27   Homi Bhabha, *The Location of Culture* (New York: Routledge, 2006); Locating culture as a primary source for architectural production, opens space for alternative possibilities and a more critical definition of what '*non-western modernism*', in particular, might constitute. Comprising complex and competing rationalities this has prompted architects to 'think through design' in relation to questions concerning the national imperative, social advocacy and identity making, most notably in relation to their own agency as designers. Such a conception of architecture gives rise to the prospect of a modern post-colonial identity making, wherein each project becomes a representation of a more critically engaged and inclusive design process. Fortunately, unlike colonialism, this phenomenon has presented itself in an indiscriminate and relatively un-systematised yet located manner across the continent. However, there may be certain areas of consistency that have contributed toward its recognition as a local tendency. Albert Memmi, *Portrait du colonisé: précédé* du portrait du *colonisateur* (Paris: ed. Buchet/Chastel, Correa, 1957). Low, 'Space and Transformation', 34–8, provides a broader discussion of this view.

28   When creatively confronted, these conditions present possibility for altering power relations through the productive reconfiguration of space. The most perceptible of these is in the critical application of individual design agency. Close reading and imaginative interpretation of the pre-existent, combined with an acute ability for design translation in respect of human purposefulness, is a rare occurrence. However, where it exists, the potential of modern processes, is to contribute toward development and transformation by re-engaging the socioeconomic possibilities within the architectural project. Citizenship, within democratically organised societies, has established space for locals to engage in international opportunities, particularly in terms of education and inevitably impacted on practice and locally situated modernism. Ironically, the free flow of individuals and ideas has permitted a more productive relationship between Africa and its former colonial powers.

29   See Appadurai, *Modernity at Large*. These few projects are not necessarily well published and admired in architectural circuits. They do not display the general trappings of architectural ambition. They possess a formal modesty that is connected to their siting and programming, and the community they are intended for. Where

they are ambitious is in their attempt to engage modernity with tradition on contemporary terms. A distinctive aesthetic has emerged from reciprocity between material and experiential sensibilities of opposing ideals. Modernism has been locally negotiated and a non-Western modern is, perhaps, in the making.

30   Iain Low, 'The First Continent: Sub Saharan Africa, an Identity into Question', in Luis Fernandez-Galiano (ed.), *Atlas – Global Architecture circa 2000* (Bilbao: Fundacion BBVA, 2007), 192–5; and Iain Low, 'Nostalgia for the Specific: Southern Africa, Local Cultures and Global Pressures', in Luis Fernandez-Galiano, *Atlas*, 14–23.

31   Kere's work is receiving critical recognition with his practice now having a global reach to four continents, and both himself and his projects being increasingly included for participation in numerous international fora and publication.

32   Appadurai. These few projects are not necessarily well published and admired in architectural circuits. They do not display the general trappings of architectural ambition. They possess a formal modesty that is connected to their siting and programming, and the community they are intended for. Where they are ambitious is in their attempt to engage modernity with tradition on contemporary terms. A distinctive aesthetic has emerged from reciprocity between material and experiential sensibilities of opposing ideals. Modernism has been locally negotiated and a non-Western modern is, perhaps, in the making.

33   Low, 'Space and Transformation – architecture and identity', *Digest of South African Architecture* vol. 7 (2003): 34–8.

34   Appadurai, *Modernity at Large*.

35   Leatherbarrow. In this instance Leatherbarrow's formal categories have been profoundly modified by adherence to local practices. Genuine architectural imagination underlays the ingenuity of interpretation that produced this work.

36   'Royal Netherlands Embassy, Addis Ababa, Ethiopia', *Digest of African Architecture* vol. 1 (2008): 56–9.

37   Leatherbarrow, *The Roots of Architectural Invention*.

38   Ricky Burdett and Deyan Sudic (eds), *The Endless City – the Urban Age Project* (London: Phaidon, 2007).

39   This is an issue that has been highlight in the Harvard Urban Studios 'Project on the City' facilitated by Rem Koolhaas. Whereas Burdett, et al., have defined this phenomenon through statistics, Koolhaas has recognised a unique African capacity for organising large populations without the aid of conventional Western infrastructure and governance systems. This observation intimates a pre-existent, yet undefinable, African urbanism in the making, that escapes conventional analysis, and that, as yet, needs to come and prove its resilience.

40   See africancentreforcities.net and www.uct.ac.za.

41   Rem Koolhaas et al., *Mutations* (Barcelona: Actar, 2000).

42   AbdouMaliq Simone, *For the City Yet to Come – Changing African Life in Four Cities* (Durham: Duke University Press, 2004).

43   Already the next wave of colonial insurgence has appeared with the arrival of Chinese construction brigades, aligned with local power elites, on the continent. As one of the next superpowers, with a growing consumer population and relatively strong economic growth, China is in a position to aggressively pursue markets for commodities, land and food resources, facilitating global trade in exchange for local 'economic growth'.

16

Global Conflict and Global Glitter: Architecture of West Asia (1960–2010)[1]

Esra Akcan

INTRODUCTION

West Asia does not sound as a familiar category of international affairs or architectural studies, and this is exactly why I tentatively propose it for an intentional non-use of the term "Middle East." Many scholars admit that the category of the Middle East has been constructed by commentators from its outside, and has been less about the experience of those who live in its vague borders, than about the West's intention to designate an "other." As Albert Hourani puts it, the geographical scope of the Middle East has always been arbitrary: while "Arab states," Egypt, Israel, Iran and Turkey are usually cited, the borders could well extend southward to North Africa, eastward to Afghanistan and westward to the Balkans.[2] This confusion has equally marked architectural historiography: in Nezar AlSayyad's words, it is necessary to demonstrate "how constructed the notion of Middle East has been and to show the fluidity of identity under both colonial and global conditions."[3] This chapter looks at contemporary architectures in parts of the "Middle East" that are grouped in an intentionally unfamiliar way, namely in Iraq, Israel/Palestine, Lebanon, Turkey, and some Gulf States, without proposing a singular and distinct identity. While many of these countries share a political destiny as descendants of the Ottoman Empire, and as the locus of major conflicts during the second half of the twentieth century, their locally and globally produced differences also set them apart. Today, the architectural and urban conditions in Istanbul are much more similar to Sao Paolo than Jerusalem, Dubai to Beijing than Baghdad. Additionally, the conflicts in this "region", like those in Israel/Palestine or Iraq are caused and shaped globally, perhaps even more so than locally. While prejudgments attached to the word "Middle East" call for alternative terms, such conditions require a discussion of these countries as heterogeneous and changing parts of an interconnected world, rather than a single and self-contained entity. The architecture culture in these countries evolved in more dialogue with the European and North American professional scene than with each other, and there is hence no unavoidable reason to treat them together as a distinct category. Due to the structure of this book that uses art historical categories based on regional affiliations, this chapter necessarily negotiates with this structure and brings together the architectural ideas and buildings in these countries, but my point is to demonstrate how these were shaped in connection with the world at large, and how global conflict and glitter affected different west Asian countries in different times and ways. I will hence discuss these countries side by side proceeding in a roughly chronological order from the 1960s till the 2000s to expose their positions in the world order and their local responses, which sometimes generated similarities due to the intertwined history of the world, and at other times differences from each other.

Many of the countries in this area came into being well after World War I and the dissolution of the Ottoman Empire: Turkey became an independent Republic in 1923, while Syria and Lebanon were placed under French mandate, Iraq, Transjordan (later Jordan) and Palestine (later Israel/Palestine) under British mandate. Among the Gulf States, the Kingdom of Saudi Arabia was established in 1932, but Bahrain, Kuwait, Qatar and the United Arab Emirates remained under foreign administration well until 1960s and 70s. Israel was founded in 1948, and continued to expand by occupying Palestinian territories since the 1967 war. By the end of the World War II, the European powers had mostly withdrawn from the region; while the United States' involvement intensified afterwards, both as a model for aspired modernization, and as an intervener to contain the cold war, to guide oil production and to control the Israel/Palestine issue. The downfall of Iran's shah regime in 1979 is usually marked as the beginning of the rise of Islamism. War and conflict never seem to have ceased in the area during the cold-war period, and later during the post-cold war and post 9/11, even though it hit different parts at different times. These include the 1967 and 1973 Arab-Israeli wars, the armed battles between left-wing and right-wing in Turkish cities, as well as the three *coups d'état* in Turkey in two decades (1960, 1971, 1980), the civil war in Lebanon between 1975 and 1990; the Iraq-Iran war between 1980 and 1988; the Gulf War in 1990–91 and the Iraq war between 2003 and 2011, not to mention the continuous Israeli-Palestinian conflict. Perhaps no other "region" illustrates the impact of war on architecture and urban development better than these countries at different moments between 1960 and 2010.[4]

At the same time, in no other country but some in focus here (and in China), can one find as many large-scale and big-budget projects, glamorous and marketable buildings designed by the most prolific international architects of our time. Developers turned their attention to major urban centers and invited cutting-edge architects in the Gulf States during the turn of the century, as well as in Turkey after the adoption of neoliberal policies following the violent 1980 *coup d'etat*, and in Lebanon after the end of the civil war in 1990. Simultaneously, the gap between the rich and the poor widened, causing some of the world's biggest squatter developments in countries like Turkey. As contradictory as this might seem at first sight, both global conflict and global glitter shaped these countries during dissimilar moments throughout the second half of the twentieth century.

MODERNIZATION THEORY AND ITS CRITIQUE

While this book covers the times after the 1960s, it is necessary to mention briefly what came beforehand, as the architecture of the 60s across the world developed in large part as a reaction to the urban and architectural tendencies of the previous decade. During the 1950s, modernization theory had swayed the world, premised on Max Weber's polarization of traditional and modern societies, and on the conviction that the Western development was a universal, neutral and linear process that each society follows. This fixed trajectory of human development persuaded many that "underdeveloped or developing" countries, including those in the "Middle East," would/should pass from traditional to modern stage by following the Western path and guidance.[5] The canonic buildings and master plans of the 1950s and early 1960s were perfect participants in modernization theory, such as the Istanbul Hilton Hotel by SOM and Sedad Eldem in Turkey (1952–55), which was an International Style box that single handedly changed the aesthetic preferences of the architects for a decade.[6] During the 1950s, the Iraqi Development Board invited Frank Lloyd Wright, Walter Gropius, Le Corbusier and Alvar Aalto to design projects in Baghdad.[7] Most prolifically, Constantine Doxiadis developed master plans for Iraq (1954–58), Syria (1958) and Lebanon (1958), with the conviction in the power of *Ekistics*—"the science of human settlements"— to civilize the world and "align architecture with development."[8] Hashim Sarkis interpreted Doxiadis' invitation to Lebanon as part of the US policy to intervene on different levels in the Middle East against the threat of communism.[9] Nonetheless, President Chehab's modernization program brought experts from other countries as well, including Oscar Niemeyer from Brazil who designed the Tripoli Fair. As part of this developmentalist program, Le Corbusier's senior collaborator André Wogenscky designed the Ministry of National Defense in Lebanon (1962–68)—an International Style prism accompanied by an ovoid shaped conference hall and minister's pavilion on a reflecting pool (Figure 16.1). In Jad Tabet's words, for the planners of this period, "the political and social project seemed to indicate that it was possible to start afresh, to rebuild the world anew, and to rid Lebanese society once and for all of the detritus of 'dead old forms'"[10]

The developmentalist ambitions, integration of modern technologies and experiments with new construction materials carried on throughout the second half of the twentieth century. The big projects designed by Western architects in Iraq continued to be built well into the 1980s. The iconic Kuwait Towers (Björn & Björn, 1969–76) and the National Assembly Building in Kuwait (Jörn Utzon, 1972–83); the factories designed by the Tekeli-Sisa firm and the first structurally ambitious skyscrapers in Turkey (e.g.İş Bank by Ayhan Böke, Yılmaz Sargın, Ankara 1976–78); and the buildings of the "Beton Brut" period in Lebanon were carried out during this time. Nevertheless, starting in the 1960s, many architects began to express their skepticism over the universalist convictions and aesthetic values of what might be called the mid-century modernization theory, but not necessarily its basic premises of development. Even though almost all of the architects and planners in the 1950s had vaguely mentioned the importance of cultural specificity,

16.1   André
Wogenscky and
Maurice Hindi,
Ministry of
National Defense,
Beirut, Lebanon,
1962–68

some in the new generation criticized their projects for being homogeneous and insensitive to existing urban conditions. In Turkey, this shift started with a criticism of the International Style box *à la* Hilton, which had by then pervaded in many cities, and was followed by the active politicization of the profession favoring the left-wing youth movements. The fact that the majority of architects enthusiastically volunteered to take responsibility for social issues infiltrated their architectural values in many ways: This ranged from a distaste for the International Style, which was associated with Americanism, to an emphasis on function that put *human* use at the center of architectural concerns; and from an intellectualist urge to find the "actual regional architecture," to an interest in historic preservation against the socioeconomic trends that threatened the older fabric of cities. This emphasis on the user, the context and the country's conditions was nothing but a blending of architecture with the political spirit of the 1960s in Turkey.[11] In Lebanon, some architects in the late 1960s questioned their peers and contemporaries for failing to understand the real forces behind architectural production, and for participating in the process where the "banal international corporate style did triumph, with its standard cheap clichés," as Jad Tabet later put into words.[12]

One of the outcomes of the rejection of the monolithic block both for aesthetic and ethical reasons was the proliferation of the fragmented block.[13] The opposition between the International Style box and the "small, multi-part approach" as it was named in Turkey was explicitly visible in an urban triangle in Istanbul's historical peninsula, whose three corners are held by the Municipality building (Nevzat Erol, 1953), Manifaturacılar Retail Center (Doğan Tekeli, Sami Sisa, Metin Hepgüler, 1959), and Zeyrek Social Security Agency (Sedad Eldem, 1962–64) (Figure 16.2).

A canonic example of the International Style prismatic block asserting itself on the area, the Municipality building was criticized during the 1960s for being a massive and forceful intrusion on Istanbul's historical wooden fabric. Instead, Manifaturacılar (small manufacturer) was composed of a series of lower-rise small blocks connected by outdoor galleries and courtyards. The courtyards open up to

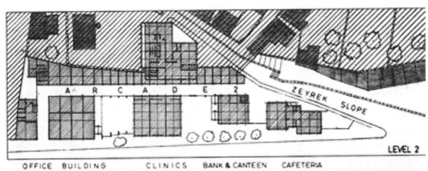

16.2   Sedad Eldem, Zeyrek Social Security Agency, Istanbul, Turkey, 1962–64

the Süleymaniye Mosque's area behind, establishing pedestrian links in between, and the fragmented blocks infuse the large complex into its context with small steps. Eldem followed the same approach in the Zeyrek building just across the road. Despite the obvious stylistic differences between these two buildings, one built with flat terraces of exposed reinforced concrete, the other with references to the "old Turkish houses," both offer an alternative to the International Style block by fragmenting the building into smaller units that do not obstruct the views of the surrounding or compete with the historical landmarks in the area. The fragmented block was soon perceived as a magic formula for all programs, places and users, and was advocated for its "human scale," dynamism and flexibility, adaptability to nature, for avoiding boring corridors, and generating case-specific results emerging out of the functional requirements of the program. Examples include such important works as the Faculty of Architecture at the Middle East Technical University designed by Behruz and Altuğ Çinici (1961–70). While the "small, multi-part approach" was a prolific theme in Turkey, similar formal strategies appeared around the world, as in the Israel Museum in Jerusalem by Al Mansfeld and Dora

Gad (1959–92), and the SOS Children's Village in Jordan by Jafar Tukan (1988–89). In Lebanon, the Mont La Salle College, by Khalil Khoury, Raoul Verney and Gregoire Serof (1969–72) became one of the landmarks of the shifting architectural values, composed as a cluster of small-scale, modular, rectangular units.[14]

A new interest in "non-rational," "organic" and "expressionistic" architecture concurrently developed during this time as another way of breaking off from the prismatic block. Architects and critics in Turkey including Şevki Vanlı and Bülent Özer participated in the debates that were taking place around organic architecture in Europe, by maintaining ties with Bruno Zevi and Rolf Gutbrod.[15] The approach that favored organic metaphors, amorphous lines and out-of-the ordinary forms found nowhere a more canonic expression than in Zvi Hecker's Spiral near Tel Aviv, Israel (1981–89), an apartment building with rotating floors, which was both a rigorous geometric exploration and a "free image that contrasts strongly with most of the rationalist architecture" in Tel Aviv (Figure 16.3).[16] The monumental Harissa Cathedral in Lebanon by Pierre el-Khoury (1970) with its curvilinear exposed concrete beams expressively rising to the sky had a quite different outcome, but expressed a similar search for an alternative to the orthogonal grids of modernism, and for an expressionistic landmark to bear the importance of its site.

MULTIPLE REGIONALISMS

Most consequential for the later decades, however, was the rise of a new interest in regional approaches to architecture, even though the underlying positions were quite diverse. This diversity is also reflected in the different words that proponents and critics used to differentiate their approaches, such as "actual regionalism," "situated modernism," "regional modernism," or "new regionalism."

The move towards regionalism in Israel took place in the context of the 1967 war and its aftermath, as Alona Nitzan-Shiftan has argued: after the Israeli capture of East Jerusalem, where the ancient core and religious sites are situated, a new master plan was immediately prepared by the Israeli experts in the "Council for the Beautiful Land of Israel." A committee of international architects, which included Louis Kahn, Lewis Mumford, Bruno Zevi, Buckminster Fuller, Christopher Alexander, Philip Johnson, Nicholas Pevsner and Isamu Noguchi was invited to comment on this plan. It soon became clear that the Israeli master planners and the international committee had different visions for Jerusalem's future. The Israeli experts continued to follow the principles of modernism, and laid their priorities accordingly: the first was the civic importance of Jerusalem, the second was the well-being of its inhabitants, and finally the third was the significance of the religious center that would have been separated from the state center. However, the international committee judged this plan for having "no vision, spirit, theme or character," and for turning Jerusalem "into a modern, International Style *ville radieuse*."[17] Instead, the committee proposed to reverse the order of priorities. A modernist plan could be implemented anywhere, but the exceptionality of Jerusalem suggested the image of a city that emanated from its religious core. "Jerusalem is more than the

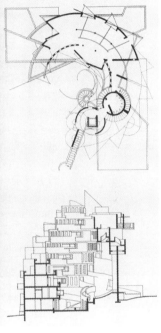

people living there," in Bruno Zevi's words; it should have remained as the center of all monotheistic religions. However, Muslims were not represented in these discussions, since participation would have meant accepting Israel's expanded borders with the 1967 war.[18] This episode had long-lasting consequences, one of which was the shift in Israeli architecture towards a more "regionalist" style throughout the 1970s and 1980s, which paradoxically borrowed from Palestinian vernacular houses. A group of architects known as the *sabra* generation advocated the cultivation of a sense of belonging, community and place in order to represent the Diaspora Jew as a "man growing out of land." Architects such as Ram Karmi and Moshe Safdie turned their attention to the Palestinian-built vernacular houses for inspiration, but justified them as Biblical architecture, their uncontaminated origin or Mediterranean heritage.[19] Housing complexes clad with the yellowish Jerusalem stone (a building regulation since 1918, but tightened with the 1968

16.3   Zvi Hecker, Spiral, near Tel Aviv, Israel, 1981–89

plan) and elaborated with big arches spread to the hills of Jerusalem, as in Moshe
Safdie's Block 38 (1979), Salo Hershman's Gilo Cluster 11, Ram Karmi's Gilo Cluster
6(1970s), and Yocov and Ammon Rechter's East Talpiot Housing (1978–82). These
marked a stark contrast with the white-washed walls of Bauhaus modernism that
was characteristic of Tel Aviv.[20] Eyal Weizman argued that the operation carried
through architecture with the 1968 master plan was much more than building
necessary housing, but a means of occupation. It was "an attempt to 'domesticate'
the occupied and annexed territories … make them [new construction] appear as
organic parts of the Israeli capital and holy city, … form a visual language that was
used to blur the facts of occupation and sustain territorial claims of expansion."[21]

After the end of the British mandate in Iraq in 1932, and following the hesitation
over the westernization programs of the 1950s, which involved Wright, Gropius,
Le Corbusier and Aalto, Iraqi architects began searching for alternative sources of
inspiration. According to Ihsan Fethi, the 1950s was "a hasty experimental phase
during which Iraqi architects abandoned their cultural roots in favor of catching up
with the western bandwagon."[22] It was these "cultural roots" that a new generation
of architects and university professors including Mohamed Saleh Makiya, Rifat
Chadirji and Hisham A. Munir embraced in the 1970s, which was interpreted by
some critics as "the liberation from foreign influences" and "transcendence of
the language of modern architecture."[23] However, far from being isolated in an
allegedly authentic culture, many of these architects were indeed participating in
the international discourse of the time, which was leaning toward the appreciation
of historical forms. Rifat Chadirji, who had worked with Le Corbusier during his
early career,[24] designed memorable buildings such as the Tobacco Monopoly
Headquarters (Baghdad, 1967–67, Figure 16.4) the Central Post Office (Baghdad,
1975), and the Hamood and Chadirji houses (Baghdad, 1972, 1979).

Brick clad cylindrical towers and façade compositions with sparsely placed, thin,
arched extension bays marked Chadirji's style, which was based on an interpretation
of local historical forms. The prolific architect Hisham Munir designed the
University City (Baghdad, 1957–), the University of Mosul (1966–) and the Mayor's
Office in Baghdad (1975–83). In the last building, Munir composed a hierarchy
of pointed arches on the four facades of a square block with a courtyard in the
middle—a revivalist strategy that would become increasingly popular with the rise
of post-modern style around the world. The regionalist and nationalist tendencies
continued well into the 2000s in Iraq,[25] but architecture was undoubtedly impaired
by the series of consecutive wars that caused many architects to leave the country.

One of the outcomes of the Civil war in Lebanon (1975–90) was an architecture
culture that was more enthusiastic about traditional ties.[26] Assem Salam and
Jacques Liger-Belair had already started advocating a better appreciation of the
genius loci since the mid-1960s, and Salam in particular had integrated historical
references in his buildings, such as the Serail of Sidon (1965). Salam also wrote
about what he perceived as the different roots of Western and Near Eastern
traditional architecture, the latter being "founded on the attitude of a community
that is profoundly governed by the religious philosophy of Islam."[27] After the 1970s,
not only Salam, but also Pierre ElKhouri and other early "modernists" increasingly

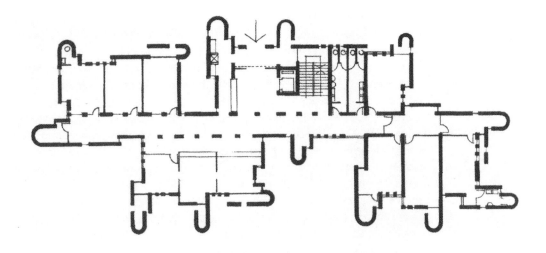

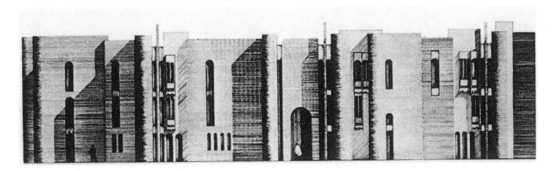

sought to combine modernism and local traditions, whether by gently inserting their buildings in the natural or urban context, by integrating textured stone and other local materials, or by referring to traditional typologies, which, in the eyes of some critics, soon relapsed into pseudo-regionalism.[28]

The "actual regionalism" movement in Turkey during this time was indeed quite different from the above developments. The influential architect Sedad Eldem had been searching for a localized modernism by directly borrowing from or integrating spatial/constructional principles of the "old Turkish houses" since the 1930s, and continued to do so during this time in many houses (Sirer, Bayramoğlu and Koç villas) and institutional buildings (Dutch and Indian Embassies, Zeyrek Social Security Agency—see Figure 16.2—Atatürk Library). But the "actual regionalism" movement was far from this call to traditionalist references or cultural roots. It was initiated by university professors and journal editors such as Bülent Özer and Doğan Kuban in the early 1960s, who argued that architecture should become an intellectual discipline, and who wanted to cultivate an informed understanding of the historical and contemporary artistic movements, as well as Turkey's own social and economic conditions. Both "copying forms from the West" and "romantic regionalism" became a target of criticism for these authors,

16.4   Rifat Chadirji, Tobacco Monopoly Headquarters, Baghdad, Iraq, 1965–67

who instead tried to carve out a definition of "actual regionalism" that responded to the "environmental conditions." This meant a rational and candid evaluation of the country's present circumstances and facts. They hence supported Turkey's developmentalist ambitions, but sought to employ realistic technologies, rather than to create excess.[29] The architecture culture in Turkey during this period was undoubtedly politicized. Many practicing architects including Vedat Dalokay, Şevki Vanlı, Cengiz Bektaş, and Turgut Cansever were vocal about architecture's political responsibility and social commitment. The members of the Chamber of Architects were in agreement more with Manfredo Tafuri's criticism of the submission of modern architecture to capitalism, than with Robert Venturi's stylistic gestures that led to the rise of the post-modern style.[30] This architecture culture came to a close with an external intervention. The 1980 *coup d'etat* undoubtedly terminated this era, forcing the hiatus of all architectural institutions and publications, not to mention the death penalties, censorship and human rights violations.

POST-MODERN STYLE AND "ISLAMIC ARCHITECTURE"

Different trajectories of regional or situated modernism soon transformed into what might be called a homogenized version of post-modern style with an increasing emphasis on the historicist use of architectural elements to bear cultural identity. Buildings that integrated references to past architectural styles gained appreciation within the context of post-modernism that was established around the world. Among the institutions that advocated modernization without detachment from cultural ties was the Aga Khan Award for Architecture (AKAA, first award cycle in 1980), which not only supported architects, communities and institutions with bounteous monetary awards, but also sought to promote knowledge about architecture in "Islamic countries." Throughout the 1980s and 1990s, the Aga Khan Award supported both canonic buildings by established or upcoming architects, and conservation projects as well as low-income housing.[31] In case of Architecture with a capital A, the Aga Khan often rewarded projects that dealt with the question of identity, and those that were evaluated as balanced syntheses between modernity and tradition. In explaining the mission of the Foundation, its secretary Süha Özkan referred to the "failure" of modernism in the Islamic societies and in the Third World, because its proponents ignored the "existence of the cultural values in the built environment, continuity between past and present, a sense of identity, consideration of climate and need for user (or community) participation."[32] In the words of Oleg Grabar, the prominent historian of Islamic art and architecture:

> Partly through the efforts and activities of the Aga Khan Award, notions of architectural identity, of reliance on native rather than imported practices and talents, of an ideologically significant rather than merely antiquarian past, of technologies appropriate to each task ... of pride in accomplishments of the past of the lands on which one builds, of locally inspired rather than imported educational objectives in professional schools, have become standard statements ... [33]

With this trajectory set during the 1980s and 1990s, the Aga Khan effectively canonized the work of Sedad Eldem, Rifat Chadirji, Hassan Fathy among others, and major projects such as the Hajj Terminal in Jeddah, Saudi Arabia by SOM (1974–82)—an unordinary airport that combines the tent typology and advanced technology to span large distances; the National Commercial Bank in Jeddah by SOM (1977–83)—one of the first climate-specific skyscrapers that was composed of solid stone facades efficiently perforated for large sky terraces and atriums in the air to help passive cooling techniques (Figure 16.5); and the Ministry of Foreign Affairs in Riyadh, by Henning Larsen (1980–84)—a large complex with a fortress-like stone-clad exterior, ceremonial entrance and a hierarchy of public and semi-private atriums, inner and outer courtyards, internal streets and semi-closed passageways.

Among the architects who anticipated the post-modern stylistic turn in the international discourse by directing their attention to the "architectural heritage of Islam" and by using "Islamic architecture" in a strategically essentialist way, the Jordanian architect Rasem Badran also holds an important place.[34] Badran designed projects in Iraq, Saudi Arabia, Lebanon, Jerusalem, Qatar, UAE, Malaysia, Yemen, and Egypt. He criticized what he perceived as "the predominant alienation characterizing our cities and rendering the Arab a foreigner in his own land,"[35] and turned his attention to traditional urban fabric and the typology of vernacular houses, using cultural symbols such as courtyards, narrow streets, projection bays,

16.5   SOM, National Commercial Bank, Jeddah, Saudi Arabia, 1977–83

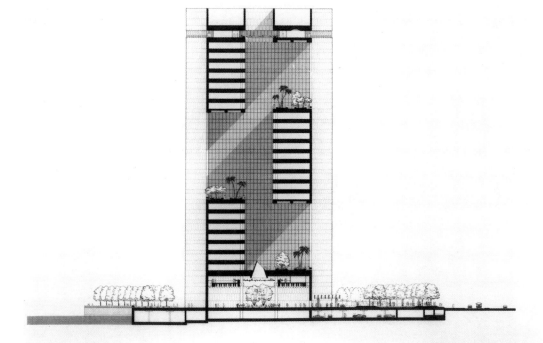

THE NATIONAL COMMERCIAL BANK
JEDDAH, SAUDI ARABIA   29 JULY, 1978

SECTION
SKIDMORE, OWINGS & MERRILL   ARCHITECTS

arches, domes and ornaments, which he represented in attractive watercolors, in many projects including the State Mosque in Baghdad (1980–81), Qasral' Hakum Complex (Great Mosque and Palace of Justice) in Riyadh (1986–92), as well as Wadi Saleh, Wadi Abu Jamil and Jabal Omar housing complexes in Jerusalem, Beirut and Makkah respectively (late 1990s-2000) (Figure 16.6).

A major debate on the contemporary mosque permeated as well, which became part of the discussion about combining Islam and modernity. The debate

16.6   Rasem Badran, Wadi Saleh Housing, Jerusalem, Israel/ Palestine, 1996

sometimes sparked angry battles between sides, as was the case in the Kocatepe Mosque in Ankara, where Vedad Dalokay's hyper-modern design—a thin concrete shell dome rising from ground with space-ship like minarets—was dynamited during construction to be replaced by an exact replica of Sinan's sixteenth-century Şehzade Mosque by Hüsrev Tayla and Fatin Uluengin, (1967–87). A wide spectrum of mosques from direct copies of classical types to de-familiarized worship places abound around the world as well as west Asia.[36] Memorable architectural examples include Mohamed Makiya's Al Khulafa Mosque in Baghdad (1961–63), the revivalist mosques of Abdel Wahed El'Wakil in Saudi Arabia, most notably the Corniche Mosque in Jeddah, (1986–88). Among the mosques that follow a more "modernist" approach, one may cite George Rayes and Jafar Tukan's Aicha Bakkar Mosque, and Assem Salam's Kashoggi Mosque (1973) both in Beirut; as well as Kenzo Tange's King Faisal Mosque in Riyadh, (1976–84) with its cylindrical praying hall sliced off at the top and slit vertically to mark the *mihrab*; and Behruz and Can Çinici's Parliament Mosque in Ankara (1989). The latter employs no recognizable traditional symbol of Islamic identity like a dome or a minaret, but takes a more metaphoric approach: The hierarchy set by a dome is interpreted as a composition with stepping rectangular prisms, the traditionally solid *qıbla* wall has been turned into a transparent screen, the traditional colonnade of a mosque courtyard is treated as a portico without columns, and a balcony implies the minaret (Figure 16.7).

Although quite different from its above ramifications, the impact of post-modern architectural style as well as the post-modern condition was nowhere more visible than in the large tourism complexes. Under the impact of global/multinational/late capitalism and the adoption of neoliberal economies in many countries, mass tourism became one of the most lucrative industries, where architects of post-modern style found matching clients who looked for spaces of "Oriental identity" as a marketing strategy. The Mediterranean, Aegean and Gulf coasts were filled with hotels and holiday resorts that globalize bourgeois comfort standards while simultaneously luring consumers with the promise of experiencing a different culture. After the mid-1980s, this has too often been materialized through theme park effects where buildings with stereotypical Orientalist facades stage allegedly authentic local lifestyles. In this commercial industry, Tuncay Çavdar tried to carve out a space for experimentation. He theorized on what he called the "Eastern way of seeing," a non-ocularcentric tradition that did not prioritize perspectival vision as the sole measure of human understanding. In translating the "Eastern way of seeing" to architectural space, Çavdar intentionally designed vistas and objects that would simulate an alienation effect as in a non-perspective Islamic painting. He deliberately fragmented buildings into an unconventional number of pieces, and increased the number of small masses that could be seen from one view point, as if they were all flattened and juxtaposed. He sought to create spaces that appeared free from gravity, as if their coordinates on the Cartesian space would be indeterminable (Figure 16.8).[37]

Not many architects, however, approached the holiday resort as an opportunity for thinking about architecture. Instead, commercial projects with post-modern

16.7   Behruz and Can Çinici, Parliament Mosque, Ankara, Turkey 1989

16.8 Tuncay Çavdar, Pamfilya Resort Hotel, Antalya, Turkey, 1984

tricks predominantly filled in the coastline of many cities. Among the tourism investments, the Palms and the World Islands of Dubai are arguably the most spellbinding. Built on landfill areas on the Gulf coast, it is roughly estimated that the projects will use up 1.1 billion cubic meters of sand and stone filled in water, and add more than 1,500 km of coastline to the city's original 67 km, although the numbers increase with each added development. Designed to be as gigantic as to be seen from outer space, and promoted by Dubai's monarchic ruler as a "poem on water," the Palms will most likely cause major environmental problems on the marine habitat. Architecturally, the Palms (concept design by Warren Pickering) are promoted to be composed of neighborhoods with countless villas, hotels, shopping malls, entertainment centers, and *32 different architectural styles* including Islamic, Mediterranean, modern and many others—a diversity and freedom of choice typical of post-modern commercial eclecticism.[38] Suitably, the Atlantis Hotel, the postmodernist icon at the far edge of Palm Jumeirah to be accessed only through a vehicular tunnel, is a stylistic mixture with references to Arc de Triomphe, Taj Mahal and Michael Graves' Disney Hotels.

GLOBALIZATION AND URBAN TRANSFORMATIONS

In addition to mass tourism, globalization had visible repercussions on the major urban centers, coupled with a changing architectural taste in favor of a less historicist and more progress-oriented, stylistically modernist approach. Globalization brought together a renewed interest in the "foreign architect" and the growing transnationalization of architecture. Out of the 100 largest projects in the Gulf region, with costs exceeding $50 billion since 1980, 88 were designed by Western firms, and only 12 by local architects.[39] Among the most ubiquitous designers are large firms like SOM, Atkins Architects and HOK, but other big firms or individuals who made a name with their experimental practice have also received large commissions including Rem Koolhaas (OMA), Norman Foster, Jean Nouvel, Zaha Hadid, Arata Isozaki, I.M. Pei, Jesse Reiser, Asymptote, Rafael Vinoly, UN Studio and others. This globalized architectural practice in west Asia at the turn of the century is most visible in the large urban development or renewal zones, such as along the Sheikh Zayed Road in Dubai, the Corniche road in Doha, the Levent-Maslak Axis in Istanbul, the city center in Beirut, and Saadiyat and Yas Islands in Abu Dhabi.

Istanbul, with a population exceeding 13 million by 2010, went through massive transformations with the adoption of neoliberal economies after the *coup d'etat* of 1980.[40] A new generation of architects appeared on the scene in Turkey during the late 1990s and 2000s, a generation which criticized the post-modern historicism of their immediate peers, and advocated tectonic sensibility and restrained expression (Nevzat Sayın, Han Tümertekin), as well as technological progress and professionalism (Emre Arolat, Tabanlıoğlu Architects). In strong contrast to the rebellious nature of the 1960s generation who were socially committed and critical of the system, most architects of the post-upheaval times preferred to seize the opportunities in the market, rather than to stay critically outside. Nowhere is the big building boom in Istanbul as visible as the proliferation of shopping malls and mixed-use "centers for good living" all around the city (an estimated 180 by 2012). For instance, those being built in the Levent-Maslak axis, the new Central Business District, have already created a new skyline of skyscrapers competing with that of the historical peninsula. Rising from a pool of Turkey's modern vernacular midrise apartment buildings, the new skyline features, among others, Metrocity by Doğan Tekeli and Sami Sisa (1995–2003)—one of the first shopping malls and business centers; *Kanyon* by John Jerde Architects with Tabanlıoğlu Architects (2002–2006)— the shopping mall with a circular semi-open street rather than a closed box; and Sapphire Tower by Tabanlıoğlu Architects (2006–10)—Turkey's highest skyscraper (261 meters) integrating some passive climate control techniques. Although not in the CBD, Foreign Office Architects' *Meydan* Shopping Center (2007) is notable due to its creative typology in contrast to the abundant generic malls with sealed walls. This building blends architecture with landscape and is organized around an open square (Figure 16.9).[41]

16.9   Foreign Office Architects (FOA), Meydan Shopping Center, Istanbul, 2007

After the civil war was over in 1990, the reconstruction of Beirut's city center became a high priority, simultaneously marking Lebanon's adoption of neoliberal economies and reintegration into the international architecture culture. The Lebanese civil war divided Beirut into Christian and Muslim sections, and turned the city center into a battlefield, making it a deserted landscape for 20 years.[42] With laws passed immediately after the war, all of the properties in the city center were expropriated, in return for private shares in the new reconstructed zone. This benefited mainly the private real-estate company and its new share-holders, Solidere, which oversaw the reconstruction of the city center with a project that encompassed 1.8 million square meters of land (of which 600,000 would be claimed from the sea by landfill areas).[43] After an initial phase of reconstructions which involved many local architects, international talents were invited, such as Rafael Moneo, Arata Isozaki, Jean Nouvel, Steven Holl, Zaha Hadid, and UN Studio. Sociologists, architects and urban planners raised questions about the privatization of the city center and the urban design decisions. This investment, according to Assem Salam, "is a high priority for symbolic reasons" in the context of municipal administration's "total bankruptcy,"[44] and, according to Saree Makdisi, is a lavish venture on high-tech infrastructure while the rest of the country is exposed to harsh economic conditions.[45] Hesitations were raised over the results of the urban design as well. In Elie Haddad's words, "under the label of urban renewal and economic growth, historic neighborhoods are being repackaged and *branded* exclusively for the upper class, dismantling the very urban structure that has made these neighborhoods come to life in the first place."[46] Nonetheless, some architects approached the topic with care, such as Rafael Moneo whose new Souks building accommodates contemporary needs but also respects the morphology of the old souks, rather than turning the area into a closed mall.[47]

At the turn of the century, many Gulf cities became major centers for architectural development, as is evident in Dubai, Abu Dhabi, Qatar, Bahrain and Kuwait. "Get a project here and it could be the *tabula rasa* of your dreams." This is how *Architects' Journal* introduced Qatar and its capital Doha as the new emerging market for architects, along with Dubai and Abu Dhabi.[48] Qatar, the richest of the Gulf countries, gained independence from Britain only in 1971. After Emir Hamad Bin Khalifa al Thani's takeover in 1995, Doha, a small pearl-fishing village, became the locus of his reforms, new institutions as well as an architectural boom. In addition to accommodating the headquarters of Al Jazeera news network, the skyscrapers rising in the West Bay along the Corniche, and Pearl-Qatar—a post-modern style high-end vacation and luxury residential development on a man-made island (just like the Palms of Dubai)—, Doha aims to turn itself into an arts and education center by also constructing museums and university buildings. Most particularly, the Museum of Islamic Art designed by I.M. Pei Architects (2003–2009), holds one of the world's finest collections in its field. Pei's stepped building holds one end of the circular Corniche road, and is in conversation with the pyramidal forms and sand-colored facades of the Sheraton Hotel at the other end—the first building to rise out of the desert in the area—as well as the Post Office in the middle. The impressive scale of the interior atrium, classically ordered and symmetrical layout, refined construction details and the geometric precision make the building a memorable public space, in contrast to the enticing exteriors, but efficient and privatized interiors that usually come out of neoliberal sensibilities. Declaredly inspired by the ablution fountain of the Ibn Tulun Mosque in Cairo, the geometry of the domed ceiling transforms from a circle to a square and to an octagon. The pattern of small domes that form the ceiling texture of the galleries is in dialogue with decent precedents in Doha such as the pattern of vaults in the Post Office and Qatar University (Figure 16.10). Other buildings in Doha's developmental leap in the last decade include the Photography Museum by Santiago Calatrava, the annex to the National Museum by Jean Nouvel; the Sports City with the canonic

16.10   I.M. Pei Architects, Museum of Islamic Art, Doha, Qatar, 2003–2008

Aspire (Torch) Tower; as well as the university buildings by Legorreta & Legorreta and Arato Isozaki in the Education City—a campus of 14 million square meters that accommodates branches of many American universities.

Abu Dhabi's skyline is mostly shaped by office skyscrapers of earlier decades, but the city is currently casting itself as a cultural and educational center, most notably by constructing an urban zone from scratch on the Saadiyat Island, for which Jean Nouvel, Frank Gehry, Norman Foster, Zaha Hadid and Tadao Ando have designed five museums, including the branches of world-famous institutions Louvre and Guggenheim. Other developmental leaps include the man-made Yas Island for entertainment and sports, as well as the Masdar City envisioned by Foster and Partners as a zero-carbon environment that runs on renewable energy. Of the buildings that have been completed to date, the Yas Hotel designed by Asymptote stands out with its amorphous shape and double surface, where the traditional sun-shading device mashrabiya is transformed into a second envelope that independently wraps the whole mass of the hotel rooms. The environmentally sensitive second layer is composed of pivoting diamond-shaped glass panels that cast shadows to protect the terrace underneath and interior spaces behind from excessive sun during the day, and that lit up with color-changing LED lighting at night (Figure 16.11).

Dubai attracted the attention of the world's richest investors and most famous architects, due to the limitless ambitions of its monarchic ruler Sheikh Mohammed bin Rashid Al Maktoum, who created a tax-free market for the global capital.[49] Determined to turn Dubai's oil revenues into a sustaining and full-fledged economic power, the authorities focused on improving the tourism and service sectors, while employing the charm of architectural excess to attract tourists, shoppers and businessmen.[50] Not only the Palm islands, but also the skyscrapers and mega shopping malls on and around the Sheikh Zayed Road follow the precedents of city building from scratch on an unmatched scale and speed. The city grew from a small fishing village to the world's most spectacular building site in a handful of years. Dubai's enthralling skyline makes it the world's most active zone for the most ambitious skyscraper design. The Burj al-Arab hotel, designed by Tom Wright from W.S. Atkins (1994–99), became the first Dubai icon that opened the curtains to a much bigger show featuring many more towers. Burj Khalifa by SOM (2004–10) is the world's tallest skyscraper to date (828 m), adding another score to the city's records. Its height presented a structural engineering challenge, which was solved by an innovative thin six-sided concrete core that is replaced by steel on the 156th floor, as well as by spiraling setbacks. Accessible only by car after security points, the tower is meant to be seen from everywhere rather than to be reached by public, however, it disappears into the mist of Dubai's humidity in most days of the year. Residues of post-modern fixation on identity have not been totally abandoned: The tower is officially promoted to have been inspired by a desert flower. Explaining his design, Adrian Smith, then at SOM, said: "Spirals come up in many forms in Islamic architecture. The tower goes up in steps in a spiraling way. In Islamic architecture, this symbolizes ascending towards the heavens."[51] Another Dubai icon, the Infinity Tower also by SOM (2006–13) takes on a structural engineering challenge: each floor plate of the 76-storey tower is rotated by 1.2 degrees, requiring the actual structure to be twisted by 90 degrees overall. Many other Gulf cities are also centers for experimental and/or iconic skyscraper design, as evident in the Doha Tower by Jean Nouvel (2005–12) that repeats the same shape as the architect's design for Barcelona Tower, but wraps it with a second layer of a mashrabiya motif to cast ornamented shadows inside; the Aldar Headquarters in Abu Dhabi by the Lebanese firm MZ Architects (2010) that attracts attention as a vertically standing disc made out of concave surfaces; as well as the Al Hamra

16.11   Asymptote Architects, Yas Hotel, Abu Dhabi, UAE, 2007–2009

Tower in Kuwait designed by the Turkish architect Aybars Aşçı at SOM (2003–10) (Figure 16.12). The latter continues the trajectory of climate-specific skyscrapers, and negotiates the desire for panoramic views through fully transparent surfaces with the need to protect the building from excessive sun. To this end, a spiraling void is subtracted from the mass of the building, which vertically runs through the tower and spirals according to the sun's path in order to cast maximum shadows on the stone-clad south façade.

Dubai has become a dreamland for both investors and designers, but it is a city where "Donald Trump trips on acid" and "Walt Disney meets Albert Speer" according to Mike Davis, and a "desperately optimist and decadent city ... of an ironically nomadic society," according to Ole Bouman.[52] Behind the spectacle that generates these polar comments, according to those who look closer, Dubai is divided into a phantasmagoric and an everyday life space.[53] According to Yasser Elsheshtawy, for one, it is not Dubai's megaprojects and icons, but rather its everyday life spaces that are indicative of the global city phenomenon: spaces of informal economies, gathering sites of underprivileged migrants, under-designed, left-over spaces with flexible functions, ethnic markets and bus stops.[54] Here is a city where shoppers from all around the world consume Western goods in mega malls that contain artificial ski slopes, ice rinks and ocean-big aquariums; but also a city with severe economic, gender and ethnic stratifications; a non-pedestrian urban agglomeration with fragmented zones that can only be accessed by car; a city with separate residential zones for Emiratis' big-family compounds, Europeans' one-bedroom apartments and South Asians' labor camps; a multicultural but non-cosmopolitan (i.e. segregated on many layers) city with a fast-growing urban zone saturated with transportation, pollution, and waste management problems.

In due course, perhaps the reason why Dubai provokes both fascination and contempt is the fact that it represents the most extreme and unchecked example of a city built out of the global capital. Rem Koolhaas not only participated in Dubai's building adventure by designing the master plan for the extra-large and ultra-dense Waterfront City (140million m² for 1.5 million people), but also theorized the global state of architecture at the turn of the century through Dubai (Figure 16.13).[55]

16.12   *c.*2000 skyscrapers of Gulf Cities (from left to right): Adrian Smith from SOM, Burj Khalifa, Dubai, UAE, 2004–10; MZ Architects, Aldar Headquarters, Abu Dhabi, UAE, 2010; SOM, Infinity Tower, Dubai, UAE, 2006–13; Jean Nouvel, Doha Tower, Doha, Qatar, 2005–12; Aybars Aşçı from SOM, Al Hamra Tower, Kuwait City, Kuwait, 2003–10

16.13   Rem
Koolhaas and
OMA, Waterfront
City, Dubai, UAE,
2006-ongoing

The Gulf is the current frontline of rampant modernization … If you want to be apocalyptic, you could construe Dubai as evidence of the end-of-architecture-and-the-city-as-we-know-them; more optimistically you could detect in the emerging substance of The Gulf—constructed and proposed—the beginnings of a new architecture and a new city …[56] The Gulf is not just reconfiguring itself; it is reconfiguring the world.[57]

Nonetheless, Koolhaas became eventually more cautious about Dubai's race to spectacle and the "architect's addiction to shape," and has taken a step in favor of minimalism.[58] "In a time frame of three weeks, a Virtually Unknown can generate the thrill that the brand-name architect couldn't even do in twelve months."[59] In this context, the critical/subversive step was to embrace simplicity and minimalism, as evident in the Dubai Renaissance Tower designed by Koolhaas and Fernando Donis of OMA (2006). In any event, far from the mid-century modernization theory which was convinced that the rest of the world should follow the Western model in order to transform from a traditional to a modern society, it is now cities like Dubai that serve either as a model for development or a cautionary tale.

While multinational neoliberalism is transforming these cities, Jerusalem has also been the focus of international architectural attention because of the global conflicts it continues to generate. *The Next Jerusalem* project (2002), for one, accepts the Palestinian nationhood as legitimate, envisions a unified city, and brings together architects and humanists from Israel, Palestine and other countries to produce visions for sharing the city. Michael Sorkin (editor), Rasem Badran, Romi Khosla, Thom Mayne, Moshe Safdie, Jafar Tukan, Eyal Weizman, Lebbeus Woods and Ali Ziadah all took part in this effort to re-envision the city, with proposals ranging from small-scale adjustments to utopian visions that re-unify or share the city.[60]

Ultimately, however, it is not only in Jerusalem that the global conflicts make an impact on architecture and urban space. Once we turn our gaze away from Architecture with a capital A especially toward the housing conditions of the low-income groups, problems under global capital and religious tension are indubitable. Thousands of construction workers migrate to Dubai almost every day, mostly from South Asia, with the hopes of finding employment, even though investors or governing authorities do not feel legally or morally obliged to subscribe to the international migrant workers' rights and housing standards—a condition which did not escape the Human Rights Watch that released *Building Towers, Cheating Workers* report in 2006.[61] More than 50 percent of Istanbul's urban fabric had been created by the rural migrants who had no option but building ad hoc houses in one night. These were recently legalized and seized by developers who turned them into multi-storey apartment buildings on weak foundations and absent infrastructure through semi-legal procedures. Fraud and shady real-estate build up a good part of housing in Istanbul, giving opportunities only to those who participate in illicit deals.[62] One-third of the population had been displaced in Lebanon either permanently during the fighting with Israel in 1978, 1982–84, or temporarily when residents left their homes due to the rising violence.[63] The southern outskirts of Beirut have been inflated with refugees during the civil war, and today, the Elisar project (1994–) undertaking its urban and architectural improvement is a constant tension and negotiation zone between the government and Hizbullah.[64] Housing settlements have served the Israeli governments as a means to conquer since 1948, as it was most openly exposed in Prime Minister Ben Gurion's words: "Settlement—that is the real conquest! The future of the state depends on immigration."[65] By building new settlements on mountain tops, Israel pushes Palestinians into isolated zones in the valleys—a situation named by Rafi Segal and Eyal Weizman a "civilian occupation that relies on the presence of a civilian architecture."[66] While these housing issues require more in-depth discussion, it would be discreditable to turn them a blind eye for any architect or scholar who wants to understand the built environment.

As I write these pages in the midst of what has been called "the Arab Spring," and the Gezi Protests in Turkey, the future is uncertain in and around these countries. Many of the facts that would help us make sense of these years remain hidden under the classified documents of state archives. These uncertainties withstanding, it seems fair to conclude that both conflict and glitter can be observed in west Asia on excessive levels, and this situation might as well be the two sides of the same coin—the human condition at the end of the twentieth century where contradictory forces pull and push a globalized world.

NOTES

1   Writing this chapter, I relied on the work of many scholars as well as direct correspondence. I would like to thank Elie Haddad in Beirut for guiding me to some of the relevant articles for Lebanon, Alona Nitzan-Shiftan in Tel Aviv for Israel, Mona Damluji in Berkeley for Iraq. Additionally, I would like to thank the institutions and

their faculty, which have been catalysts for producing most of the English doctoral and master theses on the modern and contemporary architectures in these countries, particularly Kenneth Frampton at Columbia University, Sibel Bozdoğan and Nasser Rabbat at MIT, Nezar AlSayyad at Berkeley University, and Yasser Elsheshtawy at UAE University, as well as the Aga Khan Foundation for producing many informative books on contemporary architecture in the "Islamic world," and AMO for compiling books on the Gulf Region. Nonetheless, the international scholarship on this topic is undoubtedly insufficient, and this short chapter should be read only as a brief, provisional introduction in order to guide readers to the work of relevant scholars and inspire further research.

2   Albert Hourani, "Introduction," in Albert Hourani, Philip Khoury and Mary Wilson (eds), *The Modern Middle East*, 2nd edn (London, NY: I.B. Tauris, 2005), 1–20.

3   Nezar AlSayyad, "From Modernism to Globalization: The Middle East in Context," in Sandy Isenstadt and Kishwar Rizvi (eds), *Modernism and the Middle East: Architecture and Politics in the Twentieth Century* (Seattle, London: University of Washington Press, 2008), 256.

4   The bibliography would be extensive here. For direct discussions, especially see: Oussama Kabbani, "Public Space as Infrastructure: The Case of Postwar Reconstruction of Beirut," in Peter Rowe and Hashim Sarkis (eds), *Projecting Beirut: Episodes in the Construction and Reconstruction of a Modern City* (Munich, London, NY: Prestel, 1998), 240–59; Maha Yahya, "Unnamed Modernisms: National Ideologies and Historical Imaginaries in Beirut's Urban Architecture," Ph. D. Dissertation, MIT, Boston, 2005; Rafi Segal and Eyal Weizman (eds), *A Civilian Occupation: The Politics of Israeli Architecture* (London, NY: Verso, 2003). For recent discussions on the relation between architecture and war elsewhere, see especially: Martha Pollak, *Cities at War in Early Modern Europe* (New York: Cambridge University Press, 2010); Jean-Louis Cohen, *Architecture in Uniform: Designing and Building for the Second World War* (Montreal: Canadian Center for Architecture, 2011).

5   See especially: Daniel Lerner, *The Passing of Traditional Society: Modernizing the Middle East* (New York: The Free Press, 1958). For a discussion of modernization theory as the Orientalism of the late twentieth century, see: Zachary Lockman, *Contending Visions of the Middle East: The History and Politics of Orientalism*, 2nd edn (Cambridge: Cambridge University Press, 2010).

6   Sibel Bozdoğan and Esra Akcan, *Turkey: Modern Architectures in History* (London: Reaktion Press, 2012).

7   Ihsan Fethi, "Contemporary Architecture in Baghdad," *Process Architecture* (May 1985): 112–32; Mina Marefat, "Wright in Baghdat," in Anthony Alofsin (ed.), *Frank Lloyd Wright: Europe and Beyond* (Berkeley: University of California Press, 1999); Magnus T. Bernhardsson, "Visions of Iraq: Modernizing the Past in 1950s Baghdat," in *Modernism and the Middle East*, 81–96.

8   Panayiota I. Pyla, "Ekistics, Architecture and Environmental Politics, 1945–1976: A Prehistory of Sustainable Development," Ph.D. dissertation, MIT, Boston, 2002; Panayiota I. Pyla, "Baghdad's Urban Restructuring, 1958: Aesthetics and Politics of Nation Building," in *Modernism and the Middle East*, 97–115.

9   Hashim Sarkis "Dances with Margaret Mead: Planning Beirut since 1958," in *Projecting Beirut*, 187–201.

10   Jad Tabet, "From Colonial Style to Regional Revivalism: Modern Architecture in Lebanon and the Problem of Cultural Identity," in *Projecting Beirut*, 83–105, quotation: 96.

11   Bozdoğan and Akcan, *Turkey*.

12   Jad Tabet, "From Colonial Style to Regional Revivalism," 100.

13   Enis Kortan, *Türkiye'de Mimarlık Haraketleri ve Eleştirisi (1960–1970)* (Ankara: publisher not indicated, 1974).

14   Elie Haddad, "Architecture in Lebanon (1970–2005)," unpublished paper.

15   Bülent Özer, "Ifade Çeşitliliği Yönünden Çağdaş Mimariye bir Bakış," *Mimarlık* 41, no. 3 (1967): 12–42; Atilla Yücel, "Pluralism Takes Command: The Turkish Architectural Scene Today," in Renata Holod and Ahmet Evin (eds), *Modern Turkish Architecture* (Philadelphia: University of Pennsylvania Press, 1984), 119–52.

16   Kenneth Frampton and Hasan-Uddin Khan, *World Architecture 1900–2000: A Critical Mosaic; vol. 5: The Middle East* (Wien, New York: Springer, 2000), 219.

17   Quoted in: Alona Nitzan-Shiftan, "Capital City or Spiritual Center: The Politics of Architecture in Post-1967 Jerusalem," *Cities* 22, no. 3 (2005): 229–40, quotation: 236; also see: Alona Nitzan-Shiftan, "The Walled City and the White City: The Construction of the Tel Aviv/Jerusalem Dichotomy," *Perspecta* 39 (2007): 92–104.

18   Ibid., 236.

19   Alona Nitzan-Shiftan, "Seizing Locality in Jerusalem," in Nezar AlSayyad (ed.), *The End of Tradition?* (London, NY: Routledge, 2004); Alona Nitzan-Shiftan, "On Concrete and Stone: Shifts and Conflicts in Israeli Architecture," *TDSR* XXI, no. 1 (2009): 51–65.

20   For examples, see: *Contemporary Israeli Architecture* (Tokyo: Process Architecture, 1984).

21   Eyal Weizman, *Hollow Land: Israel's Architecture of Occupation* (London: Verso, 2007), 26.

22   Fethi, "Contemporary Architecture in Baghdad," 124.

23   Udo Kulterman, "Architects of Iraq," *Contemporary Arab Architecture*, 54, 60.

24   Mona Damluji, "Baghdad Modern in Context," Conference Paper, SAH, April 13–17, 2011, New Orleans.

25   In a talk to Iraqi architects in 2001, Saddam Hussein asked them to "purify their designs of Western architecture and to concentrate on truly traditional Iraqi architecture." Hoshiar Nooraddin, "Globalization and the Search for Modern Local Architecture: Learning from Baghdad," in Yasser Elsheshtawy (ed.), *Planning Middle Eastern Cities* (London: Routledge, 2004), 59–84, quotation: 79.

26   Haddad, "Architecture in Lebanon (1970–2005)."

27   Assem Salam quoted in Tabet, "From Colonial Style to Regional Revivalism," 102–103.

28   Haddad, "Architecture in Lebanon."

29   For more discussion: Bozdoğan and Akcan, *Turkey*, chapter 6.

30   Ibid.

31   See especially: Ismael Serageldin (ed.), *The Architecture of Empowerment: People, Shelter and Livable Cities* (London: Academy Editions, 1997).

32   Süha Özkan, "Complexity, Coexistence and Plurality," in James Steele (ed.), *Architecture for Islamic Societies Today* (London: Academy Editions, Aga Khan Award for Architecture, 1994), 23–7, quotation: 25.

33   Oleg Grabar, "The Mission and its People," in *Architecture for Islamic Societies Today*, 6–11, quotation: 7.

34   Badran stated: "My understanding of Islam is that it is built upon a fixed set of principles and values and yet it accommodates dynamic change over time … This idea … has a bearing on how to deal with the concept of place and the way personal authorship can take contextuality into consideration … As far as Islamic architecture is concerned, I can say with confidence that I have adopted an Islamic approach." Rasem Badran quoted in James Steele, *The Architecture of Rasem Badran: Narratives on People and Place* (New York: Thames and Hudson, 2005), 38–9, 47.

35   Akram Abu Hamdan, "Interview with Rasem Badran," *Mimar: Architecture in Development*, no. 25 (Sept.1987): 50–70, quotation: 59.

36   For more discussion and examples see: Ismail Serageldin and Samir El-Sadek (eds), *Architecture of the Contemporary Mosque* (London: Academy Editions, 1996); Renata Holod and Hassan-Uddin Khan, *The Mosque and the Modern World* (London: Thames and Hudson 1997).

37   Bozdoğan and Akcan, *Turkey*, chapter 7.

38   Promotion brochure, author's collection.

39   Mais Mithqal Sartawi, "The Lure of the West: Analyzing the Domination of Western Firms in the Gulf Region," Master's Thesis, MIT, Boston, 2010.

40   For English books on Istanbul's recent global developments, see: Çağlar Keyder (ed.), *Istanbul: Between Global and Local* (Maryland: Rowman& Littlefield, 1999); Deniz Göktürk, Levent Soysal and Ipek Türeli (eds), *Orienting Istanbul: Cultural Capital of Europe?* (New York: Routledge, 2010); Ricky Burdett and Deyan Sujic (eds), *Living in the Endless City: The Urban Age Project by the London School of Economics and Deutsche Bank's Alfred Herrhausen Society* (London, 2011); Bozdoğan and Akcan, *Turkey: Modern Architectures in History*.

41   For more discussion, see Bozdoğan and Akcan, *Turkey*.

42   For information and photographs showing casualties, see: Oussama Kabbani, "Public Space as Infrastructure: The Case of Postwar Reconstruction of Beirut," in *Projecting Beirut*, 240–59.

43   Especially see: Saree Makdisi, "Laying Claim to Beirut: Urban Narrative and Spatial Identity in the Age of Solidere," *Critical Inquiry* 23, no.3 (Spring 1997): 661–705; also see: Saree Makdisi, "Letter from Beirut," *Any*, 1, no.5 (March–April 1994): 56–9.

44   Assem Salam, "The Role of Government in Shaping the Built Environment," in *Projecting Beirut*, 122–33, quotation: 131. Also see: Assem Salam, "The reconstruction of Beirut: A Lost Opportunity," *AA Files*, no.27 (Summer 1994): 11–13.

45   Makdisi, "Laying Claim to Beirut."

46   Elie Haddad, "Architecture and Urbanism in Beirut," *Arquitectura COAM* 359, 83–91, quotation: 91.

47   Rafael Moneo, "The Souks of Beirut," in *Projecting Beirut*, 263–73.

48   Kieran Long, "Emerging Markets: Qatar," *Architects' Journal* 229, no. 4 (February 2009): 21–34, quotation: 21.

49   Promotion publications on Dubai are excessive, which will not all be cited here. For a comprehensive history, see: Christopher M. Davidson, *Dubai: The Vulnerability of Success* (New York: Columbia University Press, 2008).

50   Oil revenues had made up to around 50% of the GDP in 1985, it was only 5.7% in 2004, and is expected to drop to 1%. Many architectural periodicals devoted special issues or extensive articles to Dubai's investments: See especially: Christine Murray, "Emerging Markets 2: Dubai," *Architect's Journal* 228, no. 21 (December 2008): 21–33; Moutamarat, AMO, Archis, *Al Manakh* (Dubai: International Design Forum, 2007); Rem Koolhaas, Tod Reisz et al., *Al Manakh II* (Abu Dhabi: Abu Dhabi Urban Planning Council, 2010). Both books are also issues of *Volume* magazine.

51   http://news.bbc.co.uk/1/hi/world/middle_east/4139094.stm. accessed: 2008.

52   Mike Davis, "Does the Road to the Future End at Dubai?" *Log* (Fall 2005): 61–4; Ole Bouman, "Desperate Decadence," *Volume* 6 (2006): 4–8, quotation: 8.

53   Many authors in newspapers and professional periodicals either condemned or celebrated Dubai, but usually based on an observation of its spectacular investments. For a book that looked behind the spectacle and did research on the city's less media-visible sites, see: Yasser Elsheshtawy, *Dubai: Behind an Urban Spectacle* (London, NY: Routledge, 2010). Also see: Ahmed Kanna, "The State Philosophical in the Land without Philosophy: Shopping Malls, Interior Cities and the Image of Utopia," *TDSR* 16, no. 2 (Spring 2005): 59–73; Ayesha al Sager, Afnan al Rubaian, Sally Khanafer, "Neither Desperate, Nor Decadent," *Volume* 6 (2006): 9–11; Alamira Reem, Bani Hashim, et al., "The Scheherazade Syndrome: Fiction and Fact in Dubai's Quest to Become a Global City," *Architectural Theory Review* 15, no. 2 (August 2010): 210–30; Vishal Pandy, "How Sustainable is Dubai?" *Urban Land* 66, no. 6 (June 2007): 60–64.

54   Elsheshtawy, *Dubai*, chapters 3, 7, 8.

55   Esra Akcan, "Reading the Generic City: Retroactive Manifestoes for Global Cities of the Twenty-First Century," *Perspecta Yale Architectural Journal*, no.41 (2008): 144–52.

56   AMO, "Argument: Introducing … ," *Al Manakh*, 198.

57   Rem Koolhhas, "Last Chance?" *Al Manakh*, 7.

58   http://www.oma.eu/index.php?option=com_content&task=view&id=344&Itemid=25 accessed: 2011.

59   AMO, "Argument: Introducing … ," *Al Manakh*, 194.

60   Michael Sorkin (ed.), *The Next Jerusalem: Sharing the Divided City* (NY: Monacelli Press, 2002).

61   Elsheshtawy, *Dubai*; Jeff Herlitz, "Workers and Housing in Dubai," *Urban Land* 67, no. 2 (February 2008): 30.

62   Bozdoğan and Akcan, *Turkey*, chapter 8.

63   Yahya, "Unnamed Modernisms," 366.

64   Mona Harb-el-Kak, "Transforming the Site of Dereliction into the Urban Culture of Modernity: Beirut's Southern Suburb and Elisar Project," in *Projecting Beirut*, 173–81.

65   Quoted in Roy Kozlovsky, "Temporal States of Architecture: Mass Immigration and Provisional Housing in Israel," in *Modernism and the Middle East*, 139–60, quotation: 142. Also see: Annabel Jane Wharton, *Selling Jerusalem* (Chicago: Chicago University Press, 2006).

66   Segal and Weizman (eds), *A Civilian Occupation*, 22. Also see: Weizman, *Hallow Land*.

17

Old Sites, New Frontiers: Modern and Contemporary Architecture in Iran

Pamela Karimi

CRAFTING A NATIONAL STYLE

Near the end of the Qajar dynasty (1785–1925), Iran's relationship with Europe greatly expanded; one effect of this was commissions by the Qajar kings for a wide range of palatial structures that were amalgams of Iranian and European styles. After 1906, when the dynasty was forced by popular unrest to provide a constitutional system, royal funding for the creation of palatial complexes was limited. Subsequently, the country was afforded a series of important new public institutions such as the Society of National Heritage, which was integral to Iran's massive project of modernization. Officially established in 1922 (then terminated in 1934, to be relaunched in 1944), the Society of National Heritage became a venue through which many preservation projects, as well as the building of a series of new public institutions, became possible.[1] With the support of the founders and members of the Society of National Heritage, many archeological sites were excavated and old monuments restored. Although those in charge were often foreign nationals, they nonetheless contributed immensely to the public awareness of Iran's national heritage.

With the rise of the Majles, Iran's constitutional parliament, in 1906, and the fall of the Qajar dynasty in 1925, as well as the commencement of Reza Shah Pahlavi's reign (1925–41), modern structures began to replace some Qajar-era buildings in the capital. Many of Tehran's Qajar structures were destroyed to make room for new government buildings. Driven in part by the ideas of Iranians like the Zoroastrian representative to parliament Arbab Keikhosrow—who was a force behind the revival of the Achaemenid and Sasanian architecture in the administrative buildings of the 1930s—and in part by contemporaneous Western trends, elevating the pre-Islamic heritage of Iran was celebrated in the form of ancient icons embellishing early Pahlavi government buildings. The National Bank of Iran (*Bank-i Melli Iran*; shown in Figure 17.11), for example, contains column capitals inspired by those found in the palaces of Persepolis, built during the Achaemenid Empire (550–330 BCE).[2] Meanwhile, the Museum of Ancient Iranian Heritage (Museye Iran-e Bastan), constructed by the French architect Andre Godard (1881–1965), showcased a monumental arch at the building's main entrance that resembles the wide-spanned and towering arch at the legendary Sassanian Ctesiphon palace attributed to the reign of Shapur I (241–72 CE). Via a series of modern buildings, Iran's nationalists portrayed their heritage as ancient and timeless, concurring with Benedict Anderson's claim that "if nation states are widely conceded to be "new" and "historical," the nations to which they give political expression always loom out of an immemorial past."[3]

ADOPTING WESTERN ARCHITECTURE

Following World War II, economic expansion was made possible by financial support from a number of local institutions and international organizations. These initiatives, introduced as national development plans,[4] contributed to large-scale housing projects such as Chaharsad Dastgah (literally, "400 units"). Occupying an area of 124,360 square meters, the complex was built in 1946 with financial support from the Mortgage Bank (*Bank-i Rahni*) and the National Bank (*Bank-i Melli*) of Iran. Chaharsad Dastgah was one of the earliest mass housing projects to provide plumbing and electricity for all tenants. However, the design of the units was not ideal: all windows were the same size, regardless of orientation, and the room arrangements lacked privacy.[5]

17.1   The National Bank of Iran under construction, 1929

Along with these large-scale developments, which provoked discontent, the work of professional Iranian architects—including Mohsen Forughi (d.1983), Gabriel Guverkian (d.1970) and Vartan Avanessian (d.1982)—helped in constructing a new identity for Iran's middle-class, white-collar population.[6] Educated in Europe, these architects returned and in the beginning of their careers designed homes for Tehran's upper and middle classes. Utilizing concrete in many of the newly built homes, as well as in public institutions such as those on the main campus of Tehran University—built by several architects, including Mohsen Forughi and Andre Godard (1881–1965)—contributed to the decline in use of traditional materials and local techniques of building and craftsmanship.[7]

The construction of these types of buildings reached its height in the last two decades of the Pahlavi regime. This was made possible by OPEC oil price increases, and was due not only to national development plans but also to the active participation of the private sector.[8] Many modern buildings constructed during these two decades followed European modernist principles, and these styles dominated the city. Meanwhile, old buildings, mostly from the Qajar period, were neglected or their historic designs altered as their facades were manipulated, for example, by additions of large glass walls.[9]

Indeed, few new structures embodied characteristics of the vernacular architecture of Iran developed, over centuries, in response to the geographical and climatic aspects of different regions of the country. Traditionally, while buildings on the northern slopes of the Alburz Mountains and the shores of the Caspian Sea featured sloping roofs and were elevated to avoid flooding, in arid areas most buildings contained flat or domed roofs and vaults constructed of mud and durable baked bricks.[10] Unlike northern homes, most desert structures were inverted, with rooms arranged around central courtyards, complete with wind-catchers and ice houses to alleviate the harsh conditions of desert life. Not only were most traditional houses built according to climatic and geographical features, they were also self-sufficient microcommunities that raised vegetables and livestock. As new products became available to fill these spaces, the economic self-sufficiency of the traditional Iranian house eroded, and the household became a fledgling locus of consumer spending.[11]

Although by the 1960s Iran was moving away from traditional methods of construction (and consequently traditional ways of life within these spaces), in the succeeding decades some architects tried to link historical Iranian architecture with modern technologies while simultaneously accommodating unique environmental characteristics of Iranian regions. Concurrent with the rise of the Post-Modern movement in the West, which allowed an eclectic array of architectural motifs from the past, the return to traditional Iranian building methods was not only a reaction to the rigidity of the imported Western Modernist styles, but also a timely response to a popular global trend.

APPROPRIATING TRADITIONAL BUILDING METHODS

In 1972, the Mandala Collaborative's Tehran's Center for Management Studies (now known as Imam Sadegh University) broke new ground as it revised aspects of traditional Iranian architecture. The chief architect, Nader Ardalan, envisioned a complex akin to a *madrasa* (religious school), with lecture halls and classrooms arranged around a central courtyard.[12] But nowhere was the "return" to traditional styles and building methods more visibly implemented than in a large residential complex partially completed in 1977 by the Iranian construction firm DAZ (headed by architect Kamran Diba). Located near the old city of Shushtar in the southern region of Khuzestan, the complex, known as Shushtar New Town, exemplifies the traditional revival approach and incorporates characteristics of the courtyard houses of southern Iran.[13]

Shushtar New Town was not fully appreciated by its inhabitants, who gradually manipulated some parts of their residences (such as dividing shared entrances and blocking unwanted views into their living rooms) to fit their conservative lifestyles. In both architectural circles and the popular imagination, the project was often regarded as a legacy of the late-Pahlavi approach (including that of Kamran Diba's favorite cousin, the Empress Farah Diba) to Iran's indigenous traditions, which is generally considered to be elitist and cliché.[14]

A more successful approach to traditional design skills surfaced in the work of Los Angeles–based Iranian architect Nader Khalili (d. 2008). Known for journeying across Iran in the 1960s and '70s to study ancient construction technologies, Khalili achieved his unique design method by using the traditional basic elements of earth, water, air and fire.[15] He focused on clay as building material to avoid cutting trees for wood or depleting the fossil fuels used to produce steel. Because Khalili used available and renewable materials, production and transportation costs were minimal in his two main projects built inside Iran: an elementary school in southern Tehran (1980) and the Sandbag Shelters in Ahvaz (1995). The school used Khalili's self-defined Geltaftan method—a system whereby the entire earthen structure is treated as a kiln and fired to form a monolithic mass[16]—while the Shelters (the winner of the ninth cycle of the Aga Khan Award for Architecture) implemented the so-called sandbag or superadobe system of packing local earth in sandbags (Figure 17.2).[17]

The work of the aforementioned pioneers has deeply influenced a generation of architects who have practiced similar techniques since the Islamic Revolution of 1979.[18] Despite the scarcity of his architectural works in Iran, Khalili earned popularity among Iranian architects through his writings. His books, translated into Persian since the late 1980s, have become a source of inspiration for students in architectural schools across the country.[19] Farhad Ahmadi's Dezful Cultural Center (completed in 1995 and nominated for an Aga Khan award) seems to have been inspired by Diba's Shushtar New Town. The center—including a bazaar, teahouse, mosque, library, visual arts and crafts school, galleries, cinema, and landscaped courtyard—fully implements formal and functional characteristics of southern Iranian architecture. While traditional wind-catchers (*badgirs*) help enhance air circulation in the building, underground spaces (*sardabs*) allow for a relaxing and cool interior environment on hot summer days (Figure 17.3).[20]

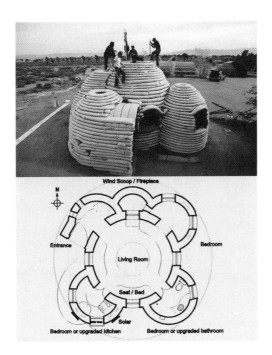

Wind Scoop / Fireplace

N

Entrance   Bedroom

Living Room

Seat / Bed

Solar

Bedroom or upgraded kitchen   Bedroom or upgraded bathroom

17.2 Sandbag Shelters in Ahvaz by Nader Khalili, 1995. Composed of arches, domes and vaults, these single- and double-curvature shell structures in Ahvaz invoke the ancient mud brick architecture of the region. While barbed wire strengthens the structures against earthquake, their aerodynamic form resists hurricanes; sandbags themselves are resistant to flood, and their earth content is fireproof. The structures are particularly suitable for temporary shelters because they are cheap and can be quickly erected by unskilled labor. Above all, this system is sustainable

Such environmentally attuned designs have not been limited to arid regions of Iran. Located 1,000 kilometers to the north, Tehran's Bagh-e Ferdows (Paradise Park) is customized to the winding site at the foot of the Alborz Mountain. Designed in the mid 1990s by architect Gholam Reza Pasban Hazrat, the park won the 1997 Aga Khan Award for Architecture for complementing the natural contours of the heights of north Tehran, complete with a series of stone structures reminiscent of those built in the northern Iranian plateau and in Kurdistan (also suitable for the relatively harsh winters of northern Tehran).

Today the younger generation of Iranian architects is fully cognizant of the importance of traditional building methods and of environmentally friendly and sustainable design. A recent hallmark of this approach is a residential complex that, despite its minimal size and private function, attracted the attention of the 2010 Aga Khan Award jury. Only 535 square meters in size, the Dowlat II Residential Complex, completed in 2007, is the work of the Tehran-based firm Arsh Design Studio. Unlike most Tehran mid-rises (see Figure 17.11) this design has a louver-like façade with a variety of openings, allowing multiple configurations decided by the inhabitants.[21] The façade calls to mind the adjustable characteristics of forms and functions of various spaces in traditional dwellings, in which division of space was based upon temporal considerations (i.e., not only did the shape of the façades facing the courtyard change as the glass and wood screens or *orosis* were constantly moved, but rooms also served different purposes at different times of the day and night). Each unit of the Dowlat II complex is split-level, and each allows access to a private roof garden (reminiscent of the rooftops of traditional courtyard homes). The architects envisaged the complex as a model that can be adapted to similar sites. Indeed, the project's low cost (a result of the use of local materials

17.3   Dezful Cultural Center, 1995. View across the courtyard fountain

and technologies) has made it a prototype for other residential neighborhoods (Figure 17.4).[22]

While the aforementioned architects have been primarily influenced by functional aspects of traditional architecture, others have been inspired by mere formal characteristics of it. The Rafsanjan Sports Complex (1994–2001) by Hadi Mirmiran (d. 2006) of Naghsh-e Jahan Pars Consulting Engineers is a case in point. Inspired perhaps by such emblematic Post-Modern complexes as James Stirling's Neue Staatsgalerie (1977–84) and Peter Eisemnan's Wexner Center for the Visual and Performing Arts (1983–89), Rafsanjan's Sports Complex is saturated with iconographical references to traditional forms.[23] Noteworthy is the facility's wrestling hall, which is housed in a monumental cone-shaped structure, resembling that of Iran's old *Yakhchals* (Ice Reservoirs) (Figure 17.5).

The structures described above have exemplified the processes of assimilation and re-interpretation of regional architecture while appropriating foreign influences. But there is more to the built environment of Iran than mere architectonics. Like all other aspects of the country's material culture, architecture has been closely tied to the country's sociopolitical conditions in the past four decades. Indeed, there is a politicized side to the architecture of Iran. The Pahlavi period offers ample evidence of how patrons (often members of the royal family) as well as architects imagined a nation unified through a number of outstanding monuments and stunning public buildings. In the official discourse of the regime, luxurious buildings such as Tehran's Museum of Contemporary Art (muse honarha-ye mo'aser), completed in 1977 by Kamran Diba (DAZ)—which houses the largest collection of Western art outside North America and Europe—were regarded as harbingers of the glory of the nation. However, many Iranians saw them as superficial.

During and after the 1979 Revolution, a few buildings—including Reza Shah's memorial—were razed and many public spaces reorganized to conform to public

17.4   Dowlat II Residential Complex, 2007. View of the façade with opened wooden panels

17.5   Rafsanjan Sports Complex in Rafsanjan (an eastern desert city and the capital of Rafsanjan County in the Kerman Province), 2001. From top to bottom: elevations and façade; below: northwest view

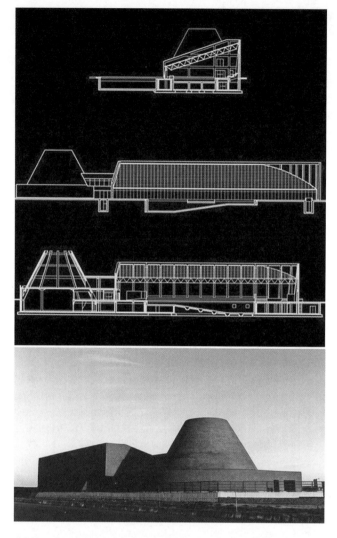

life in the Islamic Republic. In combination with propaganda murals, gender segregation and a lack of public space for entertainment become defining characteristics of urban life in the 1980s and 1990s.

MONUMENTS IN A SHIFTING POLITICAL LANDSCAPE

First-time visitors to Tehran are often impressed by a huge monument that sits right outside the Mehrabad Airport on the west side of the capital (Figure 17.6). This 45-meter-high structure encompasses both a large gallery space beneath it and a beautifully designed landscape of 65,000 square meters that wraps around it, forming an oval rotary that is now known as Meydan-e Azadi (Freedom Rotary). The monument was constructed in 1971, shortly before the 2,500-

year anniversary of the birth of the Persian Empire. The anniversary celebrations drew high-ranking delegates of the world to Iran. The festivities took place near Persepolis, the Achaemenian capital, "with royal ceremonies, exquisite dinners, dazzling fireworks, and a fantastic parade of 'Persian History.'"[24] Prior to their trip to Persepolis, guests enjoyed a tour of Tehran's new monuments, including the Shahyad, designed by the young Iranian architect Hossein Amanat, winner of a competition that had elicited more than 20 entries.[25] Although the design was jointly executed by the well-known London-based firm Ove Arup and Partners, the monument displayed its Iranian character and captured the essence of its full title, Shahyad Arya-Mehr ("the memorial of the King, the light of the Iranians").[26] After the 1979 revolution, however, the Islamic regime turned the monument into an icon of the Islamic Republic and a symbol of the Islamic Revolution's victory.

Mistreated for years and covered with anti-Shah graffiti from the revolutionary period, the monument—now renamed Azadi—was repaired and reopened by Iran's Cultural Ministry of Islamic Guidance in the early 1990s.[27] Its exhibition spaces displayed traditional arts and crafts and the whole complex was tightly controlled during pro-government rallies and annual celebrations of the Islamic Revolution.[28]

Although the symbolism of the Azadi monument had already changed by the 1990s, the Islamic Republic could not take credit for its construction—it was still a Pahlavi monument, according to collective memory. To overcome this dilemma, a proposal for a new symbol of Tehran was put forward in 1992 by Tehran's City Hall. Shortly thereafter, the city announced a design competition for a tall monument that could accommodate telecommunication facilities as well as tourist and cultural centers. Architect Mohammad Hafezi won the competition;

17.6 Shahyad Arya-Mehr (now Azadi) Monument, 1971

preliminary studies began as early as June 1993, and the new Milad Tower was completed in 2008 (Figure 17.7).

The tower was originally a component of Tehran's Shahestan Pahlavi (literally, Pahlavi Royal City), scheduled to be completed in the late 1970s. Shahestan Pahlavi was to be one of the largest urban spaces in Iran, eclipsing even the famous seventeenth-century Meydan-e-Shah of Esfahan.[29] As part of the plan, 5 million

17.7   Milad
Tower, 2008

square meters in the heart of Tehran would contain ceremonial spaces, museums, libraries, government buildings, entertainment and restaurant facilities, cultural centers, and open recreation areas, as well as a park with waterfalls. Tehran's metro system would run beneath the central boulevard in the Shahestan. Finally, a telecommunication tower was designed to embellish the heart of the Shahestan. This tower was to be placed at the so-called Nation Square, the ceremonial and symbolic center of the royal city.

Like many others, this project was halted as the clerical regime consolidated power. However, in the fall of 1995, 15 years after the Islamic Revolution, construction of the tower was launched on the heights of Gisha, a district in central Tehran that is geographically elevated. Along with its adjacent buildings, the complex now occupies a 12,000-square-meter site. Just as intended in the original Pahlavi blueprints, the 435-meter-high tower is now one of the largest telecommunication towers in the world.[30] The world's famous telecom towers—such as the BT Tower in London and the Telecommunications Tower of Berlin—have maintained their function as communication hubs. However, due to the high cost of such structures, many regions are now served by radio masts, or simple tall antennas, instead. The age of the telecom tower may be long past; the Iranian media has nevertheless generated a very optimistic image of the Milad Tower as the icon of the Islamic Republic. This pride is often coupled with the fact that the tower is the world's sixth-highest after Tokyo's Skytree (2011), Guangzhou TV and Sightseeing Tower (2004), Shanghai's Oriental Pearl (1994), Toronto's CN Tower (1976), and Moscow's Ostankino (1967).

Even before the tower was completed, the Iranian press had portrayed it as an icon of the country's independence. In the words of a pro-regime periodical, Milad Tower signifies the "potent" (mostahkam) and "everlasting" (mandegar) Islamic Republic.[31] Other newspapers have since praised aspects of the design that feature medieval Islamic patterns. According to the architect, Hafezi, a portion of the observatory component of the tower was inspired by the interlacing patterns (karbandi)found in Islamic domes of the Timurid and Safavid dynasties.[32] Subsequently, the popular newspaper Abrar Eghtesadi featured the tower in one of its 2007 issues with the headline: "Memari Irani dar Borj-e Milad [Iranian Architecture in Milad Tower]."[33]

Concern for highlighting the identity of the Islamic Republic in Tehran's monuments surfaced more strongly in a 1997 convention hall built for the eighth triennial congregation of Islamic nations' leaders. Similar to the Milad Tower, blueprints for the building came from an unbuilt 1974 Mandala Collaborative design for a symphony hall. It was a prestigious undertaking for the young Iranian firm, a landmark project that drew the interest of the Shah himself. The design concept for the symphony hall was based, Mandala claimed, on the "unifying organizational conceptions of Persian 'place making,'" especially the garden, both the "hidden garden"—an open courtyard surrounded by indoor spaces—and the "manifest garden" surrounding the building as a whole.[34] The decorative ceiling of the auditorium was at once functional—calibrated to achieve optimal reverberation— and symbolic, evoking the graded textures of the walls at Persepolis, the ruined capital of the Achaemenian empire. Outdoor rectangular gardens were intended to recall the ancient Persian ornamental gardens. Royal staircases mimicked the ceremonial staircases at Persepolis, while the stage in the main concert hall echoed Persepolis' Apadana, or audience hall. The project, which also involved the American firm of Skidmore, Owings, and Merrill, was halted in 1978, when the Shah as well as the members of the Mandala Collaborative, including Nader Ardalan and Yahyah Fiuzi, fled Iran.

Nearly two decades after his departure, former Mandala Collaborative member Yahyah Fiuzi was called back to Iran in June 1997 to design the Eighth Summit of the Organization of Islamic Conferences (OIC) based on the symphony hall's blueprints. In the wake of President Mohammad Khatami's surprise election in May of that year, the OIC summit was to be a watershed in the history of the Islamic Republic, which had boycotted the previous five OIC summits over the organization's refusal to condemn Iraq for the Iran–Iraq war, and the December summit was to be a kind of coming-out party.[35] Khatami planned to launch his "dialogue of civilizations" initiative at the summit before the assembled Muslim dignitaries, many of whom represented countries that the Republic had broken off relationships with (including Egypt, which had briefly sheltered the dying Shah two decades earlier, in the first days of the revolution).

Fiuzi, under time and budgetary constraints, created a new concept for the project, replacing the previous paradigm of "Persian placemaking" with what he called Heya'ti, or "rushed style," a process that results in temporary architecture inspired by traditional Shiite religious ceremonies.[36] Despite its shoddy look, in the end the building contributed to the Islamic Republic's rhetoric of its own glory. Interestingly enough, the decline in architectural quality—ranging from aesthetic features to technical issues—has not been viewed by political elites as a scandal but instead as a sign of Iranian independence. Whether this phenomenon is a process of de-aesthetization or a result of economic decline, the Iranian regime has constructed a positive image of it. Headlines such as "Making the Impossible Possible [mumkin sakhtan-i namumkin]," and "The Emphasis on Self-reliance [pafishari bar khud et'teka'i]," stand out on pages of an article dedicated to the building in a 1997 issue of Abadi, one of the most popular architectural journals of the time.[37] Similarly, Abrar-e Iqtisadi, a daily newspaper, later described the building as a symbol of peace (Figure 17.8).

If Khatami's "dialogue of civilizations" was not fully embodied in the Summit Conference hall, it materialized in a series of new buildings of the Iranian Embassy built in several major capitals of the world. Following the 1998 Forum of the Technical Management Group (hamayesh shoray-e hedayat-e fanni), headed by architect Mehdi Hojjat, which took place in Iran's Ministry of Foreign Affairs, a group of Iranian architects in conjunction with diplomats and the ministry's personnel put forward a proposal for renewing the buildings of the Iranian embassies around the world.[38] The goal was to project a fine image of Iran and demonstrate Iran's rich artistic and architectural heritage to the world.[39] Among all the embassies, Darab Diba's in Berlin stands out. Occupying an area of 4,509 square meters the building embodies, according to the architect, the concept of reciprocity and

بنای اجلاس سران چون نمادی از صلح بر تارک تهران می درخشد

17.8   An article from daily newspaper *Abrar-e Eqtisadi* highlights the tent-like structure of the conference hall. The caption to the image of the computer-generated model of the building reads: "The Summit Conference hall shines, like a symbol of peace, in the middle of Tehran." *Abrar-e Eghtesadi*, January 31, 2001

historical exchange of ideas that have taken place "between German and Persian poets and philosophers."[40] The solemnity of the overall shape of the building, as Diba describes it, makes reference to the spiritual dimensions of such a historic relationship, while the building's outer facade—covered with white stone plaques shipped from Iran—connote the simplicity and harmony of the verses of Hafez and Goethe (Figure 17.9).[41] The transparency of some of the interior spaces—made possible through continuous corridors and spaces divided by glass barriers—gives a sublime character to the core of the structure while simultaneously serving as a metaphorical representation of Iranians' desire for a crystal clear dialogue with the outside world.[42] Finally, the lush site surrounding the building, facing the Podbielskiallee Street in the affluent neighborhood of Dahlem in south-western Berlin, is transformed into a typical Persian *chahar-bagh* layout, consisting of plots of equal size divided by axial paths. While it is debatable whether this building has successfully communicated Khatami's concept of "dialogue of civilizations," in an era when President Mahmood Ahmadinejad has notoriously obliterated any opportunity for such a dialogue, the intentions of the architect and the rhetoric surrounding the design of the embassy (included in a glossy coffee-table book, *Diplomatic Architecture: Spatial Planning and the Architecture of Iran's Embassies*, published by Iran's Ministry of Foreign Affairs) show the extent to which political viewpoints have informed novel processes of architectural design in contemporary Iran.

17.9   Iranian
Embassy in Berlin,
2005. Above:
detail of the roof;
below: view from
south-west

(UN)COMMON PLACES AND INCONGRUOUS DEVELOPMENTS

Under the Pahlavi regime, public architecture (along with the rhetoric surrounding
it) contributed to creating an image of Iran that showcased it as a prosperous state.
But the built environment of ordinary people contradicted such an image. The last
two decades of the Pahlavi era are often associated with housing problems, which
began to be a major concern, especially after significant land reforms took place
as part of the socioeconomic improvements of the White Revolution launched in
1963 by the Mohammad Reza Shah Pahlavi. These reforms created new peasant
landowners, but even after a considerable redistribution of land, the amount
received by individual peasants was not enough to meet most families' basic needs.
As a result, the White Revolution reforms actually caused a decline in agricultural
output and forced widespread migration to large cities.[43] Many of these immigrants
were unable to own, or even rent, property in the cities. Moreover, between the
years 1968 and 1972, the price of land increased considerably; this accounted for
30 to 50 percent of the cost of housing in Tehran and other major cities.[44] These
housing problems led to a series of uprisings that eventually contributed to the
Islamic Revolution in 1979.[45] During the revolutionary years (1978–80), many poor
families appropriated "hundreds of vacant homes and half-finished apartment
blocks, refurbishing them as their own properties."[46] After the start of the war with
Iraq in September 1980, the government attempted to accommodate refugees
from border cities in the "vacant" homes of urban centers. They also turned many
public buildings, including hotels and business buildings, into residential housing
for the poor and refugees. Such appropriation was not merely the outcome of the
housing problem and the Iran–Iraq war, but signified a unique post-revolutionary
experiment in handling Pahlavi public institutions and the homes of the former
taghuties (Pahlavi bourgeois).[47]

These new arrangements, combined with the Islamic Republic's propagandist
imagery, imply a character in Iran's built environment that is exceptional.
Governmental agencies and parastatal institutions (*buniyads*) have since
contributed to the propaganda art that animates the walls of Tehran and many
other major cities.[48] Propaganda production diminished after the Iran–Iraq war and
especially during the Khatami era, when most cities were instead furnished with
commercial advertising billboards. Meanwhile, by adorning the walls of the city
with imaginative artistic murals (depicting scenes with surrealistic undertones),

many young artists negotiated unique ways of reinterpreting the political atmosphere of Tehran. Thus, as a result of freedom and opportunities developed under Khatami, a young generation of Iranian artists infused the main discourse of the regime with innovative connotations, in a form of what anthropologist Claude Lévi-Strauss has termed cultural *bricolage* (Figure 17.10).[49]

After President Ahmadinejad took office in 2005, new propaganda images came to dominate the city again. While gigantic columns supporting highways have been wrapped in verses from the Quran, vacant walls by the side of both governmental and residential buildings are now covered with revolutionary slogans and images that pay tribute to the martyrs of the Iran–Iraq war.[50] He also made a huge new mosque across the City Theatre.[51] The irony in the capital is that propaganda images and religious architecture appear not only side by side the above mentioned artistic, but also with buildings that showcase the surprising wealth of some residents of Tehran (Figure 17.11).

Such incongruous juxtapositions have become increasingly more prevalent. Perfectly suited for the Islamic Republic's ideology, religious projects such as the 2005 extension of the Holy Shrine of Hazrat Massumeh in Qom by architect Mohsen Mirheydar stand in contrast with some utterly Western-looking structures with civic functions. The latter is the consequence of the active role played by a group of architects who, despite their apolitical stances, have managed to take charge of constructing large-scale, official and governmental-funded buildings. Accommodating two large movie theatres, an exhibition hall, and a large food court, the Mellat Park Cineplex exemplifies such an approach to design. Completed in 2008 by the Tehran-based firm, Fluid Motion Architects (headed by Reza Daneshmir and Catherine Spiridonoff), the cineplex's huge undulating-

17.10   Mural by artist Mehdi Ghadiyanloo, demonstrating a pedestrian bridge that leads nowhere, Tehran, district 10, 2007

duct of concrete and glass, is lifted in the middle, allowing a sheltered open space at the edge of the Mellat Park, thus contributing to further interactions amongst the passersby (Figure 17.12).[52] Such civic spaces had been discouraged during the past decades, due to their potential for stimulating civic or revolutionary and anti-regime gatherings.

Iranian architecture since the 1960s provides a fascinating vantage point for understanding the politics of design in contemporary Iran. Architectural spaces, their adjacent sites, and the rhetoric surrounding their design processes have carried

17.11   Chenaran Park Residential Complex by Farzad Daliri. Tehran, Iran, 2008. Left to right: General view; entrance to the complex; details of façade

17.12   Mellat Park Cineplex, Tehran, 2008; north view

different meanings over the past 50 years. Many edifices have been transformed from symbols of a secular and imperial regime into artifacts of an Islamic state, and from restricted political domains into arenas for popular expressions. In the past half-century, the private and the public architecture of Iran have functioned both as sustenance to the nation state and as resistance against it; these structures have performed many roles on the various stages of Iran's unstable ideological scenes, thereby directing and shaping lived experiences of Iranians and, consequently, central to assessing the identity of the country in the past half-century.

NOTES

1   On the activities of the society see Talinn Grigor, *Building Iran: Modernism, Architecture, and National Heritage under the Pahlavi Monarchs* (New York: Periscope Publishing, 2009).

2   Kishwar Rizvi, "Modern Architecture and the Middle East: The burden of representation," in idem and S. Isenstadt (eds), *Modernism and the Middle East: Architecture and politics in the twentieth century* (Seattle: University of Washington Press), 14.

3   Benedict Anderson, *Imagined Communities: Reflections on the Origins and Spread of Nationalism* (London: Verso, 1983), 11.

4   The Ministry of Development and Housing completed two such comprehensive plans between 1949 and 1967. In addition, the High Council of Urban Planning (*shura-ye ali-e shahrsazi*) was formed in order to provide housing regulations. The development plans were primarily intended to create adequate housing. The third development plan (1968–1972) was more detailed, and proposed regulations for different types of housing, styles of architecture, construction materials, and even the renovation of old neighborhoods. See also Habibollah Zanjani, "Housing in Iran," *Encyclopedia Iranica* (2004), accessed: June 10, 2010, http://iranica.com/articles/housing-in-iran.

5   These characteristics are listed by Khadijeh Kia-Kujuri, *A Study of Nine Residential District in Tehran* (study conducted under the supervision of Building Research and Codes Division), Manuscript 2.62 (Tehran: Ministry of Housing and Development, 1351/1972), 14. Cited in Pamela Karimi, *Domesticity and Consumer Culture in Iran: Interior Revolutions of the Modern Era* (London and New York: Routledge, 2013), 69–70.

6   Mina Marefat, "The Protagonists Who Shaped Modern Tehran," in Chahryar Adle and Bernard Hourcade (eds), *Téhéran, Capitale Bicentenaire* (Paris and Tehran: Institut français de recherche en Iran, 1992), 105–108.

7   These architects also published their ideas in the journal, *Arshitect [Architect]*, which was printed from 1946 to 1948 by the recently formed Society of Certified Iranian Architects [*Anjoman arshitecthay-i Irani-i diplom-i*]. The society as well as the journal were initiated and led by Iranian architect Mohsen Forughi. Cited in Karimi, *Domesticity and Consumer Culture in Iran*, 59.

8   Nader Ardalan, "Architecture. Pahlavi, after World War II," *Encyclopedia Iranica* (1986), accessed: October 10, 2011, http://www.iranica.com/articles/architecture-viii.

9   Ali Madanipour, *Tehran: The Making of a Metropolis* (New York: John Wiley, 1998).

10   Sheila S. Blair and Jonathan M. Bloom, "Iran," *Grove Art Online. Oxford Art Online*. Oxford University Press, accessed: January 10, 2013, http://www.oxfordartonline.com/subscriber/article/grove/art/T041466.

11   Karimi, *Domesticity and Consumer Culture in Iran*, 92–3.

12   Blair and Bloom, "Iran."

13   Aga Khan Award for Architecture (Organization), *The Aga Khan Award for Architecture: The 1986 Award* (Geneva, Switzerland: Aga Khan Award for Architecture, 1986).

14   For more details regarding this issue, see Grigor, *Building Iran*; Karimi, *Domesticity and Consumer Culture in Iran*, 140–41.

15   John Sullivan and K. Lauren de Boer, "Building with Earth is Sacred Work: An Interview with Nader Khalili," *EarthLight* 32, 21, accessed: May 12, 2011, http://www.earthlight.org/khalili_interview.html.

16   The Geltaftan (literally "clay-firing") method renews traditional methods of kiln firing while encouraging the use of readily available, traditional earthen materials. See further, Aga Khan Award for Architecture, *The Aga Khan Award for Architecture*.

17   Phillipa Baker (ed.), *Architecture and Polyphony: Building in the Islamic World Today* (London: Thames and Hudson, 2004).

18   Until his death in 2008, Khalili lived and worked in California where, in 1986, he founded the California Institute of Earth Art and Architecture (Cal-Earth). At Cal-Earth, he built prototype ceramic homes and organized workshops on building efficiently and sustainably. The institute is still active today. Also see *ArchNet Digital Library*, accessed: May 20, 2012, http://archnet.org/library/files/one-file.jsp?file_id=377.

19   Khalili's *Racing Alone* was translated (*Tanha Davidan*) and taught in several undergraduate programs. Khalili's other books include *Ceramic Houses and Earth Architecture: How to Build Your Own*; *Sidewalks on the Moon*; and *Emergency Sandbag Shelter and Eco-Village: How to Build Your Own*, which include information about the building techniques Khalili researched and developed at Cal-Earth. Khalili also translated Rumi's poems in two volumes: *Rumi, Fountain of Fire* and *Rumi, Dancing the Flame*.

20   For a visual display of these spaces, see Cynthia Davidson and Ismail Serageldin, *Architecture beyond Architecture: Creativity and Social Transformations in Islamic cultures, The Aga Khan award for architecture* (Geneva, Switzerland: Aga Khan Award for Architecture, 1995). Also see *ArchNet Digital Library*, accessed: May 20, 2012, http://archnet.org/library/sites/one-site.jsp?site_id=1468.

21   See further, Aga Khan Award for Architecture, 2010; "Dowlat II Residential Building," *Archnet Digital Library*, accessed: August 10, 2012, http://archnet.org/library/files/one-file.jsp?file_id=3059.

22   This building is discussed in further detail in Karimi, *Domesticity and Consumer Culture in Iran*, 166–7. A recent similar example is a low-cost four-story residential complex designed by architect Alireza Mashhadimirza. Built in a poor neighborhood of Tehran, Mashhadimirza's building is shielded by a checkerboard façade of brick. Projecting out of this shell, the bricks cast varied shades at different times of the day, thus animating an otherwise dull façade. For more information on this project see, World Builders Directory, Online Database, accessed: January 20, 2013, http://www.worldbuildingsdirectory.com/project.cfm?id=4063.

23   The popularity of these ideas also owed to the availability of key texts, including *Deconstruction: A Student Guide* (London: Academy Editions, 1991) by Geoffrey Broadbent, whose translation became available in Iran as early as 1996. See further, Geoffrey Broadbent and Manouchehr Muzayyeni (trans.), *Vasazi (Deconstroksion): Rahnamay-e Danishjooyan* (Tehran: Shahrdari Tehran, 1375/1996).

24   The July 1966 issue of *Etelaat* newspaper reported these festivities. See further, Talinn Grigor, "Of Metamorphosis: Meaning on Iranian Terms," *Third Text*, 17, 3 (2003): 207–25.

25   Ibid.

26   Hussein Amanat, interviewed by Grigor. Cited in Grigor, "Of Metamorphosis."

27   Grigor, "Of Metamorphosis."

28   Ibid.

29   Jacquelin T. Robertson, "Shahestan Pahlavi: Steps toward a New Iranian Centre," in Renata Holod (ed.), *Toward an Architecture in the Spirit of Islam* (Philadelphia: The Aga Khan Award for Architecture, 1978), 44–51.

30   *Iran Newspaper* Editorial. 2001. *Nahveh tarrahi va ehdas borj-e milad dar Tehran barresi shod* [The Design Process in the Milad Tower], *Iran Newspaper* 2064, 1.

31   *Donyay-e Asansor* Editorial. 2005. *Borj-e milad, mostahkan va mandegar* [The Potent and Everlasting Milad Tower], *Donyay-e Asansor*, 4(20), 22; *Hamshahri* Editorial. 2000. *Hameh chiz darbareh borj-e milad* [All You Need to Know about the Milad Tower], *Hamshahri*, 8(2248), 7.

32   "Memari Irani Dar Borj-e Milad [Iranian Traditional Architectural Motifs in Milad Tower]," *Abrar Eghtesadi*, 5, 241 (2007): 16.

33   Ibid.

34   Mandala International Report, 1978, Tehran Center for the Performance of Music. Box 027. II. 98, August Komendant Collection, University of Pennsylvania.

35   The OIC has a long history and has had a particular meaning for each Islamic nation since its establishment in the early twentieth century. For more information about this conference, see Abdullah Al-Ahsan, *OIC, The Organization of the Islamic Conference: An Introduction to an Islamic Political Institution* (Herndon, VA.: International Institute of Islamic Thought, 1988), 11–13.

36   Yahya Fiuzi. Interviewed by Pamela Karimi, May 10, 2004, Washington, D.C. Cited in Pamela Karimi and Michael Vazquez, "Ornament and Argument," *Bidoun: Art and Culture from the Middle East*, 13 (winter 2008): 93–7.

37   "Moruri bar Tahaquq-i Yek Tarh [A Look at the Formation of an Idea]," *Abadi*, 7, 26 (1997): 92–5.

38   Seyyed Kazem Kharrazi, "Introduction," in *Memari Diplomatic: Barnameh Rzi Fazaie va Memari Sefarat khanehha* [*Diplomatic Architecture: Spatial Planning and the Architecture of Iran's Embassies*] (Tehran: *Markaz-e Chab va Entesharat-e Vezarat-e Omur-e Kharejeh* [The Ministry of Foreign Affairs Press], 2004), 1–14.

39   Ibid.

40   Most notably, he emphasizes the influence of Hafez's poetry on Goethe. See Aga Khan Award for Architecture, 2005; "Embassy of Iran," *ArchNet Digital Library*, accessed: May 10, 2012, http://archnet.org/library/sites/one-site.jsp?site_id=14667.

41   Ibid.

42   Such principles were likewise implemented in the design of the Consulate General of Iran in Frankfurt, which was completed in 2004 by Hamid Mirmiran of the Naghsh-e Jahan Pars Consulting Engineers. See "Consulate General of Iran," *ArchNet Digital Library*, accessed: May 10, 2011, http://archnet.org/library/sites/one-site.jsp?site_id=14672.

43   See, further, Ervand Abrahamian *A History of Modern Iran* (Cambridge: Cambridge University Press, 2008), 130–33.

44   Madanipour, *Tehran*, 394.

45   Asef Bayat, *Street Politics: Poor People's Movements in Iran* (New York: Columbia University Press, 1997); see also, Karimi, *Domesticity and Consumer Culture*, 10, 59, 114–16.

46   Ibid., 2.

47   See further Asef Bayat, "Tehran: Paradox City," *New Left Review* 66 (November–December 2010): 99–122. Online article, accessed February 10, 2012, accessed July 2011, http://www.newleftreview.org.

48   Christiane Gruber, "The Message is on the Wall: Mural Arts in Post-Revolutionary Iran," *Persica* 22 (2008): 15–46.

49   Dick Hebdige, *Subculture: The Meaning of Style* (New York: Routledge, 1979), 5–19.

50   Pamela Karimi, "Imagining Warfare, Imaging Welfare: Tehran's Post Iran–Iraq War Murals and their Legacy," *Persica* 22 (2008): 47–63.

51   On these developments, see further, Kasra Naji, *Ahmadinejad*, London: I.B. Tauris, 2008, pp. 49–51.

52   For more information on this project see, World Builders Directory, Online Database, accessed: January 20, 2013, http://www.worldbuildingsdirectory.com/project.cfm?id=1571.

18

Beyond Tropical Regionalism: The Architecture of Southeast Asia

Kelly Shannon

CLIMATE AND LANDSCAPE AS REGIONAL UNIFIER

Southeast Asia's contemporary history in the era of globalization is impossible to comprehend without links to its complexly layered history. The importance of the region arose from its intrinsic assets and geographical position, since all shipping vessels between Europe and China/Japan must pass though the Straight of Malacca—the narrow waterbody that separates Sumatra from Malaysia. The term "Southeast Asia" is of recent origin and only became popular during World War II, when the territories south of the Tropic of Cancer were placed under Lord Louis Mountbatten's Allied Southeast Asia command.[1] It presently includes and is commonly divided into "mainland" Southeast Asia: Myanmar, Laos, Cambodia, Vietnam and the peninsula of Thailand and "insular" Southeast Asia: Brunei, the Philippines, the island of Singapore, the peninsulas of Malaysia and Indonesia, the world's largest archipelago. However, it is not an obvious unit in the linguistic, historical, geographical, or ethnic senses and there are at least four different major religions: Islam, Hinduism, Buddhism and Christianity. Historically the region never underwent political consolidation as India or China did and its colonial history enhanced separate development among Southeast Asian peoples, as different European powers reigned over different territories—Dutch (Indonesia), British (Myanmar, Malaysia, Singapore, Brunei), Portuguese (East Timor), Spanish followed by American (Philippines) and French (Laos, Cambodia and Vietnam). Only Thailand remained free of colonial rule, but even its rulers appointed Western advisers to aid modernization; it is widely recognized to have had a process of self-colonization.[2]

The greater unifier is its climate and landscape. Southeast Asia is located in the monsoon belt, complicating navigation in open seas and the cultivation of crops, and with the exception of a part of Myanmar, is situated between the tropics. Historically, the contrasting topographies of mountain and plains, land and water led to the development of both maritime trade and agriculture. Port/market city morphology was marked by a transitory and temporary appearance, whereas shorelines and riverbank sites were subject to silting and relied for their wealth on the vagaries of maritime trade. As well, since such cities habitually had limited hinterlands and inadequate space for expansion, urban populations often spread over the water by houses on stilts and boathouses. As Stephen Cairns has commented, the material fabric of primarily low-rise, high-density, mosaic-like settlements with outdoor markets was generally seen to have been temporary and has been described by numerous scholars as "unsteady," "bending," "shaky," "weak," "poor," "rustic" and "wild" and written about as being in a permanent state of flux and "except in the biggest cities, life was based on the presumption of constant mobility."[3] However, one can question to what degree such descriptions coincide with material realities or correspond more with written, theoretical categories which allude to the region's history of complex negotiations of conceptual registers. Meanwhile, agricultural settlements were isolated, inward-looking, compact, frequently protected by walls and gates and self-sufficient. The productive landscapes were often closely related to sacred landscapes and the morphology of the sacred city, home of the god-king, was a representation of cosmological beliefs and adhered to practices of auspicious siting vis-à-vis geomancy. Climate and landscape also had a significant impact on the region's architecture.

According to Anthony Reid, the mild climate and availability of fast-growing trees, palms and bamboos as building materials were fundamental reasons for a low priority given to house construction.[4] Although indigenous architecture reveals a great deal of variety of house-building styles among different peoples and classes of the region, there are also startling similarities: the use of pile foundations (usually resting on the ground and not sunk into it), steep saddle roofs and gable horns.[5] Elevated housing (also known as "pole" or "stilt" housing) was necessitated as protection against flooding and floor- and wall-boards were used sparingly, keeping the structures lightweight and easy to move (Figure 18.1).

18.1   Typical landbased indigenous settlement, Toba Batak village of Tolping. Samosir Island, Lake Toba, 1986

There was a sacred importance given to heights and most dwellings were one storey; the basement was for animals, refuse and work space, the central level for human habitation and the upper (rafters) level for rice storage and ritual offerings to ancestors. And, in countries where there was a strong hierarchical, Confucian social order, the pre-colonial city was also subject to strict size regulation on buildings and plots. The style, patterns and colors of houses were closely controlled to differentiate between the social status of residents. The lightness and impermanence of domestic architecture was counter-balanced by heaviness and permanence of the region's religious architecture. Masonry and distinctive forms dominated the ruins of lost civilizations, tombs, mosques and palaces.

By the end of the eighteenth century, a colonial-urban hierarchy was in place and was characterized by stabilized settlements, garrison and trading towns. During the colonial era, the tropical vernacular traditions of the region were typically incorporated within an Orientalist gaze, as evidenced in numerous colonial exhibitions.[6] Meanwhile, cities metamorphosed with the advent of the colonial impositions and new buildings incorporated European typologies with local building traditions and vernacular motifs. At the same time, alien rule was not accepted passively in Southeast Asia. The flip-side of the colonial coin was nationalism. By the mid 1950s almost all of the countries of Southeast Asia had attained their hard won independence. Large-scale *tabula rasa* functionalist planning and orthodox Modernism represented progress and change. According to Philip Goad, the "neutrality" of Modernist vocabulary also served to diffuse inter-ethnic tensions:

> The use of reinforced concrete, the brise soleil, broad over-sailing eaves and parasol roofs to monumental pavilions appeared to indicate that monumental Modernism had been acclimatised by the tropics, and that the task of emulation had been successfully translated to the East, and, at the same time ... the historic city was effectively parcelled away and drained out of life that once ran through its streets; (the) modern Asian metropolis is largely a story of condoned disappearance.[7]

As Anoma Pieris also mentioned:

> The unguarded universalism of the post-independent period changed radically following the 1973 oil crisis, when nations were forced to become self-reliant. It also precipitated a cultural crisis fuelled by growing disenchantment with Western-educated political elites who had conceived a cosmopolitan psyche for their nations ... The specific religious and cultural characteristics of this traditionalist approach precluded the existing cultural diversity of postcolonial contexts. It promoted the culture of the majority, and marginalized ethnic minorities.[8]

TROPICAL REGIONALISM

Already then, Southeast Asian architects blended hybrid education and practical experiences. In the 1950s, many of the region's architects were trained in Great Britain (many attending the *Architecture Association*'s course on tropical architecture, led by Maxwell Fry from 1954–57 and then by Otto Koeningsberger), Australia (where in 1962, the University of Melbourne had begun a program on tropical architecture) and the United States, returning to their homeland with a heightened sense of the differences between East and West. Three books were greatly influential in this respect: Maxwell Fry and Jane Drew's *Village Housing in the Tropics* (1947), *Tropical Architecture in the Humid Zone* (1956) and Victor and Aladar Olgyay's *Design with Climate: Bioclimatic Approach to Architectural Regionalism* (1963). These studies redirected the Modernist discourse towards the vernacular traditions, which has been argued by Alexander Tzonis, Liane Lefaivre and Bruno Stagno as being anti-colonial, anti-traditionalist and anti-International Style[9] and labeled as "an architecture of resistance" by Kenneth Frampton.[10] The local insertions with decorative schemata, negotiation with local construction techniques and reinterpretation of traditional typologies and adaption to micro-differences in climatic variances resulted in what Homi Bhabha and Abidin Kusno would term "hybrid modernities."[11]

In the region there were therefore a variety of different practices—spanning from inherited colonial practices such as Booty, Edwards and Partners (now Booty Edwards and Rakan-Rakan) in Malaysia (BEP) to new practices like Malayan Architects Co-Partnership (MAC) (which later became the Singapore-based Design Partnership, now known as DP Architects) and was modeled on Walter Gropius's The Architects Collaborative (TAC), and the London-based Architects Co-Partnership. The Design Partnership was established by William Lim, Tay Kheng Soon and Koh Seow Chuan and solidified iconic success with the People's Park Complex (Figure 18.2) with a podium of shopping (1970) and slab of housing (1973) that drew from both Le Corbusier's Marseilles Unité and the work of the Metabolists in Japan.

Amongst the "masters" of this Southeast Asian architectural tendency figures Thailand's Sumet Jumsai, Singapore's William Lim and Tay Kheng Soon and Malaysia's Ken Yeang. In 1988, Jumsai's study on *Naga: Cultural Origins in Siam and West Pacific* drew attention to the region's indigenous water-based and stilt-housing, pleading for alternative architectural and urban futures for the region, while self-proclaiming his Bank of Asia Headquarters in Bangkok, the "Robot Building," as an example of post high-tech architecture. William Lim established the MAC and DP with Tay and later his own practice, from which he retired to concentrate on writing about the culture of Asian cities in the context of post-modernity. Meanwhile, Tay adopted the metaphor of "tropical cities" and Yeang the "bioclimatic skyscraper", the latter which simultaneously accepts the dominant form of global urbanity, namely the skyscraper, while adapting it locally with climatic devices—large-scale wind shields, louvered screens, overhead pergolas, sun-shading devices, wind baffles and vegetation. Tay has condemned the insertion of modernist boxes into the city, particularly in the period before the 1997 Asian financial crisis which was

18.2 Singapore's iconic tower and slab. The Design Partnership, People's Park Complex, 1970

characterized by the rush of mainstream corporate Western architects to enter the emerging market. He has boldly put forth the thesis that:

> Now it is in this context that there is a need for a more intrinsic design agenda
> for tropical Asian countries. And that to seek the design agenda from the
> environment itself, which is specific to place and time. The new technological
> environment can also be brought in as a generator of form and expression and to
> create a sense of cohesive identity, which transcends ethnicity and culture. This is
> the challenge to the creative design professions.[12]

Kusno, who has written extensively on urban space and political cultures in Indonesia, has framed the alternatives offered by Tay and Yeang in another light, giving them political implications:

> In this sense, in masking the 'modernist box," there is no immediate rejection
> of the modernist paradigm itself nor the determinants out of which it came.
> Indeed, the climatic devices are all "dependent" upon the structure of the building
> which, typologically, is not unlike those constructed all over the world. Perhaps

the obligation to come to terms with the city fabric has informed a change in the architectural sign system so that the whole cultural patterning of the city is reduced to the problem of an apolitical "climate." This climatic essentialism might as well be read, economically, as a cultural restructuring of late capitalist development whose expansion is no longer mediated by the dissemination of the old standardized "modernist box." However, this regionalist approach adopted by Tay and Yeang should also be read politically as representing the contention with primordialism in the construction of a "modern" post-colonial nation. The modernist box lying behind the climatic device is articulated to speak a language beyond that of universal Modernism. Instead, it now goes through the condition that allows the non-political climatic expression of identity.[13]

In 1989, Tay led a team to develop the "Tropical City Concept" for the Singapore Institute of Architects. They tested ideas for Kampong Bugis, a 72-hectare post-industrial riverfront redevelopment site in Singapore, and developed a scenario of a "two-level" city, where the public realm is extended to a multi-level podium that mixes shopping, entertainment, social and cultural facilities (Figure 18.3).

Housing and work places would be sectionally mixed throughout the development, reducing the need for commuting to work. The overall objective sought to densify housing in the city center and lessen the need for suburban and new town development. There were also two explicit strategies to directly address the tropical climate: (1) high-level shading to prevent heating up of the city fabric, using devices which would also operate as rain and sun energy collectors; (2) green the city both horizontally and vertically to absorb radiant and ambient insolation. It was in Malaysia that Yeang was able, in the same year, to design a tropical skyscraper that was realized, and eventually awarded an Aga Khan prize in 1995. The 15-storey Menara Mesiniaga, headquarters for IBM in Subang Jaya near Kuala Lumpur, incorporated (Figure 18.4) vertical landscaping spirals across the face of the building through the recessed terraces (used as skycourts); passive low-energy features, reducing solar heat gain in internal spaces. Yeang's development of "eco-infrastructure" has developed over the years and his firm has built numerous eco-skyscrapers and –"landscapers" in China and Southeast Asia. The DIGI Technology Operation Center in the Subang High Tech Park, in Malaysia is representative of the

18.3   Animated section for the tropical city. The Design Partnership, Kampong Bugis, 1989

move to combine advanced technologies for sequestering carbon dioxide and solar gain with low-tech devices to deal with storm water management. The building is enveloped in a "Vertical Plantscape System" which reduces solar radiation, insulates the building and bio-purifies air contaminants (Figure 18.5).

A tropical regionalism of sorts has also taken root in the region from a far less rigorous academic and ideological perspective. There are two building types that

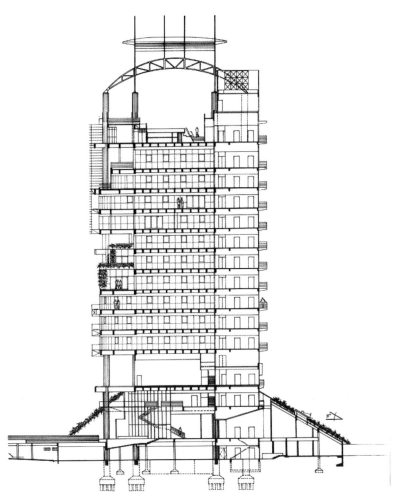

18.4 Landscape woven into the skyscraper mediates the tropical climate. T.R. Hamzah & Yeang Architects, IBM Headquarters in Subang Jaya, near Kuala Lumpur, 1992

18.5 Advanced technology is combined with soft engineering to create eco-infrastructure. T.R. Hamzah & Yeang Architects, DIGI Technology Operation Center in the Subang High Tech Park, Malaysia, 2012

have enabled architects in the region to gain international acclaim leading to a flurry of glossy publications that focused on the luxurious tropical house and the tourist resort—additive buildings as clustered pavilion forms which could successfully maintain the scale of vernacular structures. As Pieris rightly pointed out:

> Framed as refuges from the gritty reality of Asian urban life—temporal rustic retreats, these models were mini utopias projecting an idyllic lifestyle in a tropical climate. Designed for wealthy businessmen, European expatriates or multinational chains, these resorts delivered a new product for the dollar economy within developing countries, and included the local labour. The dollar economy paid for exquisite detailing, creating a resurgence in local craft traditions and a boom in local materials. It produced high standards of design unaffordable to local clients. Its consumers were a Westernized elite and Western tourists who, unaware of the irony of its transformation, envisioned the tropical experience as an extension of a moment of colonization. The local had truly become global.[14]

It is evidently quite easy to criticize resort architecture and its reinterpretation of the vernacular, popularized through lavish coffee-table monographs. However, at the same time, a number of architects, such as Peter Muller and Palmer and Turner in Bali, and Ed Tuttle in Thailand carefully crafted environments that embodied the local landscape, created incredible ambiance through carefully calibrated spatial sequences and sophistication in detail—all in an authentic reaction to rational excesses of post-war Functionalism and Postmodernism. Kerry Hill, an Australian who was renowned for his exotic hotel design throughout the region, became a mentor for a new generation of young Southeast Asian architects, "As with the OMA office in Rotterdam, which gave rise to a new generation of practitioners in Europe, so Hill's office has been a laboratory for working in the tropics, albeit with different outcomes and aims."[15]

Hill's work has not been limited to hotel commissions and other worldly escapes; the entrance plaza of Singapore's Zoo (2003) is an exemplary public project that rigorously orchestrates an arrival sequence that transcends the cliché. The Miesian asymmetrical plan pinwheels around a central courtyard (Figure 18.6) that boasts tropical shade trees and a reflecting pool; other structuring elements of the design are a portico that signals arrival, a plaza for festival activities and colonnades to direct pedestrian flows. The timber posts, translucent slatted screens, Balau-column cladding and Balau floor planks contrast with the long walls of warm-colored granite. The shifting horizontal and vertical planes of elemental repetition, cleverly exploit the Southeast Asian courtyard at a public scale and truly blur the inside/ outside threshold, creating a tempered city/ nature relationship before the zoo experience.

The Tropical Regionalism that arose in Southeast Asia in the 1950s was a counterpart to Modernist discourse, yet it continues to prevail in various forms until now as countries in the region seek alternative identities for their modern societies; in the background of the past decades which have witnessed an Asian economic boom. At the same time, a new environmental awareness has taken

18.6   Elegant
simplicity and
dignity of the
entry portico with
Balaucolumn
cladding. Kerry
Hill Architects,
Singapore
Zoo, 2003

hold and the atmosphere of tropical architecture has become synonymous with health and healing as part of its commodification process. The work of Asma Architects, a Cambodian-French office (led by Lisa and Cyril Ros with Ivan Tizianel) has developed a series of elegant projects in Siem Reap, the small city just outside the great Angkorean archaeological ruins, in addition to a series of resorts and restaurants. In 2001, they worked on the Kantha Bopha Conference Center, with their father Ros Borath. Borath left Cambodia during the country's brutal civil war and completed his architectural education in France. Returning temporarily to his native land in the 1990s, he served as Deputy Director General of the Authority for the Protection and Management of Angkor and the Region of Siem Reap, advising and supervising the restoration of the temples and complexes in the area. In their design for Kantha Bopha, a Swiss Foundation which provides free medical care to children, there is a clear influence of the architecture of Henri Ciriani, cross-hybridized with elements of Angkorean architecture and urbanism. The complex sits on a large corner site sandwiched between existing pediatric and maternity hospitals. Two large conference rooms which double as concert halls, theaters and cinemas are rendered in red brick and anchor the corner at the street; the other programs—four classrooms, a press room, library and cafeteria—are developed as an L-shape at the other corner of the site, creating both an interior open promenade and a courtyard (Figure 18.7). The exterior façade is enveloped by a frame of rough concrete with an infill of bamboo. Three large reflecting pools are used symbolically in the project and also serve as a natural barrier, eliminating the need for a fence, and demarcating the boundaries of public, semi-public and private spaces while also recycling graywater. All the materials are local and Asma Architects has successfully bought a sense of calm, modernity and muted restraint for an urgently needed program to a country in the midst of reconstruction and to a city that faces destruction by senseless over-development based on mass tourism.

18.7   Local material married with modern expression of the external courtyard. Asma
Architects, Kantha Bopha Conference Center, Siem Reap, Cambodia, 2001

NEW DIRECTIONS

Although Tropical Regionalism has been the most visibly identified movement in the region, it is clear that rapid urbanization is in the midst of shifting practices, prompting new directions in architecture. Three major directions have appeared in contemporary Southeast Asian Architecture: first, a predictable stance in relation to the region's aggressive global positioning which has resulted in an architecture of luxury high-rises (for living, work and as investment opportunities) and detached villas for the economically mobile and culturally independent wealthy middle class; second, a new experimentation with local building materials, particularly bamboo; and third, a small, but dedicated body of work that addresses the issues of social justice and the growing underclass.

A major market in Southeast Asia has also opened up for Western corporations, giving them the opportunity to produce architecture in abundance and it is doing so, to various degrees of quality. Well-established American and European firms have been working in the region already for decades and many countries still seek to have the "stamp" of Western stars in their cities in addition to a number of well-known Japanese firms including Nikken Sekki and Arata Isozaki. The goal is to join the club of "global cities"—generating a numbing sameness of the sanitized urban condition and a flattening of social and cultural spheres.[16] According to Richard Marshall, such global urban projects in Asia share a common characteristic—the conscious pursuit of "an 'absent urbanism' … the deliberate construction of city form through the articulation of buildings, roadways, streets, parks and sidewalks without any attempt to foster a social sphere. This avoidance guarantees that the global agenda will not be undermined."[17]

Perhaps the most emblematic example of the drive towards international high-rise stature is Kuala Lumpur's Petronas Towers, designed by César Pelli, with Deejay Cerico, in 1997. The 88-floor, 452 meter super-high-strength reinforced concrete with a steel and glass façade of geometric designs mildly invoking Islamic motifs, remains the world's largest twin towers and tallest building (until that title was taken by Taipei 101 in 2004) (Figure 18.8). Meanwhile, younger Western firms are discovering the region as a new market, open to new ways and modes of working—while, at the same time, inexperienced firms, without local partners often have troubles managing the bureaucratic difficulties that still arise through the various processes of the construction industry.

In Singapore, the high-rise condominium type has led a number of relatively young firms towards experimentation and the development of new apartment and high-rise typologies. WOHA Architects (established in 1994), led by Wong Mun Summ, and Richard Hassell, has developed a practice with elegant detailing that moves beyond tropical regionalism yet does not forget its lessons. Their 28-story Moulmein Rise Apartments (2001–3), which received an Aga Khan award in 2007, addresses the climate via its southern façade's "monsoon windows" which flank the living and dining areas. The windows conceal horizontal ventilation grilles, which intelligently trap and distribute convection currents without exposing the interior spaces of the apartment to monsoonal rains. The compositionally coherent urban

18.8   Skyscraper with international-style and Islamic motifs. Pelli, Clarke, Pelli
Architects, with Deejay Cerico, Petronas Tower, Kuala Lumpur, Malaysia, 1997

object is of finished exposed concrete, aluminum and wood window and abstractly perforated aluminum screens of the north façade. The slender tower with its crown of a cantilevering pergola and penthouse apartments meets the ground plane with a swimming pool on three tiers and a lobby as an open-air veranda with bamboo grove (Figure 18.9). Lincoln Modern, a 30-storey condominium by SCDA, a firm established in Singapore by Chan Soo Khian, shares affinities with the distinguished soaring WOHA modern tower. Chan portrays his work as "Neo-Tropical" and the Corbusier-inspired housing has 6-meter high split-level interlocking units, yet without apartments crossing over the full-dimension of the tower width. The curtain wall louvers and aluminum cladding is visually accentuated by two bright orange fins which anchor the service core to the ground and emphasize the vertical slenderness of the tower. Resort-style landscaping, replete with palms, a swimming and reflecting pool reveal a surface richness that denotes both luxury and poetry (Figure 18.10).

The second trend that is evident in the region is that of experimenting with materials. Representative of such a direction is a young Japanese-trained Vietnamese architect based in Ho Chi Minh City, Vo Trong Nghia, who has been creating elaborate structures of bamboo for cafes and bars in Hanoi and in the Mekong Delta. Among his works is also the transformation of a warehouse into the Vietnamese pavilion for the Shanghai Expo 2010, built out of bamboo. His Water and Wind Cafe in Binh Duong province has a graceful dome shape, created by 48 frames, 10 meters high, with a 15-meter span and a 1.5-meter diameter oculus. The mud-soaked and smoked bamboo was woven together using traditional Vietnamese techniques and covered with high fire-resistant water-coconut material; without using any nails in the construction (Figure 18.11). In 2011, Vo Trong Nghia also completed, in the same province, an 800-student, 5,300-square meter school building. The sinuous plan wraps onto itself to create two courtyards, one which collects the teachers' rooms, gym, laboratories and library and the second the classrooms. The continuous volume is constructed of pre-cast concrete and louvers and sun-shading devices create natural ventilation and playful light patterns (Figure 18.12).

This second trend ties into the third—architects who are explicitly seeking to implement social justice though their work. This approach is explored by practitioners in a number of countries, and in Indonesia specifically, two architects stand out for their social work, in parallel with their mainstream client-base of wealthy patrons. Eko Prawoto, based in Yogyakarta in central Java has been reinterpreting the region's traditions and crafts for houses for artists, museums and churches with unassuming monumentality and modernity. In 2005, he had the opportunity to volunteer his skills to rebuild a village that was wiped out in a devastating earthquake. Prawoto's skill as an educator and organizer came through as he was able to mobilize the villagers of 120 households and work with them to design a standard house with an earthquake-resistant structure, using local skills and a rotating system of collective labor so that all dwellings could be constructed simultaneously. The Ngibikan village, which had all but one house destroyed by the earthquake, was reconstructed in three months, while other villages in the Yogyakarta region struggled merely to have temporary shelters delivered (Figure 18.13).[18]

18.9   Distinctive façades mark a new type of residential development in
Singapore. WOHA Architects, Moulmein Rise, Singapore, 2003

18.10   Interlocking units are visible in the façade. SCDA, Lincoln Modern Tower, Singapore, 2003

18.11   Open-air café with raised water planes and curving bamboo screens. Vo
Trong Nghia Architects, Water and Wind Café, Binh Duong, Vietnam, 2007

18.12   Sinuous open air-like plan with generous "in-between" spaces.
         Vo Trong Nghia Architects, Binh Duong School, 2011

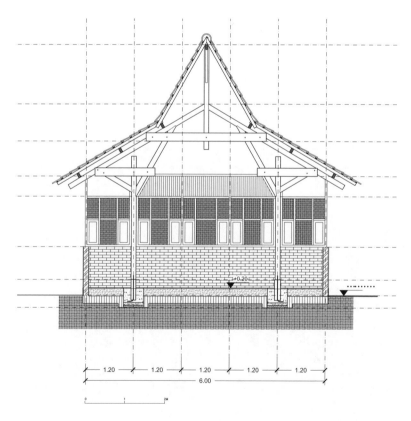

18.13   Learning from tradition in the framing for earthquake-resistant
         house. Eko Prawoto Architecture Workshop, 2005

Andra Matin Architect (AMA) perhaps best represents the new breed of Southeast Asian architects. Born in Bandung and educated locally, he moved to Jakarta to gain experience in one of the city's most established firms, Pt. Grahacipta Hadiprana, eventually setting up his own firm with Avianti Armand in 1998. AMA straddles the fast-moving world of the upper class of the region's arts and humanities professionals who are eager to create a new niche in Jakarta's city core. AMA was commissioned to design a museum and library for East Indonesian artifacts and culture, Gedung Dua 8 (1999), commissioned by the ethnologist and documentary filmmaker Dea Sundaram. The circulation system draws on the local *kampung* structure and bold geometry offsets to create more subtle local responses to climate through plays of texture and light. At the other spectrum of the economic gamut, AMA also works with the less fortunate; for example their temporary rental houses for low-income workers in Bintaro (2002–3) on the outskirts of Jakarta is a project where formal architecture has been reduced to its most essential. The four simple box units with shared kitchen, laundry and bathrooms sit on a platforms modestly covered by a frame structure that embraces existing trees and supports a sloping metal roof and roll-down bamboo blinds that modulate a semi-private threshold (Figure 18.14). From the upper class to commuters and even migrant workers, AMA is concerned about the architecture of the city, the architecture in the Southeast Asian metropolis that is in a state of rapid transformation.

CONCLUSION

As Southeast Asia continues its forceful play on the world stage, the urban and architectural challenges only promise to increase. Cities are metamorphosing at a rapid pace, where references to an idealized vernacular have been deliberately abandoned; the kampong is gradually disappearing, leaving only the Chinese shop-house as a surviving vernacular urban form. At the same time, densities

18.14 Modest yet intelligent "existence minimum" housing on the periphery of Jakarta. Andra Matin Architect, Rental Housing, Bintaro, 2002–03

are increasing far beyond carrying capacities and cities are once again becoming differentiated by race, class and gender; migrant workers commute from distant but affordable satellite centers, creating potentially volatile social and political conditions. With every natural disaster that strikes the region, the fragility of mankind's relationship with nature becomes ever more clear, reminding us of the predictions of climate change and the delicate interplay between human interventions and natural cycles. A recent report by the World Bank[19] predicted that the region will suffer immensely from the climate change's impact on population, GDP, urban extent and wetland areas. The once "hydraulic civilization"[20] of the region is mutating rapidly since economic liberalization. Yet the architecture of the city in Southeast Asia is known for its resilience to its hybrid history, for its ability to absorb and maintain contradictory versions of itself—and without a doubt this is what its architects will continue to do in the face of the challenges of the future: create a regional architecture of resilience.

NOTES

1   In October 1943, Winston Churchill appointed Lord Louis Mountbatten as the Supreme Allied Commander of the South East Asian Commend (SEAC); he held the post until it was disbanded in 1946. The contemporary political imagining of the unity of region has been bolstered ASEAN, the Association of Southeast Asian Nations, which was established by the Bangkok Declaration on August 8, 1967 as a loosely organized pact providing collective regional security against communist subversion. The founding members were Indonesia, Malaysia, the Philippines, Singapore and Thailand. Brunei joined on January 8, 1984, shortly after its long-standing protectorate agreement with the British ended. On July 28, 1995 it embraced still-communist Vietnam, the perceived danger which triggered its initial founding; communist Laos and defiantly undemocratic Myanmar were admitted on July 23, 1997 and finally Cambodia joined the group on Cambodia on April 30, 1999. The ASEAN Declaration states that the aims and purposes of the Association are: (i) to accelerate the economic growth, social progress and cultural development in the region through joint endeavors in the spirit of equality and partnership in order to strengthen the foundation for a prosperous and peaceful community of Southeast Asian nations; and (ii) to promote regional peace and stability through abiding respect for justice and the rule of law in the relationship among countries in the region and adherence to the principles of the United Nations Charter.

2   See Thongchai Winichakul, *Siam Mapped: A History of the Geo-body of a Nation* (Honolulu: University of Hawaii Press, 1994).

3   Stephen Cairns, "Troubling Real-Estate: Reflecting on Urban Form in Southeast Asia," in Tim Bunnell, Lisa B.W. Drummond and K.C. Ho (eds), *Critical Reflections on Cities in Southeast Asia* (Singapore: Brill and Times Academic Press, 2002), 114–15.

4   Anthony Reid is a renowned historian of Southeast Asia and his most well read books are *Southeast Asia in the Age of Commerce, 1450–1680. Vol. 1: The Lands below the Winds*, New Haven: Yale University Press, 1988 and *Southeast Asia in the Age of Commerce, 1450–1680. Vol. 2: Expansion and Crisis* (New Haven: Yale University Press, 1993). The first one includes an entire chapter on "material culture" where he explains in quite some depth the indigenous architecture of the region.

5   See Roxanna Waterson, *The Living House: An Anthropology of Architecture in South-East Asia* (Oxford: Oxford University Press, 1990).

6   See, for example, A. Patricia Morton, *Hybrid Modernities: Architecture and Representation at the 1931 Colonial Exposition, Paris* (Cambridge: MIT Press, 2000); Anne Maxwell, *Colonial Photography and Exhibitions: Representations of the "Native" and the Making of European Identities* (London and New York: Leicester University Press, 1999); Tim Barringer and Tom Flynn (eds), *Coloinalism and the Object: Empire, Material Culture and the Museum* (London and New York: Routledge, 1998); Panivong Noridr, *Phantasmatic Indochine: French Colonial Ideology in Architecture Film and Literature* (Durham: Duke University Press, 1996); Marieke Bloembergen, Beverly Jackson (trans.), *Colonial Spectacles: The Netherlands and the Dutch East Indies at the World Exhibitions 1880–1931* (Singapore: Singapore University Press, 2006); Joost Cote, "Staging Modernity: The Semarang International Colonial Exhibition, 1914," in *RIMA: Review of Indonesian and Malaysian Affairs*, vol. 40, no. 1, 2006: 1–44.

7   Philip Goad, "New Directions in Tropical Asian Architecture," in P. Goad, A. Pieris and P. Bingham-Hall (eds), *New Directions in Tropical Asian Architecture* (Singapore: Periplus Editions, 2005), 17,12.

8   Anoma Pieris, "The Search for Critical Identities: A Critical History," in Architecture' in Goad, Pieris and Bingham-Hall, *New Directions in Tropical Asian Architecture*, 26.

9   See Alexander Tzonis, Liane Lefaivre and Bruno Stago, *Tropical Architecture: Critical Regionalism in the Age of Globalism* (Chichester: Wiley-Academy, 2001).

10   Kenneth Frampton, "Towards a Critical Regionalism," in H. Foster (ed.), *The Anti-Aesthetic: Essays on Postmodern Culture* (Seattle: Bay Press, 1983), 16–30.

11   Homi Bhabha, *The Location of Culture* (London: Routledge, 1994); Abidin Kusno, *Behind the Postcolonial: Architecture, Urban Space and Political Cultures in Indonesia* (London: Routledge, 2000).

12   Kheng Soon Tay, *Megacities in the Tropics: Towards an Architectural Agenda for the Future* (Singapore: Institute of Southeast Asian Studies, 1989), 8–11.

13   Kusno, *Behind the Postcolonial*, 201.

14   Pieris, "The Search for Critical Identities," 31.

15   Goad, "New Directions in Tropical Asian Architecture," 19.

16   Rem Koolhaas, "Singapore Songlines," in Rem Koolhaas and Bruce Mau (eds), *S,M,L,XL* (Rotterdam: 010 Publishers, 1995), 1008–87.

17   Richard Marshall, *Emerging Urbanity: Global Urban Projects in the Asia Pacific Rim* (London: Spon Press, 2003), 192.

18   Graeme MacRae, "Globalisation and Indonesian Architecture: A Critical Regionalist Approach to National Identity," in unpublished manuscript, 2010.

19   N. Prasad, F. Ranghieri, F. Shah Zoe Trohanis, E. Kessler and R. Sinha, *Climate Resilient Cities: A Primer on Reducing Vulnerabilities to Disasters* (Washington DC: World Bank, 2009).

20   In coining the term "hydraulic civilizations," Karl Wittfogel (1896–1988), the renowned Frankfurt School historian and sinologist, recognized that the urban and rural conditions of the higher agrarian civilizations of the East followed a pattern of development decidedly unlike that of the West. For him, China's centralized state authority emerged from the needs for water engineering and control; good water management and despotism were interdependent. See Karl Wittfogel, "The Hydraulic Civilizations," in W.L. Thomas (ed.), *Man's Role in Changing the Face of the Earth* (Chicago: University of Chicago Press, 1956); Karl Wittfogel, *Oriental Depotism: A Comparative Study of Total Power* (New Haven: Yale University Press, 1957).

19

Internationalism and Architecture in India after Nehru

Amit Srivastava and Peter Scriver

India was one of many new 'developing' nations emerging from colonial pasts in the second half of the twentieth century in which the ideals and forms of an ostensibly universally applicable modern architecture were initially embraced with conviction and relative success. But the direct and particularly fertile engagement of several celebrated masters of modern architecture in new India was to secure, for this most populous of the post-colonial world's fledgling democracies, a conspicuously significant role in the canonical narrative of the internationalisation of architectural modernism. Regionalist and neo-traditional digressions in the works of some of India's own most-esteemed modernist architects were to be accorded comparably exemplary status in the critical estimation of late twentieth century commentators, who recognised these as architectural expressions of a putatively authentic resistance, from a position of geographical and cultural autonomy, to the received norms and forms of what had come to be regarded as the Eurocentric hegemony of modernism. Somewhat ironically, it was this same renewed sense of cultural pride and potency that was to underpin the aggressive opening-up of India's previously insular developing economy, beginning in the late 1980s. But globalisation would also serve, paradoxically, to compound and confuse the once confident and distinctive architectural signature of modern India through possibilities for international *bricolage* in the contemporary global culture of consumption, for which India's IT industry – among its most influential architectural patrons in the early twenty-first century – had become a prime-mover.

INTERNATIONAL EXCHANGE AND MENTORSHIP IN THE 1950S AND 60S

In the Spring of 1965 a rather extraordinary exhibition was mounted at the Union Carbide Building in New York City. Comprised of hundreds of artefacts and over 1200 photographs in which architecture featured prominently, the exhibit explored the emerging story of nation-building and modernisation in India through the life of the new country's first prime-minister, the late Jawaharlal Nehru. Fittingly, perhaps, it was a simple, even humble installation composed of free-standing panels and pavilions constructed out of plain poles and Indian printed cotton. Reviewers nevertheless praised the creative pragmatism and sophisticated layout of the exhibition panels in particular, which had been designed by a team of architecture graduates at India's newly established National Institute of Design (NID) under the guidance of the American architect/designer couple, Charles and Ray Eames.[1]

Due in part to the impact of such deft and evocative representations, the discourse on India's post-colonial architectural history has been dominated by the techno-scientific paradigm of development associated with Nehru and his era (1947–64) in which state-sponsored modernisation programmes pursued industrialisation and urbanisation on a large scale. But the broader framework of international engagement and outlook within which such collaborations between leading international designers and budding Indian architects was made possible is an integral but much less well-known part of India's architectural history in the second half of the twentieth century.

Among the many large-scale building and infrastructure projects undertaken in the first two decades after India gained her independence in 1947, the building of Chandigarh, the new capital for the Indian state of Punjab, was widely watched and recognised internationally as a project of outstanding architectural significance. For post-war champions of modern architecture as an antidote to cultural and political chauvinism, Nehru and the new Indian State would be regarded collectively as a visionary patron that had finally given a master modernist an opportunity to demonstrate the ideals of the movement in a work of unprecedented scale and symbolic importance. But whilst the authorship of this seminal project is generally ascribed to Le Corbusier and his team of European and Indian collaborators, it was also a palimpsest of an initial scheme that had been developed between 1949 and 1950 by the American planner/architect team of Albert Mayer and Matthew Nowicki.[2] The original commission had reflected Nehru's strategic focus on building post-colonial India's relationship with America, whose technological achievements and still relatively unsullied status as a non-imperial power he valued as India's preferred ally in the push to modernise.[3] India's direct engagement with the architectural culture and principles of mid twentieth-century high modernism must also be interpreted, therefore, in the context of the US-dominated international exchange that marked India's development during the Nehru era.

With the concurrent Cold War policy to persuade the world's largest democracy to align with the free-world, US Aid was already crucial to many of the large-scale infrastructure projects developed in India during this period.[4] But it was the cultural agenda of the Ford Foundation, an ostensibly independent American NGO, that had particularly significant implications for later developments in the fields of architecture and design.[5]

Among a series of Ford Foundation supported studies that profoundly influenced India's strategic development policy and investment in various technical and cultural disciplines was a seminal 1958 report by Charles and Ray Eames on the state of 'design' in India. In their recommendations the Eames strategically positioned architecture as the key profession in the integrated field of design disciplines that would be instrumental in bridging between India's crafts based past and industrialised future.

With the subsequent establishment of the National Institute of Design (NID) – another of the Eames's key recommendations – at Ahmedabad in 1961, architecture graduates were recruited as the core of the teaching staff and the development of their design knowledge was entrusted to their engagement with collaborative design commissions where they would be mentored by international architecture and design gurus.[6] These were to include a range of both established and emerging architects from both sides of the Atlantic, but ultimately the most influential of these collaborations was to be with another American.

Louis Kahn came to India in 1962 to consult for the NID on its commission to design the new Indian Institute of Management (IIM) – a prestigious sister institution that was also to be built in Ahmedabad with Ford Foundation backing. With Kahn playing this mentor/designer role and the Harvard School of Business advising on curriculum, the IIM project was an exemplar of the open and multifaceted exchange of culture and technical expertise that modernising India was keen to cultivate with the international community.[7] Kahn's mentorship at IIM resulted in extended working sojourns in his Philadelphia office for some of his closest Indian associates. There, among others, Anant Raje and Chandrasen Kapadia, two of the most influential designers and teachers of the next generation, collaborated in framing the ideals and formal language that defined the mastery of Kahn's mature work and from which they would later distil their own. The IIM project further enabled another local associate, Balkrishna V. Doshi, to establish a worldly new School of Architecture at Ahmedabad (Figure 19.1) that would rapidly become one of India's most influential forums for architectural education and debate. Doshi was no stranger to international collaboration having previously worked directly with Le Corbusier both in Paris and India, and his new school took full advantage of access to Kahn, during his periodic visits to Ahmedabad, as well as his professional and collegial networks.

Between the NID and its new architecture school, Ahmedabad had become the focus of a bourgeoning international architectural scene by the mid-1960s, and through further working collaborations on design commissions and curriculum development succeeded in attracting a host of other notable architectural, engineering and design mentors from the US and Europe over the next decade.[8]

In a developing economic environment where foreign currency was scarce, this local-global mode of exchange brought the ideas of an international discipline to a broader set of Indian architecture students who could not afford to go abroad. This pattern of exchange remained, for the most part in the 1960s, the basis for the education of a new breed of Indian architects who regarded themselves as direct participants in the development of this international discipline from the self-conscious but confident point of view of an emerging modern nation that was regarded as a leader of the 'Third World'. This, then, was an exchange in which foreign expertise was not received unquestioningly, but engaged in a form of dialogue (Figure 19.2).

However, this rich and equitable pattern of exchange could not be sustained indefinitely with subsequent changes in political and diplomatic climates, and associated national sentiment.

19.1 The School of Architecture at Ahmedabad was a direct outcome of the conjunction of entrepreneurial institution-builders and foreign technical and cultural aid that made Ahmedabad a nexus of international exchange in the 1960s. Built incrementally beginning in 1966 to designs by founding director, B.V. Doshi, the campus and its buildings embodied a dialogue between Doshi, Le Corbusier, and Kahn, with both of whom the architect had enjoyed a close working relationship

19.2 The interior of architect Hasmukhbhai Patel's own residence (1969) in Ahmedabad is a typical modernist living space from the period, with traditional Indian textiles and craft objects juxtaposed with iconic Modern furniture including chairs by Eames and Mies

INTROVERSION: LOCAL VS SOCIAL FOCI IN THE LATE 1960S AND 70S

Behind the Nehruvian ideal of Modern India was a complex political and cultural coalition that had been brought together in resistance to foreign imperialism. After Independence, however, the solidarity of this tenuous union had immediately begun to wane as regional loyalties predating colonial rule came back into play. Regional resistance to the centre had been kept in check by Nehru's government, but soon began to re-define the pattern of development after his death. Consequently, while technical exchange with the West continued to open-up new design desires and possibilities for Indian architects, these were increasingly to serve regional aspirations for political and cultural autonomy rather than a common national ideal – as Nehru had envisioned, for example, in the case of Chandigarh. Architects who enjoyed the patronage of worldly and independently wealthy regional elites were encouraged to reflect a more direct dialogue between local and universal criteria for a modern architecture, bypassing national concerns.[9] Even some who had already established themselves as leaders among the first generation of foreign-trained modernist architects had begun to experiment early on with regionally associated forms and allusions. A conspicuous example, designed as it was by a former student of Walter Gropius, was Achyut Kanvinde's stylised reference to a vernacular thatched-hut roof form in the Azad Bhawan (1958–61) for the Indian Council for Cultural Relations in New Delhi (Figure 19.3).[10] Charles Correa's ascetic memorial museum for Mahatma Gandhi, the Gandhi Samarak Sanghralaya, built in Ahmedabad between 1958 and 1963, and the exposed concrete reference to a wooden *haveli* (traditional Gujarati townhouse) in Doshi's Institute of Indology (1957–62), also in Ahmedabad, are other early examples that signalled this regionalist propensity.

19.3   The curved bangle roof form of the Azad Bhawan building, designed for the Indian Council for Cultural Relations by Achyut Kanvinde (1958–61), is an early example of experimentation with regionally associated forms by an established modernist architect

An emergent regionalism was also becoming apparent by the later 1960s in India's evolving and diversifying construction culture. In the Northern region centred around Delhi, skilful Corbusian acolytes such as Shivnath Prasad in his designs for the Shriram Centre (1966–69) and Akbar Hotel (1965–69), and J.K. Choudhary at IIT Delhi (1961–84), continued to explore the expressive sculptural potential and texture of exposed in-situ concrete in the tradition of nearby Chandigarh. On the other hand, the emerging school of Ahmedabad-centred practitioners in the Western-central state of Gujarat used their direct experience with Kahn and Le Corbusier's other more atavistic tradition, exemplified in his Sarabhai villa in Ahmedabad (1956), to develop a contemporary regional architectural identity that privileged exposed brick – of which Doshi's buildings for the School of Architecture in Ahmedabad (1966–68) (Figure 19.1) were prime exemplars. This bid for regional distinction was also apparent, albeit in a more oppositional manner, in the work of leading south Indian architects, Bennet Pithavadian and S.L Chitale, based in Chennai (formerly Madras), whose steadfast commitment to a more generic international style functionalism expressly resisted the more idiosyncratic tendencies that were distinguishing the work of their north Indian colleagues, specifically those working along the dominant axis connecting Mumbai, via Ahmedabad, to Delhi and Chandigarh. Thus a culture of international exchange was sustained well into the 1970s, but this served to access and diffuse modernist ideas in distinctively selective and discerning ways, simultaneously enabling the development of new regionalist identities which continue to define the way some professionals of one region relate to those of another, even today.

However, the India of the 1970s, under the prime ministership of Nehru's daughter Indira Gandhi, was a very different political context from the immediate post-independence era, with significant implications for the nature and scope of architectural work. With her landslide electoral victory in 1971, buoyed equally by a promise of radical policy changes to tackle poverty, and India's decisive victory in its latest war with Pakistan, Indira Gandhi had firmly established the basis for a new political epoch distinct from the officially 'non-aligned' but nevertheless internationally oriented and westward leaning development strategies of her father's era. Indeed a series of military and diplomatic developments over the preceding decade had resulted in a progressive distancing from the West, counterbalanced by a much closer new relationship of technical and cultural exchange with the USSR. Internally this was reflected in a clear shift towards radical socialist policies characterised by Soviet-style, strongly centralised technocratic action on a national basis.[11] Partially contributing to this rise of the political left, the birth centenary of Mohandas K. Gandhi in 1969 had also renewed critical reflection among socially committed professionals, including many architects, concerning the wisdom of Gandhi's thwarted alternative approach to development through self-reliance and traditional technologies. Seminal propositions of a low-cost, passively acclimatised approach to contemporary architectural design, drawing pragmatically from regional building traditions, that were built by the expatriate British-Indian architect and Gandhian follower Laurie Baker in southern India in the early 1970s, were later to have significant wider recognition and influence

(Figure 19.4). For the time being, however, the centre's renewed commitment to modernisation as a tool for universal social reform was to keep closely in check any notions of transcendent traditional values and regional differentiation that had been developing in the immediate post-Nehruvian period.

In this introverted context of nation-centric self-reliance, government programmes targeting the housing crisis of India's rapidly growing urban poor were quick to embrace the more technocratic strategy of so-called 'sites and services' projects, widely promoted by agencies such as the United Nations and the World Bank, in which the individual occupants were responsible for building the actual fabric of their dwellings upon standardised plans and infrastructure provided by the authorities. The early 1970s also saw the completion of a number of innovative architect-designed public housing projects as well as autonomous 'townships' designed for various government-controlled industrial and institutional clients. These were to have nationwide impact on the housing typology and norms that would be propagated over the next couple of decades by public works departments and other public sector agencies concerned with housing and urban development.

Among these seminal prototypes was a pair of townships designed concurrently by B.V. Doshi's Ahmedabad practice, Vastu Shilpa, for the Gujarat State Fertiliser Company (GSFC) (1964–69) in nearby Baroda, and the Electronics Corporation of India Ltd (ECIL) (1968–71) (Figure 19.5) in the historic south Indian city of Hyderabad, a future hub of India's global IT industry. These schemes made some of the boldest moves yet in post-colonial Indian architecture towards a contemporary architectural morphology responsive to the distinctive materiality and tectonics of their immediate regions, but experimenting at the same time with typological analogies and permutations of deeper and more universal notions of community form and structure – an investigation that reflected an active dialogue with the

19.4   View of water court with brick jali work in the Centre for Development Studies, Trivandrum (1972–75), designed and built by Laurie Baker. Baker's inventive path-breaking work with low-cost building materials in the south Indian state of Kerala marked a return to Gandhian ideals in the 1970s, and concurrent engagement internationally with the Appropriate Technology movement

parallel work of European colleagues of the Team 10 generation, such as Giancarlo de Carlo, with whom Doshi had maintained close contact since representing India in some of the seminal final congresses of CIAM in the 1950s. Prompted by such commissions at the scale of entire settlements, Doshi's growing practice among others was encouraged to commit significant portions of their professional time and resources to further not-for-profit research and implementation of innovative housing strategies suited to the socioeconomic realities of developing India, in collaboration with government agencies, academic partners and other NGOs.

Returning to India in the early 1970s from post-graduate architectural studies and work experience overseas, a new generation of prospective professional leaders who had experienced the revolutionary student activism in the West in the late 1960s found themselves in a timely position to drive potential change at home. By 1974 a group of these younger architect-activists who had come together under the name of *Greha* (Sanskrit for 'house') had already begun debating the state of the profession in the nation and were rethinking its engagement in the growing crises of equitable access to low-cost housing and basic amenities and infrastructure in India's rapidly growing cities.[12] Under the renewed socialist ethos of the 1970s modern professionals felt a prerogative to address their knowledge and skills to the needs of the greater underprivileged section of the population. Such a change was also enabled in part by parliamentary legislation of the Architect's Act of 1972, which legally established the professional status and authority of the Indian architectural profession at a national level for the first time, and this had further impact in the next few years with the rise of architect-dominated urban design commissions in various major cities.

One of the most significant outcomes of this engagement of avant-garde professionals in public projects through public–private collaborations was the proposal for a 'New Bombay'. First projected by Charles Correa, with colleagues

19.5   The housing for the Electronics Corporation of India Ltd. (ECIL) in Hyderabad designed by architect B.V. Doshi (1971) was an influential prototype on which many later company 'townships' and public housing projects were based

Pravina Mehta and Shirish Patel, as early as 1964, the plan was finally put into action beginning in 1971 in the context of the new Left-leaning central government's technocratic assault on poverty, through the establishment of the City and Industrial Development Corporation (CIDCO) with Correa undertaking an initial three-year term as the official Chief Architect for New Bombay. The innovative scheme, which proposed a multi-nodal strategy for future development that would relieve the acute pressures on the overcrowded city centre, was subsequently emulated in new plans for greater Madras and Calcutta as well.

On the other hand, the growth of government and the public sector in the 1970s also encouraged the emergence of a bold and structurally precocious new public architecture expressing the technological advancement of the urbanising nation. One of the most iconic but unintentionally ironic examples of this structural expressionism was the group of permanent exhibition halls designed by Raj Rewal for Pragati Maidan, the national fair grounds in New Delhi (Figure 19.6). Completed in 1972, the bold structural design of the octahedral lattice space frame system clearly emulated precedents from the recent World Fairs at Osaka and Montreal. The structures were intended for both local and international audiences and aimed to represent modernisation and productivity in the key national industries exhibited within in the most progressive light. Yet necessarily constructed for reasons of cost, not of the prefabricated hi-tech components implied, but by the locally cheaper labour-intensive technique of cast in-situ concrete, the somewhat tired style and predictable symbolism were inadvertently given a visceral new vitality by the sheer monumentality of the construction feat. Successfully accomplished on-time and within budget through such proto-industrial methods, the project emphasised the prevailing drive for technological development and self-reliance that would underpin India's economic power in the globalised future, countering the sagging morale of the early 1970s in which the nation was still struggling with the social realities and increasingly critical environmental challenges of underdevelopment in an ex-colonial economy.

19.6 The Permanent Exhibition Structures designed by architect Raj Rewal for the 1972 International Trade Fair in New Delhi embodied a tenuous marriage between hi-tech aspirations and humble means

THE CULTURAL TURN: COMMODIFICATION AND EXCHANGE IN THE 1980S

By the 1980s distinctive regionalist references and ideas were once again shaping new architectural work, but this time the primary focus on cultural forms and practices also reflected significant social and economic developments in the greater Middle Eastern and South Asian regions. Most directly influential within the discipline itself was the advent of the Aga Khan Award for Architecture (AKAA). Launched in 1977 with the first round of triennial awards announced in 1980, this prestigious and unprecedented international awards programme was ostensibly dedicated to contemporary Islamic architecture. Significantly, however, it also sought to recognise the central role of architecture in building and shaping community and cultural life. Together with its associated journal, *Mimar: Architecture in Development*, launched in 1981, the AKAA effectively aspired to represent a far broader discourse among architects and their patrons across the 'non-Western world' concerning questions of national and regional identity and the need to redress the balance between modernity and tradition in the context of economic and cultural globalisation.[13] The impact of the AKAA in India as well as neighbouring Islamic countries was therefore significant, not least because influential South Asian architects including Charles Correa and Muzharul Islam of Bangladesh had been involved in setting-up the AKAA programme as members of the Award's Steering Committee.[14]

The selection of the Mughal Sheraton Hotel in Agra, home of the Taj Mahal, as one of the recipients of the AKAA in its first cycle, identified a seminal Indian precedent for new work in this vein that was to prove particularly influential. The award in the category 'continuation with history' lauded the deft reinterpretation of the functional planning and contemporary formal vocabulary of an international hotel using 'available regional materials and technology, the abundant labour force and traditional crafts'.[15] Soon the basic strategy of re-interpreting contemporary building forms and programmes in traditional material – especially red sandstone – had become a formula of choice. An important example of this shift is Raj Rewal's landmark State Trading Corporation (STC) building, completed in Delhi in 1989. Rewal had won the commission well over a decade earlier through a competition in 1976 and the structurally expressive design with massive Vierendeel trusses was originally intended to have an unadorned finish of raw striated concrete, indicative of his work from the period. However, by the time the building was finally constructed in 1989 it had acquired a sandstone veneer.[16] Rewal subsequently developed this vocabulary of polychromatic sandstone into an extended and unabashed rhapsody on the theme of traditional Mughal and Rajput architectural and urban patterns over a series of major institutional buildings and campuses designed and built in Delhi in the 1980s. These included, most notably, the campus of the National Institute of Immunology (1983–90), and the massive SCOPE office complex (1980–89) (Figure 19.7).[17]

The eagerness with which the AKAA's mandate to renew continuity with historical and regional context was adopted by Indian and other South Asian architects reflected passionate home-grown arguments for sustaining regional craft

19.7   The SCOPE government office complex, New Delhi (1980–89) by architect Raj Rewal employed sandstone polychromy and undisguised references to the *chatris* and ramparts of historic Rajput fortresses to ennoble the labour of the army of humble civil servants employed within

traditions and resisting the hegemony of a modernity unilaterally defined by the West. However, in the religiously resurgent postmodern ethos of South Asia and the Middle-East in the 1980s that had been catalysed by the 1979 Islamic Revolution in Iran, this retaliation to Westernisation based on religious identity had also found a parallel in contemporary Indian culture and politics with the rise of the Hindu right. Encouraged if not compelled by the ensuing culture-conscious climate of patronage in the 1980s, the notions of regional and religious identity were increasingly to be conflated in the works of Indian architects. While, on the one hand, this led to the rise of a new resistance to the avant-garde modernist professional in the form of *vastu* consultants, who revisited the Vedic Hindu traditions of *vastushastra* (dwelling treatise) to provide strategic spatial guidance in the design of new projects, on the other hand, this also saw established professionals introducing new formal and symbolic possibilities into the spatial and technical conventions of late modernism to align themselves with the new patronage.[18]

Again, the work of Charles Correa in this period was a particularly influential though controversial case in point. Correa's widely published design for the Jawahar Kala Kendra in Jaipur (1986) combined the ideal types of the *navgraha mandala* (nine-house cosmogram) and the *vastupurusha mandala* (cosmogram of the primeval man) with the poetically discontinuous grid of the actual mandala-based plan of Jaipur, a celebrated historic example of spatial planning according to Vedic principles (Figure 19.8).[19] Similarly, his British Council building in Delhi (1987–92), developed a layered ritualistic pathway of foreign encounters symbolised through the *shunyabindu* (mark of void or energy centre) and a huge *banyan* tree mural produced by the British artist, Howard Hodgkin. Correa wrote explicitly of his introduction to the mythic values of India's past, from the Vedic 'analogy of Cosmos' to the more recent 'myths of Rationality, Science, Progress', and claimed that 'these patterns have been generated by an age old deep structure of more explicit myths: the *yantra*, the *mandala*, the *charbagh*'.[20]

This cultural shift in the work of such leading modernists was to pave the way for a stronger focus on aesthetic concerns and symbolic criteria in contemporary design more generally, and the late 1980s offered numerous further examples of a distinctive new formalism in contemporary Indian architecture rationalised on the grounds of increasingly overt cultural and religious symbolism.

While this value shift within the discipline had some concordance with contemporary identity politics, it is also necessary to take into account the local

19.8   In his design for the Jawahar Kala Kendra (1986), a multifaceted centre for visual and performing arts in the historic Rajput city of Jaipur, architect Charles Correa employed ancient Hindu cosmological diagrams as planning grids and pattern-generators, enabling the superposition of traditional and modernist design reasoning to be felicitously exploited for both pragmatic and aesthetic purposes

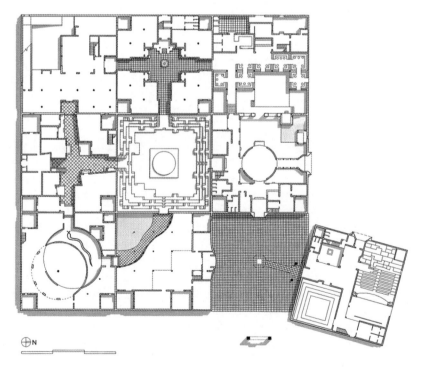

economic conditions that allowed this struggle for identity to manifest itself in peculiar ways. With the Western resolve to encourage private ownership as a Cold War response to the Communist world, the 1960s had already witnessed a rise in consumer culture in the West and by the 1970s this had led to a significant rise in international tourism. In a bid to attract the much needed foreign exchange, the Indian Government sought to develop tourism as a means to attract this international flow of capital and further encouraged private investment. Both regional identity and cultural heritage thus became valuable economic commodities which a plethora of new hotels among other commercial and cultural complexes designed during the early 1980s were to take full advantage of. Exemplary were Correa's Cidade de Goa (1982), Satish Grover's Oberoi Hotel in Bhubaneshwar, Orissa (1983), and the Oberoi Udaivilas Hotel in Udaipur (1985-) by Zhaveri and Patel (Figure 19.9) which made colourful and explicit references to local culture and architectural heritage. In Correa's case such references were even overtly theatrical, reminiscent of the propensity for witty pastiche characteristic of the contemporary work of American postmodernists such as Charles Moore and Michael Graves. But these projects nevertheless celebrated the belated economic benefit that tourism was now bringing to under-industrialised regions such as Orissa, Goa and Rajasthan.

While on the one hand the architectural commodification of culture allowed the tourism industry to enable these backward regions to gain a place in the national economy, on the other hand, it also helped attract further investment in the conservation of surviving architectural heritage. Not coincidentally, the cause of conserving India's monuments and sites of cultural significance was given new institutional authority with the establishment in 1984 of the Indian National Trust for Art and Cultural Heritage (INTACH). Departing from long standing conservation biases upheld since the colonial era by the Archaeological Survey of India, the growing appreciation of architectural heritage as an economic commodity was also beginning to allow for the surviving colonial edifices of the British Empire to be accorded new recognition and value as part of the diverse and rich cultural history of India.[21]

19.9   The Oberoi Udaivilas Hotel in Udaipur (started in 1985) was a result of the rise in international tourism and the corresponding commodification of heritage, allowing architects Nimish Patel and Parul Zhaveri to engage and explicitly reconstruct elements of Mewari architecture in a palatial modern luxury hotel

The potential to market India's distinctive architectural culture, both historic and contemporary, was further exploited in the Government of India's unique programme of international cultural diplomacy launched in the early 1980s through the so-called 'Festivals of India'. Politically, these festivals were conceived as a strategy to build national pride and counter dissenting factions within the nation, but their formulation as a celebration of a culturally heterogeneous notion of *Indianness* was equally beneficial in marketing the idea of this emerging new Asian economic powerhouse to a global audience of future trading partners and consumers. Architecturally, the most significant of these festivals were the 1985 Festival and *Mela* in France, with a special exhibition on architecture curated by architect Raj Rewal along with Ram Sharma and Malay Chatterjee, and the Festival of India in the Soviet Union, Sweden and Switzerland launched in 1987, featuring the architectural exhibition *Vistara*, curated by Charles Correa.[22] Whilst these exhibitions clearly reflected the cultural turn in the contemporary work of their curators, they were developed within the framework and ideology of the larger festivals programme and were therefore compelled to represent architecture as a part of a matrix of Indian crafts traditions, with the consequence that the rationalities unique to the discipline tended to be subsumed in an uncritical admixture of folklore and mythology that would persist in colouring the discourse through the later 1980s.

While these developments in the 1980s clearly aligned with the concurrent rise of interest in international discourse in the notion of a 'critical regionalism' within late-modern architectural production, discussion of regionalism within the Indian architectural discipline in this period remained anchored, as we have seen, in the regionalist politics and perspectives of the subcontinent, and still largely disconnected from wider debates. It was not until further fundamental changes in policy initiated by the government of Rajiv Gandhi following his mother's assassination in 1984, but not fully realised until the early 1990s, that this trend would change significantly and establish the framework which defines the developments of the current era.

GLOBALISATION AND INTERNATIONALISM SINCE THE 1990S

Arising in parallel with tourism in the 1980s was another private sector enterprise that had been overlooked in the grand designs of post-Independence economic planners for the growth of heavy industry but which was now poised to catapult India into the global economy of the late twentieth century.

The rise of computers in the 1970s had already sparked a few entrepreneurs to start exploring India's potential to develop and export competitive information technology (IT) services.[23] But with the dramatic new growth in the consumer culture of the West in the following decade, the need for affordable IT expertise and technical support had stimulated dramatic new development across India's IT sector.[24] By the end of the century, the leading Indian IT corporations were accessing exponentially expanding international markets for their services – including, importantly, not only software development but global call-centres and other modes of digitally enabled business process outsourcing – attracting unprecedented levels of foreign investment. This provided capital and incentive to commission a wave of trend-setting new architectural designs, from both local and international architectural firms, to house and brand the expansive new facilities required. Typically concentrated in extensive but exclusive campuses on the outskirts of major IT hub-cities, the architecture of these IT parks and related developments including new airports, hotels and luxury housing, was among the most conspicuous indices of the rise of global India as an economic powerhouse of the twenty-first century.

In various flagship projects commissioned since the late 1990s, Tata Consultancy Services (TCS) sought to represent its outward looking yet firmly grounded stance as the IT arm of one of India's longest established and most powerful global brands by commissioning internationally renowned designers, including Swiss architect Mario Botta and New Yorkers Tod Williams and Billie Tsien, noted for their particular sensibilities for building craft and tectonics. Botta's design for TCS in Hyderabad, completed in 2003, for instance, featured characteristically bold Platonic geometry clad in pristine sandstone that simultaneously provided the client with an iconic building of international stature and also resonated with India's multiple traditions, historic and modern, of monumental masonry construction (Figure 19.10).

On the other hand, maverick competitor, Infosys, fostered a close relationship with the local but comparably entrepreneurial Mumbai-based architectural firm of Hafeez Contractor. In a series of large-scale commissions for software development and training facilities, Contractor experimented with a diverse array of forms, styles and newly available building materials. Whilst the generic corporate globalism of California's Silicon Valley was the benchmark, these designs ranged dramatically from the wilder hi-tech exhibitionism of the Infosys Software Development Block 4 in Mysore to the ersatz neo-colonial classicism of the Infosys Global Education Center, also in Mysore – which, with its $65.4 million price-tag, was the largest IT training facility in the world at the time of its completion in 2005 (Figure 19.11).

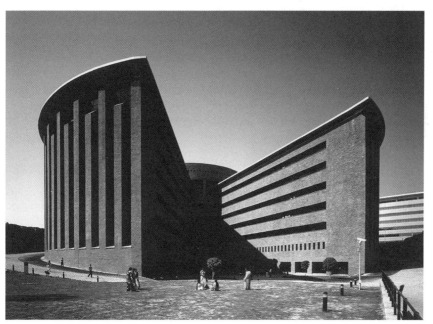

19.10 Mario Botta's flagship office block for Tata Consultancy Services (TCS) in Hyderabad (2003) celebrates the Swiss starchitect's stereotomic sensibility for solid geometric sculpture and masonry construction, acknowledging India's monumental masonry traditions in the same gesture

19.11   The (upper) hi-tech style Infosys Software Development Block 4, Mysore (2005–2006), and the (lower) contrasting neoclassical style Infosys Global Education Center, Mysore (2005), were both designed by the Mumbai-based architectural firm of Hafeez Contractor for the same corporation within the same two-year period

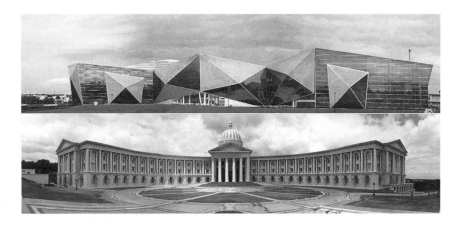

Through the global ambition of this entrepreneurial new clientele, the Indian architectural profession has thereby been finding new possibilities, since the 1990s, to reverse the introversion of the preceding generation and engage again with international practice, albeit in the often strange new clothes of current global fashion. But to a significant degree such external engagement has also been imperative. With the sheer scale and intensity of development, the norms and models of global practice have enabled the procurement of quick and reliable architectural responses to the demands of 'impatient capital'.[25] On the one hand the predictability required by international investors encourages local architectural practitioners to adopt international design norms and construction methods. Thus, new commercial and infrastructure projects boast of steel frame structures finished with glass and other prefabricated cladding materials which have previously been alien to the local construction industry and are often necessarily imported in large quantities to meet rising demands. On the other hand, the shortage of established larger architectural firms in India, with sufficient experience to fully and efficiently implement these projects, obliges the importation of project management expertise. In these cases, it is often corporate architectural practices based in other more advanced Asian business cities such as Kuala Lumpur, Singapore, Taipei, and Shanghai that provide the managerial support and international cache for Indian firms working as local collaborators (Figure 19.12). Accordingly, younger architects returning from overseas studies and work experience are increasingly tending to establish such corporate style practices in collaboration with foreign partners from the outset.

Despite some similarities between this early twenty-first-century exchange and the cosmopolitan internationalism of India's modern architectural scene in the 1960s, it is a substantially different phenomenon. With the demise of state patronage and the grand ideals of a nation-building project, the Indian architectural profession now serves the requirements of its international investors, finding itself less and less bound by the needs and means of the local environment or community, or the inspiration it might offer. In an open economy, imported processes and materials may effectively address immediate market and construction exigencies but may not offer sustainable engagement with the locale in the long term. Whilst aspiration for

19.12   The projected skyline of the Gujarat International Finance Tech-City (GIFT), under design development by the East China Architectural Design and Research Institute (ECADI) (c.2011) and planned for completion near Ahmedabad in 2017, is typical of large-scale Shanghai and Dubai-style commercial developments driven by global finance and increasingly designed by large Indian and East-Asian consortia

ever 'greener' building credentials is indeed a growing and increasingly marketable trend in Indian corporate architecture, typically measured by international standards such as the American LEED rating scheme, the symbolic allure of hi-tech approaches to a greener Indian architecture of the future is at risk of overlooking the extensive experience in developing passive low-cost strategies for the design of energy-efficient buildings and cities within the modern Indian tradition that have been incorporated over half a century in the work of senior doyens of the Indian architectural profession such as B.V. Doshi and the late Laurie Baker.

Similarly, the hi-tech allure and monetary rewards of working in the growing architectural sector of India's globe-straddling digital services outsourcing industry is at risk of effectively exporting a growing proportion of the best home-grown technical talent in the Indian profession into 'virtual' foreign service. Firms like Delhi-based Satellier, which as of 2006 had grown from 3 to over 300 employees in less than 5 years, have mirrored some of the commercial success of the Indian IT industry itself by focusing exclusively on providing design development and documentation services to the global architecture, engineering and construction industry. Yet such spectacular international success from a professional standpoint has so far had little if any substantive impact on new architecture actually being built in India today.[26]

With the lack of a grander national allegiance, or indeed any larger agenda to align themselves to, contemporary Indian architectural practitioners are becoming increasingly individual players in a corporate economy who work to serve a clientele and do not engage in professional debate. As a result, the last two decades have seen little to no importance being accorded to professional journals and public debates on issues concerning architectural directions in the nation. This contrasts greatly with the ethos of discourse and engagement of the 1960s when emerging Indian modernists worked alongside foreign professionals to develop creative but critical context-specific architectural responses to the demands and opportunities of the times.

While contemporary architectural professionals struggle to ascribe meaning to their work in the absence of any politically neutral debate about national or regional identity, a new kind of internationalism has emerged from the unlikely combination of conservative values and global monetary flows. The rise of a large economically mobile expatriate population and an open market economy has resulted in greater exchange with overseas Indians all over the globe. With their competing national affinities and identities, what binds these groups together is often their allegiance to religious centres and institutions located within the subcontinent. Architecturally this has resulted in the construction of a large number of religious institutional projects in India funded by overseas donors. These projects, however, remain the domain of traditional builders who generally do not engage with the modern profession. Accordingly, structures like the Akshardham Temple in Delhi are constructed under the guidance of a group of *swamis* using ancient stereotomic practices and avoiding modern materials like steel and concrete. Such large-scale constructions have led, furthermore, to the rise of an industry of stone workers developing temple parts for export all around the world. This international nexus now stands in defiance of the modern profession and exploits the new wealth of its worldly patrons to make the case for a return to ancient practices.

Between these separate and contradictory worlds of current international exchange, where the new temples of corporate India with their splendid cladding of imported steel and glass rise adjacent the export-revived temple stone yards of old, a small group of practitioners still vie for the patronage of enlightened elites and NGOs in negotiating a creative resistance to such global flows. In centres such as Delhi, Ahmedabad, and Mumbai, where the practice of regional modernism had flourished a generation ago, the lessons learnt from the works of Rewal, and Doshi, Correa are intermixed with more contemporary materials, forms and techniques in the work of younger practices such as Morphogenesis, Matharoo Associates, Studio Mumbai, and Rahul Mehrotra Associates to poetically interpret the possibilities of architectural cosmopolitanism, past and present. As yet limited to smaller institutional and residential commissions, however, these aesthetically refined and ethically engaged practices have had little opportunity to make a significant impact on the development of public space and infrastructure more broadly (Figure 19.13).

Outside the urban centres, the legacy of Laurie Baker is carried forward in regional and rural localities where alternative practitioners such as Yatin Pandya in Gujarat, and Anupama Kundoo in Tamil Nadu resist global norms by engaging waste materials, unskilled labour and local communities in the design process. As socially engaged and ethically minded practices, these provide some of the most valuable lessons for the sustainable future of architecture in India, but once again are limited to small NGO funded commissions, the impact of which is limited. It remains to be seen whether these regionally grounded, sustainability focused practices can recruit a sufficient following among both clients and fellow professionals to steward a renewed cultural resistance, in the context of the current open market, to the ever-growing allure of international design fashion and consumption.

19.13   Weekend retreat for a film-maker, Alibag, Maharashtra (2002) by Rahul Mehrotra Associates

India is poised to confirm its place on the world stage as one of the largest of the new economic powers that is re-centring the global economy in Asia in the early twenty-first century. But, in contrast to post-colonial India's critical early encounter with the Eurocentric mastery of mid twentieth-century 'international' modernism, global India's long-anticipated moment of economic take-off is already engaging Indian architects and builders in a very different constellation of international competition, influences and exchange. What substantive architectural legacies will emerge from the mirage of present prospects and possibilities are, as yet, uncertain.

NOTES

1   The team included another American designer, Alexander Girard, who had collaborated previously with the Eames on other Indian commissions. *National Institute of Design Documentation 1964–69* (Ahmedabad: National Institute of Design, 1969).

2   It was only after Matthew Nowicki's untimely death in a plane crash in 1950 that the more illustrious French architect had been invited to take over the project.

3   Nehru's relationship with the West and its impact on India's foreign policy has been widely examined by both Indian and foreign authors. For a specific study of Nehru's attitude towards the United States in the pre-independence years, see Kenton J. Clymer, 'Jawaharlal Nehru and the United States: The Pre-independence Years', *Diplomatic History* 14, no. 2 (1990): 143–61.

4   For the involvement of American institutions like the CIA in the funding of cultural projects in Europe and Asia as an effort to turn the intelligentsia away from communism and toward an acceptance of 'the American way', see Frances Stonor Saunders, *Who Paid the Piper?: The CIA and the Cultural Cold War* (London: Granata Books, 1999).

5   The Ford Foundation's first president, Paul Hoffmann, had previously served as the Administrator for the Marshall Plan for the reconstruction of post-war Europe. Upon

his appointment to the Foundation he met with Indian prime minister Jawaharlal Nehru in 1951 to discuss the possibility of the Foundation's involvement in India's central development ventures, and subsequently chose the Indian capital as the base for the Foundation's first international field office, which was established in New Delhi in 1952. For details of Ford Foundation activities in India, see Eugene S. Staples, *Forty Years, a Learning Curve: The Ford Foundation Programs in India 1952–1992* (New Delhi: The Ford Foundation, 1992).

6   Charles Eames and Ray Eames, 'The India Report (April 1958)', (Ahmedabad: National Institute of Design, 2004).

7   Letter, Gautam Sarabhai to Louis Kahn, April 5, 1962, 'IIM – Sarabhais Correspondence (Vikram-Gautam)', Box LIK 113, Louis I. Kahn Collection, University of Pennsylvania and Pennsylvania Historical and Museum Commission. Gautam Sarabhai's letter explained Kahn's role in the context of the setup of NID's 'service-cum-training' programme and drew upon the ideas formulated in Eames's *India Report* extensively to explain this peculiar arrangement. According to the letter, then, Kahn was primarily invited to be 'a consultant teacher to the architectural team on the staff of the Institute'.

8   These included Harry Weese, Buckminster Fuller, Enrico Peresutti, Heinrich Kosina and Frei Otto. NID also engaged in consultations regarding design curriculum and method with the Ulm School of Design in Germany, and the Royal College of Art in London. NID records also mention a proposed collaboration with the AA School in London, but this never came to fruition as the initial idea of starting a programme in 'Industrialised Architecture' was dropped in 1969. *National Institute of Design Documentation 1964–69*.

9   Viewed through this regionalist lens, institutions like the NID can be recognised as the playgrounds of ambitious institution-building elites who used modern architecture in their struggle with the centralised nation state to define regional centres of power. Originally intended as the national centre of design, NID was acquired for Ahmedabad by the city's industrial elite who sought to boost the historic Gujarati mill-town's economic and cultural status as a prospective regional counterpoint to Mumbai (formerly Bombay), India's premier commercial metropolis.

10   Achyut Kanvinde's decision to include the *bangla* form was almost certainly influenced by the neo-orientalist formalisms that had crept into the later work (in Baghdad) of his former mentor, Walter Gropius, with whom he had studied at Harvard in the mid-1940s.

11   Within the Indian Parliament, this was further cemented by a strategic alliance between Indira Gandhi's centrist Congress Party and the Communist Party of India.

12   M.N. Ashish Ganju and A.G. Krishna Menon, 'The Architect: A Symposium on the New Disciplines of a Profession', *Seminar (India)* 180 (Aug, 1974). Looking inwards and beneath the surface of mere technological fixes, *Greha* members, including H.D. Chhaya, Vasant Kamath, Romi Khosla and Ashish Ganju, sought to harness what they perceived was the 'collective spirit' inherent in traditional dwelling forms and patterns, simultaneously substituting the idea of the architect as a designer with that of a facilitator responsible for stimulating and coordinating the development of space by the inhabitants themselves.

13   *Mimar* itself was soon emulated in India with the establishment in 1984 of another glossy architectural journal, *Architecture + Design* (A+D), which quickly became the key forum for debate about contemporary architectural ideas and practice in India over the following decade.

14   And others like B.V. Doshi, who had worked alongside Moshe Safdie and Nader Ardalan to co-author the Habitat Bill of Rights submitted by the Government of Iran at

the seminal 1976 Vancouver conference of the UN, were already part of the movement in the Middle East which sought to promote, as reported in a *New York Times* article on 8 June 1976, 'vernacular architecture as opposed to the often abstract quality of much modern design'.

15   'Awards 1978–1980: Mughal Sheraton Hotel, Agra, India', Aga Khan Award for Architecture, accessed 20 December 2012, www.akdn.org/akaa_award1_awards.asp.

16   A similar response to the burgeoning demand for greater regionalist affinities is also evident in Charles Correa's LIC (Life Insurance Corporation) building in Delhi. Begun in 1975, it would have undoubtedly followed in the line of his previous designs for high-rise projects in exposed concrete such as the Kanchenjunga Apartments (1970–83) and Visvesvaraya Towers (1974–80). However, by the time the project was finally constructed in 1986, it was rendered in red sandstone.

17   In various projects from the 1980s onwards, beginning with *Sangath* (1980) in which he housed his own atelier, B.V. Doshi also incorporated many traditional building materials and skills in innovative and unconventional ways. In *Sangath* these included the use of recycled glazed tiles to develop a mosaic on the exterior vault, and locally sourced hollow hand-made pottery tiles for the construction of the self-insulating vault.

18   The rise of the traditional methods of *Vastuvidya* was greatly assisted by Vaidyanatha Ganapati Sthapati's efforts as the Principal of the Government College of Architecture and Sculpture in Tamil Nadu, India. He was responsible for establishing the Vaastu Vedic Trust and the Vaastu Vedic Research Foundation and was accordingly awarded the Padma Bhushan in 2009. He further went on to establish The American University of Mayonic Science and Technology in Santa Fe, New Mexico.

19   For an extended critique of the use of the nine-square *mandala* form in the design of the Jawahar Kala Kendra, see Vikramaditya Prakash, 'Identity Production in Postcolonial Indian Architecture: Re-Covering What We Never Had', in *Postcolonial Space(s)*, ed. Gülsüm Baydar Nalbantoğlu and Wong Chong Thai (New York: Princeton Architectural Press, 1997), 39–52.

20   Charles Correa, 'Vistara: The Architecture of India', *Mimar* 27 (Mar 1988): 24–6.

21   Swati Chattopadhyay, 'Expedient Forgetting: Architecture in the Late Twentieth-century Nationalist Imagination', *Design Book Review* (Fall 2000): 27.

22   A substantial catalogue was published by Electa Moniteur in Paris for the 1985 exhibition which became the first major publication to offer an overview of contemporary architecture in India. Catalogue, *Architecture in India: A Festival of India Publication* (Paris: Electa Moniteur, 1985).

23   These included Hindustan Computers Limited (HCL), established in 1971, and the Tata Group, initiators of the Santacruz Electronics Export Processing Zone (SEEPZ) in Mumbai, which had already become a major centre for the export of IT services by 1973.

24   Key home-grown Indian IT corporations include Wipro Technologies set up in 1980, and Infosys Technologies founded in 1981. With the changing pattern of market forces and mounting pressure from the World Bank, Rajiv Gandhi's government had made an initial attempt, as early as 1985, to relax India's still highly regulated economy. So by the time that economic liberalisation was fully implemented in 1991, India was already leapfrogging conventional industrialisation to fully embrace the new knowledge economy as a primary engine for growth.

25   Rahul Mehrotra applies the apposite notion of 'impatient capital' in his fuller critical overview of these recent developments in Rahul Mehrotra, *Architecture in India Since 1990* (Pictor, 2011).

26   Paolo Tombesi, Bharat Dave and Peter Scriver, 'Routine Production or Symbolic Analysis? India and the Globalization of Architectural Services', *The Journal of Architecture* 8, no. 1 (Spring 2003): 63–94; Paolo Tombesi, Bharat Dave, Blair Gardiner and Peter Scriver, 'Rules of Engagement: Testing the Attributes of Distant Professional Marriages', *Journal of Architectural Engineering and Design Management* 3 (2007): 49–64.

20

Architecture in China in the Reform Era: 1978–2010

Tao Zhu

In December 1978, China launched a program of economic development that would lead to dramatic changes in the built environment. These reforms proceeded cautiously, given the country's lack of experience with market economies, under the slogan, "Cross the river by touching the stones; take one step and then watch for the next one."

1980S: INITIAL REFORM, NEW ENLIGHTENMENT

Between 1979 and the mid 1980s, the Chinese Communist Party set out on a "river-crossing" expedition of increasingly ambitious measures. It launched agricultural reform, established township and village enterprises, and implemented fiscal decentralization to encourage local governments' development. The efforts most relevant to China's building industry were the opening of international trade, the establishment of Special Economic Zones in coastal cities, and the acceleration of investment in nationwide housing construction.

China's building industry started to boom in 1980, when Deng Xiaoping declared it one of the main pillars of the economy. This quickly triggered the reform of the state-owned architectural design institutes, most of which were closed under Mao's command during the decade-long Cultural Revolution, when about three-quarters of Chinese architects, along with millions of intellectuals, were banished to farms or factories to work as laborers. In the early 1980s, the "sent-down" architects who had survived were allowed to return to their design institutes and apply their professional skills to the reconstruction unfolding nationwide. In 1983, the design institutes migrated from state funding into self-supporting units that were actively engaged in the building industry.[1]

In the 1980s Chinese intellectuals and the general public enthusiastically embraced a miscellany of Western literature, including aesthetic and theoretical discourses. Chinese architects eagerly devoured Western architectural polemics which, stripped of their historical and cultural contexts, created an information explosion that often threw Chinese architects into a state of "epistemological disorder." For instance, Le Corbusier's *Toward a New Architecture* (1923), Bruno Zevi's *Architecture as Space* (1948) and Charles Jencks' *The Language of Post-Modern Architecture* (1977) were all translated between 1981 and 1982, leading to an intellectual quandary: when Chinese architects faced a "Big Roof"—the nickname for a pitched roof built with modern materials that imitated the classical Chinese roof, should they quote Le Corbusier and Zevi to condemn it as a pre-modern, historical pastiche, or should they wave Jencks's pamphlet to adore it as a post-modern gimmick?

The central theme of modernity versus tradition—often phrased as Modernism versus National Form—dominated debates among architects. Proponents of Modernism argued that the International Style represented social progress. They associated abstract and undecorated building forms with an open, forward-looking, democratic and uncompromising modernity. They identified traditional forms with authoritarian, conservative and reactionary politics. Supporters of the National Form argued that Chinese architecture should only be modernized with a "national identity." They generally focused on three traditional formats: the pitched roof (or Big Roof), which was primarily adapted from the roof-forms of Chinese royal palaces, ancient temples, or vernacular houses; the picturesque garden, which was mainly inspired by the classical gardens in the Jiangnan area; and historical decorative motifs.

These diametrically opposed positions shared a set of problems. First, neither side produced any imaginative or skillfully executed formal experiments. This problem was particularly acute in the early 1980s, when most architects were mired in making buildings in either a monotonous International Style or a superficially imitative National Form. The situation improved in the mid 1980s as Chinese architects rapidly improved their design skills. However, the second problem was more serious and to a large extent remains unresolved: neither group was able to support its position through critical historical analysis. Proponents of Modernism reduced the multilayered and complex meanings of "modern architecture" to a simplistic formal language. They failed to consider it as part of a complex historical process, in which architects had developed a series of diverse ideas and formal expressions when they were confronted with modernity and tradition at different moments and within different contexts in the twentieth century. Supporters of the National Form failed to acknowledge that for China, a large continent with a long history and a population composed of diverse ethnic groups and cultural traditions, the idea of a single Chinese nationality (*Zhonghua Minzu*) possessing only one "mainstream" tradition and "official" identity, was a myth that had been propagated by Chinese intellectuals and politicians in the late nineteenth century along with the emerging stream of Chinese nationalism. Most importantly, the disjunctive experience of so many political upheavals left both groups unable to situate their discussions in a historical genealogy. In fact, the dispute over concepts of Modernism and National Form recalled earlier arguments between advocates of Modernism and those of national tradition that evolved during the cultural debates in the May Fourth New Cultural Movement in the 1920s, were quickly interjected into the architectural practice in Republican China in the 1930s, and suspended by the Sino-Japan War (1937–45) and the Civil War (1945–49). These debates resurfaced in the 1950s, when Chinese architects became embroiled in an ongoing struggle to devise a style that would be suitable for Mao's new socialist regime.[2]

In the early 1980s a series of culturally attuned works that went beyond the reductive opposition between Modernism and National Form appeared in port cities like Shanghai and Guangzhou, historically known for their more relaxed cultural environments. The most articulate of these was the Songjiang Square Pagoda Garden designed in 1980 by Feng Jizhong, Head of the Department of Architecture at the Tongji University in Shanghai. Located in Songjiang, a small town on the outskirts of Shanghai, the garden was ample evidence that even after the Cultural Revolution had shattered so many aspects of Chinese culture, a renewed and ingenious appreciation of the Chinese local building tradition set within a modern modality was still attainable.

As "an open-air museum," the garden displayed antique structures, including a Song-dynasty Square Pagoda, a Ming screen wall, a Yuan bridge that had originally been on the site plus a Qing temple and Ming house that were relocated there. Feng organized this collection of antiquities into a contemporary garden with a fluid pedestrian network and intricate spatial experience that incorporated both the undulating topography, zigzagging pathway and sinuous waterscape of a typical Chinese garden, and such modernist gestures as the "cubic" stone treatment of the retaining wall, the two perpendicular wall segments sliding away from each other to create an open corner, and the long straight stone bench boldly stretching across a space from the Bamboo Observing Pavilion to the perimeter of the outside landscape. At the southeast corner of the garden, the Helouxuan Pavilion featured an audaciously modern free plan and open space, while maintaining compatibility with the surrounding landscape.[3]

During the 1980s, the greatest impact on Chinese architecture came from abroad. The Fragrant Hill Hotel, designed by the Chinese American architect Ieoh Ming Pei, became the central focus of debate among Chinese architects as soon as its plans were unveiled in 1980. The hotel's significance was twofold. First, it epitomized the first group of "*Shewai* hotels"—high-end hotels built in several first-tier cities to house

20.1   Feng Jizhong, Helouxuan Pavilion, Songjiang Square Pagoda Garden, 1987. Plan and exterior view

foreign visitors during the opening-up of China in the early 1980s, along with other celebrated places such as the White Swan Hotel in Guangzhou, the Jinling Hotel in Nanjing, and the Jianguo and Great Wall Hotels in Beijing. Since most ordinary citizens were only allowed to wander around the grounds, these buildings embodied the phantasmagoric imagery of "an advanced civilization and life style" to which they did not belong, but all yearned to join in the near future. The Fragrant Hill Hotel served an important didactic role. Whereas other contemporary architects simply inserted a Chinese classical pavilion into the generic modern hotel lobby, delivering a superficial message of "Chineseness," Pei recognized that this critical moment in Chinese history provided an opportunity to explore "a third way" alternative to the International Style and Chinese Classical architecture.

In 1978, when Pei was invited by Beijing officials to design a high-rise hotel in the vicinity of the Forbidden City, he persuaded his clients to build instead a low-rise hotel at the bottom of Fragrant Hill, a popular resort area 20 kilometers from Beijing city. He designed the hotel in a quasi-symmetrical layout, locating the lobby on a central axis that linked the four-storied block of guestrooms and amenities around a series of courtyards on both sides. Quite different from the traditional Chinese architectural plan in which symmetry was usually prevalent and courtyards were often enclosed, Pei's design deliberately offset the symmetry and enclosure on a local level with various architectural and landscape elements. Pei applied a small amount of flush gable and shed roofs to decorate the edge of the largely flat roof. For the central lobby atrium named the "Four-seasons Garden," an analogy to the traditional open-air courtyard, he designed the skylight with a steel space-frame and glass reminiscent of a group of Chinese gabled- and-hip roofs. The building's facade refers to Tang and Song styles of post-and-lintel trabeation and the whitewashed wall surfaces of Jiangnan gardens.

While some Chinese architects celebrated Pei's success at combining abstract modern forms with traditional emblematic elements, others criticized the building's high cost and its location, which they believed was injurious to the mountainous landscape. They also questioned Pei's formal strategy of composing the building masses in a modernist manner and then decorating the wall surfaces with motifs transplanted from the gardens and vernacular houses in southeast China, which they thought unconvincing. Yet they applauded his experimental spirit, and Pei's formal skill left a lasting impression on Chinese architects.

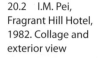

20.2   I.M. Pei, Fragrant Hill Hotel, 1982. Collage and exterior view

Since the mid 1980s, one can perceive the marked improvement in the formal quality of the architecture produced by adherents to Modernism as well as National

Form. The former is best represented by the China International Exhibition Center, Halls 2–5 in Beijing designed by Chai Peiyi. With a "stereotomic" (stone-cutting) approach, Chai cut away a few sections of the monolithic building mass to enliven its facade with a rhythm of a solid-void contrast and light-shadow play. The latter is typified by the Queli Hotel, designed by Dai Nianci and located next to the prominent historical monument of the Confucius Temple and Kong Family Mansion in Qufu, Shandong. In order to submerge the new hotel into the adjacent historical building fabric, Dai distributed the mainly two-storied guestrooms around a series of courtyards that were organized into a quasi-symmetrical design, a layout similar to Pei's hotel plan but more restrained by symmetry and enclosure. For the building's elevation, he chose the Big Roof as the principal motif. Particularly for the central roof crowning the hotel lobby, Dai took great pains to resolve the contradictions

20.3   Chai Peiyi, China International Exhibition Center, Halls 2–5, Beijing, 1985

20.4   Dai Nianci, Queli Hotel, Qufu, 1985

between traditional timber framing and the reinforced concrete structure that he actually used. His solution was ingenious but not without a certain irony: externally, the roof appeared to be an "authentic" traditional cruciform gable-and-hip roof; however, from its interior, it revealed itself as a concrete shell supported at four points.

1990S: SPEEDY DEVELOPMENT, CULTURAL DIVIDE

Early in 1992, after a three-year period of economic depression and political uncertainty that began with the 1989 Tiananmen Square Movement, Deng Xiaoping made his Southern Tour to the Special Economic Zones (SEZs). Recapturing regional support, Deng was able to restart China's economic reforms. The Central Government established another set of ambitious goals for the transition towards a market economy, including greater separation between state and Party, establishing rigorous rule of law, and creating a multi-centered network of independent systems of scrutiny and accountability of the market operation.

The 1990s saw the monotonous architectural culture of the 1980s dissipate under the impact of three major trends: the expansion of market consumption, the emerging group of young Chinese Experimental Architects, and the influx of foreign architects. The Special Economic Zones established along the coastline of the South China Sea in the 1980s and the Economic Development Zone set up in Shanghai's Pudong New Area in 1992 provided important new sources of patronage for architects. The government began converting the socialist welfare housing system into a nationwide market system, and in 1994 reformed the tax-assignment system (*fenshuizhi*) in a way that encouraged rapid real-estate development. The Business Fever (*Xiahai Re*) of the 1990s had replaced the Cultural Fever of the 1980s.

The ponderous ideological interpretation of both the International Style as representing modernity as well as National Form indicating core cultural tradition were no longer valid amid the free-market impulses of the 1990s. Both government officials and developers freely promoted the practice of juxtaposing a sleek Modernism with a hodgepodge of a Big Roof or "European continental style" (*Oulu Fengqing*), or whatever cultural references they wished, onto their building facades. Within architectural academia, the imported post-modern theories of semiotics and the "decorated shed," often applied simplistically, spurred the mania of architects who transformed numerous Chinese cities into "Potemkin towns."

Many young Chinese architects dissatisfied with this state of affairs began to open small private studios in the mid 1990s, thanks to market reforms that allowed alternatives to the collective, anonymous, normative practice model carried out by the massive design institutes and companies. Culturally, they attempted to construct a body of "autonomous" architectural discourses that were removed from any explicit figurative expressions or ideological connotations. Yung Ho Chang, who returned to China in 1994 after more than a decade of studying and teaching in the US, played a leading role in this group of emerging architects when he returned to China. Although his work was limited to theoretical speculation and small-scale installations, his clear articulation of a theoretical position, conceptual approach toward design problems, abstract and elemental formal language, and proactive attitude toward both the professional and mass media, brought a fresh perspective to the discipline. With the Beijing-based Chang serving as a catalyst, several young Chinese architects, including Liu Jiakun in Chengdu, Wang Shu in Hangzhou, Tang Hua in Shenzhen, and slightly later, Ma Qingyun in Shanghai and Zhang Lei in Nanjing, and others, began discussions that led to the formation of the Experimental Architects group.

In the mid 1990s the Experimental Architects began to develop new theoretical subjects and design strategies based in part upon Western discourses. These included "conceptual design," which allowed architects and students to make novel designs through personal conceptual speculation rather than to flow with the prevailing conventional functionalism or subjective expressionism. Chang was primarily responsible for introducing this approach to China, which had been prevalent in architectural schools in the US at the time. Other theoretical subjects discussed by the Experimental Architects included "elementary form," a reduction

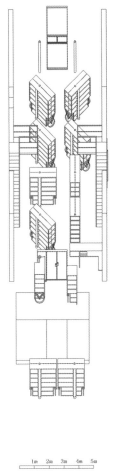

1m   2m   3m   4m   5m

20.5   Yung Ho Chang, Xishu Bookstore, 1996

of form to its essential elements to resist superfluous figuration or symbolism, "space," in which internal spatial composition is more important than external shape making, "tectonics," as inspired by Kenneth Frampton's seminal study of the "poetics of construction," and "critical regionalism," also influenced by Frampton, which encouraged Chinese architects to explore the notion of "an architecture of resistance" through the mediation between "universal civilization" and regional specificity. All these discourses offered promising opportunities for Chinese architects to construct a cultural identity in a period of rapid modernization.

The phrase Experimental Architecture was coined by architectural critics Wang Mingxian, Rao Xiaojun and Shi Jian, who considered it equivalent to the then flourishing "avant-garde" movement of Experimental Art in China.[4] Although Experimental Architecture was viewed as a liberating tool by many young Chinese architects and students who had undergone a rather orthodox, dogmatic education, at its core the concept contained an inherent paradox: the Experimental Architects were inspired by and frequently collaborated with their artist friends, and both groups shared some common interests, such as constructing physical installations. But the architects' concern with regrounding the discipline in its fundamental principles often contrasted with the artists' more subversive approaches. In the late 1990s, Experimental Architecture's alliance with Experimental Art helped to establish quickly a cultural identity against the normative architectural practice. Its inherent contradictions were not immediately recognized until the early 2000s.

China's rapid urbanization in the 1990s, a period of accelerating neoliberal globalization, produced a frenzied desire to replicate the "Bilbao effect" which led to prominent cultural commissions for numerous foreign architects. Pei, who refused to build high-rise buildings in Beijing's historical center, appeared too "conservative" compared to the new group of architects who, like Zaha Hadid, viewed the entire country "as an incredible empty canvas for innovation."[5] This period climaxed in 1999, when French architect Paul Andreu's design for the National Grand Theater of China, a gargantuan titanium dome covering three auditoria, was selected to be built at the edge of Tiananmen Square. China sought to attract prominent architects from all over the world to produce the dazzling architectural icons in cities throughout the country.

THE 2000S: THE CHINA MODEL, ANYTHING GOES (?)

Beginning in 2004, China's spectacular economic development over the past three decades prompted many international journalists, scholars and policymakers to discuss the so-called China Model of Development. This phrase suggests that after 30 years of wading across the river of reform by "touching the stones," China had managed to innovate a coherent and unique modernization model: a kind of state capitalism based on a mixture of an authoritarian state and a capital economy. Some critics viewed the China Model as a serious challenge to the Western model, which combined liberal democracy with a free-market economy.

China's tremendous economic growth—nearly 10 percent average annual growth in GDP between 1978 and 2010, the longest period of sustained economic growth in modern times—lifted 235 million people out of poverty.[6] The country's simultaneous urbanization, unprecedented in speed and magnitude, saw metropolitan growth from 172 million residents in 193 cities to 665.57 million in 654 cities over the same period, with the urbanization rate swelling from 17.92 percent to 49.68 percent.[7] Yet the chilling absence of institutional progress for human and civil rights, has not fostered an equitable system. Instead, the close integration of Party members and business elites has created a hybrid economy with features of both "crony capitalism" and "crony socialism." The resulting corruption, as well as ruthless exploitation of the country's natural resources and brutal demolition of the social welfare system, have profoundly impacted Chinese architecture.

The Built Experimental Architecture and its Discontent

The most powerful breakthrough made by the Experimental Architects in the early 2000s was the Luyeyuan Stone Sculpture Museum in Chengdu designed by Liu Jiakun. Liu designed the museum, which displays a collection of antique stone sculptures, as an "artificial stone." Similar to Chai's steretomic approach in the Beijing exhibition center, Liu divided the building into a group of smaller masses with a series of recessed vertical window slits, simultaneously composing the exterior, planning the interior spaces and organizing the program. Recalling Louis Kahn's concept of separating "servant" and "served" spaces, Liu subdivided the building into a cluster of two-storied mass-spaces in various sizes, using the large central one as an exhibition space and the string of smaller cells on the periphery for offices and amenities. Liu further pushed his idea of artificial stone-making through a bold experiment of wall construction. In contrast to Chai's whitewashed walls, which were ubiquitous in China during the 1980s and 1990s, Liu chose to apply raw concrete, a rarely used material in China at that time. Just as Feng used his rotation of podium plans in the Helouxuan Pavilion to symbolize the society's "loosening-up" during the 1980s, Liu intended to make his use of raw concrete a manifesto for a critical resistance to the vulgar commercialism prevailing in China at the turn of the twentieth century:

> The raw concrete is an important part of the 'artificial stone.' The designer hopes to obtain the frugality and unity, to obtain a solemn 'monolith' ... Moreover, in an age in which architectural makeup is fashionable, the use of raw concrete is not only an issue of architectural technique, but a matter of aesthetic tendency and spiritual quality.[8]

Whereas Liu's museum strove to maintain a high level of spatial and material unity, Wang Shu's Ningbo Museum, built in 2008, demonstrated a very strong tension between the building's overall volumetric unity and its inherent spatial and material fragmentation. Standing in a desolate new development zone of Ningbo, Wang imagined the building as "an artificial mountain." It consists of a single cubic volume at the bottom that "cracks" into five individual "hills," or exhibition pavilions, on top. In the middle section, the museum offers an Acropolis-like outdoor podium for visitors to view the building's surrounding landscape, including diminishing rice fields, neighboring new city development, and a distant mountain range. Internally, the building's mass is carved into various exhibition "caves," circulation "canyons" and sunken courtyards that create a labyrinthine walking experience. The building's exterior surface is covered with raw concrete cast by bamboo formwork as well as over 20 different types of recycled bricks and roof tiles collected from numerous demolition sites. Wang's museum is a mammoth monolith containing a huge collection of material and cultural fragments.

The two museums by Liu and Wang highlight the continuity and transformation across a two-decade span of Chinese architects' steretomic approach towards shaping a freestanding building. Wang's China Academy of Art Xiangshan Campus, with its two phases built respectively in 2004 and 2007, represents a fascinating architectural meditation upon the concept of "National Form." Similar to Dai's hotel, Wang worked with three formal tropes—the pitched roof, garden, and decorative motif. However, in contrast to Dai's direct adoption of the formal language of China's imperial palaces and ancient temples with a strong emphasis on the central axis, symmetry and figurative imitation of the classical pitched roof, Wang's campus, which was inspired by the Jiangnan garden and vernacular housing, was more fragmented, picturesque, and irregularly composed. Wang's complex shares a spirit with Feng's garden, with its dispersed individual fragments, old artifacts juxtaposed with new buildings, and picturesquely composed landscape. Wang defined the building units as U-shaped or zigzag perimeter blocks with their inner courtyards facing either the periphery of the site or a well-preserved hill in the center of the campus. He offset the immense scale of the building blocks with alternating window patterns, long zigzag stairs, horizontal louvers, and vertical wood panels to subdivide the large wall surfaces. As at the Ningbo Museum, Wang incorporated millions of recycled bricks and tiles collected from numerous province-wide demolition sites, adding a layer of "fragmentation" to the project. Wang's tendency toward fragmentation has been the most extreme among the Experimental Architects. In the end, his campus became a miniature city with numerous fragments colliding with each other and without reaching any reconciliation. For Wang and many architects working in China today, reconciling the inherent tension between the construction of a heroic freestanding building and the comprehensive planning of a coherent community capable of maintaining a certain cultural continuity within the tradition of Chinese habitation remains an elusive goal.[9]

20.6   Liu Jiakun, Luyeyuan Museum of Stone Sculpture, Chengdu, 2002

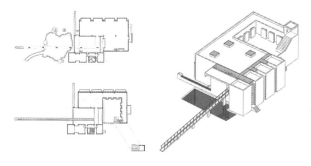

20.7   Wang Shu, China Academy of Art Xiangshan Campus, 2004 and 2007. Site plan and exterior view

20.8   Wang Shu, Ningbo Museum, 2008

Other notable realized projects by Experimental Architects also include Yung Ho Chang's Split House and Ma Qingyun's Father's House, which explored both elementary form and tectonic expression, as well as Zhang Lei's Nanjing University Library and Student Dormitory, which employed a more abstract, purist language. These works injected new energy into Chinese architecture by prompting young architects to seek fresh ideas and expressions and motivating critics to forge a new approach to architectural criticism in China. A more disciplined criticism that both engaged with and was independent from architects' positions also began to emerge in China in the early 2000s, in opposition to the overly general and often dogmatic cultural, ideological debates between Modernism and National Form in the 1980s, and the celebratory promotional writing in support of the Experimental Architecture in the 1990s.

From a somewhat "post-critical" position, Li Xiangning considered the Experimental Architects too abstract and idealistic. He argued that in light of China's dramatically changing society, the Experimental Architects' fascination with critical regionalism and Chinese cultural identity had become obsolete. Instead, Li supported an emerging group of younger Chinese architects, such as Urbanus, Atelier Deshaus, Bu Bing, Chen Xudong, Hua Li, Ma Yansong, Zhang Bin, Zhang Ke and Zhu Xiaofeng, who had begun to adopt a more flexible, programmatic, internationalist approach, which he named a "make-the-most-of-it" strategy.[10]

Shi Jian was another active critic who offered a more contextualized analysis. In 2003, while celebrating Yung Ho Chang's ten years of practice in China, Shi pointed out the apparent limitation of Experimental Architecture:

> ... overall, it had a mark of the academia (academic architecture). Amid the strong waves of China's ultra-urbanization, they (Experimental Architects) did not adapt a more proactive responsive strategy, but mostly obsessed with a state of "cultural architecture' construction, continuing the experiment in the 1980s' context.[11]

Bigness in the State Capitalist Style

The architectural phenomenon that captured the imagination of the Chinese public in the 2000s was the unprecedented nationwide construction of monumental buildings using public funds. Stadiums, opera houses, museums and governmental complexes have been built in cities of every size, fueled by China's economic boom and reflective of its aspirations for increased international stature. As China's development model has been identified as a form of state capitalism, combining an authoritarian state and a capital economy, its contemporary mega-building boom can also be conceived as a conflux of two major strands: Communist China's own legacy of building-big and the "Bilbao effect" that has been propagated by the currents of globalization. Exemplified by Beijing's 2008 Olympics, the 2010 Shanghai World Expo, and the Guangzhou 2010 Asia Games, "building big" has offered the Chinese government an opportunity to glorify its own power and authority, boost both national pride and local GDP growth, and gloss over any social contradictions created by the country's swift economic rise.

Since the 1990s, Chinese officials have been particularly eager to demonstrate their ultra-modernity and progressiveness through the embrace of foreign architects.[12] Paul Andreu's National Grand Theater, Rem Koolhaas' CCTV Headquarters and Herzog and de Meuron's National Stadium exemplify the government's interest in using avant-garde design to mask political and social problems. While the influx of foreign architects has had a positive influence on Chinese architecture by introducing sophisticated discourses, formal skills and construction techniques to Chinese architects and fostering a cosmopolitan architectural culture in many Chinese cities, the exacerbation of China's extravagant "bigness," has had disquieting results. The crown of CCTV's new skyscraper cantilevers 70 meters away from the two leaning towers in order to create "a continuous loop" to demonstrate the "collective" embedded in the CCP's gigantic propaganda machine. In the Bird's Nest, the Beijing National Stadium, the outer mesh woven by numerous colossal steel components was structurally independent from the inner concrete stadium, supporting nothing other than the columns themselves and fire stairs. Zaha Hadid designed the Guangzhou Opera House with a free-floating outer skin that required the addition of enormous steel stiffening, and whose exterior cladding of brittle black granite panels, many of which had complex curved surfaces, required manual polishing. Such excessiveness and unethical use of materials typify a new type of National Form, a state capitalist style marked by arbitrariness, indulgence and extravagance.

20.9 Herzog and de Meuron, National Stadium, Beijing, 2008

20.10 Rem Koolhaas and OMA, CCTV New Headquarters, Beijing, 2008

20.11 He Jingtang & Architectural Design and Research Institute of SCUT, China Pavilion, 2010 World Exposition, Shanghai, 2010

Toward a Civil Architecture

Two events in 2008 raised profound questions about the function and value of architecture and its relationship to society: the Beijing Olympics and the Sichuan Earthquake. The preparation for the Olympics produced a massive array of glitzy, awe-inspiring architectural icons, while the Sichuan Earthquake destroyed tens of thousands of substandard civic structures, including more than 5,000 school buildings and resulted in an extraordinary death toll. While the mega-buildings in Beijing and many other cities were staged to represent China's emergence as a superpower, the collapsed schools revealed the fragile state of the country's "infrastructure."

The shocking experience of the Sichuan Earthquake has triggered a social consciousness among Chinese architects that was absent over the previous two decades. Liu Jiakun, overwhelmed by the rubble and scent of death in the quake zone, donated and designed a memorial house to commemorate Hu Huishan, one of the more than 5,000 children killed when their schools collapsed. Diametrically opposite to China's practice of constructing enormous heroic monuments, Liu dedicated his memorial to a young and ordinary life, which, at 19 square meters in size, may be the smallest museum in China.

Taiwanese architect Hsieh Ying-chun made the most effective contribution to the reconstruction through his exceptional professional skill and social engagement. Hsieh and his Rural Architecture Studio had gained extensive experience over the previous nine years through their participation in grassroots community reconstruction in central Taiwan after the 1999 earthquake, and constructing prototypical ecological farmhouses, assembly halls and toilets in China's Hebei and Henan provinces in 2004–06. Hsieh's team developed a building system (combining standardized lightweight steel framing system and local infill materials) that can be built by residents, and which replaced the construction industry's slower and more expensive methods. Better adaptable to local customs, Hsieh's houses promote ecological sustainability by using materials with low embodied energy and techniques that reduce energy use.

20.12 Liu Jiakun, Hu Huishan Memorial House, Sichuan, 2008–09

20.13 Hsieh Ying-chun, reconstruction of Yangliu Village, Mao County, Sichuan, 2008

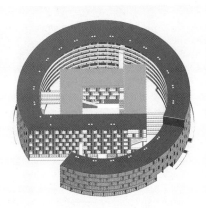

The China Architecture Media Awards (CAMA), launched in late 2008 by the *Southern Metropolis Daily* in collaboration with a group of major Chinese architectural magazines, criticized the extravagance of the Olympics projects and the plight of the collapsed schools in Sichuan quake zone by awarding the first Best Architecture Award to the Maoshi Elementary School, designed by the Hong Kong Wuzhiqiao Charitable Foundation and built with rammed earth in rural Gansu Province. The CAMA also recognized Hsieh for his reconstruction work.

The biannual CAMA program bestowed its first Special Award for Residential Architecture on Urban Tulou, an experimental affordable housing project designed by Shenzhen-based Urbanus. The six-story apartment building at the edge of Guangzhou was inspired by the traditional Hakka Tulou (earth building), whose

20.14 Urbanus, Urban Tulou, Guangzhou, 2008. Axonometric drawing and exterior view

circular outer walls were built with thick rammed earth. Urban Tulou's approach to low-income rental housing generated significant debate among Chinese architects and the mass media about an important building type that had been neglected in public discourse.

The 2008 CAMA program included a Lifetime Achievement Award for Feng Jizhong, one year before his death. The 94-year old championed the ideal of civil architecture in his acceptance speech:

> All architecture is civil architecture, especially in our era as such, and only the civil architecture is true architecture. Other architecture, if it does not represent the citizens' interests, is not true architecture.[13]

Yet government policies threaten this goal. Liu Jiakun's Hu Huishan Memorial House was never allowed to open, and in late 2010 the phrase "civil society" was discouraged by the Central Ministry of Propaganda in an attempt to avoid the term's focus on civil rights. China's continuing urban growth (its cities will have one billion residents by 2030) will both require a greater level of social engagement on the part of its state and corporate patrons, and potentially confront the regime …

NOTES

1   Between 1966 and 1976, China's universities had mostly shut down and architectural training was eliminated. A whole generation of qualified architects was missing. Faced with an urgent demand by a revitalized industry, China rushed to reopen its universities to train architects. The expansion of architectural programs in tandem with increased student admission was dramatic: in 1977, there were only eight colleges in China offering undergraduate degrees in architecture with an admission of 321 students: the following year, there were 46 programs that had accepted 1,914 students. See *China Architecture Yearbook* 1984–1985, 1988–1989 (Beijing, China Architecture & Building Press).

With the National Higher Education Entrance Examination resumed in 1977, China started to restore its higher education, including its architectural curriculum. The new architecture students swarmed into classrooms and libraries that were still in a state of ruin, eagerly grasping whatever knowledge they could find among the scattered resources. They would soon become major players in China's architectural modernization.

2   The discussions were greatly politicized and each style was either capriciously embraced or strongly attacked as a result of China's fluctuating political currents. First, Modernism was criticized as bourgeois decadence in the early 1950s, when China was under the influence of the Soviet Union that had vigorously promoted Socialist Realism. This was followed by an alternative pursuit of National Form by Chinese architects that was condemned in 1955 by Mao as feudalistic revivalism. Furthermore, Socialist Realism also had to be purged due to the Sino-Soviet split in the early 1960s.

3   Feng Jizhong, *Staying with the Ancient and Becoming New* (Beijing: The Eastern Publishing Co. Ltd, 2010), 73–108.

4   Rao Xiaojun, "The Marginal Experiment and Architectural Reform," *New Architecture* 3 (1997), 12–15; Wang Mingxian and Shijian, "China's Experimental Architecture in the 1990s," *Literature and Art Studies* 1 (1998), 118–27.

5   Susan Jakes, "Soaring Ambitions," *Time Asia*, April 26, 2004.

6   *China Daily*, 8 March, 2010.

7   *The State of China's Cities: 2010/2011* (Kenya: UN-HABITAT ITATITAT, 2010), 8; "Press Release on major Figures of the 2 010 National Population Census," April 28, 2011, accessed: June 23, 2011, http://www.stats.gov.cn/english/newsandcomingevents/ t20110428_402722237.htm.

8   Liu Jiakun, *Now and Here* (Beijing, China Architecture & Building Press, 2002), 111.

9   Wang Shu was awarded the Pritzker Prize in 2012, for "producing an architecture that is timeless, deeply rooted in its context and yet universal."

10   Li Xiangning, "'Make-the-Most-of-it' Architecture: Young Architects and Chinese Tactics," *Times + Architecture* 6 (2005), 18–23.

11   Shi Jian, "The Ten Years of FCJZ in the Context of Hyper-Urbanization," *Architect* 2 (2004).

In the past decade, I also criticized Experimental Architecture on both cultural and social grounds. Culturally, I considered its aesthetics often too reductive, even escapist, and not courageous or complex enough to confront the tremendous cultural contradictions bursting forth from China's turbulent reality.

From a social standpoint, I noticed that some of the Experimental Architects had quickly morphed from a group of "avant-garde" subversists into a cluster of star-architects who pandered to the nouveau riche, and primarily devoted themselves to an exclusive range of projects such as countryside villas and elite clubs; they remained rather distant from China's stark social conditions at a time when the country was enmeshed in housing crisis, environmental deterioration and social injustice. See Zhu Tao, "The Promises and Assumptions of 'Tectonics'," *Times + Architecture* 05 (2002); "Eight Steps toward FCJZ Atelier," *Architect* 08 (2004); "'Chinese Dwelling,' or Chinese Opportunism + Cynicism?" *Time + Architecture* 03 (2006); "The 'Criticality' Debate in the West and the Architectural Situation in China," *Time + Architecture* 05 (2006).

12   The Chinese Communist Party (CCP) emerged in the 1920s with a firm nationalist belief that a strong state is the ultimate arbiter of power. This belief emanated from two different streams of thinking: the "self-strengthening and save-the-nation" mentality from the late Qing, and the May Fourth radicalist belief that China's "backward" cultural tradition was preventing it from achieving modernity. In contrast to Hitler and Stalin, both of whom had a strong faith in the architectural blending of European classicism with national tradition, the CCP's ultimate leader Mao had an extreme distaste for China's architectural tradition, which he considered a residue of feudalism. From the 1950s to the 1970s, while in pursuit of a "proletarian revolutionary" style of city and architecture, Mao launched a series of campaigns against China's architectural heritage. These capricious political campaigns, as mentioned earlier, drove Chinese architects and officials into making further desultory decisions as they freely chose one style or combined several together, depending upon the particular political and economic circumstances of the moment. This arbitrary behavior, which turned into a self-protective eclecticism and streak of cynicism during a tumultuous period, such as the Cultural Revolution, could easily lead to an appearance of openness. This was especially true during the first decade of the twenty-first century, when globalization rather than revolution became China's zeitgeist.

13   Feng Jizhong, "All Architecture are Civil Architecture," *Southern Metropolis Daily*, December 30, 2008.

21

Architecture in Post-World War II Japan

Ken Tadashi Oshima

The future city lies in ruins.[1]

Arata Isozaki

The built environment in Japan has continuously oscillated between visionary aspirations and constructed realities. This dynamism has resulted in constantly changing diverse expressions of contemporary form shaped by global-local technological developments in modern building and the tremendous forces of political, economic and social change of the second half of the twentieth century— from the rise of the "economic miracle" with a skyrocketing GNP and population to the realities of "post-economic bubble" period.

Following the destruction of World War II, massive reconstruction plans of this defeated nation soon rekindled modernist fervor from the decades before the War. In Japan during the immediate post-war period, such rational building methods facilitated the construction of prefabricated dwellings to alleviate a housing shortage of 4.2 million units. Early examples were primarily barrack-type structures. Le Corbusier's disciples Junzō Sakakura (1901–1969) and Kunio Maekawa (1905– 1986) both actively sought to realize their master's ideals. In 1941 Sakakura began to develop an A-frame "assembly architecture" (*kumitate kenchiku*), and Maekawa pursued his own prefabricated housing scheme, which he named Premos, and produced more than 1,000 units between 1945 and 1952.[2] While maintaining the living unit of the tatami mat as the basis for these minimal 52-square-meter living units, Maekawa incorporated a system of self-supporting three-*shaku* (2.98 feet) honeycomb panels covered by plywood sheeting and used shallow wood trusses to support the roof. By 1947 the architectural profession earnestly pursued the dream of prefabrication with articles promoting "pre-assembled houses," "standard premade houses," and "panelized houses."[3] The minimal typical 12-*tsubo* (427-square feet) houses met the needs of the housing crisis, and made an easy transition from traditional wood frame construction to prefab through the use of modules suited to tatami mats and *shoji* and *fusuma* screens.

The economic severity and social changes of the immediate post-war period resulted in the rise of minimal nuclear-family dwellings such as Makoto Masuzawa's Hara House (1953) and Kiyoshi Seike's one-room My Home (1954). The 1950s also witnessed the emergence of individual minimal dwellings as experimental prototypes for mass production. Architect Kiyoshi Ikebe (1920–1979) drew from his work experiences with Sakakura from 1944 to 1946 and Maekawa as a member of NAU: New Architects' Union. Ikebe developed a series of numbered case study houses that totaled 98 in which he incorporated now common industrialized elements such as standard steel sash windows. These designs simplified Le Corbusier's Modulor to reach a broader audience in Japan through Ikebe's GM (General Module) system, based on simple multiples of two, and subsequently became a touchstone in the industrialization of modular coordination in housing. In 1952 Makoto Masuzawa (1925–1990), developed his own two-level minimal house that through its simple, straightforward design was ripe for prefabrication but not realized until after his death.

Developments in reinforced concrete, steel and glass technology brought about a new-generation of sleek, refined works. The influence of American culture during the Allied Occupation of Japan (1945–52) can be seen in Antonin Raymond's exposed reinforced concrete Reader's Digest Building (1951) on a site adjacent to the Imperial Palace in central Tokyo. An innovative cantilevered tree-like structure by Paul Weidlinger facilitated an unprecedented openness between the offices and sculptured landscape by Isamu Noguchi.

The realization of new public institutions and Le Corbusier's modern architectural principles of volumes lifted up on pilotis can be seen in Junzō Sakakura's Museum of Modern Art, Kamakura (1951). Kenzō Tange, working within his master-plan for rebuilding Hiroshima (1946–47), realized his landmark Peace Memorial Museum in 1955 that fused Le Corbusier's language of pilotis and *brises-soleil* with traditional Japanese details. Bare reinforced concrete lifted above the ground took on symbolic meaning in the Peace Memorial Museum linked on axis with the hyperbolic paraboloid peace arch. A debate on the role of tradition in modern Japanese architecture re-emerged highlighted by Kenzō Tange's brutalist reinforced-concrete Kagawa Prefectural Office (1955–8) that clearly recalls traditional Japanese post-and-beam construction. Maekawa extended Le Corbusier's model of Unité d'Habitation (1945–52), Marseille to successfully integrate Japanese domestic living within his monumental housing block at Harumi, Tokyo (1956–58). Le Corbusier himself finally built in Japan, completing the Museum of Western Art in 1959.

The year 1960 marked the ascent of Japanese designers onto the world stage at the World Design Conference held in May in Tokyo that attracted leading designers from 26 countries. During the conference a group of young architects including Kisho Kurokawa and Kiyonori Kikutake launched the Metabolist group, promoting their visions of organic megastructures. Its initial members were the architects Takashi Asada, Kiyonori Kikutake and Kishō Kurokawa, journalist and critic Noboru Kawazoe, industrial designer Kenji Ekuan and graphic designer Kiyoshi Awazu; the architects Fumihiko Maki and Masato Ōtaka soon joined them. Metabolism was critical of orthodox Modernism as represented by C.I.A.M., advocating instead a more dynamic, organic approach in which urban and architectural infrastructure could embrace short-term replaceable elements. Following the conference, Kenzō Tange unveiled his visionary 1960 Tokyo Bay Plan as a cellular structure connecting the existing urban fabric and extending it out into Tokyo Bay. Following biological metaphors, the plan expressed "the evolution of radial cellular bodies into vertebrates …" The publication of "A Plan for Tokyo, 1960," in March 1961 advocated the primary aim "to shift from a radial centripetal system in a system of linear development."

While many of the visionary urban schemes of the1960s were not built in their entirety, many individual buildings were realized. Tange realized his megastructural core/open slab vocabulary in the Yamanashi Cultural Center (1967). Metabolist works include Kikutake's Sky House (1958) with changeable "movenett" living units and Tōkōen Hotel (1965) and Kurokawa's plug-in Nakagin Capsule Tower (1972). Nevertheless, with the introduction of the government's income-doubling program in 1960, Japan achieved its celebrated "economic miracle" and subsequent building boom symbolized by Kenzō Tange's design of sweeping tensile-roof National Gymnasia for the 1964 Tokyo Olympics. The symbolic strength of the hyperbolic paraboloid structures built on the precedents of Le Corbusier's Philips pavilion for Brussel's World Fair (1958) and Eero Saarinen's Yale Hockey Stadium (1958), also placed Japanese architecture on the world stage. The completion of Japan's first

21.1 Junzō
Sakakura, Museum
of Modern Art,
Kamakura, 1951

21.2   Kenzō Tange, Hiroshima Peace Memorial Museum, Hiroshima, 1955

21.3   Le Corbusier, Museum of Western Art , Ueno, Tokyo, 1959

21.4   Kisho Kurokawa, Nakagin Capsule Tower, Tokyo, 1972

21.5   Kenzō
Tange, Tokyo
Olympics National
Gymnasia,
Tokyo,1964

high-rise, the 36-story Kasumigaseki building (1968) in Tokyo marked the mastery
of seismic construction, ascent of the national economy and urbanism from low-
rise to high-rise districts.

Within the context of 1960s economic and technical take-off accompanied
by skyrocketing land prices, architect Takamasa Azuma set out to create his
manifesto for living in the city. The 1960 U.S.–Japan Security Treaty was followed
by the income-doubling program and most prominently, the 1964 Tokyo
Olympic Games. As the Japanese capital prepared itself for the Olympics with
the construction of major avenues and elevated highways, residents increasingly
fled to the suburbs to escape congestion and pollution. Azuma countered
this trend by building his home in the heart of the urban environment on the
largest plot he could afford: an approximately 100-square foot triangular plot on
Killer Dōri, a broad avenue constructed within the urban Aoyama district by the
Tokyo Metropolitan Government in preparation for the Olympic Games. Azuma's
house became expressive of what he called the "one *tsubo* movement." As Azuma
himself explained, "No matter how limited the land, it is still possible to find an
architectural method that expresses the life style of the individual human being or
of the family. Indeed, the closer the site comes to the absolute minimum, the more
conspicuous will become the expression of the family's way of life." Azuma's Tower
House is a six-story reinforced concrete dwelling with a total square footage of less
than 600 square feet. Rooms are literally stacked on top of each other in a manner
recalling traditional lacquer boxes. The spaces are carefully intertwined from the
basement storage space, to the ground floor carport/entry, second floor living/
dining/kitchen space, third floor bath, fourth floor master bedroom, and fifth floor
children's bedroom and roof terrace.

At the apex of this boom, the designs at Expo 70 (Osaka, 1970), highlighted by the central Festival Plaza with huge space-frame roof by Tange, Arata Isozaki and the Metabolists expressed the optimistic technological positivism of the era such as the Expo Tower by Kiyonori Kikutake and Takara Beauty-Rion and Toshiba IHI Hall designed by Kisho Kurokawa. Expo 70 was an international event that celebrated Japan's rapid economic growth during the 1960s. The Festival Plaza, as its centerpiece, served as a theatrical space; it brought together a great number of performers and visitors for large-scale ceremonies and performances using the new technologies of the time. Under the leadership of Kenzo Tange, Isozaki participated in drawing up the Expo's master-plan and conceived of the concept and programmatic activities of the central plaza as a cybernetic environment that celebrated the period of "giant technology." Rather than construct solid architectural form, Isozaki sought to realize the potential of ephemeral architecture as a momentary and experiential place. Below the giant space-frame roof designed by Tange and URTEC that could be opened to the sky, Isozaki orchestrated robots that swirled around on the ground with movable seating and dramatic sound and lighting controlled by computers. Using then cutting-edge equipment, Isozaki utilized hundreds of speakers and synthesizers coordinated by computers to create a three-dimensional matrix of sound. Although the technology would soon become outdated, the concept of the "festival plaza" as a variable and continually responsive architecture has continually inspired Isozaki's design.

The 1970s became a period of polarization and diversification among architects as Japan witnessed a value shift from science, technology, and macroeconomics to non-physical and spiritual concerns. The glorious future predicted in the 1960s faded away under the impact of the "oil shock" economic crisis of 1973, and widespread urban problems such as overpopulation, air pollution, and industrial waste.

The younger, "radical" architects of this period, unlike the Metabolists, searched for an improved quality of life within the existing environment rather than reaching for monumental, technologically based conceptions. The multiple options for practice included pursuing architecture as an ideologue, artist, or artisan. The ideological trajectory could be seen in the work of the informal ArchiteXt group including architects Aida Takefumi and Minoru Takeyama supported individualistic, experimental architecture. The architects Aida Takefumi, Takamitsu Azuma, Mayumi Miyawaki, Makoto Suzuki and Minoru Takeyama were born in the 1930s and were formed in the early post-war period in Japan. The group's name is a parody of other groups including Archigram and Team X, with "X" as a satirical reference to the reading of "texts." Representative buildings include Takeyama's Ichi-ban Kan and Ni-ban Kan (1970) housing bars and clubs in Tokyo's Kabuki-cho area of Shinjuku in reinforced concrete volumes brightly painted with abstract, dynamic supergraphics.

Rejecting the urban environment, many architects looked inward to the design of small private houses. Hiroshi Hara's own Reflection House (1973–74) embedded an ideal city inside a simple wooden box illuminated from within through a series of cloud-shaped acrylic skylights. Tadao Andō exposed concrete Row House at Sumiyoshi (1976) completely closed off contact with its neighborhood to focus on the central courtyard open to light and rain. The curved concrete enclosure of Toyō Itō's White U House (1976) also lacks openings to the continuous internal living space with only selected views of the central courtyard to accentuate the purity of space and light.

Other architects looked to the purity of Platonic geometric form free from direct structural or historical meaning in projects. Representative projects include Kazuo Shinohara's Cubic Forest house (1971) and Sei-ichi Shirai's oval block Noa Building (1974) finished with smooth blackened bronze plates on top of a rusticated red brick base. Arata Isozaki's Gunma Prefectural Museum of Fine Arts (1974) was based on a series of 12-meter cubic frames in which he conceived of the "art gallery as void." As Isozaki described, "wrenched from all context, the new gallery offers a

21.7   Minoru Takeyama, Ichi-ban Kan, Tokyo, 1970

mooring for art works "floating" around the world. The aluminium-covered cubic frame established the basic envelope; exhibition and circulation facilities reveal a supplemental structure; a museum is born of the complex interactions between them." The series of cubes form a primary rectangular block housing the main exhibition spaces and two shorter projecting wings. The entry block intersects the rectangular block perpendicularly, while the double-cube block elevated above a square reflecting pool housing a gallery for traditional Japanese art intersects the block at 22.5 degrees. The south façade is clad in 1.2-meter square panels of glass and 2-mm-thick aluminium panels that cover the structural columns to create a glistening gridded surface. The effect of the abstract geometric form evoke multiple interpretations, as Isozaki elaborates on in the essay "The Metaphor of the Cube," ranging from Kasimir Malevich, Piet Mondrian, Sol Lewitt and Superstudio, to Japanese *tateokoshi* plan drawings.

In the 1980s, the unprecedented economic boom led to skyrocketing land prices, fueling a "bubble economy" and rekindling a building boom under the influence of Post-Modernism which brought the Metabolism of post-war modern Japan to an end. This pluralistic architecture freely interpreted history and style, incorporating elements of locality and popular culture. Escalated construction activity and intensified urbanization brought on the multiplicity of built forms in which everything seemed to be realizable.

21.8   Arata Isozaki, Tsukuba Center Building complex, Tsukuba, Ibaraki Prefecture,1983

Arata Isozaki pursued an ironic, mannerist ideology in the design of his Tsukuba Center Building complex (1983). Seeking to break free from a totalizing compositional system, Isozaki followed non-hierarchical principles to bring together classical precedents, modernist elements and references to his own previous work. The design employs the Platonic elements of the square, circle, and triangle and the three-dimensional translations of cubes, spheres and cylinders in the exterior and interior forms and surfaces. At the center, Isozaki consciously transposed the Western precedent of Michelangelo's Piazza del Campidoglio (1538–1650) in Rome by submerging a central oval plaza accessed along the north–south axis or along an organic cascading waterfall. The juxtaposition of geometric and organic forms is reinforced by the contrasting material expression of rough and smooth locally quarried granite in the plaza, glazed and unglazed silver exterior tile juxtaposed with aluminum panels and exposed concrete. One can read classical references to Claude Nicholas Ledoux (1736–1806) in the exterior columns or to Francesco Borromini (1599–1667) in the elliptical windows, while also experiencing abstract illusory spaces such as the detached hotel banquet hall that evokes the illusion of being in a sphere within a cube through tricks of lighting or the illusion of transposed cubes in the concert hall foyer. For Isozaki, the fragmented assemblage consciously evokes the image of ruins to create "a schizophrenic state of suspension. The fragments lose their birthplaces and points of origin. Dispersed as forms, shapes, elements and pieces devoid of meaning in the space called contemporary time, they flash on and off through the operation of metaphor. The effective method in this case is assembling fragments, as in a collage or a patchwork quilt."[4]

The increasingly heterogeneous urban character of Japan during the late 1980s informed architects' bold architectural world views. Fumihiko Maki addressed the dynamic character of Tokyo through the assemblage of Eastern and Western elements in the geometric façade and spatial organization of the cultural complex known as the Spiral Building (1985). In the urban hinterland of metropolitan Tokyo, Hiroshi Hara's Yamato International Building (1987) as the headquarters of a fashion company evoked the image of a virtual urbanscape inspired by vernacular hilltown and Itsuko Hasegawa's Shōnandai Cultural Center (1989) expressed a "second nature" through a composition of globes and crystalline forms, and fairytale silver trees along a vibrant river plaza. Extending the fantastical limits of science fiction, Shin Takamatsu's Kirin Plaza Osaka (1987) composed of four illuminated towers and shimmering details reflecting the vibrancy of the surrounding entertainment district and Kazuo Shinohara's aluminium-clad Tokyo Institute of Technology Centennial Hall (1988) evoked images of the animated Gundam robot or a crashed plane fuselage connecting the railway station with campus. Tadao Andō's Church on the Water (1988) and Church of Light (1989) provided minimally tranquil worldviews through exposed concrete enclosures focused simply on natural elements.

The effects of the Japanese "bubble economy" greatly inflating real estate and stock prices transformed Japanese urbanism vertically at varied scales. Individual residences became pencil buildings in projects such as Waro Kishi's House at

21.9   Fumihiko Maki, Spiral Building, Tokyo, 1985

21.10   Shin Takamatsu, Kirin Plaza Osaka, 1987

21.11   Kazuo
Shinohara,
Tokyo Institute
of Technology
Centennial
Hall,1988

Nipponbashi (Osaka, 1992) with four levels stacked within its 2.5-meter width. The former water treatment plants of western Shinjuku became the site of the new high-rise office district symbolically crowned by Kenzō Tange's neo-gothic twin tower Tokyo City Hall (1991). In Osaka, Hiroshi Hara's Umeda Sky Building (1993) connected twin towers by a dramatic circular sky bridge.

Nonetheless, the great rise of buildings in Japan has been accompanied by an equal descent or "what goes up must come down."[5] Tange's first Tokyo City Hall(1957) was torn down to make room for Rafael Viñoly's Tokyo International Forum (1992–96). Despite the seemingly timeless geometrical character of Kazuo Shinohara's House in Yokohama (1984) and Toyō Itō's White U, they were both torn down—1994 and 1997 respectively. As one of the most extreme examples, Masaharu Takasaki's spaceship-like Crystal Light Guest House stood for a few short years (1986–89).

21.12   Waro Kishi, House at
Nipponbashi, Osaka, 1992

21.13   Kenzō Tange, Tokyo City Hall, Tokyo, 1991

21.14   Rafael Viñoly, Tokyo International
Forum, Tokyo,1992–96

Following constant cycles of boom and recession, Japan's post-bubble period has witnessed the longest recession on record and stimulated renovation and reuse projects. The positivism of post-war Japan has been replaced by a period of reflection on the structural paradigms of the economy, society, and even building regulations. Japan now faced a rapidly aging and shrinking population. The shift between pre and post-bubble Japan follows a shift from industrial to service and information based society. 1995 was marked by the wide-scale destruction caused by both the Kobe Earthquake and the Aum Tokyo subway gassing attack. The end of the century witnessed the end of "lifetime employment" in Japan. The subsequent generation of architects addressed smaller-scale issues such as Atelier Bow Wow "pet architecture" or Shigeru Ban's work with cardboard tubes and residential projects such as the Furniture House (1995) or Curtain Wall House (1995). In contrast to the visionary Metabolist megastructures of the 1960s, micro-urban designs have embraced the dynamism of the heterogeneous city as articulated in Atelier Bow Wow's *Made in Tokyo* (1998) and through the design of individual dwellings such as their own House and Atelier Bow Wow (2005) nestled on a tight urban Tokyo site.

In the twenty-first century planners once again have contrasting visions for the twenty-first century ranging from a great number of high-rise projects throughout Tokyo to more radical ones such as Toyō Itō's Sendai Mediatheque (1995–2001), with its seaweed-like steel tube structure, or SANAA's circular glazed 21st Century Museum of Contemporary Art (2004) that reconsider fundamental principles, programs and conceptions of architecture. High fashion and luxury brands have most recently supported architectural experimentation in works as Jun Aoki's metal screen Louis Vuitton Store (2002), SANAA's crystalline Dior Omote Sando (2001–03) and Herzog and De Meuron's glazed diamond grid Prada Store (2003). These architects' practices have become increasingly global, seen in SANAA's undulating concrete slab Rolex Learning Center (2010) in Lausanne, Switzerland and Shigeru Ban's Center Pompidou-Metz (2010). SANAA's architectural achievements have been acknowledged by their winning of the 2010 Pritzker Prize and Kazuyo Sejima's directorship of the 2010 Venice Architectural Biennale. The exhibition featured Sejima's protégé Junya Ishigami in his Golden Lion-winning minimal installation of a 0.9mm diameter carbon fiber structure that infamously was knocked down by a cat almost immediately after completion. With global economic changes including the 2008 bankruptcy of Lehman Brothers and the devastation caused by the 2011 Great East Japan earthquake, architects in Japan are reminded of Isozaki's assertion that "the future city lies in ruins."

21.15   SANAA, Dior Omote Sando, Tokyo, 2001–03

NOTES

1   Published as "Ruins" in *Architectural Apocalypse: Ryuji Miyamoto*, Heibonsha, 1988. 「廃墟論」「建築の黙示録」（宮本隆司写真集、１９８８、平凡社）, 4–11.

2   "Premos" derived its name from "pre" for prefab, M for Maekawa, O for Kaoru Ono, who was a structural engineer and professor at Tokyo University, and S for the San' in Manufacturing Company. See Jonathan Reynolds, *Maekawa Kunio and the Emergence of Japanese Modernist Architecture* (Berkeley: University of California Press, 2001), 146–49.

3   Nishi Kazuo, "Prehabu jûtaku no dai ikkan wo miru (Looking at the first period of prefab houses)," *"Gendai kenchiku no kiseki" Shinkenchiku*, special issue (December 1995): 146.

4   Arata Isozaki, *The Island Nation Aesthetic* (London: Academy Editions, 1996), 51–2.

5   Botond Bognar, "What goes up, must come down: Recent urban architecture in Japan," *Harvard Design Magazine*, 1997 Autumn 1997, 33–43.

22

Edge of Centre: Architecture in Australia and New Zealand after 1965

Philip Goad

Long regarded, often romantically, as an edge condition both intellectually and geographically, the architectures of Australia and New Zealand have, over the past 50 years, charted theoretical and material practices that have realized a unique place in contemporary architectural production. Two former British settler colonies, highly urbanized and highly modernized, with divided historical, economic and political allegiances to the United Kingdom and the United States but placed within the context of Asia and the Pacific Ocean, possessing natural landscapes of profound beauty and climatic challenge, yet beset by ethical and competing crises of national identity and indigenous reconciliation, the architectures of these two countries are sustained by an archipelago of discrete urban cultures rooted in deeply self-aware local critique and frequent anxiety for participation in a broader global conversation.[1] This chapter maps the extrapolations of and inclusivist deviations from modernism since the 1960s: the rediscovery of the vernacular; the embrace of indigenous culture; the modernist shaping and Post-Modernist re-shaping of the Antipodean city and the rediscovery of the suburb; the regionalist 'answer' of form-determining climate, and most recently, the deployment of digital techniques as part of a search for significant form. The result, in both countries, is threefold: the perpetuation of and mythologizing of the detached house (as an 'elegant shed', to use the clichéd New Zealand term);[2] the ongoing conundrum of civic representation; and the need to address the realities and social inequities of intensification in the face of inevitable urban growth. In short, these are two worldly architecture cultures alternately celebrated and riven by artifice and ethics.

Separated by the Tasman Sea, over a distance of around 1,500 km, Australia and New Zealand are physically very different. An island continent, Australia has a land area of 7.6 million square kilometres (the sixth largest country in the world) and a population of just 22.7 million. By contrast, New Zealand is 28 times smaller with a land area of 268,000 square kilometres, spread over two islands, the North and South Islands, and with a total population of 4.4 million. But there are remarkable similarities. Both are developed countries hence privileged within the Asia-Pacific region, highly urbanized, each with major urban centres attended by sprawling suburbs. In Australia, for example, the state capitals of Adelaide, Brisbane, Hobart, Melbourne, Perth, Sydney and Canberra account for 65 per cent of the population, while in New Zealand, the two major cities of Auckland and Wellington in the North Island and Christchurch in the South Island accommodate 52 per cent of the population. At the same time, both countries culturally identify with their respective landscapes. For New Zealand, this includes alpine peaks, rolling plains and volcanoes, and a land subject to earthquakes. It also includes the ever-present Pacific Ocean, from where Polynesians migrated to New Zealand between AD 1250 and 1300 and thence developed their aesthetically refined Maori culture. In Australia, given its vast size, landscapes range from tropical jungle and sub-tropical savannah in the north, to huge uninhabitable expanses of desert in the west and centre, and temperate bush plains in the southeast, where the major cities hug the coast. Both countries were settled by the British: Australia as the penal colony of New South Wales from 1788 and New Zealand from the early nineteenth century peripatetically when it was visited by whalers, sealers and traders, then settled first by missionaries and later as a colony of New South Wales (i.e. ruled from Sydney) before becoming an independent Crown colony in 1841.

Both countries have a history of conflicted relationships with their indigenous communities. In New Zealand, the British signed the Waitangi Treaty with the Maori in 1840; and despite the bloody wars of the 1860s and 1870s, the gradual understanding, acceptance and celebration of Maori culture has become an intrinsic part of modern-day New Zealand culture, despite tensions owing to poverty and alienation amongst urban Maori. The significance of Maori art and architecture has developed a sophisticated scholarship, and especially since the mid 1970s with research by Mike Austin, and later by Peter Shaw and Deidre Brown.[3] Ethical awareness of indigenous architectural forms, rituals and spatial habits has enriched, on the whole, highly articulate theoretical positions amongst successive generations of progressive architects that also include a small but influential number of architects of Maori extraction. By contrast, in Australia, the mostly nomadic aboriginal population was largely submissive, eradicated in total in Tasmania, and for the most part, subjugated, forced off their homelands and subject to European disease, alcoholism or converted to Christianity. Though subject to intense scrutiny by anthropologists like Baldwin Spencer, the spatial and architectural traditions of the aboriginal tribes who had lived on the Australian continent for more than 40,000 years, were almost totally ignored. It was not until the 1980s that practitioners and academics like Col James, Paul Pholeros and Paul Memmott began to work with local peoples (urban and ex-urban) and document familial patterns, spatial typologies and the architectural aspects of aboriginal encampments. Memmott's *Gunyah, Goondie and Wurley: The Aboriginal Architecture of Australia* (2007) is a seminal work[4] but also an indictment on the fact that Australia's first comprehensive architectural history, which appeared in 1968 had no indigenous content at all.[5] At that time in architectural circles, all focus in Australia, as it was in New Zealand, was on a local embrace of modernism.

THE 1960s: LOCAL VIEWS OF MODERNISM

By the late 1960s, architectural commentators in the two countries could point to the emergence of distinctly local, regional forms of modern architectural expression. Robin Boyd, for example, detected a flourishing of architectural invention by a group of Sydney architects, later labelled as the Sydney School (Figure 22.1).[6]

This architecture of clinker bricks, skillion roofs of terra cotta tiles and stained timber structure and trim would emerge from the houses, schools and university buildings by firms like Ancher, Mortlock, Murray & Woolley and individuals like Ian McKay, Philip Cox, Tony Moore and Peter Johnson as well as by Michael Dysart with the NSW Government Architect's Branch, all of whom shared interests in British responses to Brutalism, where many young Australians had gained their post-war experience, as well as long-held interests in Scandinavian architecture, especially the institutional and religious buildings of Finnish architects Alvar Aalto and Heikki and Kaija Siren. Reasons for this affinity with Scandinavia could be found in local sympathies with landscape and in a recognition that construction and craft techniques drawn from the domestic vernacular did not preclude but instead invoked a humanized modernism.

Such a regionalist argument was not limited to Sydney. Scholars in both Australia and New Zealand have since indicated a similar reaction and empathy for site-based planning, the honest use of materials and texture and expressed structure

22.1   Ken Woolley, Exterior, Woolley House, Mosman, NSW, Australia, 1962

(especially in reinforced concrete) that was endemic to work found in all regions at the time. In 1967, Peter Beaven published an article on 'South Island Architecture' in the *RIBA Journal*, in which he made a strong case for acknowledging the climate, materials and geology of the Canterbury Plains as well as the local architecture culture's ties to English and Scottish ideals. Beaven also stressed the region's 'refinement in concrete technique and structural clarity' as earthquake precaution, hence a design dexterity in the use of fair-faced concrete beams and blockwork, singling out Warren & Mahoney's Student Union Building at the University of Canterbury in Christchurch (1964–67) for special attention (Figure 22.2).[7]

Beaven's own work differed from that of Warren & Mahoney. While still employing vigorous material and structural articulation, his multi-storey Manchester Unity Friendly Society Building in Christchurch (1964–67) with its mansard roof and precast struts on ground level, and his Canterbury Arcade Building in Auckland (1965–67) both indicate a close affinity to the work of Italian architects like Belgiojoso Peressutti & Rogers (BPR), and a desire to introduce European urbanism and contextual response to the historic city in the Antipodes (Figure 22.3).

In Australia too, the growing confidence in formal expression was explored by architects with small-scale municipal buildings in landscape settings like Edwards, Madigan, Torzillo & Briggs's Warringah Shire Library in Dee Why, NSW (1967) and Borland and Jackson's Harold Holt Swimming Centre in Glen Iris, VIC (1969) where off-form concrete and large-span interiors, were progenitors of much larger, monumental works to come (Figure 22.4).[8]

At the same time Yuncken Freeman's Victorian State Offices in Melbourne (1962–70) indicated a clear understanding of the historic colonial city in its careful arrangement of offices and offset tower to respect the axial view of JJ Clark's Renaissance Revival Treasury Building. It was clear that within the architecture cultures of both countries there was a latent *rapprochement* with history and the city.[9]

22.2   Warren & Mahoney, Student Union Building, University of Canterbury, Ilam Campus, Christchurch, New Zealand, 1964–67

22.3   Peter Beaven, Canterbury Arcade Building, Auckland, New Zealand, 1965–67

22.4   Edwards
Madigan Torzillo &
Briggs, Warringah
Shire Library,
Dee Why, NSW,
Australia, 1967

THE 1960s: AMERICAN INFLUENCE

At the same time, the 1960s saw American influence on Australian and New Zealand popular culture and politics reach its peak.[10] Since WWII, Australia and New Zealand had looked to the United States more than ever before – and not only politically. In 1966 and 1967, the Australian and New Zealand currencies went decimal and allegiance to British pounds and pence was dropped. From the 1950s, the wholesale adoption of American-derived forms of popular architecture like motels, shopping centres, drive-in cinemas, take-away food restaurants, and bowling alleys became widespread. In the 1960s the promotion of international tourism and the design and construction of large high-rise hotels like the Southern Cross Hotel in Melbourne (1962) by Leslie M. Perrott & Partners with Los Angeles architect Welton Becket, and Skidmore Owings & Merrill's Wentworth Hotel in Sydney (1962–66), as well as the Intercontinental Hotel in Auckland (1966–67) promised and delivered American glamour to the Antipodean city.

The popular love affair with things American had been a prophecy forecast with some dismay by Robin Boyd in *The Australian Ugliness*, his 1960 book, which became a bestseller on both sides of the Tasman.[11] On the one hand, Boyd's eloquently argued tract was part of a general push by the late 1950s for a new environmental awareness, finding champions for wilderness in architect-turned activist Milo Dunphy and a heightened awareness of the urban environment in books like Boyd's and also Don Gazzard's *Australian Outrage* (1966), whose message borrowed directly from *The Architectural Review's* campaign for urban beautification in the 1950s.[12] On the other hand, Boyd was acutely aware that the Australian city was rapidly being remade in the face of corporate capital.

Increasing affluence and growth characterized the two countries in the 1960s. Despite a credit squeeze in 1961, major Australian and New Zealand cities grew upwards and their suburbs spread outwards. In response to what appeared to be unmitigated suburban sprawl, some architects like Ken Woolley, Michael Dysart and Graeme Gunn were enlisted by progressive project house builders such as Pettit & Sevitt in Sydney and Merchant Builders in Melbourne to design good quality houses for the middle and outer suburbs, and unusually often combining landscape designs that incorporated Australian native plants, and planned around existing trees.

As distant landscapes of the Australian continent were ruthlessly engineered for their mining resources, there were also accompanying developments, which had architectural implications. Company mining towns, designed as idealized Radburn-

22.5 Yuncken Freeman, BHP House, Melbourne, Victoria, Australia, 1967–72

styled suburbs in remote tropical or arid locations like Weipa (1967) in far north Queensland by Don Hendry Fulton, or Bill Howroyd's Shay Gap in the Pilbara, WA (1970s) were matched by their parent corporations erecting iconic skyscrapers in the city. Yuncken Freeman's BHP House in Melbourne (1967–72) was the epitome: a Miesian steel and glass shaft tapered for aesthetic effect, its steel carapace indicative not just of the firm's main product – steel and iron ore – but also doubling as formwork and cladding. This was a significant technical advance, typical of an Australian penchant for lean constructive means. BHP House was also a formalist temple-tower in the spirit of Mies, at once affirming and dissolving the colonial grid of its site (Figure 22.5).[13] In Wellington, the Bank of New Zealand (BNZ) built its own version of BHP House, a 30 storey black glass tower by Stephenson & Turner (1972–73, 1974–84), taking 10 years to complete, by which time architectural ideas had moved on, rendering its mute darkness incomprehensible to a new generation of architects.

HARRY SEIDLER: A LIFELONG MODERNISM

An architect with a lifetime commitment to a very specific form of modernism and the city and who was unfazed by the inexorable march of architectural ideas was Viennese émigré Harry Seidler (1923–2006), classmate of IM Pei and Edward Larrabee Barnes at Harvard.[14] Instead of finding patronage within government, Harry Seidler's relationship with developer Dick Dusseldorp (1918–2000) was the key to a modernist urbanism based on speculative capital and the particularities of the Sydney landscape, capturing its panorama for private consumption, and wherever possible producing a luxuriant, Brazilian-inspired landscape at ground level. It was Dusseldorp who was the first developer[15] to use site amalgamation, which enabled Seidler to design freestanding towers that wrested central Sydney's urban morphology from its original chaotic street pattern and instated new public landscapes that responded to Sydney's harbour-side topography and included works of public art by international (rather than local) modernist artists.

22.6 Harry Seidler, Australia Square, Sydney, NSW, Australia, 1961–67

The early climax of this collaboration between architect and developer in Sydney was the completion of Australia Square (1961–67), a site formed by the consolidation of 31 small properties. Australia Square was an ensemble of buildings and spaces: a 50-storey circular office tower, a separate lower slab office block of 13 floors, an urban plaza with fountains, and a series of commissioned artworks. At the time of its completion in 1967, the tower stood as Sydney's tallest building and the world's tallest lightweight concrete building, a feat achieved with the assistance of Pier Luigi Nervi (Figure 22.6). Visually, the tower need not be considered altogether rational – it could be considered as a cylindrical rod held in visual counterpoint by a lower level prism (the office slab) and further contrasted with, at ground level, a circular fountain, circular planting beds and a piece of abstract sculpture – as it eventuated an abstract black steel piece by Alexander Calder. In other words, at a giant scale, the whole complex could be read as the deft arrangement of a series of objects. It was a new form of urban art.[16] With the plaza and its different levels, the fountain and circular beds, the edges of which could also be seats, Seidler had created the sort of urbanism which Sigfried Giedion had hoped for – a space worthy of the Baroque in its overlay of art, sculpture and architecture in service of the city. The difference being that instead of the ideology of the Church being the generator for such a confluence of the arts as it was during the Baroque period, in 1960s Sydney it was driven by a new form of real estate development whereby corporations would seek to be tenants of an iconic 'designed' development rather commission a new building in their own right.[17]

Seidler's work with Dusseldorp and his conception of the modernist city in Australia proved to be resilient, despite Post-Modernist criticism in the 1980s. His subsequent skyscrapers in Sydney, Melbourne, Perth and Brisbane to the late 1990s increasingly adopted the Baroque curves of Niemeyer and Burle Marx at podium and ground level to create artful public landscapes financed by private speculation that in each case attempted the modernist dissolution of the historic city. His last, Riparian Plaza, Brisbane (1999–2005) was a tripartite composition of parking, office and residential functions, each part identified sculpturally, graphically scaled for the immediate, middle and distant view, all celebrating the panorama: Seidler's dramatic swansong for a tropical skyscraper.

ARCHITECTURE AND GOVERNMENT, 1960s–1970s

If the United States formed a potent model for the formal transformation of the central city, it also held sway as Australia's national capital, Canberra, was being consolidated in the 1960s. While buildings such as Bunning & Madden and Tom O'Mahoney's colonnaded and marble-clad National Library of Australia (1964–68) constituted examples of a prim modern classicism also favoured in Washington DC, the competitions for the National Gallery of Australia (1967, 1973–82) and the High Court of Australia (1972, 1975–80), both won and realized by Edwards, Madigan Torzillo & Briggs, suggested a different, more confident form of internationalism – in effect a late flowering of state-sponsored Brutalism. The return to Australia of Toronto-based expatriate John Andrews, from his hugely successful Canadian American practice, to work on the Cameron Offices at Belconnen in Canberra (1969–77) was another signal that off-form concrete, systems thinking and large-scale megastructural approaches to planning and building, with a sensitive adaptation to topography, were to find full favour, especially in Canberra, which had embarked on an extraordinary programme of monumental buildings for the nation and for its burgeoning satellite suburbs. The election in 1972 of a new Labor Federal Government under Gough Whitlam would see many of these projects finally commence construction, and usher in a new generation of young architects whose work, while commissioned under a Liberal Government, would come to be associated with Canberra's reformist years under Labour.

In New Zealand, the scale of nation building through architecture was understandably more modest. The controversial commissioning in 1964 of British architect Sir Basil Spence to extend New Zealand's Parliament Building, designed in 1911 by Campbell & Paton, attested to the country's persistent and strong Anglo-ties. When finally opened in 1977 (but not completed until 1982), the distinctive shape of the building – a tapering cylinder atop a three-storey drum with a copper crown housing a Cabinet Room and offices – confirmed its nickname 'The Beehive', and its image as 'perhaps New Zealand's most recognized of the twentieth century' (Figure 22.7).[18] While the analogy with the traditional European 'skep' or woven basket for a beehive can be easily made and has been the subject of research by others,[19] Spence may also have been alluding to New Zealand's North Island landscape of

22.7   Sir Basil Spence, Executive Wing, Parliament Buildings, Wellington, New Zealand, 1964–77

remnant and active volcanoes. A form such as this, while functionally problematic, may have been imbued with a stronger symbolic intention on Spence's part: to reconcile a once indigenous landscape with an irredeemably colonized one.

Public works in New Zealand in the late 1960s and early 1970s, handled largely by the Ministry of Works, were focused on buildings for the tertiary education sector, most notably the University of Waikato campus in Hamilton (1963–1970s), the Ilam campus of the University of Canterbury (1960s-1970s), and Turitea campus of Massey University, Palmerston North (1960–78). Australian universities also experienced unprecedented expansion during this period, including the creation of new institutions like Curtin University (WA), James Cook University (QLD), Monash University and La Trobe University (VIC), in addition to architecturally significant buildings – almost all, in a vigorous Brutalist idiom – produced on campuses across the nation by architects like James Birrell, Dickson & Platten, Eggleston Macdonald & Secomb, and especially, the NSW Government Architects Office under Chief Architect E.H. (Ted) Farmer. At the University of Western Australia in Perth, Gus Ferguson's Law Building (1964–67) was a mature expression of contextually and climatically appropriate Brutalism. It was on these campuses, for the most part, planned as idealized pedestrian environments, that a young generation of architects either chanced their arm at megastructure or explored the lessons of propinquity. In both countries, the university in parallel to the dream of the single-family house became the laboratory for the sort of experiment that the speculative city would rarely countenance.

AUSTRALIA: THE SHIFT TOWARDS POST-MODERNISM

In most Australian cities in the 1970s, there was a sense of disillusion with what the brightness of the 1960s had promised. Slum clearance programs dreamt about in the late 1930s finally came to pass at the hands of various housing commissions. Great swathes of inner city terrace houses, especially in Melbourne and Sydney, were swept away in the name of social progress and replaced by low-income, often high-rise and high density housing. In central business districts across all state capital cities, nineteenth and early twentieth-century streetscapes were decimated as buildings were toppled in favour of urban tower and plaza concepts. The community was not unaware of such hazards and from the mid 1950s, state branches of the National Trust were formed in Australia and in 1954 the New Zealand Historic Places Trust was established. But it was only in the early 1970s that a coherent heritage movement would emerge and result in the formulation of internationally significant conservation principles such as the Burra Charter (1979) and the growth of a branch of the architectural profession, which was devoted to conservation and the adaptive reuse of existing or historic buildings.

The early 1970s were critical years in Australia. The premature death of architect-critic Robin Boyd in 1971 and the opening of the Sydney Opera House in 1973, completed by Peter Hall after Danish architect Jørn Utzon's controversial departure in 1966, appeared to turn the page on the modernist chapter in Australian architecture. Three strands of architectural interest, often intertwined, were to develop by the early 1980s. All three in most respects abdicated a role in the city, which had become a frequent battleground for the retention of historic buildings and landscapes. Significantly all three strands were indicative of local architecture cultures intent on reflection.

The first was a return to scientific or socio-psychological principles either related to the making of architecture according to climate and landscape through a renewed interest in passive solar energy, alternative energy sources, alternative lifestyles and intensive community participation, each in many respects a counter-culture to the already embattled aesthetic counter-currents of orthodox modernism. This was exemplified by the participatory practices of Morrice Shaw in building community playgrounds in Sydney in the 1970s, the diverse practices of architecture student activism across all university campuses like Tone Wheeler's low-energy sustainable 'autonomous house' (1974) made entirely from recycled materials and designed to generate all its power and recycle all its waste,[20] Sydney Baggs's earth constructions, and the open studio practice of Melbourne architect Kevin Borland, whose master work with Bernard Brown, the Clyde Cameron Union Training College at Wodonga, VIC (1975–57), in off-form giant concrete sewer pipes, concrete block and industrial glazing, was a free-wheeling Metabolist design, a sort of low-tech Pompidou Centre for the workers.[21]

The second was a resurfacing of a latent interest in the 'honest' functional tradition of Australia's nineteenth- and early twentieth-century rural and regional architecture. Architects since the 1970s like Glenn Murcutt and Philip Cox in NSW, and Rex Addison, Gabriel Poole and John Mainwaring in Queensland, and Troppo Architects in Darwin (after 1981) had begun to critically re-examine earlier prototypical vernacular architecture, not just for its aesthetic virtues but also for its appropriateness as regards climate, structure, materials, formal typologies and spatial traditions (Figure 22.8). The rediscovery of the verandah and corrugated iron, for example, was just one part of this reconsideration. The work of these architects, located mostly outside urban centres, became significantly influential and well-known internationally. Murcutt's houses, for example, reaffirm the ideology of the villa, as a contemporary interpretation of the Palladian ideal, situated within a romantic pastoral landscape or standing heroically amidst untouched wilderness.

The third was related to an emerging Post-Modernism. Influenced largely by events in the United States, this was a move by a younger generation of architects to return to the artifice of architecture and a re-engagement with the city. While Charles Moore's Sea Ranch (1965) was well known and reinterpreted across Australia in a variety of idioms, firms like Heffernan, Nation Rees & Viney in Tasmania, Cocks & Carmichael and individuals like Peter Crone in Victoria experimented in the 1970s with individual house designs, producing local interpretations of the work of the New York Five.[22] In Sydney Douglas Gordon had been designing Venturi-influenced houses since returning from the United States in 1964.[23] Peter Corrigan wrote about the work of Robert Venturi in *Architecture Australia* in 1972.[24] In October 1974 Charles Jencks visited Australia and gave lectures and interviews.[25] In 1979, the exhibition 'Four Melbourne Architects' was set up in Melbourne as a cheeky

22.8   Troppo Architects, Green Can House, Darwin, Northern Territory, Australia, 1980

inclusivist Post-Modern challenge to the decade-old New York phenomenon of sleek neo-Corbusian formalism.[26]

It was also in Melbourne that the critical journal *Transition* appeared in 1979, featuring articles by Australian academics on Post-Modernism. For the next 20 years, the journal celebrated a decidedly local and arguably parochial focus on Melbourne's critical design culture, with satellites of criticality revisiting the modernist project in Perth at the University of Western Australia.[27] In 1980, the RAIA National Convention in Sydney, orchestrated by Andrew Metcalf, under the theme 'The Pleasures of Architecture' featured keynote speakers Michael Graves, Rem Koolhaas and George Baird. The Australian profession, it seemed, had officially gone Post-Modern.[28]

AUSTRALIA: DISCOURSE AND DIVISIONS FROM THE 1970s TO 2000

From the mid 1970s, the Melbourne practices of Edmond & Corrigan, Norman Day, academic Conrad Hamann,[29] and an even younger generation of architects like Richard Munday, Ian McDougall and Howard Raggatt (later founding partners of Ashton Raggatt McDougall), intellectualized the shift towards accepting the suburban vernacular and its ordinary everyday qualities, along with the importance of acknowledging aesthetic intentions behind a work of architecture. The Expressionist plans and strident polychrome brickwork forms of Edmond & Corrigan's Resurrection Church in Keysborough, VIC (1976–81) and the Chapel of St Joseph in Box Hill, VIC (1976–78) constituted key moments in Australian architecture, where the certainties of orthodox modernism were completely swept away (Figure 22.9). From the 1980s onwards, this group of Melbourne architects often played a controversial role in their advocacy of radical formal and semiotic experiments. Their embrace of the 'ugly and ordinary' was often visceral, while the rest of the nation looked on at these developments – largely with suspicion.

22.9   Edmond
& Corrigan,
Resurrection
Church,
Keysborough,
Victoria, Australia,
1976–81

At the same time, in Sydney and elsewhere around Australia there were few advocates of Melbourne's upturning of style and taste. Seidler, for example, remained an active and outspoken opponent of Post-Modernism. Others like Espie Dods and Alec Tzannes shifted with the times, but revisited the urbane manners of 1920s architects Leslie Wilkinson and John D Moore in carefully controlled villas and townhouses, encouraging an interest in the city's urban morphology that would be pursued 20 years later by Philip Thalis, Peter-John Cantrill and the firm of Durbach Block.[30] Glenn Murcutt's presence in Australian discourse was undeniable in the mid 1980s, highlighted through Philip Drew's best-selling *Leaves of Iron: Glenn Murcutt, Pioneer of an Australian Architectural Form* (1985).[31] In the context of Post-Modernism and Kenneth Frampton's anxious call for a critical regionalism (1983), Murcutt's lean linear villas satisfied, for many, a dual longing – for history on the one hand, and for a romantic resistance to the speculative city on the other. Murcutt's most notable works, located outside the city and hence heroically disengaged, soon gained a mythical status (Figure 22.10). These were complemented by the teachings of Richard Leplastrier in Sydney and Newcastle, whose small number of exquisitely crafted houses in Arcadian landscapes reinforced a persuasive theoretical position based on phenomenology and place.[32] In Brisbane, Brit Andresen and Peter O'Gorman pursued similar themes, building a small number of seminal detached houses on evocative sites and landscapes.[33] Thus for successive generations of young graduates in Sydney, Brisbane, and Newcastle, the key problem of Australian architecture appeared to be the finely crafted domestic pavilion, placed delicately in the landscape.

22.10   Glenn Murcutt, Magney House, Bingie Bingie, NSW, Australia, 1982–84

AUSTRALIA: THE NEXT GENERATION INTO THE TWENTY-FIRST CENTURY

However, that assumption about Australian architecture being epitomized by the romantic ideal of the single-family house did not prove to be entirely the case. Instead, the current generation of Australian architects, educated through years of Post-Modern revisionism, and having experienced the rise of digital design and sustainability, has brought to architectural practice a decidedly mature outlook. In some cases this has included not just a critical review of modernism itself but also an acute understanding of landscape, the importance of the city, and an aspiration for some form of *civitas*. It was in Melbourne that the semiotic possibilities of digital architecture were explored most vigorously by firms such as Ashton Raggatt McDougall (ARM), reaching its zenith at the National Museum of Australia in Canberra (2001),[34] then by others like Lyons, McBride Charles Ryan and Minifie Nixon in startling formal expositions that continue to draw the awe and ire of local tastemakers, while appearing internationally at the forefront of experimentation in digital design and limited only by Australia's relatively unsophisticated construction practices (Figure 22.11).

For the most part, however, the younger generation of Australian architects tread a fine line, literally edge of centre. There is no sense of intellectual distance from the architectural centres of Europe and the United States. Digital communication and rapid air travel has banished any sense of inferiority: the badge of having studied or worked overseas no longer seems relevant. Instead, practice is knowingly local but concerns are universal. In Brisbane, m3 architecture led by Michael Banney, Michael Christensen and Michael Lavery use materiality and digital manipulation

22.11   Ashton
Raggatt
McDougall,
Storey Hall,
RMIT University,
Melbourne,
Victoria,
Australia, 1995

for experiential effect, as in the Creative Learning Centre at Brisbane Girls Grammar
School (2007) and at the Barcaldine Tree of Knowledge, in Barcaldine, Queensland
(2007–9, with Brian Hooper), where 3,600 individual pieces of recycled timber
outline the canopy of the tree that once grew at the founding site of Australia's
Labor Party (Figure 22.12).

In Victoria, Sean Godsell's linear houses clad in carapaces of recycled timber or
rusted steel revisit modernism as weathered, site responsive monuments while
his RMIT Design Archive (2010–12) flirts with the ornamental possibilities of glass
discs as sunshades. In Sydney, Chenchow Little's 'Pitched Roof House' (2010),
in black steel louvres with clear and milky white glass, appears with its folded
roof not only to suggest comfort with the parametric folds endemic to digital
architecture but through a process of reduction transcends facile sculptural form
(Figure 22.13).

In Brisbane, Donovan Hill's State Library of Queensland (2006, with Peddle
Thorp), explores the eroded monument with a Scarpa-esque attention to detail
through timber battens, off-form concrete and the creation of monumental
indoor-outdoor spaces in its benign sub-tropical climate. John Wardle's numerous
buildings for universities across Australia do the same with astonishing formal
dexterity, reminiscent of the work of Moretti and Ponti, while in Melbourne Wood
Marsh, deploys architecture as large-scale urban art. Other firms such as Neeson
Murcutt in Sydney, Kerstin Thompson, and NMBW in Melbourne advocate a more
earnest return to the essentials of materials, type and place. While self-consciously
austere, the work of these three firms exhibits a Spartan quality that smacks of an
ethics of restraint within an urban environment and a popular culture saturated
with image.

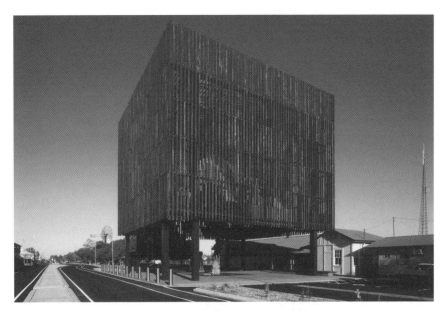

22.12   m3 architecture and Brian Hooper, Tree of Knowledge, Barcaldine, Queensland, Australia, 2007–09

22.13   Chenchow Little, Interior, Pitched Roof House, Sydney, NSW, Australia, 2010

NEW ZEALAND: THE SHIFT TOWARDS POST-MODERNISM AND BEYOND

A similar 'young maturity' is found in the work of contemporary New Zealand architects, who also experienced the full force of Post-Modern revisionism in the 1980s. Two key figures in Zealand's embrace of an alternative form of modernism and described by Paul Walker as 'New Zealand's last modern architects'[35] are Ian Athfield (1940–) and Roger Walker (1942–), who since the late 1960s, have used New Zealand domestic vernacular references and the striking topography of Wellington's steep sites to create compositions that, on one level seem to be free Metabolist/Pop compositions and on the other, highly romantic 'modern' Mediterranean villages. Athfield's work especially has drawn international attention.[36] His own white-plastered house and office (1965–) continues to grow on the side of a hill in Khandallah, Wellington like a never-ending architectural doodle (Figure 22.14). Walker's architecture was and is similar: Pop-scale porthole windows, turret roofs in blue, red and yellow, and expressive timber props at the 30-unit development of Park Mews, Wellington (1974), while his Britten House at Karaka Bay (1974) tumbles, castle-like, over ten levels down a 45-degree slope.

In the 1980s, a new and different generation of architects emerged in New Zealand and from 1990 onwards, the critical journal *Interstices* started its publication out of the University of Auckland. A Maori architect like Rewi Thompson in Auckland tackled mute monumentality in one-off houses, especially his own – a glowering ziggurat plywood box in Kohimarama (1985) – and the challenges of group housing for Maori in South Auckland. Others like Fearon Hay and Mitchell/Stout carved houses into the landscape, a habit Paul Walker and Justine Clark claim as being distinctively different from that of Australian architects,[37] and part of a house-nature dialogue that has conditioned the reception of New Zealand architecture both internally and externally for decades.[38] Such conditioning as exotic, 'other' and different from the centre (a habit applicable to much Australian architecture as well) translated into an acute and self-conscious criticality, particularly on the part of New Zealand architectural scholars, and especially in relation to issues of Maori influence, ideas or authorship in New Zealand's post-war modern architecture. As a result, buildings such as John Scott's Futuna Chapel in Karori, Wellington (1958–61) and JASMaD's Samoa House (Maota Samoa) in Auckland (1977–78) have been much studied for their ability to impart messages about indigenous architectural forms such as the wharenui or the traditional Samoan fale. More recently, the Museum of

22.14   Ian Athfield, Athfield House, Khandallah, Wellington, New Zealand, 1965–

New Zealand, Te Papa Tongarewa, in Wellington (1990–98) by JASMAX Architects, attempted to embody the nation's biculturalism (i.e. Maori and European Pakeha). The museum was planned along easily legible organizing lines that were meant to recognize Maori concepts of landform, city and common or shared earth. The result was a building of noble intentions but disappointingly, an unsurprising collection of ordinary forms.

AUSTRALIA AND NEW ZEALAND: LOCAL AND GLOBAL IN THE TWENTY-FIRST CENTURY

In Australia, the self-conscious acceptance of a complex place in the world and within global architectural discourse has been a long time coming, and arguably with less intensity and less scholarly scrutiny than in New Zealand. There are many reasons for this, not least due to the fact that for decades, indigenous presence and a contested, frequently unpleasant past, was politically and culturally ignored. Ironically, representation across multiple cultures appeared in the 1980 winning entry for the new Parliament House in Canberra by Mitchell Giurgola & Thorp. Designed by Romaldo Giurgola and completed in 1988, Parliament House brought together a range of design themes, both classical and modern. It featured a Beaux Arts plan and echoed the design and landscape intentions of Canberra's original designers Walter Burley Griffin and Marion Mahony. Significantly, facing the nation as it were, a vast 90,000-piece stone mosaic was laid out in its forecourt. Created by indigenous artist Michael Nelson Jagamarra, it was a critical acknowledgment of the indigenous population and its culture (Figure 22.15).

The recognition of aboriginal identity and presence through architecture had arrived late. The Christian missions of the early twentieth century had been the

22.15   Mitchell Giurgola Thorp, Parliament House, Canberra, ACT, Australia, 1980–88

outcome of an earlier attempt by European culture to integrate indigenous people into its society with little understanding of their visual and socio-spatial habits. While artists and architects sporadically included aboriginal motifs in their work in the 1930s, there was little real engagement, either through building or research, until the 1970s. Works by architects like Peter Myers on Tiwi Island in the Northern Territory in the early 1980s were followed by landmark projects by Gregory Burgess at Brambuk Living Cultural Centre in Victoria (1986–90) and Uluru-Kata Tjuta Cultural Centre in Uluru, Northern Territory (1990–95), but also through real collaboration between indigenous people and architects by firms like Tangentyere Design and individuals such as Paul Pholeros, as well as the formation of the Merrima Aboriginal Design Unit by the NSW Public Works Department in 1995.

The acknowledgment of indigenous presence and the concomitant reassessment of the importance of the Australian landscape have played a critical role in the development of Australian architecture in the last decade. The completion of Federation Square in Melbourne in 2002, designed by LAB Architecture Studio, was the nation's largest built project to commemorate the centenary of the Federation of Australia (1901). It evoked not just the qualities of the minor laneways of the adjacent city and the accumulation of its European history but also the colours, materials and spatial qualities of the remote Kimberley landscape in Western Australia, as well as the constructive and aesthetic possibilities of digital architecture.[39] Such a reading of Australian architecture represents a new maturing in understanding the place, a process that will be ongoing. It also suggests that being at edge of centre might represent being part of the new. A similar acknowledgment has occurred and continues within New Zealand architecture.

If indigeneity has played a key role in pricking the intellectual conscience within both countries, there has also been over the last two decades a parallel challenge and different form of professional engagement. The forces and opportunities of globalization have enabled practices like Denton Corker Marshall (DCM), Fender Katsalidis, Woods Bagot, the Cox Group and Architectus to gain significant commissions across Great Britain, Europe, the Middle East, and importantly, throughout Asia and the Pacific, commissions often larger than those that might have been earned at 'home'. Professional expertise has been sought after, deployed and in some cases earned accolades like DCM's multi-awarding winning Manchester Civil Justice Centre, UK (2003–7). The success of international practice has meant the growth of two forms of practice in both countries: one large and multinational with sophisticated 3D documentation sometimes outsourced to countries such as India; the other form of practice is small to mid size, experimental and committed to the 'difficult' project. The result is a discourse divided not along intellectual lines but along modes of practice and procurement. In the end however, architecture itself sometimes transcends these boundaries of practice, digital processes and identity construction. In Melbourne, DCM and artist Robert Owen deploy sophisticated digital compositional techniques to construct the lightweight steel lattice members of the sinuous Webb Bridge (2000–3), whose tube-like form resembles an Aboriginal eel trap, an echo of former activities that once took place in the Yarra River. While in New Zealand, Architecture Workshop's

Christopher Kelly designed the Waitomo Caves Visitor Centre (2010) where a 'sky shell' canopy designed like a hinaki (Maori eel trap) and described by the surface of a toroid opposes the dark of the caves beneath. (Figure 22.16) Both projects use twenty-first century technology and both, at the 'edge of centre', also find the new in the time honoured meeting of landscape and culture.

22.16   Architecture Workshop, Waitomo Caves Visitor Centre, Waitomo, New Zealand, 2010

NOTES

1   Philip Goad, *New Directions in Australian Architecture* (Balmain, NSW: Pesaro Publishing, 2001), 12–13. See also Jennifer Taylor, *Australian Architecture since 1960* (Red Hill, ACT: RAIA National Education Division, 1990), 9–12.

2   The 'elegant shed' is the title of the David Mitchell's book *The Elegant Shed: New Zealand Architecture since 1945* (Auckland, New York: Oxford University Press, 1984).

3   See Mike Austin, 'Polynesian Architecture in New Zealand', PhD thesis, University of Auckland, 1976 and 'Polynesian Influences in New Zealand Architecture', *Formulation Fabrication: The Architecture of History*, Papers from the 17th Annual Conference of the Society of Architectural Historians, Australia and New Zealand, Wellington, 2000; Peter Shaw, *New Zealand Architecture from Polynesian Beginnings to 1990* (Auckland: Hodder & Stoughton, 1991); and Deidre Brown, *Maori Architecture: from Fale to Wharenui and Beyond* (Rosedale, NZ: Raupo/Penguin, 2009).

4   Paul Memmott, *Gunyah, Goondie and Wurley: The Aboriginal Architecture of Australia* (St Lucia, Qld: University of Queensland Press, 2007).

5   James Freeland, *Architecture in Australia: A History* (Melbourne: Cheshire, 1968).

6   Robin Boyd, 'The State of Australian Architecture', *Architecture in Australia*, 56: 3 (June 1967): 454–65.

7   Peter Beaven, 'South Island Architecture', *RIBA Journal* (September 1967): 375–82.

8   Hannah Lewi and David Nichols (eds), *Community: Building Modern Australia* (Sydney: UNSW Press, 2010), 84–111.

9   Philip Goad, 'Absence and Presence: Modernism and the Australian city', *Fabulation*, Papers from the 29th Annual Conference of the Society of Architectural Historians, Australia and New Zealand, Launceston, July 2012.

10   The ANZUS Treaty, for example, was signed in September 1951.

11   Robin Boyd, *The Australian Ugliness* (Melbourne: Cheshire, 1960).

12   Don Gazzard (ed.), *Australian Outrage: The Decay of a Visual Environment* (Sydney: Ure Smith, 1966).

13   Philip Goad, 'BHP House, Melbourne', in Jennifer Taylor (ed.), *Tall Buildings, Australian Business Going Up: 1945–1970* (Sydney: Craftsman House, 2001), 260–81.

14   Gevoork Hartoonian, 'Harry Seidler: Revisiting Modernism', *Fabrications*, 20: 1 (January 2011): 30–53.

15   This claim is made in Alice Spigelman, *Almost Full Circle: Harry Seidler* (Rose Bay: Brandl & Schlesinger, 2001), 188.

16   Philip Goad, 'Australia Square', entry in Philip Goad and Julie Willis (eds), *The Encyclopedia of Australian Architecture* (Melbourne: Cambridge University Press, 2011), 50–1.

17   Goad, 'Australia Square', 50.

18   Jessica Halliday, quoted in Julia Gatley (ed.), *Long Live the Modern: New Zealand's New Architecture 1904–1984* (Auckland: Auckland University Press, 2008), 217.

19   Robin Skinner, 'A Search for Authority: The Sketch Design of the Beehive', *Additions to Architectural History*, Papers from the 19th Annual Conference of the Society of Architectural Historians, Australia and New Zealand, Brisbane, 2002.

20   Tone Wheeler, 'The Autonomous House', *Architecture in Australia*, 63: 4 (1974).

21   Andrew Hutson, 'Architects Groups and the Pipe Dreams of Clyde Cameron College', *Progress*, Papers from the 20th Annual Conference of the Society of Architectural Historians, Australia and New Zealand, Sydney, 2003, 158–62.

22   Conrad Hamann, 'Seven in the Seventies', exhibition notes, Monash University Gallery, Clayton, Vic., 1981.

23   Douglas Gordon (1933–2006) graduated from the University of Sydney in 1959 before completing a Master's degree from the University of Pennsylvania (1959–61). He then worked for Gordon Bunshaft at Skidmore Owings & Merrill (New York), Mitchell & Giurgola and Robert Venturi before returning to Australia. See Howard Tanner, 'Gordon & Valich', in Philip Goad and Julie Willis (eds), *The Encyclopedia of Australian Architecture* (Melbourne: Cambridge University Press, 2011), 282.

24   Peter Corrigan, 'Reflections on a New North American Architecture: The Venturis', *Architecture in Australia*, 61:1 (February 1972): 55–67.

25   'AA Interview: Charles Jencks', *Architecture Australia*, 64: 1 (February 1975): 50–59.

26   The exhibition 'Four Melbourne Architects', held at Powell Street Gallery, South Yarra in Melbourne in 1979, featured the work of Edmond & Corrigan, Norman Day, Greg Burgess and Peter Crone. What was significant about this exhibition was the diversity of aesthetic position adopted by each architect, despite the unified title, which highlighted the striking difference between the 1967 MOMA exhibition in New York of the work of Richard Meier, Gwathmey Siegel, Peter Eisenman and John Hedjuk and its subsequent book, *Five Architects* (1972).

27   An important series of monographs on the Perth architects Jeffrey Howlett, Geoffrey Summerhayes, Gordon Finn, Krantz & Sheldon, and Perth's 1950s houses was produced in associations with exhibitions at the Cullity Gallery, University of Western Australia between 1992 and 1997.

28   For a detailed analysis of the implications of the 1980 'Pleasures of Architecture' conference, see Paul Hogben, 'The Aftermath of 'Pleasures': Untold Stories of Post-Modern Architecture in Australia', *Progress*, Papers from the 20th Annual Conference of the Society of Architectural Historians, Australia and New Zealand, Sydney, 2003.

29   An important article highlighting Melbourne's receptiveness to Post-Modernism is Conrad Hamann's 'Off the Straight and Narrow', *Architecture Australia* (June 1984): 61–6.

30   See, for example, Philip Thalis and Peter John Cantrill, *Public Sydney: Drawing the City* (Sydney: Faculty of the Built Environment, University of New South Wales and the Historic Houses Trust of New South Wales, 2013).

31   Philip Drew, *Leaves of Iron: Glenn Murcutt, Pioneer of an Australian Architectural Form* (Sydney: Law Book Co., 1985).

32   Rory Spence, 'Sources of Theory and Practice in the Work of Richard Leplastrier', M. Arch thesis, University of NSW, 1997.

33   *Andresen O'Gorman – Works 1965–2001, UME*, 22 (2011).

34   Dimity Reed (ed.), *Tangled Destinies: National Museum of Australia* (Mulgrave, Vic.: Images Publishing Group, 2002).

35   Paul Walker, 'Modern Architecture in New Zealand', *DOCOMOMO*, 29 (September 2003): 46.

36   Robin Skinner, 'Larrikins Abroad: International Account of the New Zealand Architects in the 1970s and 1980s', in Andrew Leach, Antony Moulis and Nicole Sully (eds), *Shifting Views: Selected Essays on the Architectural History of Australia and New Zealand* (St Lucia, Qld: University of Queensland Press, 2008), 103–11.

37   Justine Clark and Paul Walker, 'Making a Difference: New Zealand Houses at the Beginning of the 21st Century', in Geoffrey London (ed.), *Houses for the* 21st Century (Singapore: Periplus, 2004), 63.

38   Paul Walker, 'Here and There in New Zealand Architecture', *Fabrications*, 14: 1 & 2 (December 2004): 33–46.

39   Norman Day and Andrew Brown-May, *Federation Square* (South Yarra, Vic.: Hardie Grant, 2005).

Index

(Illustrations indexed in bold page numbers)